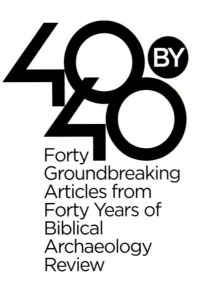

Forty
Groundbreaking
Articles from
Forty Years of
Biblical
Archaeology
Review

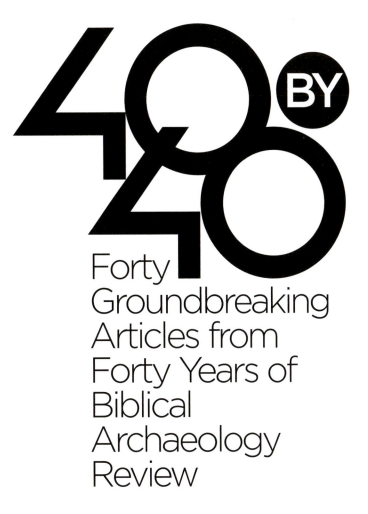

40 BY 40

Forty
Groundbreaking
Articles from
Forty Years of
Biblical
Archaeology
Review

VOLUME TWO

HERSHEL SHANKS, EDITOR

BIBLICAL ARCHAEOLOGY SOCIETY
WASHINGTON, DC

Library of Congress Cataloging-in-Publication Data

40 by 40: forty groundbreaking articles from forty years of
Biblical archaeology review / edited by Hershel Shanks.
pages cm
Includes bibliographical references.
1. Bible—Antiquities. I. Shanks, Hershel.
II. Biblical archaeology review.
III. Title: Forty by forty
BS621.F65 2015
220.9'3—dc23
2014042393

Printed in Canada
Design by AURAS Design, Silver Spring, MD

ISBN 978-0-9796357-7-9 for Soft Cover Set
ISBN 978-0-9796357-6-2 for Hard Cover Set

This book could not have been produced
without the enthusiastic, encouraging
and generous support of

George Blumenthal, USA

Major Jan Brown, Ret., USA

Lois England in memory of Richard (Dick) England, USA

Juergen Friede, Germany

Susie and Michael Gelman in memory of Avraham Biran, USA

Eugene and Emily Grant, USA

David and Jemima Jeselsohn, Switzerland

Marvin and Dolly Kay, USA

Atis and Lynda Krigers, USA

Lanier Theological Library, USA

P.E. MacAllister, USA

John and Carol Merrill, USA

Jeanette and Jonathan Rosen, USA

David Rosenstein, USA

Samuel D. Turner, USA

T A B L E   O F

V O L U M E   I

C O N T E N T S

V O L U M E II

7

Water and Burials

When digging in Israel, archaeologists must be prepared to encounter either of these underground features that are crucial in life and significant in death. A pair of articles explored these two complex systems in the First Temple period.

The work of archaeologists usually requires digging underground to reveal the material remains of ancient life. But some things were always underground, even in antiquity—such as water systems and burials. They are the stuff of life and death, both of which BAR has covered extensively.

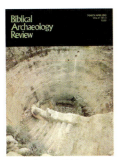

MARCH/APRIL 1980
How Water Tunnels Worked

Water is essential, and it is often scarce in the Holy Land. In this thorough overview American archaeologist Dan P. Cole explained how ancient Israelites wrung water from the land even during the long dry season and how they sought to protect their water supply even during times of siege. His article is one of the most widely cited we have published.

This article appeared in 1980, nearly 35 years ago. Continuing excavations are refining our understanding of Israel's ancient water systems, but at least two details in this article would have to be modified today. The latest views on Warren's Shaft in Jerusalem establish its existence in the Middle Bronze Age and show that it is a natural shaft that was not used to draw water. Otherwise the article elucidates why these water tunnels were absolutely necessary and how they were constructed.

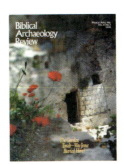

MARCH/APRIL 1986
Jerusalem Tombs from the Days of the First Temple

Tombs from the First Temple Period (eighth–sixth centuries B.C.E.) are extremely rare discoveries. Perhaps the most impressive of these are in a cave complex at the Monastery of St. Etienne in Jerusalem, which houses the École Biblique et Archéologique Française. Until the study reported in BAR by Gabriel Barkay and Amos Kloner, two young Israeli scholars fresh from their army service at the time, it was widely thought that these tombs dated hundreds of years later, to the Second Temple period. Now there is no question of the earlier dating.

These tombs also preserved the bones of the deceased. They have yet to be studied, but it seems clear that the tombs belonged to important, wealthy people in the days when kings still ruled Judah.

The bones of these ancients now share space with some of the most distinguished names in the modern study of ancient Israel—Louis-Hugues Vincent, Felix M. Abel, Roland de Vaux and others, all Dominican Fathers at the École—for the cave complex also shelters the cemetery of the monastery.

HAZOR—A YOUNG WORKMAN stands near the rubble-filled entrance of the great 9th century B.C. tunnel.

Archaeologist Yigael Yadin came to Hazor expecting to find a water system comparable to the one discovered at Megiddo: that is, a vertical shaft, inside the city walls, connected to a tunnel leading to a spring *outside* the city.

Yadin found the Hazor water shaft and tunnel, but instead of leading toward a water source outside the city wall, the tunnel descended to the water table beneath the city. The confident tunneling of these ancient Israelite engineers suggests that they knew that by heading toward the water table, they could create a water system which would be completely enclosed and secure within the city walls.

How Water Tunnels Worked

Jerusalem, Megiddo, Hazor, Gezer and Gibeon all had systems to bring water safely within their city walls during time of siege — Cole offers new suggestions on how this technology developed.

DAN P. COLE

"A CITY SET ON A hill cannot be hidden," said Matthew (5:14). Neither can it easily be supplied with water.

Cities were built on hilltops because of the obvious defensive advantages. These advantages were somewhat offset by the disadvantage that the city's springs or wells were normally at the base of the hill, outside the city walls. As the size of urban populations grew and the height of the cities themselves grew through successive rebuildings—creating higher and higher "tells"—the water supply moved progressively farther away.

In peacetime, this distance was merely an inconvenience for women and slaves; in time of war, it could be a fatal weakness. Under siege the city could be deprived of its water supply. No city can last for long without water.

Because almost no rain falls from March until October Palestinian cities were particularly vulnerable to prolonged sieges. Cisterns and other rain collectors inside the city walls were not replenished for six months or more.

Some ancient Departments of Defense solved the problem of bringing fresh water inside the city walls by means of massive engineering projects involving tunnels and shafts hewn through bedrock beneath their cities.*

Over the past century archaeologists have uncovered a dozen examples of such ambitious projects at various cities in ancient Israel. Now, a

*For the sake of clarity, the term "tunnel" will be reserved for *horizontal* cuttings, "shaft" for *vertical* ones, and "stepped tunnel" for *angling* ones.

sufficient number of these engineering operations have been revealed to enable us to begin to reconstruct the development of hydraulic technology in ancient Palestine.

Probably the most famous of these water systems are the two cut into the Ophel Hill of Jerusalem

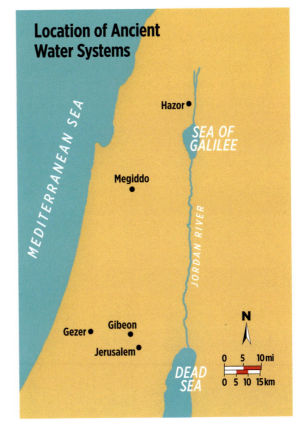

Location of Ancient Water Systems

(the so-called City of David). The earlier system is "Warren's Shaft" (named for Charles Warren, who discovered it in 1867); it is also referred to as the "Jebusite Shaft" on the common assumption that it dates to the pre-10th century B.C. Jebusite city.* This system consisted of four elements. 1. A *tunnel* which was cut to direct water from the plentiful Gihon Spring (in the Kidron Valley east of the city hill), into a chamber deep within the hill. 2. *A stepped tunnel* which was cut downward from the street level behind the city's defense wall and which led to 3. *an almost horizontal tunnel ramp* running out under the city wall to a point directly above the water chamber where 4. a shaft connected the end of this upper tunnel to the water chamber. A jar could then be lowered down the shaft by a rope and filled from the spring-fed chamber below.**

Later—in the 8th century B.C.—King Hezekiah replaced this earlier water system with a 1750-foot tunnel under the city which was cut by two crews starting at either end. This underground tunnel was graded or slanted so that it carried the water from the Gihon Spring, located outside the walls, to a pool inside the city. (See "How the Blind See the Holy Land," BAR, May/June 1979, "Queries & Comments," BAR, November/December 1979, and Hershel Shanks, *The City of David* [Biblical Archaeology Society, 1975].)

Next to Jerusalem, the best-known Israelite water system is the shaft and tunnel at Megiddo,[1] which writer James Michener incorporated into his fictional "Tel Makor" in his novel *The Source.*

The famous Megiddo water system involved two elements: First, a large vertical shaft with steps cut down around its sides was sunk through the debris layers of earlier periods into the bedrock, going down 115 feet to the level of an already-known nearby spring. Second, a horizontal tunnel, 200 feet long, was dug, running from the bottom of the shaft out under the city wall to connect with the spring. As at Jerusalem, this tunnel was cut by two teams of pick men working toward each other, one from the bottom of the shaft and the other from the spring.

Dating an ancient water system which is cut into bedrock is no easy task. The pottery and other objects found in it can only suggest when it went out of use, not when it was originally constructed. The most reliable indication of the date of construction comes from the stratigraphy at the entrance to the system inside the city. It is a safe assumption that a shaft was cut after the latest stratum of the tell through which it cuts. This is not helpful, however, for dating a later system where ancient erosion has destroyed the uppermost strata.

The University of Chicago team which excavated Megiddo in the late 1920's dated its water system to the 12th century B.C. because the latest stratum clearly cut by the shaft dated to that time. Unfortunately, several later occupation levels had eroded from around the top of the shaft, as we now know from other areas of the mound; the shaft should have been connected stratigraphically with the so-called "Solomonic stables" which the excavators uncovered immediately to the east of the shaft and with the inset-offset[†] city wall which they traced around the mound from the Solomonic gateway on the north. Had Chicago's excavators correctly connected the water shaft to the "Solomonic stables" and to the inset-offset wall, they would have dated the water shaft not to the 12th century B.C., but to the Solomonic period (10th century B.C.). This dating however, would also have been wrong, because the "Solomonic stables" and the inset-offset wall with which it was associated proved not to be Solomonic at all, but in fact dated to the 9th century B.C. In the late 1950's Yigael Yadin became suspicious of the Megiddo excavators' date for the inset-offset city wall and the buildings (including the

---

*There are reasons to question this early a dating, but they need not concern us here.

**This shaft and tunnel system has been described and illustrated in "Digging in the City of David," BAR, July/August 1979.

---

† An "inset-offset" wall is one which has periodic zigzag vertical cutbacks along its face. This device gave defenders a line of fire against attackers at the base of their wall; it became popular in Israel in the 9th century B.C.

How to Read Plans and Sections

The plans and sections printed with this article are the tools of professional archaeologists. We have attempted to use them to give the reader a three-dimensional picture of a site.

A plan is a picture which shows what is seen when looking straight down at the site. The limitation of a plan is that it cannot show depth: thus the height of two walls cannot be compared.

The function of a section drawing is to show the vertical relationship of the structures excavated at a site. A section drawing takes a vertical slice through an area. This slice may be taken through any two points on the plan at any angle. This means there are an infinite number of possible section drawings. That is why it is important to indicate on the plan where the slice or section was made.

On our plans of Hazor and Gezer the points marked A-A on the plan show the position of the section. The slice is taken from one A to the other A.

Jebusite (pre-10th century B.C.) and Hezekiah's (8th century B.C.) Water Systems

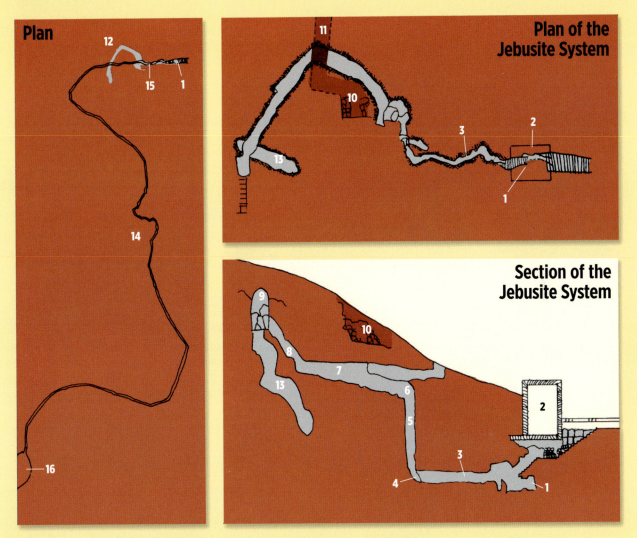

Plan

Plan of the Jebusite System

Section of the Jebusite System

JERUSALEM—BEFORE THE 10TH CENTURY B.C., the Jebusites settled near the plentiful water supply of the Spring Gihon (1) on the Hill of Ophel. They constructed a water system with four elements: *a tunnel* (3) cut into the hill to direct water from the spring into a chamber (4) within the hill; *a stepped or sloping tunnel* (8) cut downward from street level (9) behind the Jebusite city wall (10); an almost *horizontal tunnel* (7) passing under the city wall to a point above the spring filled chamber (4), and *a shaft* (5) connecting the end of the upper tunnel to the chamber below. Water carriers could stand at the top of the shaft (6) and lower buckets to bring up water.

In the 8th century B.C. King Hezekiah built a graded 1750 foot tunnel (14) under the city. It carried the water of the Spring Gihon (1), located outside the city wall, to a pool (16) located inside the city. A portion of this tunnel (15) nearest to the spring was part of the earlier Jebusite system.

1. Spring Gihon
2. Modern house
3. Spring-filled tunnel
4. Water chamber
5. Shaft
6. Place from which bucket was lowered to water below
7. Horizontal tunnel
8. Stepped-tunnel
9. Entrance to Jebusite tunnel
10. Jebusite wall
11. Probable course of Jebusite wall
12. Successful shaft and tunnel system
13. First unsuccessful Jebusite shaft
14. Hezekiah's Tunnel (8th century B.C.)
15. Tunnel common to Hezekiah's and Jebusite systems
16. Pool of Siloam

THE ORIENTAL INSTITUTE, UNIVERSITY OF CHICAGO

MEGIDDO—THE WATER GALLERY is a narrow passage made of well-dressed ashlar stones. It is just over three feet wide and up to six feet tall and originally was roofed. The gallery started inside the city, then cut through the 10th century B.C. Solomonic casemate wall, and ended at a point above the spring outside the city wall on the southwest slope of the mound. From there, stairs, which were probably hidden with a covering of wood and earth, linked the gallery to the spring chamber entrance.

In the 9th century B.C. the Solomonic gallery was blocked and covered over by a solid "inset-offset" wall—probably at the same time that the shaft-and-tunnel water system was engineered.

the only water system in evidence at the site: the Chicago excavators found earlier, less technically developed water systems at Megiddo. One, just north of the 9th century B.C. water shaft is known as the "gallery"—a narrow passage leading from inside the city, through the earlier Solomonic casemate city wall. This gallery was directly above an old entrance to the same spring which the later shaft and tunnel system served. Steps descended from the end of the gallery, down the slope to this old spring entrance. A wood and earth roofing originally concealed the steps leading down the slope to the spring entrance.[4]

At the base of the slope, this covered stairway had connected with an even earlier set of steps. These steps descended into the face of the hillside to a water chamber cut out of bedrock around the spring.

Thus we can now reconstruct three stages of the water system at Megiddo: (1) Sometime in the Late Bronze or Early Iron Age—surely before the 10th century B.C. gallery—steps were cut into the base of the slope down to a natural spring; the area of the spring was enlarged by a chamber cut out of the bedrock. (2) When Solomon fortified the city in the 10th century, a narrow passageway or gallery led from inside the city, through the Solomonic casemate wall to a point above the spring; from there stairs, which were probably covered, led down the slope and connected the gallery to the old spring chamber entrance. (3) In the 9th century B.C., King Ahab replaced this system with the huge vertical shaft inside the city and the horizontal tunnel system leading from the shaft to the spring.

After King Ahab's shaft and tunnel were cut, the old stepped entrance to the spring could be blocked up to prevent access from the outside. In fact, the excavators found this entrance blocked by a wall of huge stones.**

"Solomonic stables") related to it. Digging at Hazor, Yadin had found that the 10th century Solomonic gateway (strikingly similar to Megiddo's) had been connected to a casemate wall* *over which* a solid inset-offset wall had been laid in a 9th century rebuilding of the city (presumably by King Ahab).[2] Yadin reasoned that if at Hazor a Solomonic gateway was connected to a casemate wall over which a solid inset-offset wall was built a century later, the same thing was probably true at Megiddo.

Yadin re-investigated the Megiddo walls in the 1960's and clearly demonstrated that the inset-offset wall (and the so-called "Solomonic stables") belonged to a rebuilding of the city after Solomon. Yadin uncovered at Megiddo, as he had at Hazor, beneath the inset-offset wall, a casemate wall from King Solomon's time (10th century B.C.) which connected to the Solomonic gate in its initial phase.[3]

The Megiddo water system was not, however,

*A casemate wall consists of two parallel walls connected by periodic cross walls. The effect is to create a line of narrow rectangular rooms, but the main purpose probably was to provide a wall system with sufficient space on the top for defenders to maneuver easily. We know that this wall style was most characteristic of Israel in the 10th century B.C.

**Sometime after the 9th century B.C. shaft/tunnel system was cut, the tunnel was deepened and graded so that the water then flowed from the spring to the base of the shaft inside the city. This saved steps for the water carriers who no longer had to walk through the tunnel, but the arrangement apparently proved unsatisfactory. Perhaps the water became fouled at the shaft end since it had no place to flow off. So the tunnel floor was again recut and regraded so the spring water no longer flowed to the base of the shaft.

The Megiddo Water Systems

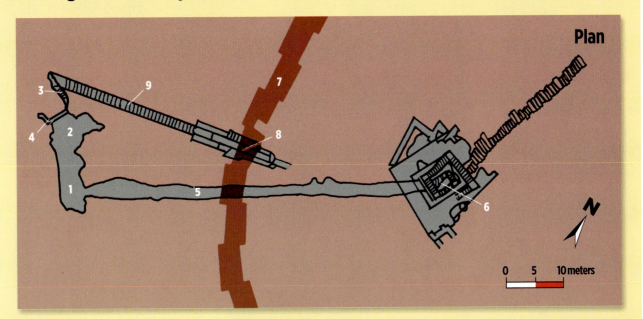

Plan

0 5 10 meters

MEGIDDO—THE FIRST OF THREE water systems at this site was constructed before the 10th century B.C. It was very simple. It consisted of a stairway (3) at the base of the tell descending to the spring chamber (2) which was filled by a spring (1). To obtain water, one had to go outside the city walls.

King Solomon constructed the second water system in the 10th century B.C. as part of his large fortified city. He cut a gallery (8) through the casemate city wall extending from inside the city to the outside. (Here the casemate is covered by the later inset-offset wall (7).) Camouflaged with a dirt and wood roof, the gallery led to a set of stairs (9) which were also covered. These stairs joined the earlier set of stairs (3) which in turn connected with the spring at the base of the tell.

The latest water system at Megiddo was constructed by King Ahab in the 9th century B.C. A shaft (6) 115 feet deep was sunk inside the city. At the bottom of the shaft, a 200-foot long tunnel (5) led to the spring chamber (2) at the base of the hill. To prevent entrance into Ahab's water system from outside the city walls, the earlier hillside entrance to the spring chamber was blocked by a wall (4).

1. Spring
2. Spring chamber
3. Pre-10th century B.C. stairs to spring chamber
4. 9th century B.C. blocking wall at entrance to chamber
5. 9th century B.C. tunnel
6. 9th century B.C. stepped shaft
7. 9th century B.C. inset-offset wall
8. Solomonic (10th century B.C.) gallery
9. Solomonic (10th century B.C.) covered stairway

The steps of this outside entrance are now unblocked, so the modern visitor to Megiddo can enter the water system from inside the city, climbing down the 9th century shaft an d follow the tunnel to the spring and then exit by way of the much earlier steps leading out to the base of the hill.

As we have seen, Yadin used what he had learned on his Hazor excavations to redate at Megiddo the inset-offset wall, the "stables" and therefore the water system with which it was associated, all to the 9th century B.C. Conversely, when Yadin returned to Hazor for renewed excavations in 1968, he was able to use the Megiddo water system to help him find a similar water system at Hazor.[5]

Yadin reasoned that Israelite Hazor *should* have had

a comparable water system to Megiddo's because of Hazor's strategic military position controlling major highways and because of its strong fortifications in the 10th and 9th centuries B.C. Having already exposed a palace within the walls at the western end of the mound and having found the Iron Age city gate on the east, Yadin deduced that the only available place for a water shaft (and the most likely place based on the mound's present topography) was midway along the south side of the tell.

A shallow depression in the mound at this point confirmed this reasoning. The depression was comparatively close to a wadi below, where water still flows today. In addition, earlier soundings in the depression had revealed no structures, only a deep

MEGIDDO—THE 9TH CENTURY B.C. water tunnel is part of the latest and most technologically advanced of Megiddo's three water systems. To create this 200 foot long passageway, two teams of workers, one starting at the bottom of a 115 foot deep shaft behind the city walls, and one starting at the base of the hill by the spring, dug toward one another through the hill. By descending the shaft and walking through this underground tunnel, the residents of the city could reach the spring. Thus, during times of siege, water could be drawn without going outside the city walls.

HAZOR—AN AERIAL VIEW of the shaft and stairs. The three people standing on the stairs provide a scale for the massive shaft.

fill. In short, it seemed the perfect place for an Iron Age water shaft.

Removing the tons of debris which had gradually filled the shaft after the 8th century B.C. destruction of Israelite Hazor was a mammoth operation and something of an act of faith on Yadin's part. But his hunch was right. The water shaft was there. In the upper portion it was similar to the water shaft at Megiddo. As at Megiddo, it proved to have been dug *after* Solomon's time, since the ramp leading down to the shaft and the retaining walls around it cut through buildings containing 10th century pottery. Moreover, these buildings were clearly associated with the 10th century casemate wall along the south slope of the mound. So the water shaft must have been dug *after* the 10th century.

More than 95 feet below the surface, Yadin finally reached the bottom of the shaft. Next he expected to find a tunnel branching off from the shaft to the south, in the direction of the water source *outside* the city, as was the case at Megiddo. This time his expectation proved wrong. Instead, he found a stepped tunnel leading *down* to the west, going 80 feet farther into the heart of the bedrock beneath the tell. There, indeed, Yadin found water—as had

Ahab's engineers 2800 years before: the natural water table over 130 feet below the city street!

Ahab's engineers at Hazor apparently knew in advance that if they dug deep enough into the hill they would strike water; there is no evidence of false starts or fumbling on the part of Ahab's diggers.

The Hazor shaft and stepped tunnel system was completely secure from an enemy because it was all inside the walls. It was thus a considerable improvement over the water system at Megiddo (and at Jerusalem, for that matter).

A military man himself, Yadin was immediately aware of the strategic importance of this ancient technological advance. He realized that as soon as hydraulic engineers at one city discovered the water table beneath their city, this type of water system would be copied and used elsewhere if conditions permitted. (It is unlikely that the discovery was made at Hazor because the Hazor engineers seemed to know ahead of time just what they were doing). This realization led Yadin to reexamine the date which had been assigned to still another water tunnel, one that R. A. S. Macalister had discovered at the beginning of this century at Gezer.

Macalister excavated at Gezer from 1902 to 1909.

The Hazor Shaft/Tunnel

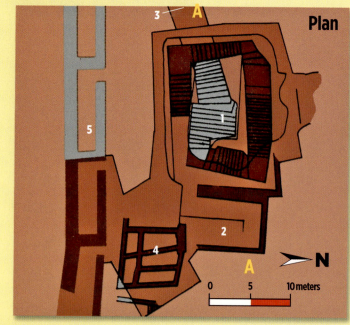

Plan

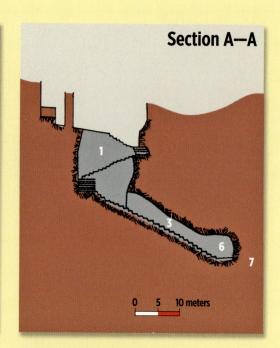

Section A—A

HAZOR—THIS WATER SYSTEM was built in the 9th century B.C. some time after the completion of the Gibeon water system.

Five flights of stairs encircling the shaft (1), led to the entrance of a stepped sloping tunnel (3) at the bottom of the shaft. The tunnel descends an additional 65 feet before reaching the water table chamber (6) 125 feet deep under the Hazor streets.

The Hazor engineers may have learned the stepped-tunnel-to-water-table technique from Gibeon where the latest water system used this technology. The engineering at Hazor appears confident and purposeful—not accidental.

A–A mark position of the section.
1. Rock-hewn shaft with steps
2. Entrance structure
3. Stepped (or sloping) tunnel leading to water table
4. 9th century B.C. 4-room Israelite house
5. 10th century B.C. Solomonic casemate wall
6. Chamber on water table
7. Pool on water table

There he found a step-lined shaft which led into a tunnel, also stepped, which sloped downward into the heart of the hill until it ended in a long chamber at the water table level.[6] All this was inside the city wall. Macalister dated the tunnel to his "Second Semitic" period—which we now call the Middle Bronze Age—about 1650 B.C. Macalister's dating was based principally on some Mycenaean sherds from his "Third Semitic" period (the Late Bronze Age, 1550 B.C.–1200 B.C.), which he had found in the debris from the tunnel. He thought the tunnel must have pre-dated the pot sherds debris found in the tunnel. He was, however, wrong. We now realize that in the erosion that occurs after the breakdown of the retaining walls around the top of a shaft, sherds from almost any period can and often do make their way into the shaft cavity.

Yadin's excavation of the Hazor shaft suggested to him that Gezer's tunnel really belonged to a later period. He argued that the Gezer shaft and stepped tunnel, like the Hazor shaft and stepped

tunnel, reflected the engineer's knowledge that the water table could be reached inside the city. Since this technology, once discovered, was likely to be copied at various sites, Yadin expected that the Gezer tunnel should be dated close to the period of the Hazor water system, which he had clearly dated to the 9th century B.C.[7]

William Dever, who directed renewed excavations at Gezer from 1965 to 1971, maintained, however, that the Gezer water system probably dated to the Late Bronze Age.[8] He thought the Middle Bronze city gateway too close to the shaft head to date the construction that early. On the other hand, Dever pointed out, Iron Age walls appear on Macalister's plans above the area of the shaft, suggesting the water system had gone out of use before that time.* Therefore he thought the Late Bronze Age the most

*I am not convinced by Dever's argument against a 9th century date. One of the Iron Age walls which on Macalister's plan appears above the shaft looks as if it could have been a retaining wall around the top of the shaft steps.

HAZOR—IN THIS AERIAL view, the reader can appreciate the bottleshape of the tell. As seen here, the "bottle" is upside down. The dark depression in the light excavated area of the tell is the entrance to the shaft which was carved from bedrock in the 9th century B.C. At times of siege, the inhabitants of Hazor could draw water, without emerging from the protective city walls, by descending this shaft to a connecting tunnel which led underground to the water chamber.

AT THE NARROW end of the "bottle" is a small part of the glacis which enclosed the "lower city," inhabited only in the Middle Bronze Age (18th through 13th centuries B.C.); to the left of the glacis is a dark area which was once a moat.

The Gezer Shaft/Tunnel

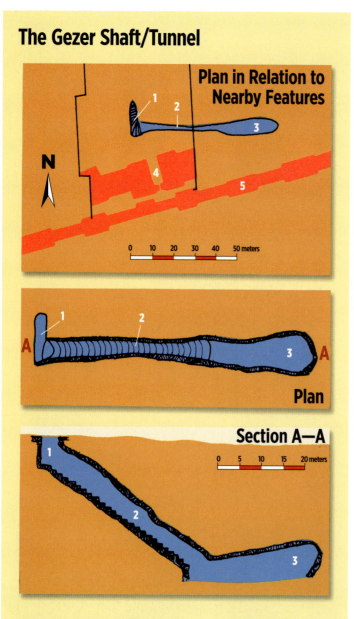

Plan in Relation to Nearby Features

N

0 10 20 30 40 50 meters

Plan

Section A–A

0 5 10 15 20 meters

GEZER—IN THE 14TH or 9th century B.C. a shaft (1) was sunk 35 feet into the ground. From it a sloping stepped tunnel (2) 48 feet long was carved. The tunnel terminated in a chamber (3) on the water table. The engineers of the Gezer water system probably knew before they began this project that they would find water if they dug deeply enough, suggesting that the people of Gezer may have learned the stepped-tunnel-to-water-table technology from other Mediterranean civilizations or from a similar discovery at another Israelite site such as Gibeon.

1. Rock-cut shaft
2. Stepped (or sloping) tunnel
3. Chamber on water table
4. Southern Gate in Middle Bronze wall
5. Late Bronze wall (initial phase built c. 1400 B.C.)

likely candidate for the Gezer water system.

Because Macalister had cut through all the building layers around the head of the water shaft at Gezer, there is no way to obtain new stratigraphic evidence to determine the last stratum through which the shaft was originally cut. This, unfortunately, is the only way to confidently date the system.

But whether the Gezer water system dates from the Late Bronze Age, as Dever argues, or from the Iron II Age, as Yadin argues, Yadin's basic thesis still remains viable. Perhaps the stairs-to-water-table concept was known as early as the Late Bronze Age at such a major Canaanite city as Gezer. The Late Bronze II Age was a period of active trade among eastern Mediterranean cultures. Fine Mycenaean pottery from this period has been found in Palestine and Egypt and large Canaanite storage jars have turned up in Greece. Ideas as well as merchandise travel the same trade routes. We know that in this period Mycenae, Athens, and other cities in Greece had water stairs inside their walls which cut directly to the water table rather than out to springs. Thus, the Canaanites could well have learned from the Mycenaeans this technique of digging down to the water table inside the city walls.

The Gezer water system could have been dug at Canaanite Gezer in the Late Bronze II Age; it could then have been abandoned and choked with rubble at the end of the Bronze Age and have remained that way through the 12th–11th century B.C. Philistine occupation. Perhaps the top of the water shaft was still visible during later periods, but Israelite engineers of the 10th or 9th century B.C. would not have known about the water table concept on which this underground water system was based. In short, Israelite engineers may have had to rediscover this knowledge. Yadin may therefore still be correct in stating that once the stairs-to-water table concept was discovered (or rediscovered) by the Israelites in Iron II, this idea was likely to be quickly copied in other Israelite cities of the period. Thus, other Israelite water systems of this type probably should be dated to about the same time as Hazor's 9th century B.C. system.

Naturally, it would be interesting to know where the Hazor engineers got their stairs-to-water-table concept. In other words, where was this type of water system first used by the Israelites?

A re-study of the complicated water systems and associated excavations at Gibeon (modern el-Jib) suggests to me that it was at Gibeon that Israelite engineers discovered—or *re*-discovered—the possibility of locating a source of fresh water inside the city, safe from enemy control during a siege.

The discovery of a huge pool-like shaft at

JERUSALEM—WAIST DEEP IN the water of the Spring Gihon, a young man stands between the well-hewn walls of Hezekiah's Tunnel. Carved in the 8th century B.C. this impressive engineering project carried the water of the Spring Gihon which is outside the city to a pool within the defensive walls of the city.

HERSHEL SHANKS

Gibeon in 1956 came as a complete surprise, both to the excavators (led by James B. Pritchard of the University of Pennsylvania), and to the local villagers. It had been completely sealed from view under tons of fill and debris for over two and one-half millennia.[9]

When Pritchard and his colleagues began excavating the site, they were already inclined to identify it as ancient Gibeon, as Edward Robinson had proposed in 1838[10] based on his explorations of the area and the similarity of the modern name (el-Jib) to Gibeon. This identification was confirmed dramatically during the first season of Pritchard's excavation with the discovery of storage jar handles inscribed with the name of Gibeon.[11]

Pritchard naturally knew about the famous "Pool of Gibeon" which is referred to in 2 Samuel 2:13–17. For a period after King Saul's death (c. 1000 B.C.) David reigned over Judah while Saul's son Ishbosheth ruled over Israel. David's army led by Joab, and Ishbosheth's army led by Abner met at the Pool of Gibeon. Each side appointed 12 young champions who faced each other on either side of the Pool of Gibeon. They were evenly matched, however, and in the bloodbath that ensued all 24 were killed—deciding nothing.

Despite this famous Biblical reference to the Pool of Gibeon, the discovery of the great shaft surprised Pritchard because another plausible candidate for the Pool of Gibeon had already been suggested.

Robinson had noticed on the northeast slope of the hill a large rectangular reservoir (37 x 60 feet across and 8 feet deep) which caught the overflow from a nearby spring. It seemed to him likely that this was the "Pool of Gibeon" mentioned in the Bible. Most scholars who accepted Robinson's identification of the site as Gibeon also accepted his suggestion about the location of the pool. When Pritchard later excavated part of the reservoir, however, he found that none of the pottery sealed beneath the plaster lining pre-dated the Roman period, so the reservoir could not have been a "pool" from King David's time.

Pritchard spent his first days at el-Jib investigating a long-known stepped tunnel which went from the spring at the base of the mound upward into the side of the hill. (This was the same spring which fed the as-yet unexcavated reservoir from

the Roman period).

Pritchard had no reason, therefore, to suspect that the site would yield a second water system. The spot where he decided to begin digging on the summit of el-Jib, in fact, was dictated by his desire to uncover the upper end of the stepped tunnel which led from the spring. He found the upper entrance exactly where he expected it, directly inside a massive fortification wall.

He did not, however, expect that less than ten feet beyond the entrance to the stepped tunnel he would encounter the top of another water system, one so ambitious that it would take the rest of that first summer and all of the next to clear. The upper portion alone spanned some 37 feet in diameter and extended 35 feet down. To construct it required the

cutting and hauling away of approximately 1100 cubic feet (almost 3,000 tons!) of limestone bedrock. This second water system is now almost universally identified as the Biblical "Pool of Gibeon" (see cover photo on p. 299).

When fully cleared, the "Pool" revealed two distinct segments. The upper portion consisted of a 35-foot-deep cylindrical shaft with almost vertical sides and a relatively flat floor. One descended into the shaft by 40 steps which spiraled down around its side. All but the top three of these steps are cut from the living rock and are approximately five feet wide. They are well cut and not very worn. A low balustrade effect is created by a rim about 20 inches wide and averaging a foot or so high which was left on the inside edge of the steps. Pritchard suggests that this balustrade might represent the level of the initial workmen's steps cut during the original quarrying out of the shaft.[12]

But the stairs do not end at the floor of the shaft. The steps continue downward for another 45 feet through a narrow, slanted tunnel which spirals down as if following the outline of the broad shaft above. This slanted, stepped tunnel reaches the water table within the hill at step 79, 80 feet below street level. There, a kidney-shaped water chamber had been hollowed out, about 22 feet long and 11 feet wide. (In addition, two small vertical shafts extend down from the floor of the pool shaft to the stepped tunnel, at its mid-point and near its termination. Presumably these had the function of providing light on the tunnel steps [see p. 315].)

This shaft/stepped-tunnel system leading to the water table inside the city should not be confused with the other water system at Gibeon. That water system consists of three elements: (1) a 146-foot-long stepped tunnel[13] from inside the city down to a water chamber outside the city walls; (2) the cave-like water chamber with an entrance from

MEGIDDO—THE TELL OVERLOOKS the Jezreel Valley where ancient and modern armies clashed and where today fields of wheat, corn, cotton, and sugar beets blanket its well-watered plains. The fortified 20 acre site protects the outlet of the Wadi 'Ara, a pass connecting the Mediterranean coastal road with routes continuing to the north and east.

The dark depression at the base of the light colored excavated areas (right, center) is the 115-foot deep shaft King Ahab constructed in the 9th century B.C. This shaft connects to an underground tunnel which leads to the spring at the base of the hill. Directly below the shaft is a short, light beige incision which is the 10th century B.C. Solomonic water gallery (see p. 305). Directly below the gallery is a spring, the ancient city's life supply.

In the upper right half of the picture and directly behind the depression of the water shaft is another round depression marking an Iron II Israelite grain silo.

GIBEON—JAR HANDLES INSCRIBED with the word "Gibeon" were found in the debris of the water shaft. Written from right to left in 7th century B.C. Hebrew script, many of the inscriptions on the handles have next to the word "Gibeon" the phrase, "the enclosed vineyard" and the name of the owner of the vineyard. The discovery of an extensive wine production and storage complex at Gibeon confirmed that the Gibeonites stored wine in the jars to which the inscribed handles were once attached.

outside the hill slope (similar to the earliest system at Megiddo); during times of siege, the entrance to the water chamber could be blocked; (3) a horizontal zigzag tunnel, 110 feet long, following the natural fissures in the bedrock leading to the spring—the source. By following the natural fissures in the rock, the flow from the source to the water chamber would be greatly increased. The source of the spring lies almost directly under the city wall.

Just before the stepped tunnel ends inside the city, it takes a sharp right-angle turn. This brings the entrance of the tunnel and its top steps parallel to and flush with the inside of the city wall. If the stepped tunnel had not taken this right-angle turn, it would have extended into the huge pool-shaft, barely 10 feet away.

Pritchard reasoned that the seemingly inconvenient 90-degree turn at the top of the stepped tunnel was probably necessary to avoid the rim of the pool-shaft. The pool-shaft, Pritchard concluded, must therefore have pre-dated the stepped tunnel

The Gibeon Water Systems

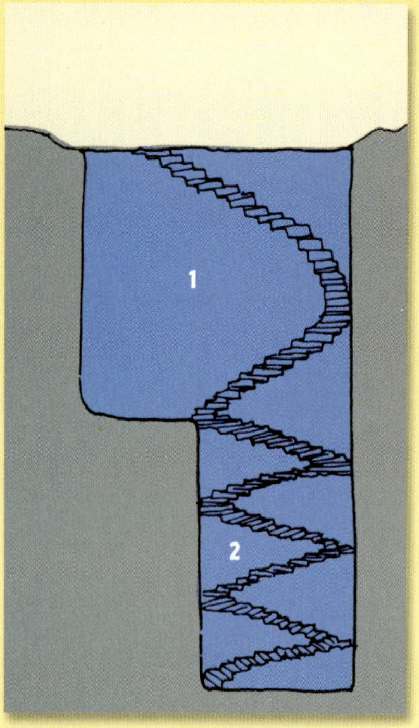

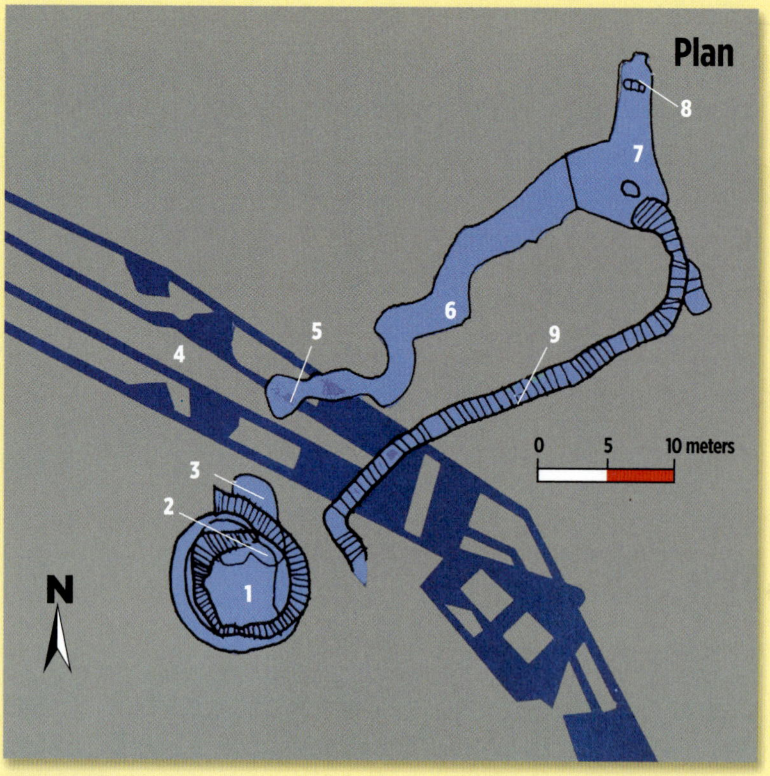

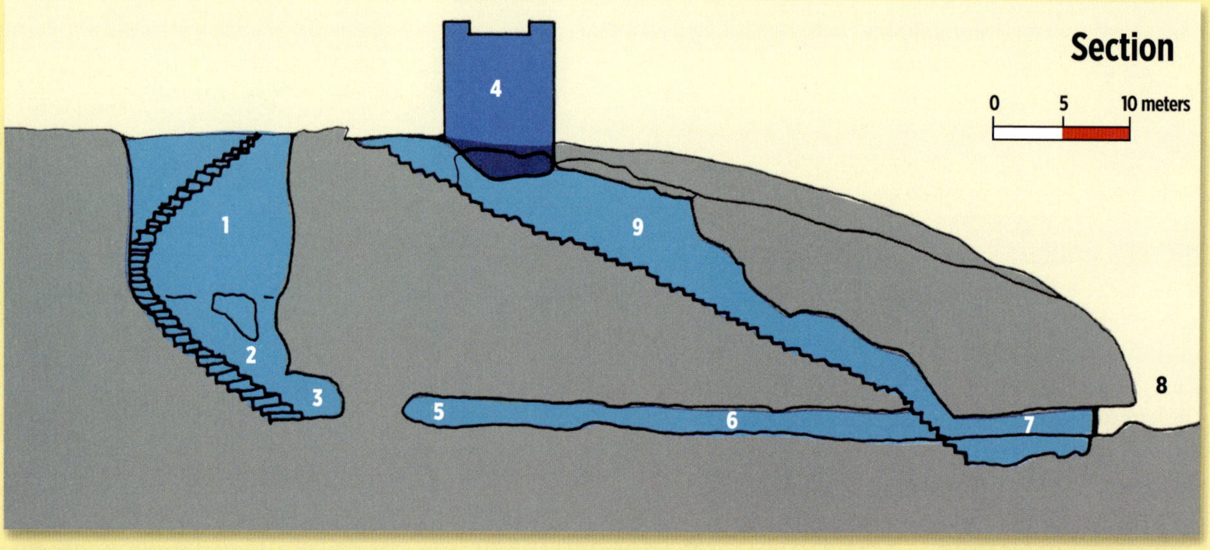

Plan

0   5   10 meters

Section

0   5   10 meters

GIBEON—THE EARLIEST OF THREE water systems was the pool, a large cistern which stored rain water (1). The pool was carved from solid rock some time before the 10th century B.C. During the long rainless summers this cistern probably stored an inadequate amount of water for the city.

The Gibeonites then constructed a second system to increase their water supply. This system consisted of a stepped sloping tunnel (9) leading from just inside the city wall to a water chamber (7) outside the city at the base of the hill. In order to avoid the pool, the upper portion of the stepped tunnel abruptly turned 90 degrees, flush with the city wall after it passed under it. The water chamber at the lower end of the stepped tunnel was filled by fresh water from the spring (5) under the hill. The water flowed from the spring to the water chamber through a feeder tunnel (6) which increased the flow.

After completing this feeder channel, the Gibeonite engineers may have realized that they had tunneled to a point almost directly under their cistern pool. They then decided to dig below the cistern pool to the level of the spring (2), intending to dig a tunnel to the spring. Before reaching the spring they hit the water table, thus discovering an abundant source of water without tunneling to the spring. There they carved out a kidney shaped water chamber (3).

1. Pre-10th century B.C. "pool"
2. Stepped shaft to water table
3. Chamber at water table
4. City wall constructed in 12th–10th centuries B.C.
5. Spring
6. Feeder tunnel to increase flow of spring to water chamber
7. Water chamber
8. Outside entrance to water chamber
9. Stepped (or sloping) tunnel from inside city to water chamber

GIBEON—CARVED COMPLETELY FROM bedrock, the steps and curving balustrade lead to the bottom of the great pool. The lowest portion of the balustrade at the bottom of the pool-shaft may originally have been part of a platform. At that time the pool may have been used as a cistern in which the water carriers stood on the platform while they drew water.

Later, after the feeder tunnel had been dug from the base of the hill to the spring, the Gibeonites may have realized that the spring was almost directly below the floor of the cistern. A stepped tunnel was then dug below the cistern floor (the opening is seen on the left) to try to reach the spring. The tunnel struck the water table—on the same level as the spring—where abundant water was found, providing a reliable water supply completely within the city walls.

Under the ladder are two vertical shafts through which light entered the tunnel.

THE UNIVERSITY MUSEUM, UNIVERSITY OF PENNSYLVANIA

system which he dated to the 10th century B.C.

Pritchard's dating of the stepped tunnel was based on the following evidence: just outside the city walls, the stepped tunnel appears to have been deliberately opened to the ground slope surface during the cutting, perhaps to make it easier to steer the picking teams. (After completion, the exposed portion of the stepped tunnel was covered with huge slabs and concealed from sight.) The city wall at this point shows two phases. The inner wall is dated, by the latest pottery beneath it, to the Iron I Age (12th—11th centuries B.C.); the outer wall appears to be a strengthening of the fortifications in the 10th century: Since the stepped tunnel to the spring was cut through the bedrock beneath both *walls* (apparently in order *not* to undermine them), Pritchard concluded that the stepped-tunnel-to-spring system was built after the second of those walls, but probably not by much—i.e., late in the 10th century.

But if the Gibeonites already had a completely secure stairway down to the water table inside the city (the pool-shaft system), why would they later have built a more vulnerable stepped tunnel leading under and outside the city wall? Pritchard answered that perhaps the water flow in the pool-shaft system was not sufficient to meet the city's needs. Such circumstances might have required the cutting of the second stepped tunnel directly to the spring outside the city wall, after which the pool-shaft and its stepped tunnel continued in use only as a supplementary system.

Pritchard recognized that the huge pool-shaft and its lower stepped tunnel represent two distinct phases of construction, but he argued that they are part of a single construction project. He believed that the engineers' intention from the beginning was to cut a broad stairwell to the water table, but that a change in political or economic conditions (a new king? an increase in labor costs?) caused the Gibeonites to alter their plan and to complete the project along less ambitious lines, i.e., by the

YIGAEL YADIN AND THE ISRAEL EXPLORATION SOCIETY

HAZOR—AFTER COMPLETING EXCAVATION of the water shaft and tunnel, the archaeologists constructed heavy wooden scaffolds to prevent rocks from falling on visitors. Because they were often immersed in spring water, the steps at the end of the sloping stepped tunnel were made of hard basalt rather than of the softer and faster weathering limestone. These steps are visible in the foreground.

narrower stepped tunnel instead of by extending the broad and vertical pool-shaft. The threat of an enemy attack could have had the same effect, impelling the Gibeonites to change design in order to speed up the pace of their descent to a secure water source.

Whatever the reasons for the differences between the upper pool-shaft and its lower stepped tunnel, Pritchard was convinced that the two phases of the project were executed relatively closely in time because the steps in the pool-shaft show no more wear than the steps in the stepped tunnel below.

I should like to propose another solution to the Gibeon puzzle. Perhaps the pool-shaft and its continuation, the stepped tunnel that goes to the water table, were two distinct projects separated by a century or more. I suggest that the pool-shaft was originally dug only as a cistern for the collection of rain water—that in David and Abner's time it was indeed a "pool" and nothing more than a pool.[14]

Following this suggestion further, the other stepped tunnel, leading to the spring outside the walls, was built after the pool-shaft in order to supplement the water supply by making the fresh water of the spring accessible inside the city (that is, through the stepped tunnel to the spring).

When, as part of that second project, the Gibeonites cut the horizontal feeder tunnel back into the hill from the spring to increase the flow of water, they certainly must have realized that they had reached a point almost underneath the earlier cistern shaft, which we have been calling the pool-shaft. Note the proximity of the inner end of the feeder tunnel to the area of the pool-shaft. The engineers might have thought that they were closer than, in fact, they were. Because of its zigzag course, the horizontal feeder tunnel extended some 16 feet less in actual distance than its 110-foot length.

The Gibeonites might have decided to cut a stairway tunnel down from the base of their earlier cistern (the pool-shaft) with the intention of reaching the level of the horizontal feeder tunnel and then cutting out horizontally to connect with it. The water chamber at the base of the pool/stepped-tunnel system does, in fact, extend in the direction of the feeder tunnel. Before reaching that goal, however, the Gibeonites hit the water table! They thus discovered a fresh water supply wholly secure inside the city walls. This project—and the discovery it led to—should be dated *after* the 10th century stepped-tunnel-to-spring system. An early 9th century date would be quite plausible.

The news of this remarkable discovery would have quickly spread. It could easily have become the model for Hazor, whose engineers opted for this system

GIBEON—THE ZIGZAG FEEDER tunnel was cut from the cave-like water chamber at the base of the tell to the spring under the city wall, so that the spring water would flow more freely into the water chamber. Although the spring is only 94 feet from the water chamber, the feeder tunnel covers about 110 feet. The meandering path of the tunnel suggests that the original diggers followed a trickle of water as it flowed through fissures in the rock.

instead of the Megiddo shaft and tunnel system which led to a spring outside the city wall. This could explain why the Hazor system reflects such confidence in the result. After the Gibeon experience, the Hazor engineers would have known precisely what they were doing. (If Yadin's dating of the Gezer water system is correct, Gibeon could have served also as the model for Gezer where the engineers also proceeded to their goal with confidence.)

My theory about the Gibeon water system assumes that the pool-shaft was first built as a cistern. Pritchard considered this possibility but rejected it because the fissured bedrock would probably not

GIBEON—THE STEPPED TUNNEL, with its 93 steps cut from solid rock, leads underground from a spring chamber at the base of the hill up to the city; it passes beneath the city wall, then opens within the city. Worn stone treads and polished walls are vivid evidence of the nameless carriers of Gibeon who climbed the steps and touched the walls for support as they carried water up into the city.

been washed away over time.[15]

Pritchard also argued that the pool-shaft and its lower stepped tunnel could not have been separate projects because of the balustrade left on the steps. The balustrade alongside the pool-shaft steps seems to continue as a rim around the top of the stepped tunnel cavity. According to Pritchard, "The balustrade left in the live rock at the point where the steps go below the floor of the pool indicates that the circular stairway into the [stepped] tunnel was a part of the plan of construction when the floor of the pool was leveled off. The floor on the east side is carefully smoothed, while on the south and southwest provision was obviously left for the descent of the stairway into the [stepped] tunnel."[16]

But this same evidence might be used to argue the opposite interpretation. Why plan for a balustrade around the top of the tunnel steps? The water carriers on the steps would hardly need it at that point. If it was to protect persons standing on the pool floor from falling into the stepped tunnel, why wasn't a similar rim left around the two holes in the pool-shaft which provide light to the stepped tunnel below? Why finish off the bottom of the pool-shaft at all if the intention had been to tunnel deeper?

Perhaps the balustrade at the bottom of the pool-shaft represents the lowest level of the earlier cistern steps, which had terminated in a platform slightly above the cistern floor to allow water carriers to fill their jars without stepping into the water when the water was at its lowest levels. Pritchard found a shallow, almost square basin hollowed out of the pool-shaft floor alongside the bottom segment of the balustrade. This might have been an installation to facilitate filling jugs when the water level was low. Perhaps when the stepped

have retained water for long without plaster, and he found no trace of plaster in the pool shaft. But the Gibeon engineers may not have known this when they dug it. Perhaps they hoped that the bedrock would be as impermeable as it is in some other places in the region. Or perhaps the Gibeonites inhibited percolation out of the pool by periodically applying a clay mortar lining, all traces of which would have

tunnel project was initiated below the pool-shaft, the earlier pool stairs were sufficiently worn to lead the pickmen to re-cut them, creating the balustrade effect in the process as an afterthought. The stepped tunnel which extended the line of the steps down through the earlier platform was made narrow enough to leave the outer edge of the platform as an incidental rim—not necessary, but also not in the way.[17]

One cannot say for certain that the stepped tunnel beneath the pool-shaft provides the specific "missing link" which prepared the way for the Hazor shaft-to-water-table system. But it is clear that the Hazor project presupposes an awareness of the subterranean water table deep beneath the Israelite city. The Gibeon water system, on the other hand, does *not* demand such prior knowledge. The groping of the diggers who accidentally found the water table under the city is apparent. Gibeon it seems, then, is the most likely model for the Hazor engineers who, with sure and steady picks, dug directly through bedrock beneath the city streets to the water table level, 146 feet below.

The water tunnels of ancient Israel—whether in Jerusalem, Megiddo, Gezer, Gibeon or Hazor—are records through which modern day tourists may wander. They are unique archaeological remains—testimony to the engineering prowess of the ancient inhabitants of Israel. 𝄢

[1] For fullest description see Robert Scott Lamon, *The Megiddo Water System* (Chicago, 1935).

[2] Yigael Yadin, *Hazor: the Rediscovery of a Great Citadel of the Bible* (New York, 1975), pp 168, 187–193.

[3] Yadin, *Hazor*, pp. 207–220.04 A stairway of similar concept was excavated by James G. Pritchard at Tell es-Sa'idiyeh in the Jordan Valley in 1964; see *Biblical Archaeologist* XXVIII:1 (Feb., 1965), 12–14.

[5] Yadin, *Hazor*, pp. 233–247.

[6] R. A. S. Macalister, *The Excavation of Gezer* (London, 1912), II, 256–265; III, Plate LII.

[7] *Biblical Archaeologist* XXXII, 3 (September, 1969), 70.

[8] Ibid., 71–78.

[9] For the fullest description of the Pool and its discovery, see James B. Pritchard's *Gibeon, Where the Sun Stood Still* (Princeton, 1962), pp. 64–74.

[10] Edward Robinson, *Biblical Researches in Palestine* (London, 2nd ed. 1860), Vol. I, pp. 454–456.

[11] Pritchard, *Gibeon* pp. 45–52.

[12] James B. Pritchard, *The Water System of Gibeon* (Philadelphia, 1961), p. 8. See this volume for the most complete technical description of both the Pool and the stepped tunnel to the spring at el-Jib.

[13] The same general concept (stepped tunnel through bedrock to already-known spring source) is exhibited in modified form in "Warren's Shaft" at Jerusalem. An even closer analogy may be the tunnel at Khirbet Bel 'ameh (ancient Ibleam) near Jenin, but it has not been fully exposed or dated (see G. Schumacher in *Palestine Exploration Quarterly*, 1910, 107–112, Pl. 2).

[14] If the pool had been used originally as a cistern, we should not necessarily find traces today at the top of the shaft of the channels which led water into the reservoir. When it was converted to its later use the channel endings would have been dismantled to prevent water from flowing into the cavity.

[15] Alternately, the upper shaft may have been a grain silo. A silo of similar shape, complete with spiraling steps, is preserved at Iron Age Megiddo The installation at Megiddo, however, only entailed cutting through earlier earthen debris layers and then lining the silo walls with small stones. It seems unnecessarily ambitious of the Gibeonites to have hewn through solid bedrock merely for grain storage.

[16] Pritchard, *The Water System of Gibeon*, p. 10.

[17] A secondary cutting of the upper stairs would explain why they appear less worn than those of the stepped tunnel to the spring in spite of the fact that the pool appears to predate the stepped tunnel and yet to have been still in use right up until the city's destruction at the end of the Iron Age. There is a further reason to suggest that the upper shaft may have been originally a reservoir. The Hebrew word identifying the early 10th century installation at Gibeon in 2 Samuel 2 and translated "pool" (*berekah*) seems to be used elsewhere in the Bible for places where water is *collected*: basins into which water flows, natural pools in which rain water collects and so forth, for instance Isaiah 22:9, 11; Ecclesiastes 7:5. I find no place where the meaning is clearly a *source* of water or a place *from which* water flows. One verse is particularly striking. In Nahum 2:8 the prophet writes, "Nineveh is like a pool (*berekah*) whose waters run away." The implication, of course, is that the waters should *not* run away from a *berekah*: they should be held by it.

For an interesting exchange about this article between a reader and author Dan Cole, see the Queries and Comments section in the January/February 1981 and March/April 1981 issues.

Related Reading

Yigal Shiloh, "Jerusalem's Water Supply During Siege—The Rediscovery of Warren's Shaft," BAR, July/August 1981.

Terence Kleven, "Up the Waterspout: How David's General Joab Got Inside Jerusalem," BAR, July/August 1994.

Dan Gill, "How They Met: Geology Solves Long-Standing Mystery of Hezekiah's Tunnelers," BAR, July/August 1994.

Ronny Reich and Eli Shukron, "Light at the End of the Tunnel," BAR, January/February 1999.

Hershel Shanks, "I Climbed Warren's Shaft (But Joab Never Did)," BAR, November/December 1999.

Avraham Faust, "Warren's Shaft," BAR, September/October 2003; Aryeh Shimron, "Response: Warren's Shaft," BAR, July/August 2004.

Hershel Shanks, "The Siloam Pool," BAR, September/October 2005 (see p. 502 of this book).

"Did Ancient Jerusalem Draw Water Through Warren's Shaft?" BAR, March/April 2007.

Hershel Shanks, "Sound Proof," BAR, September/October 2008.

Eyal Shalev, Amihai Sneh and Ram Weinberger, "The Fault Beneath Their Feet," BAR, September/October 2010.

Hershel Shanks, "Will Hezekiah Be Dislodged from His Tunnel?" BAR, September/October 2013 and works cited.

Jerusalem Tombs from the Days of the First Temple

A few hundred yards from Damascus Gate and over the wall from the Garden Tomb, a magnificent burial cave lies beneath a Dominican monastery.

GABRIEL BARKAY AND **AMOS KLONER**

DAMASCUS GATE, THE MOST IMPORTANT entrance to Jerusalem's Old City, fairly bustles with activity inside and out. Arab men in their robes and keffiyehs; Arab women in long embroidered dresses; priests from a dozen different Christian denominations, Eastern and Western, each with his distinctive gown or collar or hat; Orthodox Jews with long beards and black garb walking to the Western Wall of the Temple Mount to pray; young Israelis; and tourists from everywhere—all mingle and brush shoulders. As a dozen languages blend together, honking taxis and braying mules create a cacophony. Odors typical of Near Eastern bazaars—sweet Turkish coffee, roasted nuts, spices and sheepskin—float through the air.

As its name implies, Damascus Gate opens onto the road to Damascus, 140 miles away. In Hebrew, the gate is called *Sha-ar Shechem*, Shechem Gate, because the road also leads to Shechem, modern Nablus, on the way to Damascus.

Within a block of the gate, on the right going north, is a large, walled compound—the monastery of the Dominican fathers. Within its walls is not only the Monastery of St. Étienne (St. Stephen), but also the famous École Biblique et Archéologique Française, or the French School, as it is sometimes called.

Walking through the small opening in the massive monastery wall is like passing from one world into another. Noise and bustle are left behind and serenity and calm take their place. In the spacious gardens of the monastery, shaded by tall old pines, one hears only the sound of birds or the turning of an ancient folio page in the school's world-renowned library. White-robed priests move silently amid columned porticos. The atmosphere is holy.

Although one is hardly aware of it as one enters the Monastery of St. Étienne today, the monastery compound sits on the slope of a hill. This hill is separated from the walled Old City to the south by Nablus (Shechem) Road, which runs along the outside of the wall. Toward the end of the last century, this hill was identified by the famous English general Charles George Gordon as Golgotha, the site of Jesus' crucifixion. Today, the southern face of the hill is obscured by the East Jerusalem bus station. A Moslem cemetery occupies the summit. North of the bus station is the so-called Garden Tomb where, some have proposed, Jesus was buried. Still further north, the Monastery of St. Étienne adjoins the Garden Tomb.

In one of St. Étienne's gardens a flight of stairs leads down to the monastery's underground burial chapel. Here are buried some of the legendary figures in the history of Biblical scholarship, ancient geography and Jerusalem archaeology—Roland Guerin de Vaux, Louis Hugues Vincent, Felix M. Abel, Raphael Savignac, Charles Coüasnon—all Dominican priests. Their names reverberate in the hushed burial chapel as scant sunlight reveals the inscribed plaques on the wall behind which their mortal remains lie.

The burial chapel is, in fact, directly in front of

DOMINICAN PRIESTS BURIED in the underground chapel of St. Étienne's Church include many of the great figures in the history of scientific research in the Holy Land: Louis-Hugues Vincent, who excavated the ancient burial caves next to this chapel in the late 19th century, Roland de Vaux, excavator of Qumran and Tirzah (Tell el-Farah), Raphael Savignac, known for his studies in Arabia and the Negev, and Felix M. Abel, founder of modern geographical study of the Holy Land.

RICHARD NOWITZ

CONCEALED BY MODERN JERUSALEM, an ancient cemetery within these rocky hills covers much of the area of this aerial photo.

All the tombs named on the locator drawing are part of the same complex of burial caves, hewn from the bedrock in the eighth and seventh centuries B.C., when the First Temple stood about a half mile to the south, on the Temple Mount.

(1) École Biblique
(2) St. Étienne Church
(3) entrance to St. Étienne Cave Complex 2
(4) entrance to St. Étienne Cave Complex 1
(5) entrance to Garden Tomb
(6) Garden Tomb compound
(7) Moslem cemetery
(8) Skull Rock (Golgotha)
(9) old East Jerusalem bus terminal
(10) new east Jerusalem bus terminal
(11) Nablus Road (the road to Damascus)
(12) White Sisters Convent burial cave
(13) Conder's Cave

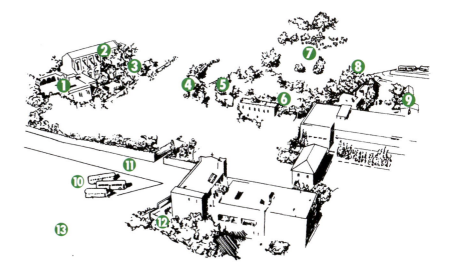

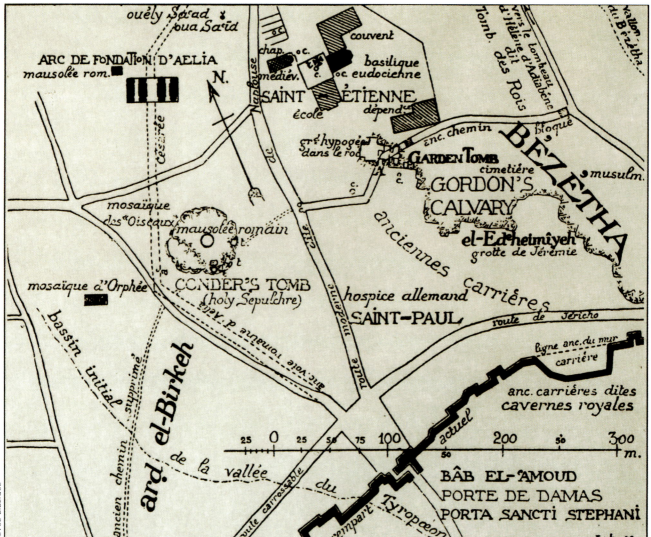

another burial cave complex, a very ancient one. In 1885, shortly after the monastery was established here because it was the traditional site of the martyrdom of St. Stephen, this burial cave complex was excavated by the Dominican fathers. They found another burial cave complex near a church they were building in memory of St. Stephen. The cave complex behind the fathers' burial chapel is called Cave Complex 1; the other, Cave Complex 2.

The results of these 19th century excavations were published by Roland de Vaux (1885), Marie Joseph Lagrange (1894) and Louis-Hugues Vincent (1926), who dated the burial caves to the Second Temple period (first century B.C. to first century A.D.) or the Roman period (first to third centuries A.D.). No special importance was attributed to the caves.

However, during the last 100 years, and especially recently, we have learned an enormous amount about burial caves and customs in different

IN 1925, THE *REVUE BIBLIQUE* published this map of Jerusalem, showing the monastery of St. Étienne and the Garden Tomb. Another cave tomb on this map was identified as the Holy Sepulchre in 1881 by Claude Conder, but is no longer a contender.

Biblical periods. On the basis of this scholarship, even a cursory examination of the tomb complexes at St. Étienne cast grave doubt on Lagrange and Vincent's dating. It therefore seemed appropriate to undertake a thorough reinvestigation of these burial caves. In 1973, the authors, with the kind permission of Père Pierre Benoit, then head of the École Biblique, initiated a detailed survey of these caves (see the sidebar "How We Happened to Re-Explore the Caves at St. Étienne").

The entrance to Cave Complex 1 is behind the altar of the modern burial chapel. The first room of the ancient burial cave is the entrance chamber. This entrance chamber measures about 14 feet by 17 feet. The ceiling is about ten feet high. These measurements are significant, and we will return to them later (see the sidebar "Measurements in the Bible—Evidence at St. Étienne for the Length of the Cubit and the Reed").

Inside the doorway to the entrance chamber is a step that forms an additional threshold. In this rock-hewn step there are carved two three-quarter-circle sockets; these sockets originally held the hinges of a double door that controlled access to the burial cave. Steps like this one, with similar sockets, are known from various Iron Age II (eighth to seventh century B.C.) structures. They are usually found at palace throne room entrances—for example, at Arslan-Tash, at Zincirli (ancient Samal) and Tell Halaf in northern Syria; at Nimrud (Biblical Calah) (Genesis 10:11–12), and Nineveh in Assyria, and at Megiddo and Gezer in Israel. The implication, as we shall see again and again, is that this impressive cave complex dates to the First Temple period (eighth or seventh century B.C.), rather than to the Second Temple period (first century B.C. to first century A.D.).

A careful examination of the walls of the entrance chamber reveals that they are decorated with shallow sunken panels, rectangular in shape, that were hewn into the rock faces of the walls. These rectangular panels are probably stone copies of wooden panels that typically covered the walls of Judean palaces during the Israelite period. Until this discovery, archaeologists had not seen any Israelite or Judean palace (or other building) of this period with a preserved superstructure of walls. At best, they had found only wall stubs. The walls of this St. Étienne burial cave can therefore teach us a great deal about how palace walls were decorated in Iron Age II. Such decoration was probably used on the walls of Solomon's Temple. In 1 Kings 6:9, we read that after Solomon finished building the Temple, he covered the walls with "beams and planks of cedar." This is how the New Jewish Publication Society translation renders the passage, but a note to the verse tells us that the "meaning of the Hebrew [is] uncertain." The Hebrew word translated as "beams" is *gebim*; for "planks" the word is *sderot*. *Gebim* probably refers to the sunken panels, and *sderot* to the raised strips between the panels. Who would have thought that an examination of the stone walls of a burial chamber would elucidate a hitherto obscure Biblical passage and would tell us how the walls in Solomon's Temple might have been decorated.

Incidentally, this method of wall decoration continued to be used to the end of the Divided Monarchy (586 B.C.). Jeremiah prophesies against Jehoikim, king of Judah (italics added):

SUNKEN PANEL. Carved into a stone wall of the Cave Complex 1 entrance chamber, panels, doorway frames and a double cornice running along the top of the wall display the stonemasons' skill. Chisel marks are invisible, a strong indication that this tomb was carved in the First Temple period. During the Second Temple period, by contrast, rock surfaces were dressed with chisels that left clear "comb" marks.

"Ha! he who builds his house with unfairness
And his upper chambers with injustice,
Who makes his fellowman work without pay
And does not give him his wages,
Who thinks: I will build me a vast palace
With spacious upper chambers,
Provided with windows,
Paneled in cedar,
Painted with vermilion!
Do you think you are more a king
Because you compete in cedar?"
(Jeremiah 22:13–15).

It seems that the same wall decoration was being used in Jeremiah's time.

Another point of interest in the entrance chamber is the cornice that decorates the top of the walls where they meet the ceiling. The cornice is carved from the rock, as is everything else in the burial cave. It consists of two strips running horizontally, the upper of which protrudes more than the lower. Cornices like this one have been found in other Iron Age burial caves. One such burial cave, known as the Tomb of the Royal Steward, was hewn for one of the highest ranking officials in the kingdom of Judah in the late eighth or seventh century B.C. Located in Silwan Village, the tomb lies across the valley from that part of Jerusalem called the City of David. An inscription deciphered by Professor

RICHARD NOWITZ

RICHARD NOWITZ

HEDY YEHUDAIOV

AN ANGULAR CORNICE decorating a chamber in St. Étienne's Cave Complex 2 is examined by co-author Barkay (left). This decoration and double cornices such as the one (below left) in Cave Complex 1 closely resemble the cornice on the ceiling of the royal burial cave at Van, in Urartu (modern Turkey) (above). Although much bigger than the St. Étienne tomb, the caves at Van date to the same period, the eighth century B.C., and follow the same basic plan of burial chambers leading off a central entrance chamber.

Nahman Avigad identifies the Tomb of the Royal Steward* and allows it to be securely dated to the period of the Judean monarchy. Other tombs with this same type of cornice were excavated at the site called the "Shoulder of Hinnom" overlooking the Hinnom Valley, next to St. Andrew's church in the western necropolis of Biblical Jerusalem.

Another tomb with a similar cornice was found southwest of Jerusalem in Khirbet Beit Lei, near Amatziah. An ancient Hebrew inscription in this tomb, published by its excavator Joseph Naveh, allows us to date the tomb with confidence to the Iron Age. Thus the St. Étienne cornice helps establish this cave complex as a First Temple burial tomb.

The entrance chamber of the St. Étienne burial cave, like its other rooms, has been carved with exceptional skill and care. This tomb complex was obviously the final resting place of an important and wealthy family. The walls are dressed so smoothly that we could not see any evidence of tooling. In Second Temple period tombs, by contrast, archae-ologists easily recognize the work of metal-toothed chisels, or "claws," which were used to finish the walls. The finely finished walls provide one more indication that the St. Étienne tombs must be dated to the First Temple period, rather than to the Second

* See "On the Shorter Inscription From the 'Tomb of the Royal Steward,'" David Ussishkin, *BASOR* 196 (1969), ww8.

How We Happened to Re-Explore the Caves at St. Étienne

Our story began in 1973 when Amos Kloner and I returned to Jerusalem on leave from the army during the Yom Kippur War. We had a little time remaining before reporting back to our units, so Amos and I decided to visit the caves at the St. Étienne monastery on the grounds of the École Biblique et Archéologique Française, the French school of archaeology.

For me, the first sight of the St. Étienne tombs was especially meaningful. I had recently spent several years with Professor David Ussishkin exploring First Temple burial caves in the Silwan village opposite the City of David, about one mile from where I now stood. The tooling marks, the architectural elements and the burial customs of the First Temple period were as familiar to me as if I had lived in those times. And now, standing in the St. Étienne caves for the first time, I was struck by the clear appearance of many of these First Temple period features. We knew immediately that the elegant central room leading to seven separate burial chambers must have been hewn in the First Temple period—not in the Roman period, as scholars had thought.

When Amos and I mentioned our views to Père Pierre Benoit, the distinguished director of the École Biblique who had accompanied us to the tombs, he smiled in a tolerant, fatherly way. When we asked if we could return to study the caves, Père Benoit granted permission, as if to say, Why not? No harm could be done.

It was a strange experience for us—young Israeli scholars—to be telling Père Benoit and the other eminent scholars at the École Biblique that their tombs were almost 800 years older than they thought.

Two months later we were released from the army and began our detailed study of the St. Étienne caves. For many days we descended to Cave Complex Number 1, and on the way passed through the underground chapel where the Dominican fathers of the École Biblique are buried. Each day we read the names on the stone plaques marking the final resting place of these giants—Louis-Hugues Vincent, Felix M. Abel, Raphael Savignac, Roland Guerin de Vaux, Charles Coüasnon—whose scholarly works illuminated the Bible, the geography of the Holy Land and the archaeology of Jerusalem. Most particularly, as we carried on our work, we felt the shadow of Père Vincent, who contributed so much to Jerusalem archaeology, but whose dating of this tomb we were now challenging.

—GABRIEL BARKAY

Temple period. Indeed, carefully dressed, smooth surfaces, especially on ashlar masonry, are typical of royal architecture in both the kingdom of Israel and the kingdom of Judah during the Iron Age.

The original 1885 excavation report includes a curious item. The excavators state that they found a metal box in a pit in the rear part of the entrance chamber. It was decorated with garlands and human figures in relief. Unfortunately, we could not examine this box—it has disappeared from the archaeological collection of the Dominican fathers. According to the excavation report, the box contained animal and bird bones. It is too bad this box and its contents have been lost because from it we might have learned a great deal about burial customs, as well as about art of the period. The box may even have contained a foundation deposit buried in the entrance chamber when it was originally hewn.

Leading off the entrance chamber are six additional rooms or chambers, two off of each wall except the entrance wall. This plan—a central entrance chamber with burial chambers around it—is found in several First Temple period burial caves in the kingdom of Judah. The Amatziah burial cave already mentioned was hewn on this plan. So was a burial cave at Khirbet el Kôm, west of Hebron, where Hebrew inscriptions scratched on the wall enabled the excavator, William G. Dever, to date it unequivocally.

Much to our surprise, in the course of our research we found that this same plan, and the same style of cornice we previously described, appears in the royal burial caves of the kingdom of Urartu (Biblical Ararat) at Van in Turkish Armenia. Both the burial halls and the cornice are much larger in the Urartu caves, but the plan of the halls and the design of the cornice are the same.

The rectangular entrances to the six chambers leading off the entrance chamber are decorated with a shallow frame carved from the rock. Each entrance is nearly six feet high, and with two exceptions, all the burial chambers are arranged in the same way. On the two side walls and on the wall opposite the entrance, burial benches have been hewn from the rock. The three burial benches form a kind of upside down Π (a Greek letter *pi* or the Hebrew letter *ḥet*). During the First Temple period, bodies were placed on these burial benches.

Each burial bench has a low parapet about two inches high around its outer edge, carved from the rock, presumably to prevent the body and burial gifts from rolling off the bench. Headrests at the ends of the burial benches, also carved from the rock, indicate how the bodies were placed. The headrests are shaped like horseshoes. The two ends of each horseshoe are rounded and the central part is lower and flatter than the ends. The head of the deceased rested in the horseshoe, and the neck came through the opening.

There are four headrests carved on the three burial benches in each burial chamber—two headrests at either end of the burial bench opposite the entrance and one on each of the side burial benches. Thus,

Cave Complex One

Carved 43 feet deep into the bedrock of the grounds of the St. Étienne Monastery, this complex is typical of many First Temple period tomb caves throughout the kingdom of Judah: a central entrance chamber is surrounded by burial chambers; most of the burial chambers (3, 4, 5, 8 on the plan below) have benches lining three of the walls; generally, horseshoe-shaped headrests are positioned on the benches (3, 4, 5, 6); and under each right-hand bench, a hollowed out area for gathered bones extends under the left-hand bench of the next room (3, 4, 5, 6).

Although typical of eighth- to seventh-century B.C. tombs, this complex and Cave Complex 2 as well also have very unusual architectural and decorative features. In both complexes, the first room off the right wall of the entrance chamber is larger than the other chambers and has no burial benches. Here the body may have been prepared for burial, or the family may have gathered to perform a funeral.

Carved into the stone walls of the large entrance rooms of both complexes and some of the burial chambers are door frames, recessed panels and ceiling cornices, evidence that these tomb complexes were hewn by a wealthy or noble family. Some of these features appear in the photo (right), framed by the doorway to the entrance chamber of Cave Complex 1.

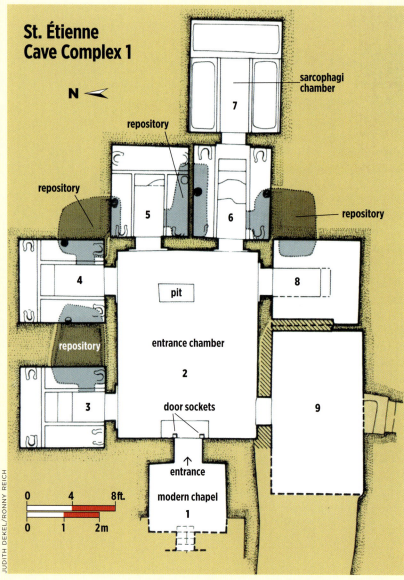

St. Étienne Cave Complex 1

N ⟨

- repository
- repository
- 7 — sarcophagi chamber
- 5
- 6
- repository
- 4
- pit
- 8
- repository
- entrance chamber
- 2
- 3
- door sockets
- 9
- ↑ entrance
- modern chapel
- 1

0   4   8 ft.

0   1   2m

RICHARD NOWITZ

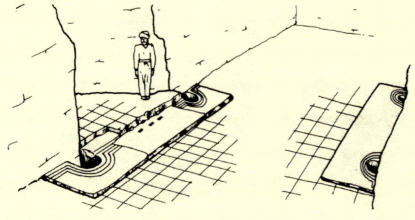

STACY MARTIN, AFTER M. E. L. MALLOWAN

Cave Complex 1, continued

On a rock-hewn threshold (left), just inside the entrance chamber of Cave Complex 1 at St. Étienne's Monastery, two three-quarter-circle, carved sockets once held the hinges of a double door. A similar doorway was constructed in the eighth to seventh centuries B.C. in the palace of the Assyrian kings at Calah (Biblical Nimrud) and at the other Assyrian capitals. An artist's reconstruction (below left) shows the Nimrud entry threshold with large sockets that originally held hinges for immense wooden doors.

In the St. Étienne tomb, pushing open the double doors and stepping across the threshold brought the visitor into a large, almost square chamber (right, above) with a ten-foot-high ceiling. In the photo (see also pp. 320–321), five of the six doorways in the room are visible; each one leads to a burial chamber. Such a configuration of entrance chamber and surrounding burial chambers is typical of First Temple period (eighth to early sixth centuries B.C.) burial caves.

Built on a grand scale—the entrance room alone measures 17 feet by 14 feet—the tomb was decorated with raised door frames, cornices and sunken panels, all carved into the stone walls. Gabriel Barkay, an Israeli archaeologist who studied the St. Étienne tombs, shows a Dominican priest a cornice of two horizontal strips that runs along the entrance room's walls where they meet the ceiling. Between the two doors on the wall facing the entrance to the complex is a sunken panel.

We read of such decoration in palaces and in Solomon's Temple in Jerusalem, described as "paneled...with beams and planks of cedar" in 1 Kings 6:9, but because no palaces or any buildings at all from Iron Age II have been found with preserved walls, we had no idea until now how these decorations looked.

This 2,700-year old St. Étienne burial cave—with its stone walls mimicking the wooden trim once used on elegant buildings for the living (artist's reconstruction, right)—shows us how some of the decorative elements in Solomon's Temple may have looked.

Cave Complex 1 revealed several unique features in addition to the doorway sockets. An empty pit was discovered in the floor of the entrance chamber. Here, according to the report published by the tomb's 19th-century excavators, a decorated metal box was buried. Now lost, this box may have held a foundation deposit set into the tomb's entrance by its original builders. Finally, deep in the hillside, a special inner chamber of three sarcophagi was hewn, where the founders of the family were probably interred. The tomb complex was apparently designed to lead those who entered to this important, innermost chamber.

RICHARD NOWITZ

JUDITH DEKEL

Cave Complex 1, continued

Most elaborate of the burial chambers in Cave Complex 1, two adjoining rooms, one behind the other (6 and 7 on the plan), are positioned nearly on a straight line of sight with the complex's entrance doorway. The innermost chamber with its unique features probably held the revered remains of the family matriarchs and patriarchs.

Burial benches with horseshoe-shaped headrests line two sides of the chamber. Under one bench (right), a hollowed-out cavity, called a repository, holds bones that the ancients had collected from the benches each time a new generation was to be buried. It's very likely that some of these bones are original burials from the First Temple period. With the discovery of these repositories (close-up below) we can understand such Biblical phrases as "slept with his fathers" and "gathered unto their fathers."

Unlike other burial chambers in Cave Complex 1, which have three benches, this room has only two benches, and they are larger than the others. This burial chamber is also distinguished by its high ceiling and by the double cornice, which can be seen clearly at the juncture of walls and ceiling.

Steps lead up to the doorway in the far wall, opening into another, candlelit burial room (photo, left). In this innermost chamber of the St. Étienne burial caves (also seen right), instead of benches, three rock-hewn coffins, or sarcophagi, were cut from the rock. A double cornice crowns the walls. The room has no repository; thus, archaeologists surmise that the family's leaders were laid to rest here, not to be moved. But at some point, perhaps in the Byzantine period, the bones were removed. The lids of the sarcophagi are missing, although the ledge on the wall that held them in piece is still visible.

The plan and the photograph on pp. 328–329 show the alignment of this special burial chamber, the sarcophagi chamber and the entrance chamber.

RICHARD NOWITZ

RICHARD NOWITZ

RICHARD NOWITZ

RICHARD NOWITZ

STONE HEADRESTS. On the burial benches of the St. Étienne cave tombs, these horseshoe-shapes cradled the heads of the deceased. Unlike the thin, simple "u"-shaped headrests in Cave Complex 1 (top), those in Cave Complex 2 (bottom) are slightly higher and thicker and curve out at the ends. This gives them the look of the wig typically worn by the Egyptian goddess Hathor, an indication of the cultural influence of Egypt in ancient Israel.

four bodies could be accommodated on the three burial benches—two on the back bench and one on each side. The headrests on the side benches were placed on ends closest to the entrance and opened toward the back of the chamber.

The headrests in the other burial cave complex at St. Étienne, Cave Complex 2, are slightly different. They are heavier and higher, with a curve at the two ends, reminding us of the wig typically worn by the Egyptian goddess Hathor.

Interestingly enough, Hathor appears on the famous eighth-century B.C. carved ivories from the palace at Samaria, capital of the northern kingdom of Israel.

Headrests similar to those found at St. Étienne are also known from the necropolis of the nobles in Silwan Village and in the western cemetery of

Jerusalem in the Hinnom Valley as well as at the burial caves of Khirbet el Kôm, and at Ṣovah, west of Jerusalem.* All date to the First Temple period. No doubt the Jerusalem tombs were the prototype; the country folk at places like Khirbet el Kôm were trying to emulate the elaborate, elegant, beautifully carved burial caves that characterized sophisticated artistic development in the royal center of Jerusalem.

As our readers will no doubt have guessed by this time, burial benches arranged around the sides of the room are typical of First Temple period tombs. Second Temple burials, on the other hand, are entirely different. In the later period, burial niches (called *kokhim*; singular, *kokh*) rather than benches, were carved perpendicularly into the rock. In addition, the Second Temple period burial caves sometimes had shelves carved into the walls with ceilings shaped like arches; these are called *arcosolia* (singular, *arcosolium*).

First Temple period or Iron Age rock-hewn tomb chambers with burial benches on three sides are very widely distributed in Judah. They have been found at Beth Shemesh, Lachish, Mitzpah, Motza and elsewhere. There can thus be no doubt that the burial complex at St. Étienne dates to the First Temple period.

In each of the burial chambers at St. Étienne, a rectangular opening was cut into the side of the right-hand burial bench. This opening leads to an irregular, hollowed out area under the burial bench. This hollowed out area extends into the next room, under the left-hand burial bench of that room, so that the space under both side benches is utilized.

These hollowed out areas are repositories. When the burial benches were needed for the next generation, the bones and burial gifts of the earlier generation were simply scooped up from the burial benches and placed in the repository under the bench. These repositories explain the Biblical phrases in which the deceased are "gathered unto their fathers" (e.g., Judges 2:10; 2 Kings 22:20) or "buried with his fathers" (e.g., 2 Kings 8:24) or "slept with his fathers" (e.g., 2 Kings 13:13). The bones of each generation were literally collected and added to the pile of bones of the forefathers. Bones have even been found in the repositories at St. Étienne, although we cannot tell whether they are from the original burials or from later burials, since the caves were reused in the Byzantine period (fifth and sixth centuries A.D.), more than a thousand years after their original use.

One room in Cave Complex 1 at St. Étienne is special. It is the right-hand room on the wall

* *Excavations and Surveys in Israel*, Vol. 1, 1982 (Jerusalem Israel Ministry of Education and Culture, Department of Antiquities and Museums).

Measurements in the Bible
Evidence at St. Étienne for the Length of the Cubit and the Reed

Our work at the burial caves at St. Étienne has yielded an unexpected bonus by clarifying the length of the cubit and the reed, units of measurement mentioned frequently in the Bible.

The cubit—actually the Egyptian cubit—was the standard measure of length in the Biblical period. The priestly tabernacle, the Temple of Solomon and many other structures are described in the Bible in cubit measurements. In fact, there were two different cubits, the long or royal cubit and the short cubit. Scholars have used various means to determine the length of the cubits, more or less with success. The long cubit is approximately 52.5 centimeters and the short cubit is about 45 centimeters.

When we began measuring the tomb complexes at St. Étienne, we immediately noticed that the entrance chamber of Cave Complex 1 measured 5.3 meters by 4.2 meters. Thus it was 10 long (or royal) cubits by 8 long cubits. The ceiling was 7 long cubits high. The width of the step at the entrance to the Cave Complex 1 is 52 centimeters, 1 long cubit; the distance between the two sockets on top of the step is also 52 centimeters. The length of the pit in which the metal box was found is 105 centimeters, 2 long cubits. The width of this pit is 50 centimeters, about 1 long cubit.

In Cave Complex 2 we were amazed to find a different measurement, the short cubit. The entrance chamber is 4.5 meters by 7.2 meters, that is, 10 short cubits by 16 short cubits. The width of the step at the entrance to Cave Complex 2 is 1.33 meters, 3 short cubits; the depth of the step is .68 meter, 1.5 short cubits.

Although the two cave complexes at St. Étienne were hewn on the same plan and most probably at almost the same time, they

```
┌──────────────────────────────────────────────────────────┐
└──────────────────────────────────────────────────────────┘
METER                                          100 cm (39.36 inches)
┌──────────────────────────────────┐
└──────────────────────────────────┘ 52.5 cm (20.67 inches)
LONG (ROYAL) CUBIT
┌────────────────────────────────┐
└────────────────────────────────┘ 45 cm (17.71 inches)
SHORT CUBIT
```

used different cubits. In Cave Complex 1, the long or royal cubit was used. In Cave Complex 2, the measurements indicate that the short cubit was used. It seems therefore that the short cubit and long cubit were both used in the eighth to seventh centuries B.C.

The use of two different cubits is reflected in the Bible. In 2 Chronicles 3:3, we are told that Solomon built his Temple according to the "first" cubit. Unfortunately, we still don't know if the "first" cubit refers to the long cubit or the short one.

We have already noted that the entrance chamber to Cave Complex 1 was 8 by 10 long cubits (about 22 square meters); the entrance chamber to Cave Complex 2 was larger, 10 by 16 (2 multiplied by 8) short cubits (about 32.5 square meters). In 1 Kings 7:10 we learn that the buildings comprising Solomon's palace area were built of stones 10 cubits long and stones 8 cubits long. Apparently the proportion 8:10 was a common one, considered most appropriate and pleasing at that time.

The reed (kâneh in Hebrew) is mentioned 19 times in the Bible; most of its occurrences are in the Book of Ezekiel, where it is used both as a unit of measurement ("the threshold of the gate which was one reed broad" [Ezekiel 40:6]) and as a measuring instrument ("He measured the east side with the measuring reed" [Ezekiel 42:16]).

Ezekiel 41:8 defines the reed as "six noble cubits."

Just as there were two kinds of cubits, the long cubit and the short one, apparently there also were two different reeds corresponding to the two cubits.

Evidence for use of the six-cubit reed is clearly present in Cave Complex 2 at St. Étienne, where we find repeated units of six cubits and fractions of six cubits, as shown in the plan. The distances between the center of each burial chamber doorway to the centers of those doorways adjacent to it on the same wall are in every case six cubits, or one reed. Measuring from each corner of the chamber to the center of the nearest burial chamber doorway we find a distance of two cubits (one-third of a reed). The reed of Cave Complex 2 is 2.7 meters long (45 centimeters multiplied by 6) because the measurements in Cave Complex 2 are based on the short cubit.

The six-cubit measurement and its multiples, 12, 18, 30, 60 and 300 appear in the Bible 31 times. (Seven cubits and its multiples appear only *three* times.) The frequent Biblical references to six cubits and its multiples, plus the on-site evidence of six-cubit units in Cave Complex 2 at St. Étienne, enable us to understand the length of the Biblical reed.

Most likely, the hewers of Cave Complex 2 and the builders of other large structures found the cubit "ruler" to be too small for convenient use and used a six-cubit reed stick instead, just as a modern builder prefers a yardstick to a one-foot ruler. —GABRIEL BARKAY

opposite the entrance to the entrance chamber. There are only two burial benches in it, one on either side of the room. These burial benches are larger than usual, and each has two headrests, one on either end, as if each burial bench was intended for a couple. The ceiling of this chamber is higher than the other rooms and certain decorative elements recall the elegance of the entrance chamber: a double cornice was carved at the top of the wall, and sunken panels were carved into the wall leading from this chamber to another behind it.

Between the two burial benches of this special

room, a flight of steps leads up to the innermost chamber of the entire burial complex. This innermost chamber has no burial benches, but three roughly hewn sarcophagi are cut from the rock in the same arrangement as the burial benches in the other burial chambers. The same sunken panels used on the walls of the entrance chamber appear on the outer faces of the sarcophagi. Narrow shelves protruding from the walls just above the sarcophagi were intended as supports for stone slabs that once covered the sarcophagi. In this innermost chamber, there is no repository for bones. The bodies of

Cave Complex Two

Cave Complex 2 differs only slightly from Cave Complex 1. The entrance chamber is considerably larger, and three burial chambers extend from the left wall, instead of two. The headrests are thicker, with ends that curl up. In the first chamber on the right wall (as in Cave Complex 1), the dead may have been prepared for burial.

These rooms were built according to a plan using the ancient cubit measurement; in fact, Cave Complex 2 was built using multiples of the so-called short cubit (45 cm) and Cave Complex 1, using multiples of the long, or royal Egyptian, cubit (52.5 cm).

LEEN RITMEYER

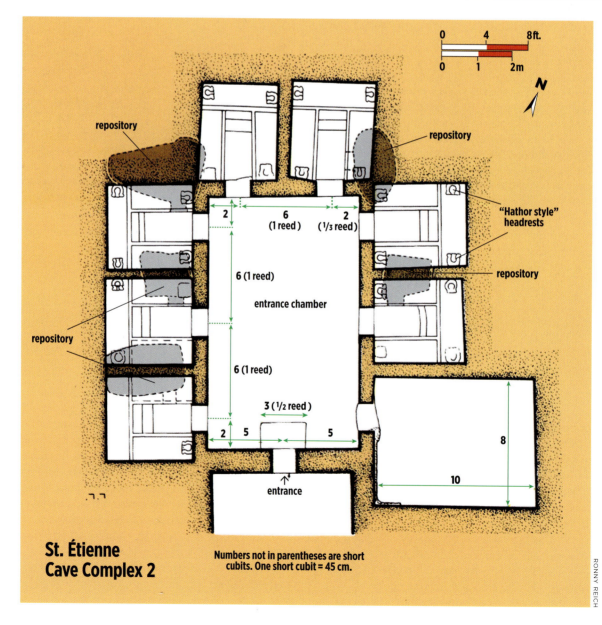

St. Étienne
Cave Complex 2

Numbers not in parentheses are short cubits. One short cubit = 45 cm.

RONNY REICH

the honored dead placed in these sarcophagi were buried here for the first *and* the last time. Their bones were not "collected" in later generations. Like the other "special" chambers of the complex, this innermost chamber also has a double cornice at the top of the walls.

If we look at the plan of the burial cave complex, we can easily see that the entire complex was organized so that people would walk directly into the innermost chamber, which was no doubt the most important room of the burial cave. We assume that the sarcophagi in this room held the bodies of the fathers or founders of the family. The rest of the immediate family members were buried in the adjacent rooms.

Another special room in this cave complex was the first room on the right after entering the entrance chamber. While it is larger and more elaborate than the other rooms, it does not include any burial installations—neither benches, sarcophagi, nor repositories. We assume that this room was used either for some kind of ceremony or as a room in which bodies were prepared for burial. In 2 Chronicles 16:14 we are told that when King Asa of Judah died, his body was laid in a resting place filled with expertly blended spices and perfumes. Perhaps this was the purpose for which this empty room at St. Étienne was used. It is interesting that in Cave Complex 2, a similar room was also found to the right of the doorway to the entrance chamber.

We now know that the two cave complexes at St. Étienne were part of a much larger necropolis north of Jerusalem in the First Temple period. Just south of the St. Étienne tombs is the Garden Tomb, which can now also be dated to the First Temple period (see "The Garden Tomb: Was Jesus Buried Here?" BAR, March/April 1986). South of the Garden Tomb there were two other burial caves published by Amihai Mazar dating to the First Temple period.

What accounts for the location of this necropolis north of the city? In 1970, Professor Nahman Avigad uncovered part of the massive, 23-foot-thick, wall that bounded Jerusalem on the north in the late eighth century B.C. Today this wall can be seen in the Jewish Quarter of the Old City, far south of the northern necropolis we have been discussing. The Christian Quarter and the Moslem Quarter of the Old City lie north of this ancient wall and south of the northern necropolis. What was in this area in the eighth century B.C.? The words of the prophet Jeremiah suggest the answer; in the future, he says, a rebuilt city would include the extramural suburbs like Gareb Hill and Goah (Jeremiah 31:38–39). The prophet may well be describing the northern suburbs of Jerusalem, located outside the wall of the city before the Babylonian destruction in the early sixth century B.C.

During the eighth and seventh centuries, the population of Jerusalem expanded tremendously.* This is suggested by the Biblical text, and it has been confirmed archaeologically. The area north of the walled city was the proposed direction of expansion. With this increase in population, more burial grounds were needed. To the burial areas west of the city (such as the Shoulder of Hinnom)** and east of the City of David (in what is now the village of Silwan) we may now add the northern necropolis in the area north of the northern suburbs.

The two burial cave complexes at St. Étienne are the most elaborate and the most spacious First Temple period burial caves known to us in all Judah. Each covers approximately 10,000 square feet. We have no information whatever about the appearance of the tombs of the kings of the House of David. It may well be that the royal tombs closely resembled the burial cave complexes at St. Étienne, designed to hold the founder of the family and generations thereafter.

The burial caves at St. Étienne have enriched our knowledge of Jerusalem, provided us with an example of elegant, wealthy tomb complexes of the First Temple period, taught us about burial customs of the times, and even instructed us about the masonry and decoration of royal palaces, the use and length of cubits and reeds and something about the topography of Jerusalem. Surely this is adequate for the moment. ⊠

*See Magen Broshi, "Estimating the Population of Ancient Jerusalem," BAR, June 1978.

**See Gabriel Barkay, "The Divine Name Found in Jerusalem," BAR, March/April 1983.

Related Reading

Hershel Shanks, "Have the Tombs of the Kings of Judah Been Found?" BAR, July/August 1987.

Othmar Keel, "The Peculiar Headrests for the Dead in First Temple Times," BAR, July/August 1987; Gabriel Barkay, "Burial Headrest as a Return to the Womb—A Reevaluation," BAR, March/April 1988.

Hershel Shanks, "The Tombs of Silwan," BAR, May/June 1994.

Hershel Shanks, "Is This King David's Tomb?" BAR, January/February 1995.

Gabriel Barkay, "The Riches of Ketef Hinnom," BAR, July/August/September/October 2009 (see p. 404 of this book).

Gabriel Barkay, "Who Was Buried in the Tomb of Pharaoh's Daughter?" BAR, January/February 2013.

Jeffrey R. Zorn, "Is T1 David's Tomb?" BAR, November/December 2012.

8

Powerful Life in the Divided Monarchy

Archaeological excavations in the sibling kingdoms of Israel and Judah have brought forth rich discoveries of prosperity and divine worship, as well as harrowing remains of death and destruction—all of which have enriched our understanding of the Biblical period.

With Solomon's death, his kingdom broke in two—the kingdom of Israel in the north and the kingdom of Judah in the south. Although often at odds with each other, they were inextricably linked by their shared heritage and their worship of the same God.

NOVEMBER/DECEMBER 1979
Answers at Lachish

Lachish was a major settlement in Judah in the First Temple period and earlier. It is best known for its destruction by the Assyrian monarch Sennacherib a short time before he marched on Jerusalem to besiege the Judean (or Judahite) capital in 701 B.C.E. In archaeological terms, the date of this conquest was determined beyond controversy by demonstrating that the destruction revealed in Level III at Lachish occurred in 701 B.C.E. In the history of archaeology this has been an extremely important datum because of the related problems it solved.

Equally dramatic, it was now clear that the destruction of Level III was depicted in the reliefs of the siege of Lachish in Sennacherib's palace, reliefs that are now a major attraction of London's British Museum.

All of this was described in this chapter's first article by Israeli excavator David Ussishkin.

If the last article produced answers, the next article produced questions. It examined a puzzling isolated site from the eighth century B.C.E. in the Sinai desert, just west of the road from Gaza to Eilat that separates the Negev from Egypt. Strangely, the ancient site was apparently ruled by the northern kingdom of Israel, rather than

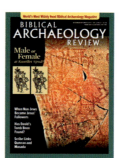

NOVEMBER/DECEMBER 2012
The Persisting Uncertainties of Kuntillet 'Ajrud

the adjacent southern kingdom of Judah.

A fortress-like religious building dominated the site. At one time it had plastered walls covered with paintings and inscriptions. Two large storage jars found in the building featured religious decorations and inscriptions—a procession of worshipers; the Egyptian god Bes; a woman playing a lyre; horned ibexes flanking a sacred tree; and inscriptions referring to Yahweh, the Israelite God, and his Asherah or *asherah* (depending on whether it refers to Yahweh's consort or Yahweh's symbol). Altogether Israeli archaeologist Ze'ev Meshel recovered more than 50 inscriptions, although many were quite small. What was the site—a caravanserai, a rest stop for pilgrims, a fortified trading post, a cult center or something else? You may have your own ideas after reading BAR's review essay of the excavation's final publication.

JANUARY/FEBRUARY 1996
The Fury of Babylon— Ashkelon and the Archaeology of Destruction

Before the Babylonians destroyed Jerusalem and Solomon's Temple in 586 B.C.E., they destroyed the metropolis of Ashkelon, which perhaps gives an idea of the devastation the Babylonians wrought on the Israelite capital. Ashkelon, of course, was a major Philistine trading center, rather than a religious center, and the remains naturally reflect this—pottery with typical Philistine decoration, a seaside marketplace, elegant tableware imported from Phoenicia, a commercial agreement for the purchase or delivery of grain, weights and a scale balance. An incense altar reflects Philistine religious activity, as does a bronze offering table engraved with bread flanked by libation flasks. As American archaeologist Lawrence E. Stager put it in his article, "At Ashkelon, commerce and religion apparently marched hand in hand."

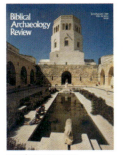

JULY/AUGUST 1989
What Happened to the Cult Figurines? Israelite Religion Purified After the Exile

Like the Philistines, Israelites once used figurines in a religious context. But this was discontinued when the Jews were permitted to return to the Holy Land from the Babylonian Exile in the late sixth century B.C.E.

A favissa is a pit in which votive objects such as small clay figurines have been discarded. The discovery of two favissae at Tel Dor led Israeli archaeologist Ephraim Stern to a larger study of these cult figurines over thousands of years. They are found all over the ancient world, including at early Israelite sites. A curious fact, however: They are not found at Jewish sites in the post-Exilic period. When the Babylonians conquered Jerusalem and destroyed the Solomonic Temple in 586 B.C.E., the Jews were exiled to Babylonia. Then, half a century later, the Persians defeated the Babylonians and permitted the Jews to return from the Babylonian Exile. At post-Exilic Jewish sites, these votive figurines are absent. This is in contrast to non-Jewish sites of

the same period. What are the implications for Israelite religion at this time? Stern explored some possibilities in the fourth article in this chapter.

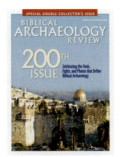

JULY/AUGUST/SEPTEMBER/OCTOBER 2009
The Riches of Ketef Hinnom

At an extraordinary burial site called Ketef Hinnom ("The Shoulder of Hinnom") outside the Old City walls of Jerusalem, Israeli archaeologist Gabriel Barkay discovered two small silver amulets. When unrolled, they were found to contain the oldest variants of Biblical texts ever to have been discovered—four centuries older than the Dead Sea Scrolls.

But this is only the end of the story. The site also produced Turkish rifles from the First World War, a colorful mosaic from a Byzantine-period church, cremation burials of the Tenth Roman Legion following the Roman destruction of Jerusalem in 70 C.E., a stone quarry used by Herod the Great, and Judahite rock-cut tombs carved in the First Temple period and used for hundreds of years thereafter. These tombs were perhaps the most dramatic finds of the excavation.

In one of them was a bone repository that had never been opened! In addition to the bones of some 95 individuals, it contained more than a thousand artifacts, including jewelry made of gold, silver and precious stones, perfume bottles, oil lamps, inscribed seals, more than 250 complete pottery vessels—and the two silver amulets with Bible-like inscriptions similar to the priestly blessing in Numbers 6:24–26.

Gaby Barkay's article was the feature story in our 200th issue of BAR, published in 2009.

Answers at Lachish

*Sennacherib's destruction of Lachish identified;
dispute over a century's difference in Israelite
pottery dating resolved by new excavations;
stamp impressions of Judean kings finally dated.*

DAVID USSISHKIN

LACHISH WAS ONE OF THE most important cities of the Biblical era in the Holy Land. The impressive mound, named Tel Lachish in Hebrew or Tell ed-Duweir in Arabic, is situated about 25 miles southwest of Jerusalem in the Judean hills. Once a thriving, fortified city, the almost 18 acre tel* today stands silent and unoccupied.

Settlement began here in the Chalcolithic period, toward the end of the fourth millennium B.C. By the third millennium Lachish was already a large city. In the Middle Bronze Age (first half of the second millennium B.C.), Lachish was heavily fortified by a glacis** which gave the mound its present prominent

*Readers may be confused by the use of the two spellings of "tel" and "tell" to refer to an ancient mound. "Tell" is the transliteration of the Arabic word and is used with an Arabic site name; "tel" is the transliteration of the Hebrew word and modifies a Hebrew site name. When speaking of *specific* mounds we use the appropriate spellings; but when speaking in general we use "tell."

**A glacis is an artificial ramp built against a slope in order to fortify it. This was the typical fortification used in the country during the Middle Bronze Age.

shape. In the Late Bronze Age (16th–13th centuries B.C.), Lachish was a large Canaanite city-state. A few letters from Lachish were found in the 14th century royal Egyptian archives at Tell el-Amarna. They were sent from the Canaanite king of the city to the Egyptian pharaoh.

Lachish played a major role in the story of the Israelite conquest of Canaan as related in Joshua 10. Japhia, king of Lachish, joined an alliance of five kings whom Joshua defeated on the day the sun stood still. After defeating these armies and killing their royal leaders, Joshua proceeded to attack their cities. Lachish was able to defend itself against Joshua's forces only for a single day. On the second day of the attack, Joshua took Lachish. He destroyed the city and killed its inhabitants. Excavations have confirmed a major destruction level at about this time (12th century B.C.). The archaeological record has also revealed that for about the next 200 years, until the 10th century B.C., Lachish was mostly abandoned.

ASSYRIAN ARCHERS MARCH in formation in Sennacherib's palace at Nineveh on one of the reliefs commemorating a military victory.

Following the division of the United Kingdom into Judah and Israel at Solomon's death, Lachish was rebuilt and heavily fortified by one of the kings of Judah, who turned it into a garrison city and royal stronghold. Undoubtedly the most important Judean city after Jerusalem, the city was defended by two massive city walls, the outer one built half way down the slope and the inner one extending along the edge of the mound. A large gate complex on the southwest side protected the city at its entrance. A huge palace-fort crowned the center of the city. Lachish played a major role in Judah until its destruction at the hands of Nebuchadnezzar's Babylonian army in 588/6 B.C. The city was rebuilt again in the Persian-Hellenistic period (sixth–fourth centuries B.C.), when it served as a district capital. Then it was abandoned forever.

A British expedition headed by James L. Starkey conducted large scale excavations at Tel Lachish between 1932 and 1938. This was one of the largest and most methodical excavations carried out in Palestine before the Second World War. Starkey systematically planned the work many years ahead. He spent the first years principally in preparatory

work, away from the mound itself. He dug ancient graveyards in the vicinity of the tel, cleared areas on the slopes, and built a convenient expedition camp. Some, but relatively little, work was done on the mound proper. The excavations, however, came to an abrupt halt in 1938. While travelling from Lachish to Jerusalem, to attend the opening ceremony of the Palestine Archaeological Museum, Starkey was forced by Arab bandits to stop near Hebron. Without warning the bandits shot him dead. After Starkey's murder, the excavation was wound down, while his assistant Olga Tufnell worked for twenty years on the data and finds, in the end producing a meticulous excavation report.

The mound remained untouched until the present excavations, except for a small dig carried out by Professor Yohanan Aharoni of Tel Aviv University on the eastern part of the mound.

One of the main areas excavated on the mound proper by the British expedition was the city gate complex and the roadway which led to it from outside the city. The city gate is situated near the southwest corner of the mound, and, in fact, the topographical lines had revealed its existence even before work began. As often happens in ancient Biblical cities, a number of city gates were found superimposed on one another, each associated with a different occupation level, each having been used during a different period in the city's history.

The first city gate uncovered by Starkey was naturally the uppermost and the latest one. It dated to the Persian period, and was in use until the final abandonment of the site. This gate and the related level, forming the uppermost archaeological stratum, was labelled Level I by the British. On penetrating further, the excavators found that the Level I gate and roadway were constructed above an earlier gate complex, which was accordingly labelled Level II. This earlier gate had been destroyed in an enemy attack, as evidenced by a thick layer of destruction debris over the remains of the Level II gate.

At that point Starkey made his most famous discovery: a small room, later called the guard room, was found within the Level II gate-complex. The floor of the guard room was covered by the ashes of the destruction. Beneath the ashes were sealed hundreds of storage jar fragments blackened by the intense fire which accompanied the destruction. Eighteen of these pottery fragments contained ancient Hebrew inscriptions written in ink. These ostraca, that is, inscribed pot sherds, are known today as the Lachish Letters. They were sent to a military commander at Lachish during the last days of the kingdom of Judah, when Nebuchadnezzar, king of Babylon, had already begun to conquer Judah.

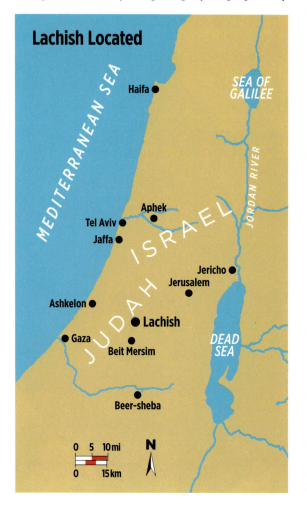

That Lachish was attacked and almost certainly destroyed by Nebuchadnezzar at that time (588/6 B.C.), is proven by the striking words of the prophet Jeremiah (34:7): "And the king of Babylon's army attacked Jerusalem and the remaining cities of Judah, namely Lachish and Azekah; for these were the only fortified cities left in Judah." The discovery of the 'Lachish Letters' in the city gate together with late Judean pottery indicate that the destruction of the Level II city-gate—and the associated city— must be assigned, in accordance with the testimony of Jeremiah, to the Babylonian conquest. From the archaeological point of view, this means that Level II was destroyed and sealed under destruction debris in 588/6 B.C.

As the excavations in the gate area continued, Starkey soon discovered that the Level II city-gate complex was built above an even earlier gate-complex, which he accordingly labelled Level III. This gate-complex was much larger and more massive, and only small parts of it were uncovered by the time the excavations ended in 1938. It was nevertheless clear that the Level III gate had been razed in an intense conflagration. Remains of this terrible destruction were also found wherever the excavator's spade reached contemporaneous remains in the city. Shops and houses built along the road which led from the gate into the city, the huge fortified palace (probably the seat of the Judean governor), and houses built beside the palace—all had been destroyed and were covered with a fiery debris. It was clear that Level III had been a fortified and densely populated Judean city which was completely destroyed in a fierce enemy attack. The question was: When and by whom was the Level III city destroyed.

By 1937 Starkey's views had already crystallized. Greatly influenced by William F. Albright's dating of the Judean levels at Tell Beit Mirsim (situated a short distance to the southeast of Lachish), Starkey suggested in a London lecture that Level III at Lachish was destroyed in the Babylonian campaign of 597 B.C. In that year Nebuchadnezzar besieged and occupied Jerusalem, deposed King Jehoiachin, put Zedekiah on the throne of Judah, and deported a large segment of the population (2 Kings 24:15 ff). Starkey believed that the close resemblance between the pottery of Level III and Level II indicated that a relatively short period must have elapsed between the destruction of the two levels. The dating of Level II to 588 B.C. seemed certain, so this observation concerning the similar pottery fit well with Starkey's conclusion that Level III must have been destroyed in 597 B.C., only about a decade before the destruction of the superimposed Level II.

JAMES L. STARKEY headed a British expedition which conducted large scale excavations at Tel Lachish between 1932 and 1938. Rarely photographed, he is shown here in the expedition camp. His excavation was one of the largest and most methodical carried out in Palestine before World War II. It came to an abrupt halt in 1938 when Starkey was murdered while en route to the opening ceremony of the Palestine Archaeological Museum (known today as the Rockefeller Museum in east Jerusalem).

When Olga Tufnell worked on the material after Starkey's murder, she reached different conclusions. In her opinion there was a clear typological difference between the pottery of Level III and Level II. Tufnell relied especially upon material from Level II which had been uncovered in the windup of the excavation after Starkey's death. Tufnell also discerned two phases in the Level II gate, each of which had been destroyed by fire. If there were two phases within Level II, this made it even more unlikely that only a decade separated Level II and Level III. Tufnell thus concluded that a much longer period must have elapsed between the two levels,

AVRAHAM HAY AND MICHAL ROCHE

THE INNER GATEWAY. The Lachish ostraca were found in a room in the outer gate of the double gate complex. In the upper right corner three people stand at the entrance leading through the gateway. The inner gateway was originally composed of four piers forming three rooms. Before the Assyrians destroyed Level IV–III in 701 B.C., an identical set of piers and rooms stood opposite. This is the largest city gate known from the Israelite period, measuring about 100 feet long by 75 feet wide.

AN INSCRIBED OSTRACON records the death throes of Lachish, just before the Babylonians razed the city in 588/6 B.C. Twenty-one ostraca, written in clear Biblical Hebrew, were buried under the debris of the Level II outer gate guard room. Lachish Letter IV poignantly portrays the last days of Lachish in a letter from a soldier (Hoshaiah) at a settlement some distance from Lachish to his commander at Lachish (one Yaosh): "And let (my Lord) know that we are watching for the beacons of Lachish…we cannot see [the beacons from] Azekah." Hoshaiah assumes that, since the beacons of Azekah no longer burn, it has already fallen. Azekah is just 11 miles northeast of Lachish. Jeremiah 34:7 records that Azekah and Lachish were the last Judean strongholds to be taken by the Babylonians.

and that Level III must have been destroyed much earlier than 597 B.C. She assigned its destruction to the Assyrian conquest of 701 B.C., a famous and well-documented historical event which will be discussed later in this article.

The dispute over the dating of Level III reflected one of the most serious and central dating problems in Palestinian archaeology. So long as it remained unresolved, scholars would disagree by more than 100 years about the dating of Level III pottery. This pottery repertoire had been found not only at Lachish but at a host of other sites as well.

The effort to resolve this dating problem focused primarily on Lachish. In scholarly shorthand the problem was put at countless scholarly meetings and conversations. What was the destruction date of Lachish Level III? The reason the spotlight was directed at Lachish Level III rather than at contemporaneous levels at other sites was because of the clear and unambiguous stratigraphy at Lachish, the rich assemblages of pottery and other finds, and the historical connections of the site. All this turned Lachish into a key site and the question of the date of the destruction of Level III became a problem of sustained scholarly attention. Many famous scholars expressed their opinion on the matter. The 597 B.C. date was supported by W. F. Albright, B. W. Buchanan, G. Ernest Wright, Paul W. Lapp, Frank M. Cross, Jr., H. Darrell Lance, J. S. Holladay, Jr. and Dame Kathleen Kenyon. Dame Kathleen based her opinion on the results of excavations at Samaria, located in the northern part of the country. Samaria, the capital of the kingdom of Israel, was conquered in 720 B.C. by Sargon, king of Assyria. Dame Kathleen assigned the destruction of Period VI to this event. The pottery of Period VI could thus be securely dated to that time. The Samaria Period VI pottery (c. 720 B.C.) differed sharply from the Lachish Level III pottery, so Dame Kathleen concluded that a long span of time must have passed between Period VI at Samaria and Level III at Lachish. To her, in light of the Samaria Period VI pottery, 701 B.C. was too early for Lachish Level III; therefore the destruction level must be assigned to 597 B.C. In this reasoning, she assumed that pottery styles changed along similar lines in

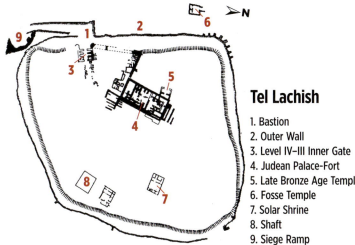

the northern and southern parts of the country—an assumption now known to be of very doubtful validity for many periods.

The 701 B.C. date for Lachish Level III was supported, on the other hand, by Ruth Amiran, Benjamin Mazar, R. D. Barnett, Anson F. Rainey, and especially by Yohanan Aharoni. For more than a decade Aharoni excavated in Judah, studying its history and material culture, and in 1966 and 1968 he carried out excavations on the eastern part of Tel Lachish, in the "Solar Shrine" area. This work added vast quantities of material relevant to the subject. Aharoni believed that sharp differences exist between the Level III and II pottery assemblages, differences which could be easily recognized in contemporary assemblages all over Judah. It thus seemed impossible to him that only a decade separated the two levels.

In 1973 Tel Aviv University's Institute of

TEL LACHISH VIEWED from the northeast. The Judean Palace-Fort appears as a raised rectangular area on the far side of the top of the mound.

Tel Lachish

1. Bastion
2. Outer Wall
3. Level IV–III Inner Gate
4. Judean Palace-Fort
5. Late Bronze Age Temple
6. Fosse Temple
7. Solar Shrine
8. Shaft
9. Siege Ramp

JUDEAN SOLDIERS DEFEND the main city gate of Lachish; below, an exodus of women enter captivity. To the right of the gate, Assyrian footmen with battering rams attack the weakened city walls. At the bottom of the wooden tracks, three hapless defenders are impaled. For more details, see the larger sketch of the relief, which appears on the following spread.

Archaeology and the Israel Exploration Society began renewed excavations at Lachish under my direction.* Six excavation seasons were conducted between 1973 and 1978. The next season is planned for the summer of 1980.

The new excavations have concentrated on three main excavation areas or fields, to use the jargon of the trade: (1) the Judean palace-fort and the Canaanite buildings underneath (under the supervision of Christa Clamer); (2) the Judean city gate and its environs (under the supervision of Y. Eshel); and (3) another area at the western part of the mound (under the supervision of Gabriel Barkay). The palace-fort and the city gate areas had already been partially dug by Starkey; here we are continuing his work. In the new area on the western part of the mound, we have dug a relatively narrow trench cutting through the edge of the mound which will eventually extend to the lower slope. Here we hope to penetrate the lower levels of the mound, and get a sectional view of the various levels down to bed rock, following the pattern set by Dame Kathleen Kenyon in her excavations at Jericho. Last year we also started an archaeological survey of the Lachish area (under the supervision of Y. Dagan).**

After a few years of systematic digging in these areas the stratigraphic picture of Lachish in the Israelite period including Level III, has now been completely clarified. All the areas uncovered by Starkey at the western part of the mound have been stratigraphically connected to our new excavation areas. All our excavation areas have now been linked to one another through monumental structures: The Judean palace-fort has been connected to the massive wall labelled "the enclosure wall." The latter, crossing our "section area," has been physically connected to the inner city-wall built along the upper periphery of the mound, which in turn has been linked to the massive city-gate. All these monumental structures may be looked upon as forming

*These excavations are sponsored by a number of public bodies, primarily by the Samuel H. Kress Foundation in New York, as well as The Northwest Christian College in Eugene, Oregon; Central College in Pella, Iowa; Florida College in Florida, and the University of South Africa in Pretoria.

**In addition to those mentioned above, the archaeological core-staff of the expedition includes A. Urweider from Switzerland, architect, and Orna Zimhoni, recorder. Song Nai Rhee from Oregon is the U.S. expedition's coordinator.

the skeleton of the mound. In turn, we established the relationship of each monumental structure to its adjacent habitation levels and accumulated debris, the latter representing the flesh of the mound and providing the relevant stratified data for the related monumental structures. At a number of points the stratigraphy of the mound was checked down to the Late Bronze Age (that is, to the latest Canaanite city level), confirming Starkey's allocation of six strata between the Late Bronze Age and the Persian-Hellenistic period. In addition, an independent—but similar—stratigraphical picture was observed by Aharoni in his trench at the eastern part of the mound. The following picture clearly emerges:

Level VI represents the final Late Bronze Age (that is, Canaanite) city. At that time Canaanite Lachish reached its prime, a prosperous and flourishing city with a rich material culture. The city came to a sudden end and was destroyed by fire in the 12th century B.C. We believe that this destruction should be attributed to the invading Israelites, as recorded in the book of Joshua 10:31–32.

Level V: Following the complete destruction of the Canaanite city, the site was abandoned until the tenth century, the period of the United Kingdom of Israel. At that time, settlement was renewed, and is represented by Level V. Many small houses were then built all over the site, but no defense wall along the edge of the mound protected the city. This settlement was also destroyed by fire. A monumental structure known as Palace A dates from this period and became the first stage of the Judean palace-fort. It is not clear whether Palace A was contemporaneous with the rest of the Level V houses, or whether it was built after their destruction. In either case, we are inclined to assign the construction of Palace A to Rehoboam, since in 2 Chronicles 11:5–12, 23 Lachish is mentioned among the cities fortified by him.

Level IV represents a royal Judean fortified city constructed by one of the kings of Judah who reigned after Rehoboam. We are not sure which one. This city was built according to a unified architectural concept, and—in comparison with other provincial Judean cities—on a grandiose scale. The summit was crowned by the huge palace-fort (Palace B). Auxiliary buildings which served as stables or storehouses flanked Palace B. The city was defended by two rings of fortification walls connected to a massive gate-complex. Many open spaces suggest that at the beginning of Level IV Lachish was probably a garrison city rather than a settlement of the usual type. The city of Level IV probably served as a royal garrison city for a relatively long period of time. Level IV came to a sudden end, but it seems

AVRAHAM HAY

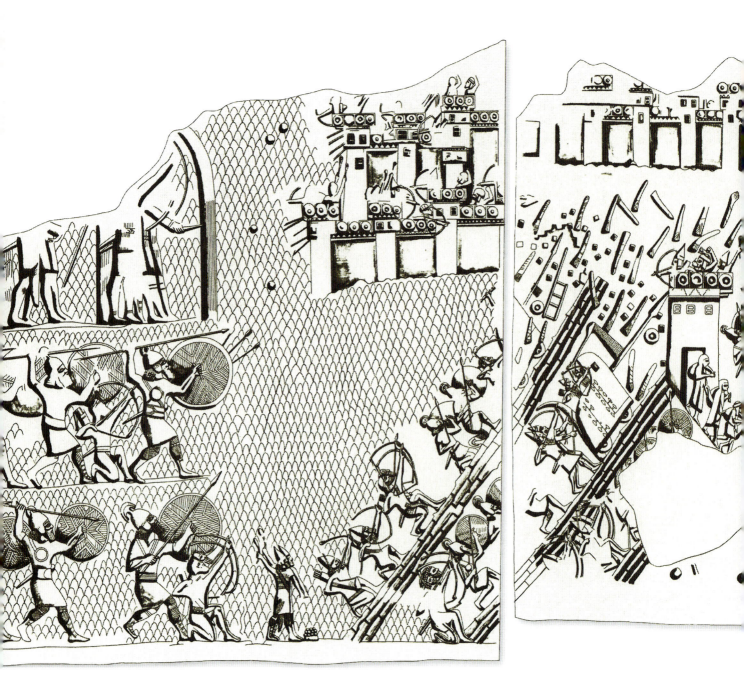

THE RELIEF OF THE SIEGE of Lachish from Sennacherib's palace at Nineveh commemorates one of the Assyrian king's greatest victories. The storming of the city gate, shown here, illustrates the powerful Assyrian war machine described in Sennacherib's annals. Preserved in several cuneiform accounts, these annals boast that Sennacherib "laid sedge to 46...strong cities...by means of well-stamped (earth) ramps, and battering rams brought (thus) near (to the walls) (combined with) the attack by foot soldiers, (using) mines, breaches as well as siege engines."

On the far left, the relief depicts soldiers from Lachish standing on the city's crenelated walls; the wall is reinforced with a series of round shields (top). Below the walls (on the far left), we see the Judean hilly terrain depicted as rows of scallops. On the bottom from the far left can be seen Assyrian archers scaling the first of seven wooden log tracks leading to the city gate. These tracks were laid on beaten earth siege ramps and were used to roll battering rams toward the walls. These battering rams, which are being pushed up each set of log tracks, are encased in a

JUDITH DEKEL

four-wheeled siege engine which not only protects the soldiers pushing inside but provides a platform for Assyrian warriors as well. Judean soldiers fighting from the walls above the Assyrian siege ramp hurl torches, slingstones, and arrows at their attackers.

Note the battering ram along the diagonal of the second track from the left. As a safety measure against the flaming torches which the Lachishites fling toward them, an Assyrian soldier pours water over the battering ram facade with a large ladle. Directly in front of this battering ram is the main city gate of Lachish.

Through it a line of Judean women leave the city. Above the heads of the Lachish soldiers on the gate are the walls of what may be the Palace-Fort. To the right of the city gate five battering rams breach the city walls; below them (bottom center) three Judean defenders impaled on posts are displayed by Assyrian soldiers.

TEL LACHISH (in an artist's rendering) with its double fortification wall, impressive double gateway complex, residences crowding the mound, and the large Palace-Fort crowning the center of the city.

clear that this was not caused by fire. In any case, the data points to the continuation of life without a break at the end of Level IV: The Level IV fortifications continued to function in Level III, and other structures of Level IV were rebuilt in Level III.

The Level III city continued to function as a royal Judean fortified city. The fortifications and the palace-fort (Palace C) continued to be used with some modifications. The main change which took place was construction of a large number of houses which were uncovered in the area between the city-gate and the palace-fort. The houses are small and densely built, and are quite different from the neighboring monumental structures. These houses, which contained an enormous amount of pottery and other domestic utensils, clearly reflect a substantial increase in the population. An intense fire destroyed all the buildings of Level III, monumental and domestic.

An intermediate stage between Level III and Level II consists of a poor habitation level lying on the ruins of the destroyed city gate of Levels IV–III; no fortifications existed at this time.

In Level II the city was partly rebuilt. A new city wall and city gate were constructed. The palace-fort, however, apparently remained in ruins. Houses were built sporadically all around. Level II was totally destroyed by fire, almost certainly in the Babylonian conquest of 588/6 B.C.

Level I represents the post-exilic remains, including the Persian city-walls, city gate, and small palace (the Residency).

Needless to say, from the beginning of our work, the paramount question in our minds was the date of destruction of Level III. It seemed to us that a satisfactory and conclusive solution to this problem could be found only by means of direct stratigraphical evidence recovered from the mound. After a few years of digging and deliberations, and after the stratigraphy of the mound has been clarified as summarized above, we think the problem has been solved. Before presenting the suggested solution, however, I should first set before the reader the events of 701 B.C., which have considerable bearing on the problem.

During the last part of the eighth century B.C. the Assyrian empire was at its prime. Centered in northern Mesopotamia, the area of the upper Tigris River, it politically dominated the entire Near East. In 720 B.C. the Assyrians conquered the kingdom of Israel; the Israelites were deported (and became the ten lost tribes) and the country became an Assyrian province. The kingdom of Judah, however, remained independent for a few more years. In 705 B.C. Sennacherib ascended the Assyrian throne. One of his first tasks was to deal with an alliance against Assyria which included Egypt, some Philistine city-states along the Mediterranean Sea, and King Hezekiah of Judah, who reigned in Jerusalem. In 701 B.C. Sennacherib took on the coalition. The events of Sennacherib's military campaign are recounted in detail both in the Bible and in contemporary Assyrian records (the different sources are, however, somewhat inconsistent). Sennacherib's army first marched south from Phoenicia along the sea coast. Here Sennacherib successfully repelled the Egyptian army and subjugated the Philistine cities. The Assyrian monarch next turned on Judah. He conquered most of the country except for Jerusalem, where Hezekiah somehow managed to withstand the siege (see 2 Chronicles 32; 2 Kings 18–19). Sennacherib tells us in his royal annals inscribed in cuneiform that he "laid siege to 46...strong cities, walled forts and to countless small villages (of Judah) in their vicinity, and conquered (them) by means of well-stamped (earth-) ramps, and battering-rams brought (thus) near (to the walls) (combined with) the attack by foot soldiers, (using) mines, breaches as well as siege engines." As to the inhabitants, he "drove out (of them) 200,150 people, young and old, male and female, horses, mules, donkeys, camels, big and small cattle beyond counting, and considered (them) booty." Other Assyrian inscriptions tell in brief that the Assyrian king "laid waste the large district of Judah." The Bible corroborates the Assyrian sources: "In the fourteenth year of King Hezekiah did Sennacherib king of Assyria come up against all the fortified cities of Judah, and took them" (2 Kings 18:13; Isaiah 36:1; also 2 Chronicles 32:1).

The city of Lachish was one of the conquered Judean strongholds, as we are informed by two different sources. First, the Bible states that Sennacherib camped at Lachish and established his headquarters there, at least during part of his sojourn in Judah (2 Kings 18:14, 17; 19:8; Isaiah 36:2; 37:8; 2 Chronicles 32:9). Second, the famous Lachish reliefs at Sennacherib's palace in Nineveh record the attack and conquest of Lachish.

When Sennacherib transferred the Assyrian capital to Nineveh (modern Kuyunjik), he devoted great effort to beautifying the city, especially by the construction of his royal palace. This extravagant edifice is described in detail in Sennacherib's inscriptions; he proudly called it the "Palace without rival"! Called the South-West Palace by Sir Henry Layard who excavated it on behalf of the British Museum in the middle of the nineteenth century, the building lends considerable support to Sennacherib's description. Unfortunately, the science of archaeology was in its infancy in the nineteenth century and Layard's methods as well as the records he left behind are far below modern standards. Layard did, however, prepare a partial plan of the building and uncovered a large number of stone reliefs adorning the walls.

A special room, centrally positioned in a large ceremonial suite of the palace, contained the Lachish reliefs depicting Sennacherib's conquest of Lachish. The walls of this room were completely covered with reliefs in this series. The length of the entire series was nearly 90 feet. The preserved part—now exhibited in the British Museum in London—is nearly 60 feet long. The slabs at the left-hand side have been lost, but according to Layard they portrayed "large bodies of horsemen and charioteers" kept in reserve behind the attacking army. Further along, in consecutive order from left to

The Stratigraphy of Tel Lachish
(as interpreted by the current expedition)

Present to 1000 A.D.	Medieval graves; remains of Israel's 1948 War of Independence
Post-exilic period (Babylonian, Persian, Hellenistic) 1st century B.C.–6th century B.C.	**LEVEL I:** fortified city in main phase; city wall and gate; Residency; Solar Shrine; houses and pits
588/6 B.C.	Destruction: Babylonian conquest
	LEVEL II: sparsely populated Judean city; city wall and gate; the Lachish letters
	Intermediate stage in deserted gate area
701 B.C.	Destruction: Assyrian conquest
	LEVEL III: densely populated city; same fortifications and rebuilt palace-fort (Palace C)
	LEVEL IV: royal Judean fortified city; two city walls and gate; palace-fort (Palace B)
Late 10th century B.C.	**LEVEL V, LATE PHASE:** Palace A—Rehoboam's fort (?)
c. 925 B.C. (?)	Destruction: Shishak's campaign (?)
	LEVEL V, EARLIER PHASE: unfortified (?) settlement; cultroom; houses
	Gap in habitation—site deserted
12th century B.C. Late Bronze Age III	Destruction: Israelite conquest (?)
	LEVEL VI: prosperous, densely populated and unfortified Canaanite city under Egyptian control; Fosse Temple III
14th century B.C. Late Bronze Age II	Destruction
	LEVEL VII: city of el-Amarna period; Fosse Temple II
Late Bronze Age I	Mound sparsely populated; Fosse Temple I
16th century B.C. Middle Bronze Age III	Destruction
	LEVEL VIII: fortified city, glacis and fosse; palace
Middle Bronze Age I–II	Mound levels not excavated
Intermediate EB–MB Period	Cemetery 2000; settlement outside mound
Early Bronze Age 3rd millennium B.C.	Mound levels not excavated; tombs; caverns; Khirbet Kerak ware
Chalcolithic Period (Ghassulian) 4th millennium B.C.	First settlement on mound
Prehistoric periods	Remains in general area of Lachish

A MASSIVE FOUNDATION WALL of the Judean Palace-Fort. Initially uncovered during the Starkey excavations in the 1930's, this wall supported one of the largest, most impressive buildings from the Iron Age. Presently crowning the central part of the mound, the palace extends over half an acre. The foundation walls, at one point preserved to a height of more than 35 feet, were filled with soil to provide a gigantic substructure for the palace.

ferocity of the attack. The city is built on a hill, and is surrounded by two high walls shown at the two sides of the relief. In the center of the relief is the city gate, depicted as a free-standing structure. Judean refugees are shown leaving it. An isolated structure above the gate seems to be the huge palace-fort whose remains were uncovered in the excavations. The main Assyrian siege ramp is shown to the right of the gate; here five battering rams, supported by infantry, attack the city wall. A second siege ramp is shown to the left of the gate, and here two more battering rams attack the gate and the wall. The defenders, standing on the walls, are equipped with bows and slings) they hurl stones and burning torches on the attacking Assyrians. Those Lachishites defending the city wall at the point of the siege ramp are throwing burning chariots down on the Assyrians below—probably a last, desperate attempt to stop the Assyrian onslaught. The fact that seven battering rams are involved in the attack—as compared to one or two battering rams which are usually depicted in Assyrian siege scenes—is a good indication of the unusual importance and scale of this battle.

The central architectural position of the 'Lachish room' in Sennacherib's palace, the unusual length of the relief series, the detailed portrayals, the scale of the attack—all this leads to clear-cut conclusions. First, the conquest of Lachish was of singular importance; it may even have been Sennacherib's greatest military achievement prior to the construction of the royal palace. At any rate, no other campaign of Sennacherib was recorded in a similar fashion. Thus, in 701 B.C. Lachish was a strongly fortified city, probably the strongest in Judah after Jerusalem. Second, we can conclude that Lachish was conquered, burnt and razed to the ground by the Assyrian army in that year. Although the burning and destruction of Lachish are not specifically recorded in Sennacherib's annals, and in fact are not shown on the surviving parts of the relief (the upper section of the relief which has not been preserved, however, may well have depicted tongues of fire coming out of the burning city), it nevertheless seems likely, considering the importance Sennacherib attached to Lachish, that the city was razed after its conquest.

In light of evidence summarized above —historical as well as stratigraphic—the crucial question of the destruction date of Lachish Level III can be resolved. In 701 B.C. Lachish was a strongly fortified city which was conquered and destroyed. Thus there must be a conspicuous burnt level representing this destroyed city. Level VI, as we have seen, is a Canaanite city that was destroyed in the 12th century B.C. and Level

right, are shown the attacking infantry, the storming of Lachish, the transfer of booty, captives and families going to exile (see cover photo on p. 340), Sennacherib sitting on his throne (see inside back cover of November/December 1979 issue), the royal tent and chariots and, finally, the Assyrian camp— almost certainly the camp mentioned in the Bible. One of the two accompanying inscriptions identifies the city as Lachish. The actual storming of Lachish is depicted in the center of the series, opposite the entrance to the room, so everyone approaching the room would see it.

We believe the detailed relief gives an accurate and realistic picture of the city and the siege. The relief conveys to the viewer an impression of the strength of Lachish's fortifications, as well as the

AVRAHAM HAY

II represents the latest Judean city, destroyed by the Babylonian army in 588/6 B.C. This leaves us with three possible "candidates" for the city destroyed by Sennacherib: Levels V, IV and III. The settlement of Level V, possibly unfortified, which is characterized by 10th century pottery, can hardly represent a large, fortified city, and cannot be dated to the end of the 8th century B.C. Level IV apparently came to a sudden end, but it seems clear that this was not caused by fire. Moreover, the city walls and city gate of Level IV continued to function in Level III, and some Level IV structures were rebuilt in Level III. These facts point toward the continuation of life without a break.

THE ASSYRIAN AND BABYLONIAN ATTACKS on Lachish took place at the southwest corner of the mound (pictured here). This is the most vulnerable point of the stronghold. The British expedition removed a large vertical section from the mound. This section appears as a light, pebbly triangle on the far right side of the tell. The outer rim of the tell and the "path" (to the left center) mark the limits of this vertical section. The current excavations have proved that this exposed section and the slope above the large boulders (center left) are part of a siege ramp built by the Assyrians. The ramp was about 55 meters (180 feet) wide at its base and 16 meters (52 feet) high—terminating at the base of Lachish's outer city wall. Depicted in the Lachish reliefs (see pp. 350–351), the ramp was mounted by Assyrian battering rams and archers during the siege of Lachish in 701 B.C.

TWO JUDEAN CITY WALLS at an earlier stage of excavation on the western edge of the mound of Lachish. In this picture the two walls are superimposed. The later wall (Level II), destroyed by the Babylonian army in 588/6 B.C., is seen as a row of stones on the top and flank of the sloping left side of the mound; the earlier wall (Levels IV–III), destroyed by the Assyrians in 701 B.C., can be seen preserved to a considerable height, with a ladder leaning against it. Two years later, when the lower picture was taken, the Judean city wall has been removed. The earlier wall consisted of a stone foundation (or socle) and a mud brick superstructure. Here most of the mud bricks of the lower, earlier wall have been completely removed, but a section of mud brick is still visible in top center. The square flat area is the stone foundation of the earlier wall. The remains of a still earlier Canaanite building (Level VI) are visible under the lower wall, on the upper left. This Canaanite building was destroyed by fire, probably during the Israelite conquest.

AVRAHAM HAY AND MICHAL ROCHE

AVRAHAM HAY AND MICHAL ROCHE

TESTIMONY TO THE FEROCITY of the battles at Lachish against the Babylonians in 588/6 and the Assyrians in 701 B.C. are these sling stones and arrowheads which the British excavated in the 1930's.

Considering that the fortifications remained intact, we can hardly identify this level with the city which was stormed and completely destroyed in the fierce Assyrian attack of 701 B.C. Level III thus remains the sole suitable "candidate," and we have no alternative but to conclude that this is the level destroyed by Sennacherib in 701 B.C.

The finds from this level correspond well with the accounts of the Assyrian attack describing the tragic fate of Lachish. The strong fortified city of this level was completely destroyed by fire. The palace-fort and the city gate were burnt down to their foundations, the city wall was razed to the ground, and houses were burnt and buried under the debris. Signs of conflagration are visible everywhere; in some places the accumulated destruction debris—including mud-bricks baked hard by the intense fire—reached a height of nearly 6 feet. The British expedition had the impression that some walls were even pulled down after the collapse of the super-structure. The large number of iron arrowheads found in this level are additional evidence for a raging battle. Pottery and other utensils were found crushed under the debris of the houses. There is no evidence that the inhabitants later tried to retrieve their belongings or reconstruct their homes.

A destruction date of 701 B.C. for Level III also accords better with the findings in the city gate area than a date of 597 B.C. We uncovered much pottery in this area, both in Level III and in Level II. Special mention should be made of two store-rooms, one destroyed at the end of Level III and the other at the end of Level II. Both storerooms contained large assemblages of pottery vessels typical of storerooms which had been crushed and buried at the time of their destruction (see photo, following pages). The pottery repertoire from the

later storeroom clearly differs from that found in the earlier one; obviously, it would have taken longer than a decade for these typological changes to have occurred. Also, we found a modest reoccupation on the ruins of the old, Level III gate, before the construction of the new, Level II gate. This reoccupation makes it all the more difficult to suggest that Level II followed Level III within a decade or so. There are simply too many changes for all of them to have occurred in so short a time.

In summary, the following picture emerges. The densely populated and prosperous city of Level III was attacked and conquered by Sennacherib in 701 B.C. Following the battle, the city most likely was sacked, burnt and razed to the ground by the Assyrian army, and then left in ruins. Most of the survivors, if not all, were forced to leave the city. Many were probably killed by the Assyrian soldiers, either in battle, or after having been taken into captivity. The British expedition found evidence for wholesale slaughter in one large tomb which contained a mass burial of about 1500 people. The Lachish reliefs also depict Judean prisoners being impaled and stabbed. Many of the remaining Lachishites were probably exiled and may be numbered among the 200,150 Judean deportees mentioned in the Assyrian inscriptions. The deportation scenes in the Lachish reliefs show large families as they are being driven out of the city, their belongings in their hands, or loaded on ox-carts or camels (see cover on p. 340).

Sennacherib tells in his inscription that the towns which he had plundered were given to the Philistine cities along the Mediterranean coast. That is, to Ashdod, Ekron and Gaza. The desolate city of Lachish was probably one of those towns. It is reasonable to assume that the city was left in ruins and deserted during a large part of the seventh

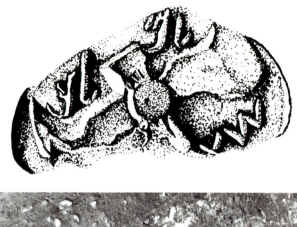

AVRAHAM HAY AND MICHAL ROCHE

THIS TWO-WINGED EMBLEM of a royal seal (drawing and photo above) was found in excavations at Lachish. Archaeologists were, however, unsure of the level from which it came. In the recent excavations at Lachish one four-handled jar, reconstructed from broken pieces of pottery found in Level III (see p. 360), had on two of its handles the two-winged royal stamp. (On the other two handles were private stamps, inscribed, *Meshulam* [son of] *Ahimelech*.) So this two-winged *l'melekh* handle should also be attributed to Level III.

The jar handle shown here has the words *l'melekh* and the name of the city Sochoh inscribed on it.

AVRAHAM HAY AND MICHAL ROCHE

THIS PRIVATE SEAL, found on a four-handled royal jar at the city gate, reads *Meshulam* [son of] *Ahimelech*. Two handles bore the stamp shown here. The other two handles on the jar bore seal impressions with a two-winged royal emblem, and the name of the city Sochoh. Over 50 handles with private stamps were found in Lachish as well as over 350 handles with royal winged emblems.

Avraham Hay and Michal Roche

LARGE STORAGE JARS lie crushed on the storeroom floor behind the gatehouse where they were buried by Level III debris at the time the Assyrians destroyed Lachish in 701 B.C. Especially important among the storage jars were those containing royal Judean stamps, so-called *l'melekh* handles. These royal stamped handles always include the word *l'melekh* ("belonging to the king") and the name of one of four towns (Hebron, Sochoh, Ziph, or *mmst*). At Lachish more than 300 *l'melekh* handles were found. Seven whole storage jars could be restored and some of these were found to contain *l'melekh* handles. By reconstructing whole pots from clearly datable strata, the excavators determined that royal storage jars of all known types—those bearing stamped handles with four-winged seals, with two-winged seals as well as with private seals—were used concurrently in Judah.

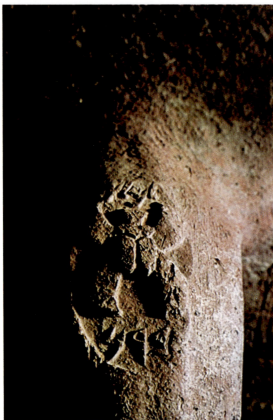

AVRAHAM HAY AND MICHAL ROCHE

century B.C., even though a few people might have continued to live in the destroyed city, as we found in the city-gate area. Similar remains may still be buried in unexcavated areas of the site.

At present we possess no archaeological data indicating when the city of Level II was built, but we may assume that it was only when Lachish was once again part of the kingdom of Judah. Tentatively, we may assign the construction and fortification of the Level II city to King Josiah, who was responsible for so many reforms in the latter part of the seventh century B.C. The Level II city was constructed along different lines from Level III and was apparently much less densely populated.

Securely dating the destruction of Level III enables us to solve many significant historical and archaeological problems. One good example involves so-called royal Judean storage jars.

Since the 19th century A.D., storage jar handles with royal Judean seal impressions have been discovered in various sites in Judah. By now more than a thousand such stamped handles are known. These seal impressions include a brief Hebrew inscription and an emblem. The inscription always includes the word *lmlk*, (the handles are often called *l'melekh* handles) which means "belonging to the king." They also include the name of one of four towns, Hebron, Sochoh, Ziph, or *mmst* (the name *mmst* is not known from any other source, and its exact pronunciation is unclear). The emblem on these royal handles is either a four-winged scarab or a two-winged symbol, which should probably be identified as a winged sun-disc. Some scholars also distinguish between emblems portrayed in a naturalistic style and those portrayed schematically.

The inscription *lmlk* indicates the direct

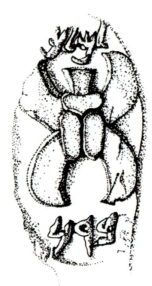

RECONSTRUCTED FROM POTTERY SHERDS found on a storeroom house floor (see previous page), the four-handled royal Judean jar (top left) bears a *l'melekh* stamp on one of its handles, and a stopper in its neck. Below the jar is a close-up of the stamp with a detailed drawing of it to its right. The four-winged *l'melekh* stamp bears the name Hebron.

All of these pottery sherds and stamped handles were found amid the crumbled walls in Tel Lachish's Level III.

connection of the jars to the government of Judah, but the nature and meaning of the connection remains obscure. Some say that the *lmlk* stamp indicates that the jars were produced in royal potteries: others say this indicates that the jars were associated with royal Judean garrisons; still others suggest that the *lmlk* stamp means that the produce kept in them belonged to the government. Perhaps the most popular view is that the *lmlk* stamp constituted a government-certified guarantee of the accurate capacity of the jar or of its contents.

Another uncertainty relates to the four cities which appear on the seal impressions. These cities are relatively unimportant ones, and one of them, *mmst*, as mentioned above, is not known from any other source. These cities could each represent a government administrative district in Judah, or they could be the sites of the royal potteries, or centers for the production of wine (if that was the commodity kept in these jars).

The distribution of the seal impressions among the various Judean sites where they have been found shows no consistent pattern with respect to the four cities. The seals are not concentrated in the areas of these particular cities, and seal-impressions bearing the names of the different cities are usually found together.

Another problem concerning these storage jars relates to their function. What were they meant to hold? Wine? Oil?

Still another unanswered question concerns the interpretation and meaning of the emblems.

A final and fundamental problem concerns the dating of these royal storage jars. During whose reign or reigns were these jars produced? Lacking stratigraphic evidence, the royal jars were usually dated on the basis of historical and epigraphical considerations. Many scholars believed that the royal seal impressions with a four-winged emblem date to the eighth century, and that those with the two-winged emblem date to the seventh century. Other scholars, notably Frank M. Cross and H. Darrell Lance, argued that the stamps of all types were contemporaneously used during the reign of Josiah (seventh century B.C.) and that their use ceased after his reign. Recently, A. Lemaire, who considered the epigraphical evidence, and N. Na'aman, who considered the historical evidence, reached the conclusion that the royal stamps of all types should be dated to the eighth century B.C.

The British excavation had already made clear that Lachish was a key site for solving the dating problems of the royal storage jars. Over 300 of these handles were recovered in the British excavation. In addition, the British archaeologists found 48 handles

AVRAHAM HAY AND MICHAL ROCHE

AN IVORY STOPPER (above) in the form of a male ibex was found in a Judean house in Level IV. The stopper is perforated and liquids, probably perfumes, were poured from a vessel through the mouth of the ibex. It is only seven centimeters tall.

from similar jars but bearing a "private" stamp (that is, a stamp with a private name). Furthermore, they even restored one jar bearing stamps with the four-winged emblem, one jar with a "private" stamp, and a few jars of that type which were unstamped. The royal storage jars had been very popular in Level III and were limited to that level. As stated by Miss Tufnell, "Nearly all the rooms attributed to city Level III contained at least one example of this vessel, and they were virtually confined to it."

Here, then, was the first clear example of the royal storage jars which were found in a good stratigraphical context, sealed under the destruction debris of

Level III. Nevertheless, the royal storage jars could not be securely dated for two reasons. First, the date of the destruction of Level III was a controversial issue. (Indeed the assumed date of the royal Judean jars based on historical and epigraphic considerations, was often used to argue for one date or another for the destruction of Level III). Second, the majority of the royal stamps recovered at Lachish had a four-winged emblem. Only a small number bore the two-winged scarab, and it remained unclear whether they were stratigraphically associated with Level III or not. The reason for this unusual distribution was not known. Some suggested that the small number of two-winged emblems may have been intrusions from a later date. Thus it was an open question as to whether jars containing the two-winged stamps were used concurrently with jars bearing the four-winged stamps. If the jars bearing stamps with a two-winged emblem were later in date (having been adopted after the destruction of Level III), this would explain why so few of them were found at Lachish.

Tufnell's report was ambiguous on the question. Lance argued that the data presented in Tufnell's excavation report indicated that the handles with the two-winged symbol originated in Level III contexts. Aharoni introduced a note of caution by emphasizing that the scholars at that time were basing their arguments not on whole vessels which could form reliable ceramic evidence, but rather with mere handles which could easily be strays out of stratigraphic context.

Our recent excavations added new data which now solves the problem conclusively. In our excavation we emphasize whole pottery restoration wherever possible. The fragments of every vessel which are lying on the ground undisturbed are methodically collected and later restored to the extent that this can be done. In this way, we were able to recover seven whole storage jars containing royal seal impressions as well as a few unsealed jars of a similar type. All these jars (like the jars uncovered and restored by Starkey) were recovered in clear loci of Level III and all of them were crushed under and sealed by the destruction debris of that level. Of special interest are two jars which bear seal impressions with a two-winged symbol. One two-winged storage jar was discovered in a storeroom situated behind the gatehouse, together with storage jars which bear royal stamps with a four-winged emblem. The other two-winged storage jar, whose lower part could not be restored, was discovered in one of the gate chambers. Two of its four handles bore seal impressions with a two-winged emblem and the name of the city Sochoh. The other two handles carried a "private" stamp

with the name "Meshulam (son of) Ahimelech," who probably was a government official associated with the "business" of the royal storage jars, whatever that was.

Thus we know that royal storage jars of all types—those without stamps as well as those bearing stamps with a four-winged and a two-winged symbol—were used concurrently in Level III prior to its destruction. This event, as shown above, occurred in 701 B.C., so we must conclude that royal storage jars of all types were used concurrently in Judah during the reign of King Hezekiah. It is difficult to decide whether the royal storage jars of all kinds were produced exclusively during Hezekiah's reign or not. It is possible that one or more kinds of these storage jars were produced prior to Hezekiah's ascent to the throne. Moreover, because Lachish was for the most part abandoned after 701 B.C., we do not know whether the royal storage jars were produced and used after that date, that is, during the later part of Hezekiah's reign, and during the p eriod following his death. In any case, by the time that Level II was destroyed in 588/6 B.C. by the Babylonian army, these vessels were not in use any more in Lachish, and probably not in the rest of Judah.

In addition to the royal Judean storage jars, we can now securely date an enormous amount of pottery found in the burnt houses of Level III, crushed and sealed under the destruction debris. These vessels were in use in these houses on the day of Lachish's destruction, so they all must date to the last decade of the eighth century B.C. Thus, we now have a large corpus of well dated Judean pottery which can serve as a bench mark for understanding pottery typology, pottery development and pottery chronology in the entire country during the period of the First Temple. Indeed, the dating of the "Lachish III pottery" (as it is now called) to the eighth century rather than to the beginning of the sixth century (as would have been the case if Level III had been destroyed in 597 B.C.) has resulted in many changes in our understanding of the development of Iron Age pottery in the land of Israel.

Finally, it should be noted that the scholarly debate concerning the destruction date of Level III continues. Our argument in support of 701 B.C., as proposed by Olga Tufnell and Yohanan Aharoni, is based on internal evidence and we strongly believe that this kind of evidence is the most convincing kind. Other scholars, however, believe that the weight of the external evidence is so great that it definitely indicates that Level III was destroyed in 597 B.C. and not before. According to this view, the evidence from Lachish itself presented above must be adapted to fit the external evidence. First and foremost among these scholars is Dame Kathleen Kenyon. She visited our excavation in the summer of 1977. During her visit we had an opportunity to analyze with her the entire question, including its various implications. In 1978 she studied the problem afresh in connection with her work on a revised edition of her *Archaeology in the Holy Land*. While she accepted the newly uncovered archaeological data as interpreted by us, she nevertheless concluded that the pottery evidence from Samaria is more important. As she wrote me on June 23, 1978, shortly before her untimely death: "I have, of course, been considering the new Lachish evidence very carefully...I still find it very difficult to accept the Lachish III remains as belonging to the Assyrian destruction of c. 700 B.C., both on the grounds given in *Samaria-Sebaste 3* (the report on the excavations at Samaria), and because it leaves the seventh century B.C. a complete blank for progress as indicated by pottery forms...I do not have a closed mind on the subject...but I do think that there are problems to be accommodated..."

Two other distingushed scholars, A. D. Tushingham of the Royal Ontario Museum in Toronto and J. S. Holladay, Jr. of the University of Toronto also believe—on the basis of the evidence external to Lachish—that Level III was destroyed in 597 B.C. In January 1979 we arranged a seminar on the question at the University of Toronto. Chaired by Dr. T. Cuyler Young, the seminar had the opportunity of hearing Tushingham, Holladay and myself present our different views. The seminar aroused much interest, and I hope Tushingham and Holladay will publish their arguments in detail so they can be judged by the scholarly world at large. Although I continue to listen with great respect, I must nevertheless restate my firm belief that the internal evidence from Lachish itself definitely carries greater weight and must prevail over the external evidence: Level III at Lachish was destroyed in 701 B.C.

The Lachish excavations will continue for many years to come. Indeed, we are following a detailed, long-term plan. We hope to uncover much more significant data in the future. 🔲

In the nearly 35 years since this article appeared in BAR, its principal conclusion—that Level III represents Sennacherib's conquest of Lachish in 701 B.C.E.—has been accepted by virtually all scholars and has become a linchpin of the chronology of Judah during the First Temple period.

On two other matters briefly adverted to in this article, Ussishkin has changed his mind, so he tells us. At the time he wrote this article, he believed the last Canaanite city (Level VI), which was destroyed by fire in about 1130 B.C.E., was the work of the invading Israelites. He now believes, with Olga Tufnell, that this city was destroyed by the Sea Peoples.

When this article was written Ussishkin believed that the first Judahite (or Judean) city (Level V) was destroyed by fire, possibly by Pharaoh Shishak. He no longer believes this city was destroyed by fire, and there is little to no evidence indicating that Shishak was the destroyer.

In 2014, Ussishkin published a popular book on Lachish, titled *Biblical Lachish: A Tale of Construction, Destruction, Excavation and Restoration*, a joint publication of the Israel Exploration Society and the Biblical Archaeology Society, publisher of BAR.

Ussishkin's excavations at Lachish concluded in 1987. A new expedition to Lachish began in 2014, directed by Yosef Garfinkel of the Hebrew University of Jerusalem and Michael Hasel and Martin Klingbeil of Southern Adventist University in Tennessee. David Ussishkin is scientific advisor to the renewed excavations.

Related Reading

Hershel Shanks, "Destruction of Judean Fortress Portrayed in Dramatic Eighth-Century B.C. Pictures," BAR, March/April 1984; David Ussishkin, "News from the Field: Defensive Judean Counter-Ramp Found at Lachish in 1983 Season," BAR, March/April 1984.

David Ussishkin, "Lachish—Key to the Israelite Conquest of Canaan?" BAR, January/February 1987.

David Ussishkin, "Restoring the Great Gate at Lachish," BAR, March/April 1988.

Philip J. King, "Why Lachish Matters," BAR, July/August 2005.

Yosef Garfinkel, Michael Hasel and Martin Klingbeil, "An Ending and a Beginning: Why We're Leaving Qeiyafa and Going to Lachish," BAR, November/December 2013.

The Persisting Uncertainties of Kuntillet 'Ajrud

HERSHEL SHANKS

EVERYTHING ABOUT IT HAS BEEN DIFFICULT. Located in the Sinai desert about 10 miles west of the ancient Gaza Road (Darb Ghazza, in Arabic) as it passes through Bedouin territory separating the Negev from Egypt, it is remote and isolated from any other settlement. In 1975, a Tel Aviv University archaeologist named Ze'ev Meshel, together with a band of nine volunteers mostly from kibbutzim and a few colleagues as staff, decided to excavate the site. It has no Biblical name. The Bedouin call it Kuntillet 'Ajrud, "the solitary hill of the water source." Hoping for relatively comfortable weather, Meshel decided to begin the excavation in October, between the suffocating summer heat and the blinding winter sandstorms. "Unfortunately, we were gravely mistaken," Meshel writes in the newly published excavation report (see box on p. 367). "The weather changed drastically from day to day, there were periods of non-stop winds, especially exposed on the summit of the hill, and the sun and dust blinded us and made excavation difficult." They were forced to move their tent camp

PREVIOUS PAGES: A remote site in the Sinai, isolated from any other settlement, the ruins known as Kuntillet 'Ajrud sit atop a natural hill miles from anything. After three short excavation seasons nearly four decades ago, the final report has now been published. The finds are spectacular, dating to the early eighth century B.C.E., yet huge questions remain.

at the base of the hill from one side to the other and back again to prevent the wind from blowing it away. The weather proved no less violent during a second season in December 1975 and a third season in May 1976. Then they departed.

The finds were fantastic. The zingers were two large pithoi, or storage jars, now reconstructed (Pithos A and Pithos B), that weighed about 30 pounds each and were painted with deities, humans, animals and symbols, as well as a number of inscriptions, including three that refer to Yahweh (the personal name of the Israelite God) and his *asherah* or Asherah, depending on your interpretation. Asherah, of course, is a pagan goddess. Was she God's wife, as one popular book by a leading archaeologist put it?[1]

Of the more-than-50 inscriptions that were recovered, 20 consist of only one or two letters. Still, that leaves 30 more-extensive inscriptions, an enormous collection. The most intriguing are painted on the pithoi. The language is Hebrew, as are the letters, although a few are Hebrew language in Phoenician script. Some of the inscriptions are incised on stone bowls; others are incised on pottery

before firing; still others are written with ink on potsherds or on the plastered walls of the major building at the site.

Unfortunately, the two scholars responsible for reading and interpreting the inscriptions in this volume, Shmuel Ahituv and Esther Eshel, were not able to examine the artifacts themselves, only photographs. The artifacts from the site became inaccessible when they were returned to Egypt in 1994 as part of the 1979 Israel-Egypt peace treaty (more on that later).

One of the few things that seem clear is the date: The building containing most of the finds and the finds themselves date to about 800 B.C.E. or shortly thereafter. Why the settlement was established or why it was abandoned is another matter.

Below an inscription on Pithos A referring to Yahweh and his *asherah* are drawings of two figures (see p. 369). Indeed, the inscription runs through the crown of one of them. Each of the figures is easily and unquestionably identifiable as Bes, a collective name for a group of Egyptian dwarf deities. They are prominently pictured here with typical arms akimbo, hands on their sides, legs bowed, grotesque facial features, feathered headdresses and nude except for a lion skin. The Bes on the left is taller than the one on the right.

Bes figures are often associated with music and dancing, of which they were patrons. And, indeed, to the right of the two Bes figures is a seated woman playing a lyre—well, you might assume she was a woman because two round circles indicate the figure's nipples or breasts. But Pirhiya Beck, who wrote the chapter on the drawings, emphasizes that this is not necessarily indicative. Little circles represent breasts or nipples on some male Bes figures also. One example, according to Beck, is the Bes figure on the right. Although it is shorter than its mate, smaller, with a less fancy headdress

COURTESY DR. ZE'EV MESHEL/ISRAEL EXPLORATION SOCIETY

IN THE WILDERNESS. Beyond this dark-robed Bedu woman and her child walking with their donkey through the desert landscape, the flat hilltop of Kuntillet 'Ajrud is visible in the distance to the north. It is located 10 miles west of the ancient Gaza Road, which passes through Bedouin territory separating the Negev desert from Egypt's Sinai peninsula, connecting the city of Gaza on the Mediterranean coast to Eilat at the northern tip of the Red Sea. The ancient name of the site is unknown, so it goes by the name the Bedouin gave it, meaning "the solitary hill of the water source."

BRACED AGAINST THE ELEMENTS. The excavators hoped that an October dig season would allow them to avoid the harshest summer and winter weather. Unfortunately, this was not so—and it only got worse in the subsequent December and May dig seasons. The changing weather, constant buffeting winds, blinding sand and extreme heat made excavations difficult. The conditions sometimes interrupted digging and repeatedly forced the team to move their tent camp from one side of the hill to the other and finally to the wadi bed below.

and has nipples or breasts depicted by little circles, Beck nevertheless regards this Bes as male. As proof, Beck points to the vertical lines below the nose (in both Bes figures); if these are intended to represent beards, "then both figures are apparently male."

The Bes on the left is also male. But not for the obvious reason. Dangling from between its legs is an appendage. It is not what you think it is, however. It is only the tail of the lion skin customarily worn by Bes, according to Beck.[2]

In the end, Beck considers it "doubtful" that the two Bes figures were meant to represent a god-and-goddess couple. Other scholars may disagree, however. One factor that might have supported Beck's conclusion has literally disappeared. Beck's contribution to this volume is a reprint of her 1982 article in the journal *Tel Aviv*.[3] At the time that Beck studied these Bes drawings, both figures were covered with black soot. So far as could be seen, it appeared to her that *both* Bes figures had appendages between their legs. If these appendages are

interpreted as penises, rather than tails, the two Bes figures can hardly be interpreted as a god-and-goddess couple. In time, however, most of the soot faded and it became clear that the Bes on the right had nothing between its legs. In this volume, the Bes on the right is drawn *without* an appendage (unlike the drawing in Beck's 1982 article in *Tel Aviv*). As the editors of this volume state, "This fact may change the interpretation of the whole scene" (p. 165). Unfortunately, Professor Beck died of cancer in 1998, so we cannot know what her reaction would be now.

An inscription above the heads of the Bes figures reads in part: "I have [b]lessed you to YHWH [Yahweh] of Shomron [Samaria] and to his *asherah*."

This raises two huge questions: (1) What is "his" *asherah*? There are no capital letters in ancient Hebrew. So we don't know whether it's "*asherah*" or "Asherah"; that is, we don't know whether Asherah is Yahweh's consort

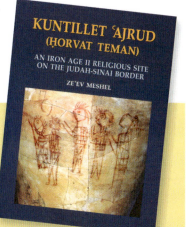

Kuntillet 'Ajrud (Horvat Teman): An Iron Age II Religious Site on the Judah-Sinai Border
By Ze'ev Meshel
(Jerusalem: Israel Exploration Society, 2012), xxxv + 364 pp., $94.95 (hardcover)

AVRAHAM HAI/TEL AVIV UNIVERSITY INSTITUTE OF ARCHAEOLOGY

FINDS ON DISPLAY. Before the Kuntillet 'Ajrud finds were returned to Egypt in 1994 as part of the Israel-Egypt peace treaty, many of the artifacts were shown in an exhibit at the Israel Museum in Jerusalem. Shown here are two reconstructed pithoi, or storage jars, weighing 30 pounds each and measuring 3.3 feet tall, as well as a large 400-pound stone basin with a Hebrew inscription on the rim (see p. 373). Although difficult to see in this photo, the pithoi, called Pithos A and Pithos B, are covered with paintings of deities, animals, humans and numerous inscriptions—a treasure trove for archaeologists.

or whether *asherah* is his symbol, like a sacred tree or a pole. (2) And how do we understand the attribution of "Shomron" to this Yahweh? Was Shomron indicative of God's dwelling place?

As noted above, the inscription partially covers the crown of the Bes on the left. Ahituv and Eshel conclude that the inscription was added after the drawings of the Bes figures were painted; therefore the inscription and the Bes figures are very probably unrelated.

The literature on Asherah vs. *asherah* is vast.* There is no question that Asherah was one of the chief female deities in the Canaanite pantheon. She was the consort of the god El. But she seems to have vanished from Canaanite/Phoenician inscriptions by the first millennium B.C.E. Whether the Biblical authors remembered her in this form is questionable; the word occasionally appears in the Bible in the masculine plural (*asherim*). It also appears in the feminine plural (*asherot*), referring to cultic objects similar to standing stones (*matzevot*). Sometimes the *asherim* or *asherot*, especially in the context of *matzevot*, are to be cut down or burned; such references must be sacred posts. The editors conclude that the blessing formula "Yahweh and his *asherah*" refers not to the goddess Asherah but to a cultic object like a sacred pole or tree. One such sacred tree is in fact depicted on the other side of this same pithos.

The geographical marker "Yahweh of Shomron" appears in the inscription on Pithos A. Another geographical marker appears in an inscription on Pithos B: "I have blessed you by YHWH of Teman and his *asherah*." The text continues: "May He bless you and may He keep you, and may He be with my

lord [forever?]." This echo of the priestly blessing from Numbers is startling, and the recognition for many will be a moving moment: "[May] the Lord [YHWH] bless you and keep you" (Numbers 6:24). The Kuntillet 'Ajrud text is two centuries earlier than the silver amulets from Ketef Hinnom in Jerusalem that likewise echo this Biblical text.**

"Yahweh of Teman" is referred to once more on Pithos B and also twice on a piece of plaster that

** See Gabriel Barkay, "The Riches of Ketef Hinnom—Jerusalem Tomb Yields Biblical Text Four Centuries Older than Dead Sea Scrolls," *BAR*, July/August, September/October 2009.

TWO BES OR NOT TWO BES. One of the most intriguing and hotly debated drawings from Kuntillet 'Ajrud is this scene on Pithos A (the relevant fragments of the pithos are pictured opposite before it was fully reconstructed). According to Pirhiya Beck, who interpreted the drawings for a 1982 article (she has since died), the two main figures on the left are both male. All agree that they are depictions of the Egyptian deity Bes with typical wide-legged stance, arms akimbo, grotesque facial features, feathered headdresses, and only a lion skin for a garment (see drawings). The seated lyre player at far right fits with Bes's association with music and dancing. Beck believed that both of the Bes figures are male, despite the apparent breasts and smaller stature of the Bes on the right, because of the lines beneath the noses of both figures, which seem to represent facial hair. Beck interpreted the appendages between the figures' legs, which appear in the 1982 drawing on the left, as the tails of the lion skin garments they are wearing. But as soot faded from the pottery over time, it became clear that the smaller Bes had nothing between its legs, and the drawing was updated accordingly, this time without the appendage (far right). This may change the whole interpretation of the scene, say the editors of this volume. Some will now see the two Bes figures as a god-and-goddess couple, although the editors of this book do not go so far.

Also visible in the photo (and the drawing on the left) is an inscription that runs through the crown of the Bes figure on the left. It reads in Hebrew, "I have [b]lessed you to YHWH [Yahweh] of Shomron [Samaria] and his *asherah*." Because it runs through the crown of the Bes figure, it must be dated later.

* These discussions also include a reference to "YHWH and his asherah" found at Khirbet el-Qom (Biblical Makkedah) near Jerusalem. See Shmuel Ahituv, "Did God Really Have a Wife?" *BAR*, September/October 2006. See also André Lemaire, "Who or What Was Yahweh's Asherah?" *BAR*, November/December 1984.

PHOTO AND DRAWINGS COURTESY OF DR. ZE'EV MESHEL AND AVRAHAM HAI/TEL AVIV UNIVERSITY INSTITUTE OF ARCHAEOLOGY

1982 DRAWING

2012 DRAWING

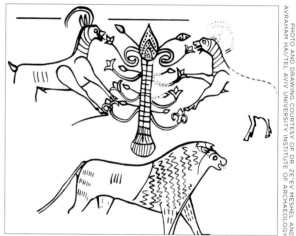

GODDESS OR TREE? Several inscriptions from Kuntillet 'Ajrud refer to Yahweh "and his *asherah*." Is *asherah* the Canaanite goddess Asherah, suggesting Yahweh had a consort, or is it simply a sacred tree or post sometimes mentioned—and condemned—in the Bible? The editors of the Kuntillet 'Ajrud volume conclude that it is the latter. Indeed, on the other side of the inscription mentioning "Yahweh and his *asherah*" on Pithos A is a drawing of a sacred tree flanked by two horned ibexes on top of a striding lion—a common ancient Near Eastern motif.

PHOTO AND DRAWING COURTESY OF DR. ZE'EV MESHEL AND AVRAHAM HAI/TEL AVIV UNIVERSITY INSTITUTE OF ARCHAEOLOGY

had fallen to the floor. The script of the latter is Phoenician, although the language is Hebrew. It reads in part: "[May] he lengthen their days and may they be sated ... recount to [Y]HWH of Teman and his *asherah* ... YHWH of the Te[man] has shown them favor, has bettered their days ..." (p. 104).

Teman seems to have a variety of ancient references. It sometimes refers to Mt. Sinai. It can also refer to part of the Negev and a city in Edom. The references here to Shomron (Samaria) and Teman indicate the areas (non-exclusive) over which Yahweh rules or where he dwells. We find the same thing in the Bible. "God is coming from Teman," reads Habbakuk 3:3 (see also Zechariah 9:14; Psalms 78:26), Such references are common not only with respect to Yahweh, but with respect to other gods as well. As the editors state: "Other gods are mentioned together with their dwelling place, as in 'Ba'al of Hermon' or 'Ba'al of Hasor,' and it is thus not surprising that the God of Israel would be referred to in this manner as well" (p. 130). The Bible also tells us poetically that "the mountains dripped before Yahweh of Sinai" (Judges 5:5).

The prayer that encapsulates Israelite monotheism, "Hear O Israel, the Lord (Yahweh) our God, the Lord (Yahweh) is One" (Deuteronomy 6:4), is thought to be a reaction to the notion that Yahweh "had various local manifestations," as the editors put it. The Kuntillet 'Ajrud texts represent this local understanding.

A drawing on Pithos B features a procession of worshipers with arms raised in a gesture of adoration or perhaps supplication. The five figures all face left. They are drawn adjacent to the two inscriptions referring to "Yahweh of Teman and his *asherah*," but, again, it is doubtful that there is any connection between the texts and the drawing.

This is only a taste of the drawings on these pithoi. Others include the drawing mentioned above of horned ibexes flanking a sacred tree, a common motif in the ancient Near East; a majestic lion with a protruding tongue; an archer; and a calf suckling its mother with her head turned back, another common motif. The bases of many more pithoi were recovered; one can only wonder what treasures were painted on them when they were whole.

In addition to the inscriptions on the two pithoi, other inscriptions were found on wall plaster. The following theophany, painted on a piece of plaster found lying on the floor, reads in part: "When God shines forth ... [Y]HW[H] ... The mountains will melt, the hills will crush ... The Holy One over the gods ... Prepare (yourself) [to] bless Ba'al on a day of war ... to the name of El on a day of [w]ar" (p. 109). The possibilities of interpretation are myriad.

Does all this help to tell us what kind of site Kuntellet 'Ajrud was? Yes and no. It surely seems to have been a religious site. But more than that is difficult to say. Oddly, despite the clearly religious nature of the drawings and inscriptions, no evidence of cultic activities was found at the site—no altar, no shovels, no incense burners or incense, no offerings or sacrifices, no idols or figurines. On the other hand, a platform in a second building on the site might be interpreted as a *bamah*, or high place. Perhaps the site was abandoned voluntarily and the inhabitants simply carried off the cultic equipment with them when they left.

On potsherds from the shoulders of 20 of the pithoi, one or two letters were incised prior to firing. Most common were the letters *aleph* and *yod*. At least two of these potsherds were labeled *kuf resh*, QR. The excavator suggests this stood for *qorban*, "sacrifice." If so, this is more evidence of the religious nature of the site. The other two single letters may have indicated the tithed quantity or quality of the contents.

The building's two kitchens each had only one *tabun* (Arabic for "oven") at any given time, which suggests that living was communal, perhaps for priests. Another fact suggestive of priests are the textiles found at the site: Most are linen; very few fragments are wool. The Bible frequently prescribes linen clothing for priests (see, e.g., Ezekiel 44:17–18).

The building in which most of the drawings and inscriptions were found is itself a conundrum. It has a fortress-like plan with four corner towers. But clearly it did not function as a fortress. It differs from the many other Israelite fortresses in the Negev. For example, it has no casemate walls (double walls periodically connected with short walls perpendicular to the long walls). Most importantly, it has a narrow room with benches

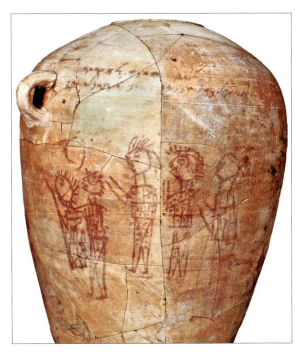

YAHWEH OF TEMAN is mentioned in two Hebrew inscriptions on Pithos B (above and right) and twice more in an inscription on some fallen pieces of wall plaster (below, right). The first, written above a drawing of five worshipers, reads "to YHWH of the Teman and his *asherah*. Whatever he asks from a man, that man will give him generously. And if he would urge—YHWH will give him according to his wishes."

To the right of the worshipers (partially visible on the right edge in the drawing at right) is a poetic text reminiscent of the priestly blessing from Numbers 6. The text on the pithos reads, "Say to my lord, are you well? I have blessed you by YHWH of Teman and his *asherah*. May he bless you and may he keep you and may he be with my lord [forever]."

The reconstructed text on the plaster fragments (right) is also Hebrew but written in Phoenician script: "May he lengthen their days and may they be sated ... recount to YHWH of Teman and his *asherah* ... because YHWH of the Teman has shown them favor, has bettered their days." These geographical references in connection with a deity (Yahweh of Teman or Shomron) were fairly common in antiquity and indicated the area(s) over which the deity ruled or where he dwelled.

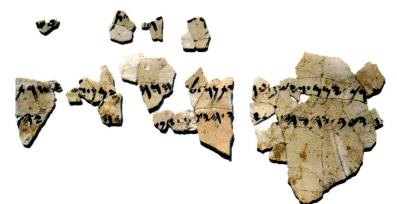

PHOTOS AND DRAWING COURTESY DR. ZE'EV MESHEL/ISRAEL EXPLORATION SOCIETY

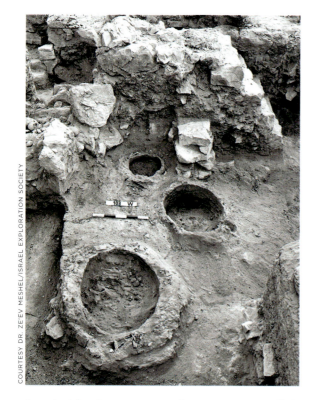

COMMUNAL COOKING. The main structure at Kuntillet 'Ajrud had two kitchens, one at each end of the site. In each, only one *tabun*, or oven, was in use at any given time. This suggests communal cooking and living, possibly for priests—or perhaps guests at a caravanserai. The western kitchen at the site has remains of three *tabuns* (shown at left), as does the eastern kitchen—but they were in separate phases. We don't know why the earlier *tabuns* went out of use, but in each successive phase, the previous oven was covered over and a new one dug out and lined with mud and pottery sherds.

Another surprising conclusion: Although the site is on the southern border of Judah, the authors connect it to the northern kingdom of Israel. And they have some pretty convincing evidence. The northern connection is reflected most convincingly in the theophoric elements of the personal names found at the site. Let me unpack this: References to deities, called theophoric elements, are often incorporated into personal names; in this case the deity is Yahweh (YHWH). These abbreviations of Yahweh take two forms: In Judah the theophoric element is YHW, usually written "-yahu," as for example in the name of Israel's prime minister, Netanyahu—literally, "gift of Yahweh." In the northern kingdom of Israel the theophoric element is spelled YW, usually written "-yo." In Hebrew the difference in spelling is small—only one letter—although when written in Latin letters the two seem quite different.

Sometimes one of these "abbreviations" is used instead of the full name Yahweh. In one inscription at Kuntillet 'Ajrud, we find it once by itself as meaning YHWH. More often, the "abbreviation" appears as the last syllable of a name. In an

just inside the entrance—the excavators call it the bench room—from which most of the finds were retrieved. This portion of the building was coated in white plaster and decorated with a few colored murals. Scholars have made a variety of suggestions as to what the structure was used for—a desert way-station, a caravanserai, a kind of inn, a rest stop for pilgrims, a fortified trading post, a pilgrimage site, a shrine, a cult center, a religious school, a retreat for priests, etc.

WHAT WAS THE ARCHITECT THINKING? The fortress-like plan of the main building—especially the four corner towers—suggests that it may have been a fortified outpost. Other suggestions for its use include a desert way station, an inn, a rest stop for pilgrims, a trading post, a shrine, a religious school and a retreat for priests. The outer court on the eastern side led to the building's only entrance. The entrance opened directly into the long plastered "bench room," where most of the finds were discovered. Many of them suggest a religious function, but no evidence of cultic activity at the site was discovered—no altars, offerings, incense burners, shovels, figurines, etc. A mass of raised stone in the adjacent building (not shown on the plan) may have functioned as a *bamah*, or high place.

tower

tower

bench room

entrance

kitchens

tower

outer court

tower

inscription on the rim of a large 400-pound stone bowl the name Obadiah is spelled 'BDYW: "Of [or "To"] Obadiah [ending in YW] son of 'Adnah, blessed be he to YHW." The consistent use of the theophoric element "yo" rather than "yahu" in names at Kuntillet 'Ajrud is a strong indication that it is an Israelite site, not a Judahite site.

Other reasons also point to Kuntellet 'Ajrud as an Israelite, not a Judahite, site—such as the occasional use of Phoenician script and the reference to Yahweh of Samaria (in Israel).

The excavator explains the Israelite identification as a result of an internecine conflict in which Joash (or Yoash [802–787 B.C.E.]), king of Israel, defeated Amaziah, king of Judah. As a result of Amaziah's defeat, Israel dominated Judah. The excavator suggests that Joash established the site of Kuntillet 'Ajrud to demonstrate his control and authority at the southern extremity of the kingdom of Judah (see 2 Kings 14:8–14; 2 Chronicles 25:17–24).*

All in all, this final excavation report is a superb volume, although inevitably it won't have the final say. The discussion and interpretation will continue far beyond its pages.

On the one hand, you can regard the book's appearance—delayed almost 40 years—as well worth the wait. On the other hand, you can ask why it has taken so long. On January 16, 2011—ten days before the Arab Spring erupted in Tahrir Square—I interviewed Egypt's then-head of the Supreme Council of Antiquities, Zahi Hawass, in his Cairo office.** Among the other subjects of the interview, I was concerned about the finds from Kuntillet 'Ajrud since they were turned over to the Egyptians in 1994 as part of the 1979 Israel-Egypt peace treaty. They had never been seen or heard from since. Reportedly, they were still in the boxes in which they were returned.

I asked Hawass what happened to them. He replied that he did not know but would look into it. He also threw a little dig back at me: "I have never seen any publication saying what you are telling me."

"You are very right," I admitted.

As a result of subsequent events—Hawass was thrown out of office, reappointed, then thrown out again; he is now facing criminal charges—he understandably never got back to me. On February 3, 2011, Hawass's office reported that there had been a break-in at the archaeological storage facility at Qantara, on the west bank of the Suez Canal, the

*See Hershel Shanks, ed., *Ancient Israel—From Abraham to the Roman Destruction of the Temple*, 3rd ed. (Washington, DC: Biblical Archaeology Society, 2011), p. 159.

**See Hershel Shanks, "Egypt's Chief Archaeologist Defends His Rights (And Wrongs)," BAR, May/June 2011.

PHOTO AND DRAWING COURTESY DR. ZE'EV MESHEL/ISRAEL EXPLORATION SOCIETY

NORTH AND SOUTH. This 400-pound stone basin, photographed during its excavation (see also, p. 368), bears an inscription on the rim: "Of [or "To"] Obadiah son of 'Adnah, blessed be he to Yahweh." Although Kuntillet 'Ajrud is located near the border of ancient Judah with Egypt, the spelling of the name Obadiah (and many other names found at the site) reflects a connection with the northern kingdom of Israel, rather than Judah. Was the basin donated by someone from the north?

most likely place where the Kuntillet 'Ajrud artifacts were stored; "six boxes were taken," Hawass reported.

Some of the stolen artifacts were quickly recovered. Then, on March 3, the Egyptian press reported that 30 truckloads of antiquities from the Qantara storage facility had been moved for safekeeping to the Egyptian Museum in Cairo. Included were "Sinai artifacts that were retrieved from Israel following the signing of the Egypt-Israel peace treaty."

Why has it taken nearly four decades to publish this final report? One reason is that everything about the site and its finds is so darn difficult to interpret—or even to see. It is striking how often in this volume a discussion ends with a question mark, if not literally then figuratively. Take the site itself:

We don't really know why it was established, what it was, who lived here or why it was abandoned. And this is nothing compared to the difficulty of interpreting the finds. As Beck writes of the drawings, "The interpretation of most of the scenes remains uncertain." But there is something else—the difficult inscriptions. Excavator Ze'ev Meshel struggled for years to address them. He consulted internationally known epigraphers like Frank Cross of Harvard, André Lemaire of the Sorbonne and Kyle McCarter of the Johns Hopkins University in Baltimore and made very substantial progress, as revealed in his path-breaking 1979 article in BAR.* Finally, however, in 2006 Meshel (reluctantly?) assigned the final publication of the inscriptions to two leading Israeli epigraphers—Shmuel Ahituv of Ben Gurion University of the Negev and Esther Eshel of Bar-Ilan University. Of course, they built on the work Meshel had already done, so he is listed as the third author of the volume's chapter on the inscriptions. Ahituv and Eshel, too, consulted experts internationally,

for whom they express their thanks. But Ahituv and Eshel are also explicit: "The final version of this chapter was authored by Ahituv and Eshel and reflects their views and conclusions." What heated discussions this statement screens we cannot know— nor do we need to.

All in all, this final excavation report is a magnificent production despite the many unanswered questions with which it leaves us. ▣

[1] William G. Dever, *Did God Have a Wife?* (Grand Rapids: Eerdmans, 2005).

[2] Beck's contribution to this volume is a reprint of her 1982 article in *Tel Aviv*: Pirhiya Beck, "The Drawings from Horvat Teman (Kuntillet 'Ajrud)," *Tel Aviv* 9 (1982), p. 38.

[3] Beck, "The Drawings from Horvat Teman," p. 38.

* Ze'ev Meshel, "Did Yahweh Have a Consort?" BAR, March/April 1979.

Related Reading

Queries and Comments: "Gender at Kuntillet 'Ajrud," BAR, March/April 2013.

Irit Ziffer, "Portraits of Ancient Israelite Kings?" BAR, September/October 2013.

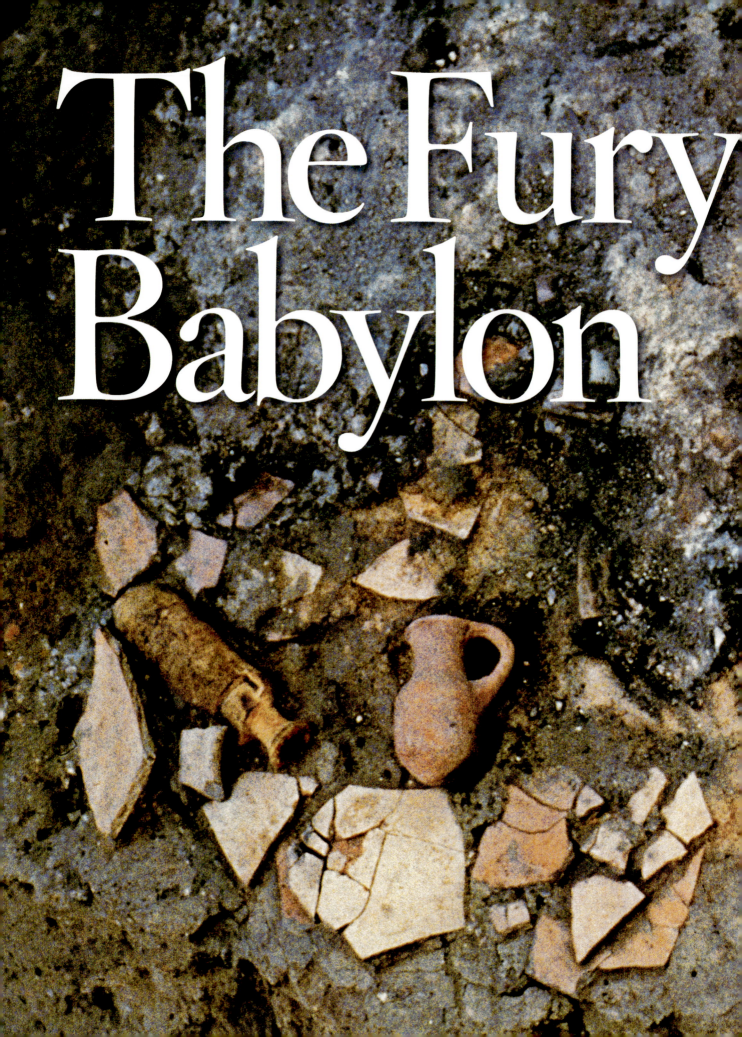

The Fury
Babylon

of

Ashkelon and the Archaeology of Destruction

LAWRENCE E. STAGER

PHOTOGRAPHS BY CARL ANDREWS,
LEON LEVY EXPEDITION

IN 586 B.C.E. NEBUCHAD*R*EZZAR (ALSO known as Nebuchad*n*ezzar II), king of Babylon, attacked Jerusalem, destroyed the Temple and burned the city. This of course is the focal point of the Biblical story. For Nebuchadrezzar, however, Jerusalem was only one of many prizes, part of a major military operation in the West extending over many years. The real battle was between two superpowers—the newly ascendant Babylonian Empire in the East (replacing the Assyrians) and Egypt in the West. Hebrew University professor Avraham Malamat has aptly applied the term "bipolar politics" to this contest.[1]

By the last half of the seventh century B.C.E., Egypt dominated neighboring countries like Philistia and Judah (the northern kingdom of Israel having already been destroyed by the Assyrians in 721 B.C.E.).

During the reigns of Pharaoh Psamtik I (664-610 B.C.E.) and his son Necho II (610-595 B.C.E.), Egypt moved into the vacuum left by the withdrawal of Assyria from the West. For four decades Egypt held sway over former Assyrian provinces as far north as Megiddo (*Magiddu*).[2] Referring to this mortal engagement between East and West, between Babylonia and Egypt, the prophet Jeremiah rebuked Judah in the harshest terms for allying itself with Egypt. Philistia made the same mistake.

> **Our excavations provide a detailed still life of Ashkelon on the eve of its destruction.**

In 605 B.C.E., as crown prince and field commander, Nebuchadrezzar led Babylonian troops in a critical battle with the Egyptians under Pharaoh Necho II at Carchemish on the Euphrates River, in what is today western Syria. A decisive Babylonian victory emboldened Nebuchadrezzar, now king, to move south. (It was to this Babylonian victory that the prophet Jeremiah referred when he predicted that Judah too would be devastated by Nebuchadrezzar [Jeremiah 25:8-11]; the stamp of the battle of Carchemish is also seen in

PRECEDING PAGES: "NEBUCHADREZZAR marched to the city of Ashkelon" and "turned the city into ... heaps of ruins," according to the cuneiform *Babylonian Chronicle*. The vitrified brick, crushed pottery and charcoal found throughout the city suggest the terror of the Babylonian destruction.

Two superpowers dominated the Near East in the late seventh century B.C.E.: in the East, the Neo-Babylonian Empire, which extended control over Syria after Assyria's decline; in the West, Egypt, which dominated the southern Levant. In 605 B.C.E., Babylon pushed west (see map, below); the newly crowned King Nebuchadrezzar II won a decisive battle against the Egyptians at Carchemish on the upper Euphrates. The next year he moved south, capturing and burning the Philistine seaport of Ashkelon.

The ferocity of the Babylonians is amply demonstrated by the archaeological evidence. Fires swept through the city's winery (where the photo was taken), leaving remnants of charred wood; brick and pottery were melted into glass; ceramic jars were smashed and strewn helter skelter. So widely known was the destruction of Ashkelon that the prophet Jeremiah wrote that Babylon rose out of the north "to destroy all the Philistines... Ashkelon is silenced" (Jeremiah 47:4-5).

explicit references in Jeremiah 46:2-6.)

After Carchemish, the new king campaigned throughout most of 604 B.C.E., right into the winter when the rains begin, sometimes falling in torrents. Ordinarily, nobody would think of conducting military operations—especially campaigns so dependent on horse and chariot—during the rainy season. But late in 604 B.C.E. Nebuchadrezzar decided to strike at the primary seaport of the Philistines—Ashkelon. At least that is what we are told in the fragmentary *Babylonian Chronicle* written in cuneiform:

The Babylonian Campaigns (609-586 B.C.E.)

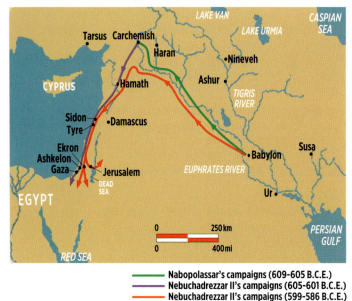

Nabopolassar's campaigns (609-605 B.C.E.)
Nebuchadrezzar II's campaigns (605-601 B.C.E.)
Nebuchadrezzar II's campaigns (599-586 B.C.E.)

(Nebuchadrezzar) marched to the city of Ashkelon and captured it in the month of Kislev (November/December). He captured its king and plundered it and carried off [spoil from it...]. He turned the city into a mound (Akkadian *ana tili*, literally a tell) and heaps of ruins ...[3]

Usually, when an ancient city was besieged, the gates and fortifications were the first features to come under attack. If the assault on these fortifications was successful, the defenders normally surrendered and the rest of the city was spared.* That was not what happened at Ashkelon, however, according to Nebuchadrezzar's version of events. For his description to be accurate, Nebuchadrezzar's armies must have advanced far into the interior of the city and reduced this major metropolis to a heap of ruins—in other words, made it a tell.

The Leon Levy Expedition to Ashkelon has given us an opportunity to test the accuracy of the Babylonian ruler's account. It has also provided us with a detailed still life of a Philistine metropolis in the late seventh century B.C.E., on the eve of Nebuchadrezzar's vaunted destruction of the city.

As a seaport (after 11 seasons of terrestrial excavations and 4 of underwater exploration, we have found anchors and ballast from several shipwrecks; however, we are still searching for the harbor), Ashkelon provides evidence of diverse international influence. Phoenician Red-Slipped Ware is abundant, as is its locally made version. (This pottery is most abundant at Philistine sites on the Mediterranean coast—Ashkelon and Ashdod—and is significantly rarer at contemporaneous sites on the inner coastal plain, such as Ekron [Tel Miqne] and Timnah [Tel Batash].)

Cargoes from Phoenician ports such as Tyre arrived in Ashkelon loaded with elegant bowls and cups of Phoenician Fine Ware, including so-called Samaria Ware as well as red- and cream-polished table ware, the latter imitating ivory or alabaster. The prophet Jeremiah was an insightful observer of the geopolitics of his day in referring to Philistia as the "helper" of Tyre and Sidon (Jeremiah 47:4). A special trading relationship between Philistia and Phoenicia, known as *ḫubūr*, has been inferred from the 11th-century B.C.E. Egyptian "Tale of Wenamon."[4] Such trading agreements persisted into the late seventh century B.C.E., and it is to those agreements that Jeremiah alludes.

*In Genesis 22:17, God assures Abraham that his descendants will be able to "seize the gates of their enemies." The implication is that once the gates were taken, the battle was over; the city might as well surrender and avoid further destruction. In fact, "gates" is often a metonym for "cities" in Biblical Hebrew (see Judges 5:11).

Phoenician (and perhaps Philistine) ships also brought amphoras and fine wares from Ionia, the Greek islands, Corinth and Cyprus. Elegant wine pitchers (*oinochoai*) decorated with wild goats, stags, and geese arrived from East Greece. Ionian drinking cups (*skyphoi*) were also on board.

At Ashkelon, commerce and religion apparently marched hand in hand. We found an ostracon, a potsherd with writing on it (see box, pp. 384-385), used as a receipt in a room with smashed jars, charred wheat, weights and a scale balance. On top of this rubble was the collapsed roof of the building, which consisted of reed-impressed and mat-impressed clay. Sitting on top of the roof debris was a small incense altar (without horns) made of sandstone and used to offer incense, such as myrrh and frankincense, to Philistine deities.

This is the first time anyone has found stratified evidence for rooftop altars. In his catalogue of Judah's sins, Jeremiah lists rooftop rituals such as incense offerings, and wine and oil libations, in worship of pagan deities. He declares that the "Chaldeans [Babylonians] who are fighting against this city [Jerusalem] shall come, set it on fire, and burn it, with the houses on whose roofs offerings have been made to Baal and libations have been poured out to other gods, to provoke me [Yahweh] to anger" (Jeremiah 32:29). Jeremiah obviously

MUDBRICK TOWERS PROTECTED Ashkelon's 10,000-12,000 inhabitants along a mile-and-a-half arc. The Philistine city's defenses consisted of as many as 50 towers, evenly spaced along a mudbrick fortification wall built on top of artificial ramparts—made of a thick sheath of sand, soil and debris—surrounding the city. These earthen ramparts, known as glacis construction, were originally built by Canaanites in about 2000 B.C.E.; they were then rebuilt in Iron Age II (1000-586 B.C.E.) by the Philistines, when these towers were also constructed.

knew what he was talking about, and we now have an example of a rooftop altar from Ashkelon.

Egyptian influence, both commercial and religious, has been documented far beyond our expectations. Among the Egyptian artifacts we found were barrel jars and tripod stands made of Nile clay and a jewelry box made of abalone shell, in which a necklace of Egyptian (or Phoenician) amulets found nearby had once been kept. But there were also Egyptian religious items found in a building we identified as a winery. A bronze statuette of Osiris lay near a cache of seven bronze bottles (*situlae*). A procession of Egyptian deities in relief files around the bottles. In the midst of the cache of bronze bottles was a bronze votive offering table engraved with what appears to be a loaf of bread flanked by libation flasks. Two baboons sit at opposite corners of the offering table. At another corner sits a falcon;

ASHKELON: AN INTERNATIONAL CITY
From Around the Eastern Mediterranean

A port of call for ancient Mediterranean mariners, Ashkelon was the destination of wares from Phoenicia, Ionia, the Greek islands, Greece and Egypt, which were traded for wine, olive oil and other goods from the surrounding regions and the interior.

Imported pottery provides evidence of trade with the Greek island of Chios (upper left) and with Cyprus (upper right). The collection of sherds above contains a number of distinctive styles, such as Wild Goat Style pottery (which includes depictions not only of goats but also of geese and stags), thought by some to be manufactured in Ionia, but more likely produced at many different centers in East Greece. The sherd with the human-headed sphinx is also from Chios, while the sherd with scallops (bottom row, second from left) is from Corinth.

Numerous cultic artifacts from Egypt, among them a faience figurine of the half human, half lion dwarf-god Bes (opposite, upper right), protector of the home and family, and an abalone jewelry box with nine small amulets (opposite, upper left), suggest that Ashkelon was home to a permanent Egyptian enclave with its own sanctuary. In the seventh century B.C.E., Philistia had strong cultural and political ties with Egypt; like Judah to the east, Philistia sided with Egypt against Babylonia in the struggle for Near Eastern hegemony. Both suffered for that choice

of allegiance: Philistine Ashkelon was sacked and burned in 604 B.C.E.; and Judahite Jerusalem, after a long siege by the Babylonians, was destroyed in 586 B.C.E.

In the ashes of Ashkelon's winery lay a cache of seven bronze bottles, called *situlae* (shown below and on this issue's cover). Each bottle contained depictions in relief of Egyptian deities.

In the midst of the *situlae*, the excavators found a bronze offering table engraved with bread and libation flasks; around the table are two baboons, a falcon, a jackal and a frog.

Situlae are votive offerings, perhaps for the revivification of the dead. The most prominent deity represented is Min, on the bottle at upper right: Min is depicted erect, masturbating himself

with his left hand while throwing his right hand up in a gesture of deepest pleasure. Lawrence Stager suggests that for the Egyptians Min's act of masturbation mirrored the original life-giving force from which all generative power derives. These phallic-shaped bronze bottles may have contained semen or other liquids, such as milk, to symbolize the power of giving life.

THE ZOOARCHAEOLOGICAL RECORD
Pigs' Feet, Cattle Bones and Birds' Wings
BRIAN HESSE AND **PAULA WAPNISH**

In the 1992 and 1993 seasons at Ashkelon, over 12,000 animal bones were found in the destruction debris now dated to 604 B.C.E.

About half of these bones were found in the street outside the square building called the Counting House (see plan, opposite). This suggests that this area was used for carcass processing, although part of the accumulation may have resulted from the fact that this area is a slight downslope and may have accumulated remains through erosion.

Several other considerations, in addition to the accumulation of bones, indicate that this was a carcass-processing area. Of the 43 articulations (bones found in anatomical relationship) that were excavated, the largest concentration (16) was found in this same area. Most of these articulations were of non-meaty portions of the carcass—"wrists" and "ankles" still attached to the toe bones of sheep or goats. This concentration of articulations indicates a scene of primary carcass processing in the months prior to the destruction of Ashkelon in the winter of 604 B.C.E.

Five of the animals represented by these feet were 16 to 24 months old when they died. Assuming they were born in the seasonal pattern typical for sheep and goats in the Near East, these feet came from animals that died in late fall or early winter. The age of the animals at death is consistent with the historical record, since Nebuchadrezzar's destruction of Ashkelon in early winter would have sealed the deposit before the feet had a chance to be scattered by exposure to the elements, scavenged by dogs or trampled by traffic.

Three vertebral column sections were also found in this area. These sections were probably also a by-product of primary butchery.

Because the societies of the ancient Near East had only a limited technical capacity to store fresh meat, slaughtered animals had to be quickly processed. Ethnographic analogies suggest that entire sheep and goat carcasses were hung up along the street, with the meat cut off at purchasers' requests. Since the most desirable portions of the carcass may have been carried off for further processing with the bones still embedded in the meat, the by-products of the initial steps of butchery (the skinning of the animal and the removal of non-meaty portions) are all that remain to mark the activity.

A cache of "ankle" bones (astragali) was also found in the Counting House. Some of these nearly cubical bones were polished on several surfaces, a common practice that allowed the bones to roll more easily when used as dice. But they also may have been used as counters. A number of other bones, mostly the articular ends of long bones, showed evidence of sawing. These bone sections are not just the by-products of butchery; they also represent the first step in the preparation of "blanks" for the large-scale manufacture of bone tools, amply evidenced from ten years of digging at Ashkelon.

In one of the shops off the Piazza Philistina (Room 431), two complete lower forelegs of cattle were found. The discovery of these meaty portions suggests that this was a butcher's shop. A second concentration of cattle remains, again including meatier portions of the anatomy, was found in another room (Room 422). The spatial segregation of cattle remains from the remains of sheep and goats suggests that these animals were purveyed through separate marketing systems. Room 422 produced another surprise: Wings and legs from at least 12 small birds were found concentrated in one area. Perhaps both of these rooms were areas where meat was further prepared for cooking.

Nearly 1,800 fish bones were also recovered, a large part of which were found in a single room, the Wine Shop. This suggests that fish, too, were marketed and consumed through a system independent of barnyard stock.

What this patterning shows is that animals arrived at market through organized channels, not through sporadic marketing by individual households.

No camel remains and only nine pig, three gazelle and five deer bone fragments were recovered. Pigs, gazelle and deer may have been part of the domestic mode of subsistence and not regularly processed commercially.

Another anomaly: Sheep and goat remains outnumber cattle remains about eleven to one, a ratio unexpected in urban Philistia, where intensive agriculture dependent on animal labor likely supported the population. We suspect that this anomaly is due to the fact that only part of the site has been excavated. In some new area of excavation, we might well find an abattoir that once specialized in beef.

a jackal crouches at the fourth corner. Between the jackal and the falcon is a frog. The most prominent deity represented on the *situlae* is Min or Amen-Re, with erect phallus. Although not especially clear from this example, from other statues of Min we can interpret what is happening here: The god masturbates with his left hand and raises his right hand in a gesture of joy or pleasure.[5] In Egyptian creation myths, divine masturbatory semen provides the initial life-giving force from which all other generative power derives.[6] These bronze bottles probably contained offerings of actual semen or liquids, such

as milk or water, symbolic of this revivifying fluid.

A "twin" of our bronze Osiris statuette was uncovered more than 60 years ago in a small salvage excavation at Ashkelon. The excavator, J.H. Iliffe, dated it to the fourth century B.C.E., but it is now clear that this statuette and 25 other bronze statuettes of Egyptian deities, as well as 14 other Egyptian bronze artifacts (including cube-shaped weights) found in Iliffe's excavation[7] were contemporaneous with our bronzes—that is, late seventh century B.C.E., not fourth century B.C.E.

What were all these Egyptian artifacts doing

THE "STREETS" OF ASHKELON, shown above, are mentioned in David's lament over the deaths of King Saul and his son Jonathan (2 Samuel 1:20). The Hebrew word ḥûṣṣōt, however, does not mean "streets" but "bazaars"; David warns the Israelites not to proclaim the news of the deaths of Saul and Jonathan in the famous bazaars of Israel's enemy, lest Philistine women rejoice at Israel's loss of its royalty.

The photo looks west toward the sea, along Ashkelon's marketplace (see plan, right). The main street runs toward the sea just to the right of the large hole (the 1921 British excavation probe) in the foreground; to the left of the street is the Administrative Center (no longer visible because the excavators have dug below it), and to the right are the shops. Beyond the shops, just past the small hole at right center, is the Plaza—an open square. To the left of the far end of the Plaza is the Counting House; some of its rooms are visible in the photo. In the Counting House excavators found an ostracon (an inscribed potsherd) that was used as a receipt for a shipment of grain (see box, pp. 384-385).

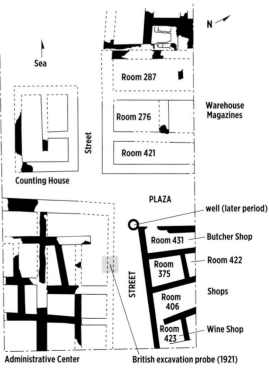

N

Sea

Room 287

Warehouse Magazines

Room 276

Street

Room 421

Counting House

PLAZA — well (later period)

Room 431 — Butcher Shop

STREET

Room 375 — Room 422

Room 406 — Shops

Room 423 — Wine Shop

Administrative Center

British excavation probe (1921)

THE EPIGRAPHICAL RECORD
A Philistine Ostracon From Ashkelon
FRANK MOORE CROSS

ZEV RADOVAN, LEON LEVY EXPEDITION TO ASHKELON

Excavators at Ashkelon recently found an inscribed potsherd that throws light on the little-known language and script of the Philistines in the seventh century B.C.E. It was dug out of debris of the destruction level left by Babylonian forces after their attack on the city in 604 B.C.E. The inscription is on the weathered body sherd of an Iron Age II jar with red slip and burnishing. The text of the inscription penned on the sherd is only partially preserved—it is broken off on both sides and the ink is only faintly preserved in some words. What little we can read, however, is of no little interest:

1.] m'br . š . tš [
2.] kّw . yš'n̊ . l [
3.] ' [.] br [.] ṣpn̊ [

1.] from the (cereal) crop which you[
2.]...they shall pay to[
3.]...(cereal) crop of Ṣapan-[Divine Name?]

The ostracon appears to be an agreement for the purchase or delivery of grain. The word 'b(w)r is rather rare in Biblical Hebrew, but it also appears in Middle Hebrew, in Imperial and

at Ashkelon? Very probably   there was an Egyptian enclave there   with its own sanctuary.

The building in which these Egyptian artifacts were found was in the center of the city. Three rooms in this monumental building contained wine presses, hence our designation of the building as a winery. The winery platforms, vats and basins were lined with cobblestones and coated with smooth, shell-tempered plaster of unusually high quality (see photo, p. 389). The best preserved wine press had a shallow plastered platform (where the grapes were pressed by foot) with a low rim on all four sides; the rim on one side had a small hole through which the grape juice flowed into a channel leading to an intermediate-sized plastered tank or vat. Another channel drained the juice into a deeper plastered vat, with a small sump or catchment in the corner. Juice from Ashkelon's wine presses was decanted into wine jars and left to ferment in adjacent storerooms. Dipper juglets and fat-bellied storage jars (amphoras) with pointed bases and protruding handles were the predominant pottery types found in the winery.

We also found in this building dozens and dozens of puzzling unbaked clay balls, some as large as grapefruits, with a single perforation through the center (see photos, p. 388). At first we thought they might be loom weights for weaving. Since wine-making is a seasonal activity that takes place during and after the grape harvest in August/September, perhaps the building was used for weaving during other seasons. But many of these clay balls are too large and heavy to be loom weights. The more probable explanation connects them to wine production: They fit nicely into the mouth of the fat-bellied storage jar, the most common Philistine wine jar found at Ashkelon. When wine ferments, it gives off gases. To prevent explosions, the gases are released, sometimes through a bunghole in the side of the wine jar or cask. Of course, a puncture in the side of a pottery vessel damages it permanently. The same effect, without damaging the vessel, could be obtained if perforated stoppers, such as these clay spheres, were sealed in the mouth of the jar, and the hole opened or closed at the appropriate time to release the gases. Israeli archaeologist Zvi Gal was the first to propose the function of these clay balls, which he found in an excavation at Ḥurvat Rosh Zayit, and we think he is right. If the clay spheres are not loom weights, then there is no reason for us to believe that the winery was converted into a textile factory during the off-season.

later Aramaic, in Phoenician and in Akkadian (ebūru), with the meanings "produce (of the field)," "crop" (especially of a cereal) and "grain." The personal name in the final line is familiar from such names as Biblical Zephaniah (ṣpnyhw) or Phoenician Ṣapan-ba'l.

According to Lawrence Stager, director of the Leon Levy Expedition to Ashkelon, the ostracon was found associated with a dozen or so cuboid weights, a scale balance and storage jars containing the charred remains of grain, especially wheat. These might well be the remains of a grain storage area and its "office" and records.

Of more interest to the epigraphist than the rather banal content of the ostracon is the script in which it is inscribed. In the Persian remains of the city of Ashkelon, the considerable number of ostraca found have been inscribed in Phoenician and (in lesser degree) in Aramaic scripts. The script of this ostracon from the late Philistine stratum before the city's fall to Nebuchadrezzar is neither Phoenician nor Aramaic. It stands very close to Hebrew, and is obviously derived from Hebrew. It also shares many traits with Edomite, a script also derived from Hebrew. However, it shows distinctive typological characteristics and must be given its own name as a local or national script.

I have been inclined to call it Hebreo-Philistine to underline its affinities with Hebrew, and to save the simple term "Philistine" for an older script, presumably a script with Aegean affinities like the Deir 'Allā clay tablets. Professor Stager has suggested "Neo-Philistine." This label would have the advantage of following the practice of naming national scripts without hyphenated names denoting their origins. We do not speak of Hebreo-Edomite, Hebreo-Moabite, Aramaeo-Nabataean or Aramaeo-Ammonite but simply of Edomite, Moabite, Nabataean or Ammonite. So I shall call the script Neo-Philistine.

Joseph Naveh in an important essay, "Writing and Scripts in Seventh-Century B.C.E. Philistia: The New Evidence from Tell Jemmeh" (*Israel Exploration Journal* 35 [1985], pp. 8-21), collects a number of texts stemming from Philistine sites, or having peculiarities in common with texts whose provenience is clearly Philistine. He proposes that the script of these texts be termed Philistine. Noting, however, that these texts are not homogeneous, he suggests that the chancelleries of the great Philistine city-states may have had slightly differing styles comparable to the situation in Trans-Jordan with Ammonite, Moabite and Edomite.

The fact that the Philistine script and orthography of this period stem from Hebrew—and not Phoenician—is surprising. It points to a period of strong Israelite cultural influence on—and most likely political domination of—the Philistines. The era of the United Monarchy of David and Solomon provides the appropriate context for the borrowing. This is the period when, according to Biblical accounts, Israel exercised hegemony over the Philistine city-states.

We hope that future seasons at Ashkelon will furnish more inscriptions in "Neo-Philistine," and that our knowledge of the Philistine script and language will increase in sophistication from its present sketchy state.

The winery at Ashkelon shatters another modern myth about the Philistines: that they were beer-guzzling louts. One of the most characteristic pottery vessels found at Philistine sites is a jug with a strainer spout, commonly referred to as a Philistine "beer jug."[8] The strainer supposedly functioned to strain out the beer dregs. The ecology of Philistia, however, favors the production of grapes over barley. The sandy soils and warm, sunny climate of the coastal plain produced many palatable wines, ranging from the light varieties at Ashkelon to the heavier ones at Gaza.[9] The winery at Ashkelon and similar contemporaneous wine presses recently excavated near Ashdod suggest that coastal Philistia was an important producer of wine both for local consumption and for export. Wine, not beer, was the beverage of choice. The "beer-jugs" really served as carafes for wine. The strainer spout acted as a built-in sieve, which filtered out the lees and other impurities. To remove even finer unwanted particles from the wine,

TERRACOTTA FIGURINES, originally 4-5 inches in height, were uncovered from the rubble of Ashkelon's destruction. Although the excavators do not yet know the name of the deity shown at right, a silver plaque of the Syrian goddess Ishtar/Ashtarte, the "Queen of Heaven," has been found at Ekron; the goddess Asherah is attested on seventh-century ostraca from Ekron as well.

FAT-BELLIED JARS, such as the four largest vessels in the photo above, were used by Philistines for fermenting and storing wine. As a port and trading center, Ashkelon was visited by ships from various places in the eastern Mediterranean, such as Phoenicia to the north: Cargo-laden ships from Sidon and Tyre arrived in Ashkelon with goods stored in ceramic jars—like the curving tapered jar at far right and the amphora in front of it. At lower left is an example of the distinctive Philistine Red-Slipped Ware. The inverted bowl combines the form of Assyrian-style pottery (characterized by a sharp shoulder and flaring rim) with the decoration of Phoenician Fine Ware (characterized by a burnished red slip and a reserve pattern resembling so-called Samaria Ware).

the pourer might have placed a linen cloth over the ceramic strainer.[10] The Philistines were not the only winebibbers to filter their wine. Egyptian wall reliefs depict royalty and nobility pouring wine through sieves into their drinking bowls or cups.

While Ashkelon produced wine, Philistine Ekron, located in the inner coastal zone, with its expansive rolling fields of deep fertile soils, was the undisputed olive oil capital of the country, if not the world.[11] More than a hundred olive oil factories lined the outer industrial belt of Ekron. The coast and interior of Philistia thus formed complementary zones for the production of two of the most important cash crops of the Levant—olive oil and wine. Largely because of these exports to Egypt and other Mediterranean countries, Philistia grew fat

from its oil and heady from its wine during the last half of the seventh century B.C.E.*

The bazaar, or marketplace, of Ashkelon overlooked the sea. A row of shops flanked the street on one side. The floor of one of the shops (Room 423; see plan, p. 385) was littered with dipper juglets and wine jars. It might well have been a wine shop. Just outside the shop lay an ostracon, which Professor Frank Cross has dated to the late seventh century based on the shape and form of the letters. The inscription lists so many units (bottles) of red wine (*yn ʾdm*) and so many units of *šēkār*. The verb-form of this latter term means to get drunk, so the noun-form is usually translated as "strong drink"; it probably refers to a particularly strong wine made from dates and known as *šakrā* in Syriac.[12] To this day, date palms thrive in the Yadin National Park, where the tell of Ashkelon is located.

Another shop (Room 431) contained cuts of meat, including two complete forelegs of beef,

*The prodigious efforts of Seymour Gitin to link the prosperity of Ekron to the Assyrian Empire have produced an anachronistic conclusion. The economic "take off" did not occur during the late eighth or early seventh centuries B.C.E., but later in the second half of the seventh century B.C.E. What propelled the olive oil industry at Ekron into the international sphere was not a dying Assyria but a rising Egypt, ever the greatest consumer of Levantine olive oil. The expansion of Ekron and the development of its oil industry occurred after Assyrian interest and power in the West had begun to wane in the late 640s.

A SAILOR'S PARADISE. Fine wines probably accounted for a good part of Ashkelon's international allure, along with products from the interior, such as olive oil. Three rooms in one large building contained wine presses (an example is shown at left) consisting of carefully constructed platforms, vats and basins (see drawing above, which is modeled on a different wine press from the one shown here). Built of cobblestones, the presses were coated with an impermeable layer of fine shell-tempered plaster. At the highest level rested the platform where grapes were pressed by foot; the juice then flowed into a channel leading to settling vats, from which it flowed into other channels emptying into larger basins. From the basins, the juice was collected in jars (like the fat-bellied amphoras shown in the photo opposite), fermented and sold.

DOZENS OF CLAY BALLS (right) found in the winery, some as large as grapefruits, posed a dilemma for the excavators. What were they? Because the balls were perforated through their centers, it was thought that they might have been loom weights, used to anchor threads while weaving. After the wine-making season of August/September, perhaps, the winery was turned into a weaving center.

More likely, however, they are wine-jar stoppers. The clay balls fit easily into the mouths of fat-bellied storage jars. Plugging the jars during fermentation, the stoppers allowed the build-up of gases to be released at regular intervals through their perforations.

The finished wines were served in a so-called "beer-jug" (similar to the earlier example shown below). Nothing could be further from the truth than the image of the Philistines as loutish, beer-guzzling thugs. Not only was their craftsmanship superb, but they drank wine: The "beer-jug" is really a wine decanter, with small perforations in the spout to strain out sediment.

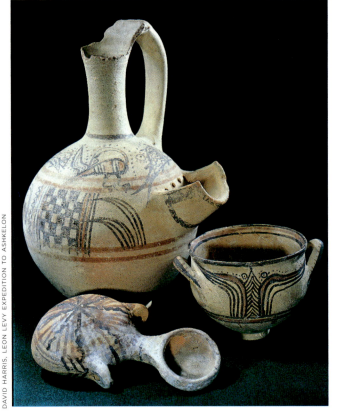

which prompted staff zooarchaeologist Brian Hesse to label this the Butcher Shop (see box, p. 382). It is easy to imagine the various cuts of meat hanging in the windows and doorway of this shop in Philistine times, much as they do today in the meat-markets of the Old City of Jerusalem.

Without doubt, the most famous reference to Ashkelon is the lament of David on the death of his friend Prince Jonathan and King Saul at the hands of the Philistines (2 Samuel 1:20):

Tell it not in Gath,

proclaim it not in the streets of Ashkelon,

lest the daughters of the Philistines rejoice,

the daughters of the uncircumcised exult.

The Hebrew word translated as "streets" is ḥûṣṣōt. It does not really mean "streets," however. As Benjamin Mazar pointed out 30 years ago, the word means "bazaars." The poet who composed this early Hebrew verse knew about Ashkelon as a great commercial center and entrepôt, where news and information traveled fast. Was it the bazaars of Ashkelon that the poet had in mind? The bazaar was the most bustling part of any Middle Eastern city, then as now. The bazaar that we uncovered from the late seventh century was probably not much different in layout or function from the earlier bazaars to which the Biblical elegist alludes.

Across the street from the shops was a major public building, probably the town's Administrative Center. As one walked toward the sea, past the shops on the right and the Administrative Center on the left, the street opened up into a square, which we have dubbed "Piazza Philistina." Bordering the west side of the plaza is a series of long narrow rooms (Rooms 421, 276 and 287), probably magazines of a warehouse,

DAVID HARRIS, LEON LEVY EXPEDITION TO ASHKELON

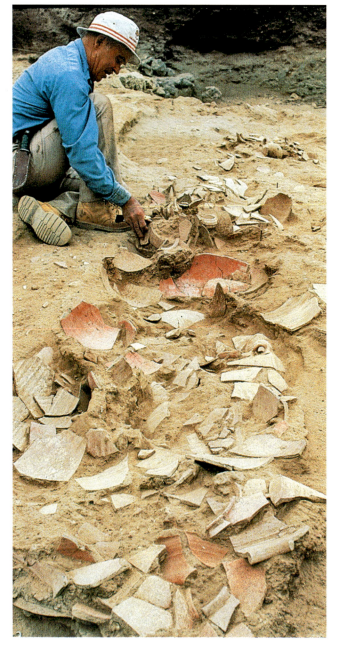

IMAGES OF DESTRUCTION. Ashkelon's excavators found evidence of Babylonian devastation throughout the city: smashed pottery (left), charcoal, vitrified brick (see photo, pp. 376-377), charred wheat, collapsed roofs and debris. The most disturbing sign of the invaders' ferocity, however, lay in one of the bazaar's shops: the skeleton of a 35-year-old woman (above), who had sought to hide from her attackers among the shop's large storage jars. Lying on her back with her legs recoiled in terror, she lifted her left arm up to her head, as if to ward off a blow. The physical anthropologist who examined this skeleton determined that the woman had been clubbed in the head with a blunt instrument.

After razing Ashkelon, Nebuchadrezzar destroyed Ekron and later battled with the Egyptians over Gaza. He then retired to Babylon in 601/600 B.C.E. A year later his troops returned to the Levant, conquering a number of Judahite cities and besieging Jerusalem. In 586 B.C.E., Jerusalem's defenses collapsed and the city, with its Temple, was completely destroyed. Many of the Jews, like the Philistines before them, were led into Exile.

where produce and goods were stored before being put on sale in the shops. Turning left at the plaza, a narrow corridor leads to a square building on the right, tentatively identified as the Counting House because of some of the small finds located there. Nearby were a dozen scale weights of bronze and stone along with two bronze pieces of pans and part of a bronze beam from a scale balance. An ostracon found there appears to be a receipt for grain paid for in silver (see box, pp. 384-385). In this period just prior to the introduction of minted coinage in the Levant, ingots, jewelry and precious metals served as currency. By the seventh century B.C.E., commodities were often paid for in silver.[13] Prices could be compared using an equivalent

unit of value, such as a shekel weight of silver.

The script on the ostracon is also interesting. It is an alphabetic script similar to, but not identical with, Hebrew and Phoenician, peculiar to Philistia in the seventh century. When the Philistines first came to the eastern Mediterranean littoral from the Mycenaean world (including coastal Asia Minor, Crete and the Cyclades, and other sites) in the early 12th century B.C.E., they probably brought with them a language related to Greek and a script that will be related to Linear B—whenever it is found; we still have no sure example of early Philistine writing. Our ostracon indicates that by the seventh century B.C.E., and perhaps as early as the time of David and Solomon, the Philistines were using a local script and had adopted a Semitic dialect as well.

One thing is clear: this large, sophisticated Philistine metropolis of the late seventh century B.C.E. was thoroughly destroyed. The destruction of Philistine Ashkelon was complete and final. The Iron Age, in archaeological terms, had ended.

Archaeology cannot be so precise as to date the destruction of Ashkelon to 604 B.C.E., but the *Babylonian Chronicle* leaves little doubt that the late seventh-century destruction we found all over the site, followed by a 75- to 80-year gap in occupation until the Persian Period, was the work of Nebuchadrezzar in 604 B.C.E.

Earlier in the late eighth-early seventh centuries the Assyrians had made a serious investment in the West. They established administrative provinces where former kingdoms and city-states had been. They developed a complex imperial apparatus and infrastructure to insure that Mediterranean wealth was siphoned into their coffers. Nebuchadrezzar probably lacked the capability of imposing an effective imperial bureaucracy on these small Mediterranean states as Assyria had done. His overriding concern was with Egypt. And his instrument of foreign policy toward real or potential allies of Egypt was a blunt one—annihilation, and for those who survived, deportation. Throughout Philistia, and later throughout Judah, his scorched-earth policy created a veritable wasteland west of the Jordan River. Those fortunate enough to survive this devastation were usually deported to Babylonia.

Philistines, Jews and many others were exiled to Babylonia by Nebuchadrezzar. He needed deportees to repopulate and rehabilitate his empire after the depletion of its manpower in the earlier Assyro-Babylonian wars.[14] In a rations list in cuneiform, dated to 592 B.C.E., we find prominent Ashkelonians serving Nebuchadrezzar in Babylon: two sons of Aga (the last king of Philistine Ashkelon), three mariners, several officials and chief musicians—all deportees from Ashkelon.[15]

A century and a half later, as we know from the Murashu Archive, masses of deportees from the West had been settled in the Nippur region, southeast of Babylon. Philistines from Ashkelon and Gaza were living in their own ethnic communities located along canals leading into Nippur, where they were doing business with a big firm run by the Jewish Murashu family.[16]

Only with Cyrus the Great, the Persian successor to the Babylonians, does the archaeological record begin again in Ashkelon (where Phoenicians settled; Philistines did not return from the diaspora)—as in Jerusalem* and in Judah, where many Jewish exiles returned to their homeland.

According to the Chronicler, writing in the fifth century B.C.E., long after Nebuchadrezzar's destruction of Jerusalem in 586 B.C.E. Judah "lay desolate" for 70 years "until the land had made up for its sabbaths" (2 Chronicles 36:20-23).

Before Nebuchadrezzar's juggernaut advanced toward Ashkelon, the Philistines probably felt secure in their well-fortified city of 10,000-12,000 inhabitants. They had refortified the seaport by adding another thick sheath of sand and debris over the mile-and-a-half arc of artificial earthen ramparts (the so-called glacis construction) around the city. We have excavated two large mudbrick towers on the crest of the glacis, about 60 feet apart. If this pattern persists along the crest of the arc, as many as 50 towers may have fortified the city when Nebuchadrezzar attacked. This fortification system was destroyed at the end of the seventh century B.C.E., presumably by Nebuchadrezzar's forces.

In the winery mentioned earlier, remnants of charred wood were all that remained of the panelling that once framed mudbrick doorjambs. Indeed, the path of fiery destruction could be traced throughout the building by carefully observing the crushed pottery, charcoal, vitrified mudbrick, and wall and ceiling fragments. There was no doubt that the building had come to an abrupt and catastrophic end. We may conclude that vineyards that took numerous generations of peace, stability and nurturing to produce were destroyed almost overnight by Nebuchadrezzar and his vandals.

As with the winery, so with the Counting House. A large container of olive oil had spilled on the floor; when the fires of destruction reached that part of the building, they burned so hot that mud bricks and other clay materials were vitrified.

The rest of the bazaar, too, was plundered and pillaged in every area. In the winter of 604 B.C.E., wailing and despair replaced the joy and laughter that had once rung throughout the Ashkelon bazaar. Everywhere in the bazaar we found smashed pottery vessels by the hundreds amid the destruction debris, much of it identical to what we saw in the winery.

Evidence of just how far into the city Nebuchadrezzar's troops proceeded came to light in one of the shops of the bazaar (Room 406), where we found the skeleton of a middle-aged woman, about 35 years old, who had been crouching down among the storage jars, attempting to hide from the attackers. When we found her, she was lying on her back, her

*Gabriel Barkay extends the use of the Jerusalem Ketef Hinnom tomb into this gap; but that does not mean the city was rebuilt or widely inhabited.

legs flexed and akimbo, her left arm reaching toward her head. The skull was badly fragmented. We removed the skeleton to the laboratory of physical anthropologist Patricia Smith of Hebrew University, who carefully reconstructed the skull and determined that the woman had been clubbed in the head with a blunt instrument.

"Ashkelon is silenced," wailed the prophet Jeremiah at the destruction of Israel's arch enemy; "For the Lord is destroying the Philistines" (Jeremiah 47:5,4).

After destroying Philistine Ashkelon, Nebuchadrezzar moved on to the inland Philistine city of Ekron (Tel Miqne), which is being excavated by a joint Israeli-American team headed by Hebrew University professor Trude Dothan and the director of the W.F. Albright School of Archaeological Research, Seymour Gitin. The devastation of Ekron at the hands of Nebuchadrezzar in 603 B.C.E. (or perhaps in 601 B.C.E.) has left an incredible yield of material remains, including thousands of whole or restorable pots, animal bones and a rich array of small finds, including several Egyptian objects.

During the seventh century B.C.E., the kings of Judah vacillated between Egypt and Babylonia half a dozen times or more. Ashkelon and Ekron cast their lots with Egypt. Although Nebuchadrezzar never succeeded in conquering Egypt itself, he was nevertheless able to reduce Egypt's actual and potential allies and client-states to rubble.** Eventually, the pro-Egyptian policy of Judah (against the counsel of Jeremiah) led to the destruction of Jerusalem and Judah in 586 B.C.E. The First Temple period was at an end.

**It was not from want of trying, however. In 601/600 B.C.E. Nebuchadrezzar over-extended his army by invading Egypt; he was defeated by Necho II, who then reconquered Gaza.

[1] Avraham Malamat, "The Kingdom of Judah Between Egypt and Babylon," Studia Theologica 44 (1990), pp. 65-77.

[2] See Malamat, "The Twilight of Judah: In the Egyptian-Babylonian Maelstrom," Vetus Testamentum Supplement 28 (1975), pp. 123-125.

[3] British Museum 21946, 18-20. In the first edition of Chronicles of Chaldaean Kings (626-556 B.C.) (London: British Museum, 1956), pp. 68, 85, D.J. Wiseman restored Ashkelon (is´?-qi?-[erasure]-il-lu-nu) as the name of the captured city. Later W.F. Albright, accompanied by Wiseman and A. Sachs, reexamined the tablet in the British Museum and concluded that Wiseman's reading was correct. More recently, A.K. Grayson, in reviewing P. Garelli and V. Nikiprowetzky's Le Proche-Orient Asiatique: Les Empires Mésopotamiens in Archiv für Orientforschung 27 (1980), declared the reading of the name Ashkelon to be "very uncertain." He apparently convinced Wiseman that the earlier reading was "uncertain" (Wiseman, Nebuchadrezzar and Babylon, Schweich Lectures of the British Academy, 1983 [Oxford: Oxford University Press, 1991], p. 23, n. 158). In 1992, my colleague Peter Machinist asked I. Finkel, curator of cuneiform in the British Museum's department of Western Asiatic Antiquities, to check the tablet once again for the name of the captured city. In a letter dated November 11, 1992, Finkel confirmed that the city referred to is indeed Ashkelon. For details, see Lawrence Stager, "Ashkelon and the Archaeology of Destruction: Kislev 604

B.C.E.," in "A Heap of Broken Images": Essays in Biblical Archaeology (Louisville, KY: Westminster/John Knox, forthcoming).

[4] Benjamin Mazar, "The Philistines and the Rise of Israel and Tyre," in The Early Biblical Period, ed. S. Ahdituv and B. Levine (Jerusalem: Israel Exploration Society, 1986 [1964]), pp. 63-82, esp. 65-68.

[5] The Egyptologist Dr. Michael Baud examined the situlae and suggested this interpretation of Min's gesture, also based on statuary of the deity.

[6] J. A. Wilson, "The Repulsing of the Dragon and the Creation," in Ancient Near Eastern Texts Relating to the Old Testament, ed. James B. Pritchard (Princeton, NJ: Princeton Univ. Press, 1969), p. 6.

[7] J.H. Iliffe, "A Hoard of Bronzes from Ashkelon, c. Fourth Century B.C.," Quarterly of the Department of Antiquities in Palestine 5 (1936), pp. 61-68.

[8] See William F. Albright, The Archaeology of Palestine (Harmondsworth: Penguin Books, 1961), p. 115.

[9] See P. Mayerson, "The Gaza 'Wine' Jar (Gazition) and the 'Lost' Ashkelon Jar (Askalônion)," Israel Exploration Journal 42 (1992), pp. 76-80; and "The Use of Ascalon Wine in the Medical Writers of the Fourth to the Seventh Centuries," Israel Exploration Journal 43 (1993), pp. 169-173.

[10] See J.D. Eisenstein, "Wine," in The Jewish Encyclopedia (New York: Funk and Wagnalls, 1904), vol. 12, pp. 532-535; Lawrence E. Stager, "The Impact of the Sea Peoples in Canaan (1185-1050 B.C.E.)," in The Archaeology of Society in the Holy Land, ed. Thomas E. Levy (New York: Facts on File, 1995), pp. 332-348.

[11] Seymour Gitin, "Incense Altars from Ekron, Israel and Judah: Context and Typology," Eretz-Israel 23 (1989), pp. 52*-67*; and Gitin, "Tel Miqne-Ekron in the 7th Century B.C.E.: The Impact of Economic Innovation and Foreign Cultural Influences on a Neo-Assyrian Vassal City-State," in Recent Excavations in Israel: A View to the West, ed. Gitin, Archaeological Institute of America, Colloquia and Conference Papers 1 (Boston: 1995).

[12] F. Brown, S.R. Driver and C.A. Briggs, A Hebrew-English Lexicon (Oxford: Clarendon Press, 1953), p. 1016. According to L. Oppenheim, date wine was added to the list of alcoholic beverages in Mesopotamia no earlier than the Neo-Babylonian period (Ancient Mesopotamia: A Portrait of a Dead Civilization [Chicago: Univ. of Chicago, 1964], p. 315).

[13] See Gitin, "Tel Miqne-Ekron in the 7th Century B.C.E.," pp. 69, 77, n. 36 for further bibliography.

[14] See I. Eph'al, "The Western Minorities in Babylonia in the 6th-5th Centuries B.C.: Maintenance and Cohesion," Orientalia 47 (1978), pp. 74-90.

[15] See E.F. Weidner, "Jojachin König von Juda, in babylonischen Keilschrifttexten," in Mélanges Syriens offert à Monsieur René Dussaud, vol. 2 (Paris: Guethner, 1939).

[16] Eph'al, "The Western Minorities in Babylonia in the 6th-5th Centuries B.C."

Related Reading

Lawrence E. Stager, "When Canaanites and Philistines Ruled Ashkelon," BAR, March/April 1991 (see p. 168 of this book).

Lawrence E. Stager, "Why Were Hundreds of Dogs Buried at Ashkelon?" BAR, May/June 1991.

Lawrence E. Stager, "Eroticism and Infanticide at Ashkelon," BAR, July/August 1991.

"From Vespa to Ashkelon," BAR, July/August 2010.

Daniel M. Master and Lawrence E. Stager, "Buy Low, Sell High: The Marketplace at Ashkelon," BAR, January/February 2014.

What Happened to the Cult Figurines?

Israelite Religion Purified After the Exile

EPHRAIM STERN

ACCIDENTAL DISCOVERIES OF TWO PITS containing cult figurines have led me to discern an extraordinary development in Israelite religious observance. This development occurred when the Jews returned from the Babylonian Exile in the sixth to fifth centuries B.C.

The first discovery took place in the opening season of our excavations at Tel Dor, on the Mediterranean coast of Israel, where we were fortunate enough to uncover a *favissa* (FAH-viss-uh). A *favissa* (plural, *favissae* [FAH-viss-ee]) is a pit into which votive figurines or statuettes have been thrown. Sometimes these figurines are made of metal or stone, but mostly they are made of clay. They are almost always broken, intentionally destroyed.

Originally the figurines from our *favissae* had stood on a shelf or bench of a nearby sanctuary. After a time, having served their purpose—whatever that was—the figurines were removed, deliberately broken, probably in some kind of religious ceremony, and then disposed of. Because they were sacred objects, they could not simply be thrown away. Instead, they were literally buried in a special pit, thus making room in the sanctuary for a new host of votive offerings. (To this day, Jews refrain from throwing away or destroying worn-out sacred texts; instead, they bury them or store them in a repository called a *geniza*.)

We found the first *favissa* at Tel Dor in 1980. Though we have dug for nine years, and have become the largest dig in Israel, the discovery of

the *favissa* in our first season will always be remembered as a special thrill. Somehow, the *favissa* had been miraculously preserved in an area near the city gate, in a very narrow space between two city walls, one from the Persian period (fifth–fourth centuries B.C.) and the other from the Hellenistic period (third–first centuries B.C.). The *favissa* itself dates to the fifth to fourth centuries B.C. We know this by comparing certain stylistic elements of the figurines with others that have established dates.

In 1982, we discovered a second *favissa*. This one (on the eastern slope of the mound—in our Area C) was dug into the clay bricks of the city wall from the Iron Age (ninth–eighth centuries B.C.). Obviously, this *favissa* was created long after the Iron Age defense wall had gone out of use. We date this *favissa* to 420–400 B.C., based on the dates of the Attic pottery that we found in it.

Each of these *favissae* attests to a nearby contemporaneous sanctuary, which we have been unable to find. These sanctuaries were probably completely destroyed in later periods.

The discovery of these two *favissae* has led me to study ancient figurines generally. Clay figurines are

HOLDING HER BREASTS and grinning broadly, this 6-inch-tall figurine represents the fertility goddess Astarte in a typical pose. Worshipped under a variety of names throughout the ancient Near East, Astarte was the consort of the storm-god Baal. The late Iron Age, Phoenician mold at right, found at Tel Dor, produced this modern cast.

COURTESY EPHRAIM STERN

TEL DOR thrusts a rocky finger into the Mediterranean about 12 miles south of Haifa in Israel (see map). Founded by the Canaanites in the 20th or 19th century B.C. and occupied by various peoples through the Roman period, Dor became an important port city that conducted extensive trade with Cyprus and the countries in the Aegean. In excavations conducted since 1980, visible in the area just above the center of the photo, a number of intentionally buried figurines have emerged. These led dig director Ephraim Stern to make a general study of such objects, which in turn led him to an original observation about the development of Israelite religious practices in the period following the return of the Jews from exile in Babylonia.

not found in nearly as great abundance as pottery vessels in archaeological excavations in Israel, but they are by no means uncommon either. They date from almost every archaeological period. Some of these clay figurines even date from as far back as the Neolithic period (eighth millennium B.C.), when pottery vessels were created for the first time in the Near East. In every succeeding period, clay figurines continued to be produced. By now they have been found not by the hundreds, but by the thousands.

Numerous studies have been devoted to the various techniques by which these clay figurines were made and to the creation of different typologies by which they can be subdivided. It is more difficult to determine their cultic significance. Thus, we can distinguish figurines that come from Israel, Judah, Edom, Philistia and Phoenicia (see map, p. 399), but we cannot so easily discuss their divine identity nor the functions they served in the various cults.

Before describing the clay figurines we found in the *favissae* at Tel Dor, let us look at the Phoenicians who lived at Tel Dor in the period of our *favissae*.

The Phoenicians were actually the heirs and descendants of the Canaanites. Indeed, they called themselves Canaanites. "Phoenician" is the term applied to them by the Greeks, beginning in about the eighth century B.C., after this fascinating people had already become a major worldwide (as the world was then known) maritime power. But originally these Canaanites were pushed by the Philistines (and related Sea Peoples) and by the Israelites into a small coastal area on the Mediterranean Sea, north of the Sea Peoples and west of the Israelite territory. This occurred as early as the 11th century B.C. and was completed by the time of King David and King Solomon in the tenth century B.C. The Canaanites—or Phoenicians, as we may now call them—were confined to a few major coastal cities, from south to north: Dor, 'Acco, Tyre, Sidon, Byblos and Arwad. Unable to expand to the east or the south, they turned to the Mediterranean Sea on the west. They became merchants, sailors and traders, ultimately establishing important colonies as far west as Spain, exporting their culture as well as their goods, and importing the goods and cultures of other peoples. Not until the Roman destruction of Phoenician Carthage in 150 B.C. did the Romans eclipse the Phoenicians.

The process of Hellenization on the coast of Palestine began in the fifth century B.C., the period of our *favissae* at Dor. The figurines in the *favissae* of Dor, consistent with hundreds of other figurines found at other coastal sites in Phoenicia and elsewhere, reflect both Eastern and Western influence. In fact, they can be generally divided into Eastern and Western types, the former exhibiting ancient Canaanite and Egyptian influence, and the latter the more recent Greek or Hellenistic influence.

The Eastern type is more common in Palestine, Cis-Jordan and Transjordan. The Western type is more common in Rhodes, Cyprus and mainland Greece. In coastal Phoenicia, the two types are mixed.

The Eastern type shows a variety of stylistic influences—Canaanite, Egyptian and even Mesopotamian-Persian, all of which were merged in the finest artistic tradition of the Phoenicians. The Western type, on the other hand, is more uniform stylistically, without an admixture of influences. Thus we can readily distinguish Greek, Rhodian and Cypriot subdivisions of the Western type.

The Eastern and Western types can also be distinguished by production techniques. In the older, Eastern tradition, the body is solid and handmade;

GRAVES FOR FIGURINES thrilled excavators when they were discovered at Tel Dor. Known as *favissae* (singular, *favissa*), such pits provided a special burial place for discarded votive figurines, whose sacredness demanded this unusual treatment. After a figurine had served its purpose, it was removed from the sanctuary and deliberately broken—probably in some ceremony—and then laid to rest in a *favissa*.

Uncovered in 1980 between two city walls near the city gate, the first *favissa* found at Tel Dor (top right) contained the figurines seen on the right side of the pit. These date to the fifth to fourth centuries B.C. The second *favissa* (right), discovered in 1982, was dug into the clay bricks of the Iron Age city wall on the mound's eastern side. This *favissa* also revealed Attic pottery dated to 420–400 B.C.

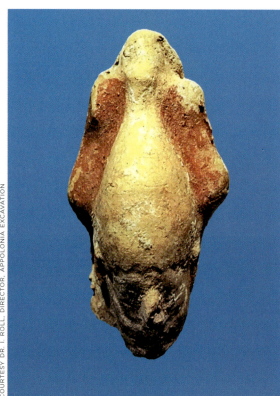

THREE BROKEN STATUETTES of the male deity Baal, excavated at Tel Dor, display the same fezlike hat, the typical Phoenician headdress of the Iron Age and Persian period (tenth–fourth centuries B.C.). Other characteristic Phoenician features of these 2-inch-high heads include large moustaches and a long beard still intact on the right-hand figurine. The latter also retains a fragment of his arm, bent at the elbow, perhaps in the act of stroking his beard, a common gesture in Baal figurines. (The numbers visible above the brow of the left-hand head are modern identification numbers.)

Baal figurines also sometimes wear the long, pointed Egyptian-style headdress known as an "Osiris" hat (left), which bedecks a head unearthed at Appolonia, an ancient city 22 miles south of Caesarea on the coast of Israel. Flaring, red-painted ornaments decorate each side of the hat.

only the head is molded. Sometimes we even find molded, solid plaques. In Phoenicia proper, we also find hollow round bodies made on a wheel ("bell-shaped" bodies) to which molded heads were attached. Beginning in the sixth century B.C., a new technique was imported from the West, probably from Greece: a hollow body molded in front, with the back sealed with smooth strips of clay.

The figurines from both East and West include both male and female deities.

Wrapped in a cloak and seated on a chair, a bearded man with a large moustache represents a common male deity. In this position, he strokes his beard. In another variation, he stands with his hands crossed on his breast. In both the seated and standing versions, he wears a round, flat headdress, the typical Phoenician headdress of the Iron Age and Persian period (tenth–fourth centuries B.C.).

A common variation of the seated form has the figure wearing a long pointed hat of Egyptian style (known as the "Osiris" hat). Despite the different headdresses in the two types of figurines, they apparently represent the same god, as indicated by the identical beard and moustache and by the same

RIDERLESS NOW, this fragmentary horse figurine probably once bore a man wearing the national headdress of the Persians. Such statuettes, known as "Persian riders," most likely depict Baal in his warrior-god incarnation. Traces of paint blotch the surface of this example found at Tel Dor.

seated attitude. Both types probably represent the most common deity in the pantheon of Phoenicia and Palestine, the god Baal. The difference in dress possibly attests to "Baals" of different localities, as was common in the Canaanite-Phoenician cult.

Another, less common, male figurine depicts a man wearing a pointed cloth hat that covers his cheeks and chin. As we know from Achaemenid (uh-KEE-meh-nid) reliefs, this was apparently the national headdress of the Persians. Whenever the body of these figurines is preserved, it is seated on a horse—hence the common scholarly term "Persian rider" for these figurines. The "Persian rider" figurines probably represent Baal in his aspect as a warrior god.

The most common figurines at Dor, however, are of the Western type. It should not be surprising that the inhabitants of Dor, whether Phoenician or Greek traders, preferred the new Greek-styled figurines to the older Eastern types. The heads of these bearded figurines were made from a mold created by a talented engraver and produced in multiple copies. But then a handmade headdress was added. The headdress varies. It may be a Greek warrior's helmet or a pointed Phrygian cap, or the figure may be bareheaded. This type of figurine may originally have represented Zeus in his various guises, but here he is turned into Baal.

Several other forms of male deities have been found at Dor, such as the Greek Heracles (here to be identified as the Tyrian Baal Melqart), as well as young boys, but these examples are enough to give you a general idea.

Most of the female figurines represent traditional fertility goddesses, either in the older form of a naked woman supporting her breasts with her hands (see photo on p. 393), or the later type wearing a drape. When she wears a drape, her head is covered with an Egyptian wig; she is either pregnant and rests a hand on her swollen abdomen, or she is nursing or

CURLY LOCKS and a jutting beard frame the face of this Greek-style figurine head. Not quite 2 inches high, the head, typically produced in multiple copies from a mold, wears a hand-modeled Greek warrior's helmet. Other examples of this sort wear a pointed Phrygian cap or remain bareheaded. Although this kind of figurine probably originally represented the Greek god Zeus, it became the Phoenician god Baal when the style was imported to Dor, where Western-type figurines predominate over the Eastern-type.

COURTESY EPHRAIM STERN

COURTESY EPHRAIM STERN

A MATERNAL ASTARTE appears in these three, 6-inch-high statuettes from Tel Dor. This later development in the traditional representation of the fertility goddess—in contrast to the earlier style seen in the photo on p. 393—shows her wearing a drape and an Egyptian wig. In this form, she is depicted pregnant, as in the left- and right-hand examples, or nursing a child, as in the center example. Figurines made in this later style incorporated new Greek production techniques, resulting in hollow bodies cast by a mold in front, with their backs sealed by smooth strips of clay.

READY TO FIGHT OFF EVIL, Bes stands in a traditional pose, arms akimbo, wearing a truculent expression and his usual feathered headdress. An Egyptian god adopted into the Canaanite-Phoenician pantheon, Bes served as the ordinary person's chief talisman against evil. He had already assumed a prominent role by the ninth century B.C. During the time of the Dor *favissae*, Bes was represented in numerous forms, including this 1.5-inch bone pendant.

carrying a child already born. Most of these later-style figurines are already made with the new Greek technique—that is, with hollow, molded bodies in front, and with the back sealed with smooth strips of clay. Thus here again we can distinguish between Eastern and Western types on the basis of technique as well as style.

Sometimes, however, elements of Eastern and

Western style are fused. For example, many female figurines display an Egyptian wig and face, but have round curls in the Greek fashion on their forehead.

Many female figurines can be easily identified in their original Greek guise as Aphrodite, Artemis or Athena, but it is beyond doubt that in Palestinian sanctuaries they all represented Astarte, the local female consort of the god Baal.

The pagan religions of Palestine, both in the older Canaanite period and in the later first millennium B.C., were undoubtedly complex. For the earlier period this complexity is clear from the 14th-century B.C. literature found on cuneiform tablets at Ugarit. For the later periods our sources are sparse. We do, however, know the names of the chief gods of the various peoples inhabiting the country, such as Qos, the chief god of Edom; Chemosh, the chief god of Moab; Milkom, the chief god of Ammon; and Baal, the chief god of Phoenicia. Each of these gods had a consort, but in no case do we know the entire pantheon.

Overall, the archaeological finds reflect three major types of figurines that appear simultaneously in all assemblages, just as we have seen at Dor: an adult male, represented as a king sitting on a throne or standing, or as a warrior on a horse; a fertility goddess holding her breasts or a child and sometimes pregnant; and young boys.

This is consistent with Sabatino Moscati's observation that the Phoenician cult was composed of "a triad of deities":

"a protective god of the city; a goddess, often his wife or companion who symbolizes the fertile earth; and a young god somehow connected with the goddess (usually her son) whose resurrection expresses the annual cycle of vegetation. Within these limits, the names and functions of the gods vary, and the fluidity of this pantheon, where the common name often prevails over the proper name, and the function over the personality, is characteristic. Another characteristic of the Phoenician triad is its flexibility from town to town."*

Thus, Baal had many local names. Some were connected with sacred mountains such as Baal Saphon (and perhaps Baal Carmel); others were connected with geographic regions as in Baal Lebanon; but mainly they were connected with different cities where Baal had different names, such as Baal Ashmun in Sidon, Melqart in Tyre, Baal Gebal in Byblos and Baal Haman in Carthage.

The same is true of goddesses. Astarte (Ashtoret)

*The World of the Phoenicians (London Weidenfeld & Nicolson, 1973), p. 62.

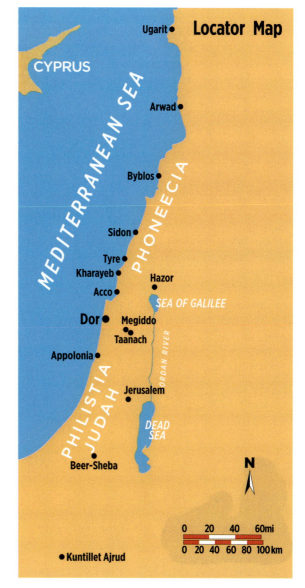

underwent similar changes from town to town: In Byblos she was called Baalat Gebal and was depicted as the Egyptian goddess Isis; in Carthage she was known as Tanit Pane Baal; and in Sarepta she was called Tanit-Ashtoret.

Occasionally, a find will point to a particular cult practice. For example, from Greek sources we know that the Phoenician cult practiced sacred prostitution. In the first Dor *favissa*, we found an almost intact figurine of a naked woman with swollen belly and drooping breasts, seated with legs apart and smiling. This figurine is unique in Palestine, although two similar, but not identical, figurines have been found in Kharayeb, farther north on the Phoenician coast (see photos, p. 401). In the Kharayeb examples, the woman sits with her legs apart, one hand on her knee and the other pointing to her genitals.

What we have been describing might be called the official cult, associated with sanctuaries where priests doubtless officiated. But side by side with this official cult was a popular religion or "popular cult" that served the people's daily need to ward off evil spirits and misfortune. The scholarly term for this is "apotropaic religion," from a Greek word meaning "to avert evil." Archaeological remains from this popular religion include such items as demonic figurines and masks, as well as associated jars and beads.

In the period of the *favissae* at Dor, the principal divinity who was invoked to ward off evil was an Egyptian god named Bes (see photo, p. 398). Bes had become a member of the Canaanite-Phoenician folklore much earlier, and now assumed the principal burden of protecting the ordinary person. Bes is a small grotesque god, always depicted naked, often with prominent genitals, arms akimbo, and with a peculiar feathered headdress. He must have already played an important role in the ninth century, as we know from his appearance on a painted vessel at Kuntillet Ajrud, an Israelite-Phoenician desert sanctuary in Sinai. Later, during the period of the Dor *favissae*, he is found almost everywhere—as clay figurines, on vases, on pendants and on stamp seals.

At Tel Dor and at nearby Tel Mevorakh, which I excavated several years ago,* we found Bes in a variety of guises—on vases, as clay figurines, as faience figurines, engraved on a particularly beautiful pendant and at the center of a complete faience necklace (the only one of its kind ever discovered in Israel). At the end of the Persian period (fourth century B.C.) and the beginning of the Hellenistic period (third century B.C.), Bes was gradually replaced by demonic representations of Greek satyrs.

A popular emblem to ward off evil spirits was the "eye of Horus," another Egyptian import into Palestine. Three pairs of Horus eyes were found on the Tel Dor necklace mentioned above, which includes the figure of Bes as its centerpiece.

Another class of apotropaic artifacts consists of clay masks, although only a fragment of one of these was found at Dor. These masks, like Bes and the eye of Horus, have a long history in Palestine, going back all the way to the Late Bronze Age (15th–13th centuries B.C.). But there is no doubt that they flourished especially in the Persian period. These masks depict both male and female apotropaic divinities, the majority with grotesque faces undoubtedly intended to frighten away evil spirits.

In the center of the forehead of some of these

*See Ephraim Stern, "Excavations at Tel Mevorakh Are Prelude to Tel Dor Dig," BAR, May/June 1979.

GLOSSARY

Achaemenid (uh-KEE-meh-nid): the dynasty of kings that ruled Persia from about 550 to 331 B.C.

favissa (FAH-viss-uh): similar to a *geniza* (see below), this is a special pit in which discarded votive figurines were deliberately buried, probably in a religious ceremony.

geniza: a storage room for worn, discarded religious books and artifacts. It is forbidden to destroy these objects or to throw them away, because they may contain the name of God.

tefillin (tih-fee-LEEN [Heb.]; tih-FILL-en [common Yiddish pronunciation]): small boxes containing scripts from the Jewish law, which observant Jews wear on the forehead and arm during recitation of certain prayers.

masks is an emblem, or totem, that varies from one to the other. Many years ago, I discussed these totems with the late Professor Yigael Yadin, who, in his brilliant, imaginative and intuitive way, immediately suggested a relationship between the totems on the foreheads of these pagan masks and the Biblical injunction to place the words of God's law as a frontlet between your eyes (Exodus 13:11–16; Deuteronomy 6:4–9, 11:13–21). Observant Jews to this day wear a small box containing the words of the law on their forehead (as well as a similar box on their arm in obedience to another part of these Biblical passages) during their morning prayers. Yadin thought that perhaps these phylacteries (*tefillin* [tih-fee-LEEN] in Hebrew), as these small boxes of scripts are called, were originally intended as a symbolic gesture in opposition to the pagan cult of the time.

As I have already noted, beginning in the Persian period and to an increasing extent in the Hellenistic period, we see the absorption of Greek deities and ideas into Phoenician culture. In the Persian period, most of the cultic finds still reflect a local or Egyptian character; in the course of time, they tend to change to a Greek character. Bes is gradually replaced by satyrs; the Astarte mask takes on Greek features. But the Phoenicians absorbed the Greek features, rather than simply adopting the Greek character. Thus, a clay figurine with the features of Heracles, Zeus or Aphrodite may be a local god—Baal Melqart or Ashmun or Astarte—with a Greek name. In the words of my teacher, the late Professor Michael Avi-Yonah, "Usually the eastern god retained his identity and only borrowed the shape of the Greek."

Now let us place these cultic artifacts in a larger

SACRED PROSTITUTION, a cultic practice intended to insure the continuing fertility of nature, is reflected in these figurines from Tel Dor (left) and Kharayeb (right), on the Phoenician coast 40 miles north of Dor. The unique figurine from Dor shows a smiling woman seated with spread legs. In the similar, but even more explicit, Kharayeb figurine, the woman points to her genitals.

COURTESY EPHRAIM STERN

setting. I have already suggested that their origin goes back long before the post-Exilic period we have been describing. As I said, clay figurines have been found by the hundreds—even by the thousands—all over Palestine in earlier periods. At Iron Age sites (12th–6th centuries B.C.), and at Late Bronze Age sites (16th–13th centuries B.C.), as well as at those from still earlier periods—including sites in the heartland of ancient Israel: at Arad, Beer-Sheva, Lachish, Megiddo, Taanach, Hazor and Dan—figurines, mostly of clay, have been found. These sites have produced quantities of clay figurines from the Israelite and earlier Canaanite periods. Even in Jerusalem, at a site overlooking the Temple Mount, a hoard of clay figurines dating from the eighth to seventh centuries B.C. was found. Thus, the use of these pagan figurines by Israelites is attested both archaeologically and in the Bible. (See, for example, Isaiah 42:17, 44:9–17; Jeremiah 44:15–25; 2 Kings 17:15–17, 23:1–15.)

Especially revealing are the drawings and inscriptions found at ninth-century Kuntillet Ajrud.** I have already mentioned the drawing of Bes on a vase from Kuntillet Ajrud. This same vessel invokes the name of the Israelite God Yahweh. Many other artifacts at Kuntillet Ajrud incorporate pagan elements into the Hebrew cult.

In time the Assyrians destroyed the northern kingdom of Israel (in 721 B.C.). Then the Babylonians conquered the southern kingdom of

Judah and destroyed Jerusalem (in 586 B.C.). Thus began the Babylonian Exile. Fifty years later, the Persians ruled the eastern world and permitted the Jews to return to their homeland. It is this period on which we have concentrated in this article.

In the Persian period (the post-Exilic period), we find a very strange phenomenon: In the areas of the country occupied by Jews, *not a single cultic figurine* has been found! This is despite the many excavations, as well as surveys, that have been conducted in Judea and, to a somewhat lesser extent, in Samaria.

This sharply contrasts with earlier periods, when it is impossible to distinguish between Israelite areas and pagan areas on the basis of the presence or absence of cultic figurines. In earlier periods we also find sanctuaries and altars in Israelite areas, despite the famous religious reforms of King Hezekiah (727–698 B.C.; see 2 Kings 18:3–6), and then by King Josiah (639–609 B.C.; see 2 Kings 23:1–15), both of whom attempted—apparently unsuccessfully—to centralize Israelite worship in Jerusalem and to ban outlying cult places. Archaeologists have failed, however, to locate either sanctuaries† or cultic figurines in areas occupied by the returning exiles.

In areas outside the region settled by the returning exiles, we continue to find a great number of assemblages of cultic figurines—in Idumea, Philistia, Phoenicia (as we have seen in this article)

** See Ze'ev Meshel, "Did Yahweh Have a Consort?" BAR, March/April 1979; André Lemaire, "Who or What Was Yahweh's Asherah?" BAR, November/December 1984.

†The Samaritan temple at Gerizim was, of course, a schismatic exception. The Samaritans were expelled from the Jerusalem Temple in the fourth century B.C. They then built their own temple on the top of Mount Gerizim. The Samaritan settlement at this site is now being excavated by I. Magen. The residential quarter is very well preserved, but not the temple itself.

and Galilee—that is, in those parts of the country still dominated by pagans. In these regions dozens of *favissae* full of clay figurines and stone statuettes have been found, most of them along the Mediterranean coast. One of the largest assemblages comes from Dor.

How can we explain the complete absence of sanctuaries (except, of course, for the Jerusalem Temple) and, even more significantly, the complete absence of these common cultic figurines in areas of Jewish settlement in the post-Exilic period? Apparently, pagan cults ceased to exist among the Judeans, who purified their worship.

This situation may also help us point to the origins of the synagogue, although we have no archaeological evidence from such an early period. (The earliest synagogue structures—at Masada, Herodium and Gamla*—date from about the turn of the era. The famous Theodotus inscription comes from a Jerusalem synagogue in the first century B.C., but it mentions that Theodotus is a grandson of an *archisynagogus*, so there must have been a synagogue in Jerusalem in the late second or early first century B.C.;** this is our earliest archaeological evidence for the existence of a synagogue.) In the post-Exilic period, the small, pagan cult sanctuaries, which produced figurines like those we have been looking at, were no longer available in areas settled by Jews. It seems logical to conclude that they were replaced by small, public prayer centers—that is, synagogues. It seems that this development occurred among the Babylonian exiles and was transferred to the land of Israel by the returning exiles. (In Egypt, the situation was different. We know from the Bible that there was an Egyptian diaspora even before the Babylonian destruction of 586 B.C. In Egypt, unlike Babylonia, the Jews continued their pagan customs, and, as we know from papyri found on the island of Elephantine

*See "Gamla: The Masada of the North," BAR, January/February 1979.

**See Hershel Shanks, *Judaism in Stone: The Archaeology of Ancient Synagogues* (Washington: Biblical Archaeology Society; New York: Harper & Row, 1979), pp. 17–20.

in the Nile, they even built their own temple and adopted Egyptian and Canaanite pagan names.)

One concluding observation: Now that we have established the fact that the Jewish exiles who returned from Babylon to the land of their ancestors no longer tolerated cultic figurines, we can use this principle to distinguish between pagan and Jewish settlements. Take, for example, the city of Lachish in the Persian period, where many such figurines have been uncovered.

In "Restoring the Great Gate at Lachish," (BAR, March/April 1988), David Ussishkin claims that Persian-period Lachish (sixth–fourth centuries B.C.), "represents the work of the returning Babylonian exiles who now governed the Persian province of Judea (Yehud)." In the same issue, Itzhaq Beit-Arieh urges that Lachish was an Edomite city in this period ("New Light on the Edomites," see p. 204 in this book).

In my opinion the latter view is correct. In the case of Lachish, we have not only the presence of many cult figurines, but also the fact that until now not a single "Yehud" stamp impression has been found at Lachish even after many years of excavations. ("Yehud" was the name of Judea in the Persian period, and stamp impressions with this designation are commonly found at Judean sites of the period.)

The study of ancient cult figurines is a fascinating one. I hope I have shown how much can be learned from such a study. ▣

This article elicited numerous letters from our readers, which were published in the Queries and Comments sections of the November/December 1989 and January/February 1990 issues of BAR.

Related Reading

André Lemaire, *The Birth of Monotheism* (Washington, DC: Biblical Archaeology Society, 2007).

Hershel Shanks, "The Persisting Uncertainties of Kuntillet 'Ajrud," BAR, November/December 2012 (see p. 364 of this book).

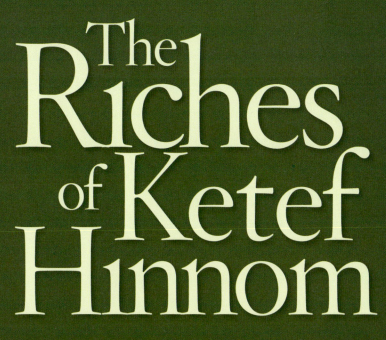

The Riches of Ketef Hinnom

Jerusalem Tomb Yields Biblical Text Four Centuries Older than Dead Sea Scrolls

GABRIEL BARKAY

I'VE LIVED IN JERUSALEM FOR MORE THAN 59 years. I sometimes feel I can put myself in the shoes (or minds) of ancient Jerusalemites. I think I can tell better than most where these ancient Jerusalemites would have located different facilities.

I came to Ketef Hinnom in the early 1970s looking for evidence of these ancients, such as quarries, farms, orchards, military encampments, burials, roads, forts—even cultic activity that took place outside the city.

Ketef Hinnom is located just opposite the Old City—to the southwest, across the Hinnom Valley from Mt. Zion. When I began collecting surface potsherds and looking for terrain features, I found evidence of human activity over thousands of years. In each period, the inhabitants had cleared away the remains and looted the treasures of their predecessors.

In 1975, we began a relatively small excavation that

Author's Note: This story is dedicated to the blessed memory of Alexander Singer (1962–1987), who participated in the first excavation season at Ketef Hinnom. An officer in the Israel Defense Forces, Alex was killed by terrorists from Lebanon in 1987 on his 25th birthday while going to the aid of his commander. He was the son of BAR contributing editor Suzanne Singer and her husband, Max.

PRECEDING PAGES: DIG VOLUNTEERS lie in an Iron Age tomb. Although they may sometimes have felt as if they were being worked to death, these volunteers revealed one of the most remarkable and long-lived tomb complexes ever discovered in the Holy City. Originally hewn from bedrock in the seventh century B.C.E., the Ketef Hinnom caves remained in use for nearly 2,500 years, serving a variety of functions and peoples, from Roman legionaries to the Ottoman-Turkish army. In this special report, Jerusalem archaeologist Gabriel Barkay, who directed the excavations between 1975 and 1996, takes BAR readers on a guided tour of the caves and the diverse array of artifacts found inside, including the oldest Biblical text ever discovered.

turned out to be extraordinary both in the quantity and the richness of the finds: an ancient church, cremation burials of the Tenth Roman Legion, burial caves from the time of the Judahite monarchy, jewelry, weapons and—the *pièces de résistance*—two inscribed silver amulets that contain the earliest texts ever discovered from the Hebrew Bible.

Ketef Hinnom ("the Shoulder of Hinnom")[1] is an elevated hill adjacent to St. Andrew's Scottish Church and Hospice, which was built in 1927 on a hill dominating a spectacular view of the Old City walls and Mt. Zion; it is now outside the walls but was once part of the Upper City of ancient Jerusalem. Beyond it to the east lie Silwan village, the Mount of Olives and the Judean wilderness. The hill rises more than 250 feet above the Hinnom Valley. To the north of the hill lies the 150-year-old Montefiore windmill that served the first modern settlers outside the Old City walls, and beyond that, the historic King David Hotel.

Ketef Hinnom also sits on the border between the Biblical tribal allotments of Judah and Benjamin: "Then the boundary goes up by the Valley of the son of Hinnom at the southern slope of the Jebusites—that is, Jerusalem" (Joshua 15:8). Ketef Hinnom is thus located on the road connecting David's birthplace, Bethlehem, with his capital, Jerusalem.

During the Second Temple period, the Roman general Pompey most probably built his camp in this area, opposite the city, when he attacked Jerusalem in 63 B.C.E. Later, in 70 C.E. during the First Jewish Revolt against Rome, the Roman army built a section of its siege wall here.[2]

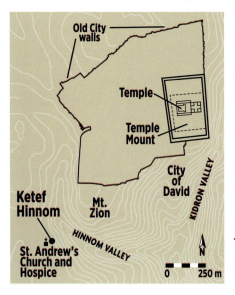

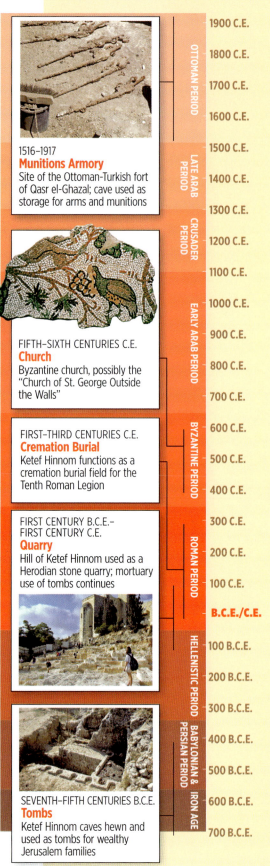

Digging Back Through Time

1516–1917
Munitions Armory
Site of the Ottoman-Turkish fort of Qasr el-Ghazal; cave used as storage for arms and munitions

FIFTH–SIXTH CENTURIES C.E.
Church
Byzantine church, possibly the "Church of St. George Outside the Walls"

FIRST–THIRD CENTURIES C.E.
Cremation Burial
Ketef Hinnom functions as a cremation burial field for the Tenth Roman Legion

FIRST CENTURY B.C.E.–FIRST CENTURY C.E.
Quarry
Hill of Ketef Hinnom used as a Herodian stone quarry; mortuary use of tombs continues

SEVENTH–FIFTH CENTURIES B.C.E.
Tombs
Ketef Hinnom caves hewn and used as tombs for wealthy Jerusalem families

1900 C.E.
1800 C.E.
1700 C.E.
1600 C.E.
1500 C.E.
1400 C.E.
1300 C.E.
1200 C.E.
1100 C.E.
1000 C.E.
900 C.E.
800 C.E.
700 C.E.
600 C.E.
500 C.E.
400 C.E.
300 C.E.
200 C.E.
100 C.E.
B.C.E./C.E.
100 B.C.E.
200 B.C.E.
300 B.C.E.
400 B.C.E.
500 B.C.E.
600 B.C.E.
700 B.C.E.

OTTOMAN PERIOD
LATE ARAB PERIOD
CRUSADER PERIOD
EARLY ARAB PERIOD
BYZANTINE PERIOD
ROMAN PERIOD
HELLENISTIC PERIOD
BABYLONIAN & PERSIAN PERIOD
IRON AGE

We excavated at the site intermittently between 1975 and 1996, for a total of seven seasons.[3]

Before the Scottish church was built in 1927, the slopes of Ketef Hinnom were covered with olive and mulberry trees. An 1852 map drawn by the Dutch geographer C.W.M. Van de Velde shows a fortified watchtower called Qasr el-Ghazal ("Fort of the Gazelle") at Ketef Hinnom.[4] Qasr el-Ghazal was probably built early in the Turkish-Ottoman period (1516–1917) and guarded the southern approach to Jerusalem.

Also from the Turkish-Ottoman period, we uncovered clay smoking pipes, coins and a Greek medallion depicting Jesus being baptized by John the Baptist.

One of the burial caves we discovered (Cave 20), originally hewn in the seventh century B.C.E., was reused by the Turkish army more than 2,500 years later (at the end of the 19th century) as an arms and ammunition depot, probably for troops stationed in the nearby fort of Qasr el-Ghazal. An explosion destroyed the roof of the burial cave. Under the collapse, we found not only coins that helped us date the explosion, but also the remains of dozens of rifles, including an American double-barreled Winchester. Along with the firearms, we uncovered fragments of porcelain coffee cups, smoking pipes, military insignia and buttons, decorative livery beads and a European pen with a gold nib.

On the northern part of the hill we excavated a previously unknown large basilical church from the Byzantine period (fifth–sixth centuries C.E.). The church had, in effect, been turned into a stone quarry during the Turkish-Ottoman period, when its handsome ashlars (rectangular stones) were reused for other purposes, probably the building of the nearby Qasr el-Ghazal.

Despite the removal of so many of its stones, we were nevertheless able to determine the plan of the church. Parts of the walls and the apse of the central nave and even the stylobates that supported two rows of pillars survived the Turkish-Ottoman quarrying. We also discovered a large stone threshold from the church, a vaulted chamber that had served as a crypt, and pieces of the mosaic floor that had decorated the church. One particularly beautiful mosaic fragment depicts a partridge pecking at a bunch of grapes, surrounded by vine tendrils and vine leaves. The hindquarters of a ram can also be glimpsed. Also of special interest were dozens of marble stone tiles in different colors cut in various shapes and sizes: rectangles, triangles, circles, squares, floral designs and even tooth shapes. These pieces once formed part of luxurious decorated floors adorned with

RØHR PRODUCTIONS LTD.

PERCHED ATOP THE "SHOULDER OF HINNOM," St. Andrew's Scottish Church and Hospice (popularly known as "The Scottie" to its guests) overlooks sweeping vistas of the Hinnom Valley and the walls of the Old City. Throughout history, the hill's commanding views over both Jerusalem and its southern approaches gave the site unusual strategic importance. The hilltop was occupied and reoccupied by successive generations of Jerusalemites from the Iron Age to the Ottoman period. Gabriel Barkay's excavations can be seen along a narrow limestone outcropping adjacent to the modern church (seen in the shade diagonally across the center of the photo).

B. FRENKEL/COURTESY OF GABRIEL BARKAY

PROTECTING JERUSALEM. During the Ottoman period (1516–1917), Ketef Hinnom was the site of a fortified watchtower known as Qasr el-Ghazal ("Fort of the Gazelle") that guarded the southern approach to the Holy City. Soldiers stationed at the fort used the hill's ancient burial caves as storage areas for arms and munitions. In one of the caves, excavators found these Turkish rifles from the end of the 19th century. Other finds included military insignia and buttons, porcelain coffee cups and smoking pipes.

This was apparently one of a series of churches along the pilgrims' road between Jerusalem and Bethlehem. Additional churches have been found along this road at Abu-Tor, just south of Ketef Hinnom, at Ramat Raḥel, and more recently the Kathisma church was discovered a little farther south, where Mary is said to have sat and rested on her way to Bethlehem.*[6]

While digging under the remains of the church, we discovered several concentrations of burnt soil and ash that appeared in the balks (sides) of the excavated squares. Later, we found some complete and intact ceramic cooking pots that had been put into the ground in an upright position, as though on purpose. These pots contained crushed and burnt bones and ash, as well as some small iron nails. This was no doubt a cemetery of cremation tombs. The concentrations of ash and burnt soil probably mark the place where the bodies were cremated. The cooking pots, typical of the Late Roman period, served as urns for the remains of the dead. Similar evidence for cremation has been found near Damascus Gate and along the northern wall of the Old City, as well as in Binyanei Ha'ūma, west of Jerusalem, and at Ramat Raḥel to the south of the city. At all these sites we have evidence for the presence of soldiers from the Tenth Roman Legion, mainly roof tiles stamped with that legion's name. No other group in the history of ancient Jerusalem is known to have practiced cremation. The Tenth Roman Legion was stationed in Jerusalem from the destruction of the Second Temple in 70 C.E. until the reign of Emperor Diocletian in the late third century. This was confirmed by a clay roof tile stamped with the letters "LXF," an abbreviation of *Legio X [Decima] Fretensis*, the official name of the Tenth Legion. The tile appears to date from the third century C.E.[7]

At a level below the cremation burials, we found a group of graves dating to the end of the Second Temple period (ending in 70 C.E.). They consisted of cists dug into the ground that were surrounded or lined with stones and covered by rough stone

inlaid designs, a flooring technique called *opus sectile*. Colored glass tesserae, many of which were gilt, represented the remains of vibrant mosaics that had once decorated the walls of the church. And below the church's narthex, the plastered walls of three graves were painted with depictions of metal crosses inlaid with colored, semiprecious stones.

East of the church we unearthed a group of structures that were apparently auxiliary buildings of the church complex. These included a large round silo. The small finds included molded oil lamps typical of the period, some decorated with crosses and one with a cruciform handle. We also found a fragment of a clay stamp that had been used to stamp impressions on loaves of Eucharistic bread.

Can we identify this Byzantine church? I believe we can. I think it is the church known as "The Church of St. George Outside the Walls" and in other sources as "St. George Outside the Tower of David." In literary accounts of the Persian (Sassanian) invasion of Christian Jerusalem in 614 C.E., this church is mentioned: Christian clergy were massacred there.[5]

*Hershel Shanks, "Where Mary Rested—Rediscovering the Kathisma," BAR, November/December 2006.

slabs. Several of the graves contained no skeletal remains, however, perhaps indicating that these had been Jewish burials from which the families of the deceased had later collected the bones and placed them in ossuaries (bone boxes), as was the custom at the time. The ossuaries would have then been placed in a family tomb. Coins from the first century confirm the date of these burials.

In two of the burial caves from the First Temple period (Caves 34 and 51) we found an abundance of Second Temple period finds—mostly made of silver and beads of different materials and colors but also a blue glass seal bearing a stylized animal design. We also found a cooking pot with a small hole perforating its side. Such perforated pots were also found in excavations next to the Temple Mount and in the Jewish Quarter of the Old City and elsewhere in Jerusalem.[8] It has been suggested that these pots were used by Temple priests for ritual purposes; the holes were intended to prevent the vessels from being used again.

One of our rock-cut burial caves originally hewn at the end of the First Temple period (Cave 34) evidenced continuous use through the Persian, Hellenistic and Roman periods. The later users of the cave simply buried their dead on top of the earlier remains. The Late Roman period (132–324 C.E.) was represented in this cave by pottery, coins and jewelry, including two golden earrings, one of which was inlaid with semiprecious stones. Next to one of the skulls, a coin dating to the reign of Emperor Maximus (286–310 C.E.) was found. This is most probably an example of the Roman custom of placing a coin in the mouth of the deceased in order to pay the fare to Charon for the ferry ride across the River Styx into the netherworld.

In the northern and eastern areas of Ketef Hinnom, we excavated parts of a large quarry from the Second Temple period. Further large areas of this quarry were excavated more recently by the Israel Antiquities Authority prior to the construction of the Menachem Begin Heritage Center built on the site in 2004.[9] Potsherds in the quarry

bed, which in some cases were found more than 13 feet below the surface, dated the quarry to the Herodian dynasty (first century B.C.E. and first century C.E.). The large ashlar blocks that were quarried here left their marks in the quarry bed: clear channels where the sides of the blocks had been carved and separated from the bedrock. We also found two iron axes used for cutting stone and a large iron wedge-shaped tool weighing about 25 pounds. Once the chiseling had separated the stone on all adjacent sides from its surrounding bedrock, workmen inserted such wedges to break the stone free from beneath.

The most prominent archaeological feature on Ketef Hinnom is the remains of seven rock-cut burial caves of the late First Temple period (seventh century B.C.E.). All of these caves were damaged in varying degrees by later quarrying. The ceilings and façades were no doubt quarried away for the construction of the Byzantine church. Other parts of the caves were probably destroyed when a Turkish-Ottoman road was constructed on the terrace situated above the burial caves. Although most of the ceilings have been destroyed, the remaining fragments are sufficient to reconstruct the height of the chambers, about 7 feet.

All the caves follow well-known patterns of rock-cut burial caves from late Iron Age Judah and Jerusalem that served several generations of wealthy families.** A step leads down from a small courtyard into a central passage of a square burial chamber. Most of these burial chambers are fairly small and square (about 10 feet by 10 feet), although two of the caves (Caves 20 and 24) are somewhat larger and have several burial chambers connected to the

**Gabriel Barkay and Amos Kloner, "Jerusalem Tombs from the Days of the First Temple," BAR, March/April 1986.

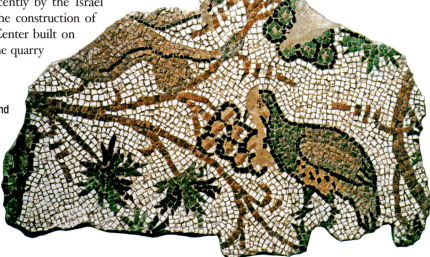

A GLIMPSE OF FORMER GLORY. This colorful mosaic fragment depicting a partridge, grape vine tendrils and the hind quarters of a ram was found amid the scattered ruins of a Byzantine church (fifth–sixth centuries C.E.) just north of the Ketef Hinnom caves. Although later quarrying disturbed much of the building's foundations, excavators were nonetheless able to identify the basilical plan of a traditional Byzantine church.

main hall. Around three sides of the burial chambers are rock-cut burial benches.

On the burial benches in two of the chambers of Cave 24 (Chambers 13 and 25) are slightly raised stone burial pillows with a scooped-out area for the neck and head, thus forming an elegant head rest for the deceased. One of the burial benches (in Chamber 13) could accommodate four bodies side by side as indicated by four headrests, two at each end. A burial bench with headrests from Chamber 25 was wide enough for six bodies. Although more than 80 carved headrests have been discovered in burial caves from First Temple Jerusalem, only Ketef Hinnom has burial benches with multiple headrests.

In five of the seven burial caves, a repository for the bones of the deceased was carved out beneath the burial bench. Perhaps a year after the initial burial, the bones of the deceased were placed in the repository to make room for the next generation of the family. Along with the bones, whatever burial gifts had been laid on the bench with the deceased were also placed in the repository.

The repositories are of different shapes: sometimes a small round space, sometimes oval, sometimes square, and in one case L-shaped. In several of the caves, a

A HERODIAN STONE QUARRY lies just down the hill from the Iron Age tombs. Well-dressed ashlar blocks were cut from the limestone bedrock using iron axes and heavy iron wedges, some of which were recovered in the excavation.

small step was hewn into the rock to allow for easier access to the repository.

The burial caves are badly damaged, but a fragment of an elegant cornice survived near the ceiling of one of the caves (Cave 20). Such cornices are known from other Jerusalem cave-tombs and were likely intended to imitate architectural elements of houses from the time.[10]

Although the burial caves had been destroyed and looted in ancient times, we did find some funerary offerings that were overlooked by the looters. For example, in Cave 34 we found a blue and yellow glass pendant that appears to show the distorted face of an oddly featured man.

Then in Chamber 25 of Cave 24, we found what can only be described as an archaeologist's dream—an untouched repository with all of its original contents intact! Interestingly enough, the hitherto-unopened repository was under the burial bench with six headrests mentioned earlier.

The repository remained undiscovered apparently because a rock layer had collapsed from the cave ceiling, thereby concealing its contents from looters. This is the only repository from First Temple period Jerusalem ever discovered with its contents intact.

The repository contained more than a thousand different artifacts. According to Professor Patricia Smith of the Hebrew University, who studied the repository's human remains, at least 95 individuals are represented.[11]

ZEV RADOVAN/WWW.BIBLELANDPICTURES.COM

PLAN OF BURIAL CAVE 24

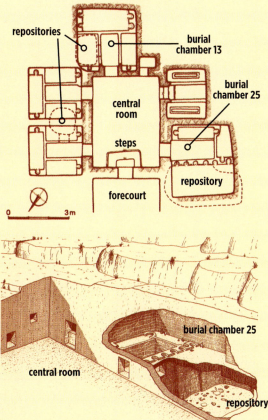

LEEN RITMEYER/COURTESY OF GABRIEL BARKAY

repositories

burial chamber 13

burial chamber 25

central room

steps

repository

forecourt

0   3m

RECONSTRUCTION BY LEEN RITMEYER

central room

burial chamber 25

repository

Anatomy of a Judahite Cemetery

The Ketef Hinnom excavation identified seven burial caves used during the late Iron Age and early Persian period (seventh–fifth centuries B.C.E.). Although the ceilings of the caves had collapsed from later quarrying and destruction, the remaining walls and features preserved the layout of an extensive necropolis that served the funerary needs of generations of ancient Jerusalem's wealthiest families.

The most elaborate of the burial caves was Cave 24, which consisted of five rock-hewn burial chambers located around a central room (see drawing at left). The tomb complex was entered from a forecourt through a small rectangular opening in the rock face, followed by steps that led down to the central room (the entrance to Cave 34 is shown at right). The walls of each adjoining chamber were lined with raised stone benches upon which the deceased were initially placed, along with burial gifts and offerings. The benches were sometimes outfitted with carved stone headrests, a common feature of Judahite tombs from this period. The headrests found in Chamber 25 of Cave 24, the largest of the cave's burial rooms, indicate that nine individuals could be interred in the room at any one time (see photo above and on p. 404).

When more space was needed for the next generation, the bones on the burial benches and the burial goods were transferred to repositories carved out beneath the benches (see reconstruction drawing of Chamber 25 and its repository at left).

FROM THE COURT OF ZEDEKIAH? The upper register of this seventh- or early-sixth-century B.C.E. seal is inscribed in ancient Hebrew script with the name "Palta" (in reverse; the drawing beneath it shows the correct orientation as it would appear on the seal impression). The lower register depicts the pointed fronds of a palm branch. Separating the two registers is a lotus bud design, a common decorative element on late Judahite seals. The name Palta is a short form of the name Pelatyahu, or Pelatiah in English. The latter appears in the Bible as the name of a high governmental official under King Zedekiah, the last king of Judah (Ezekiel 11:1,13).

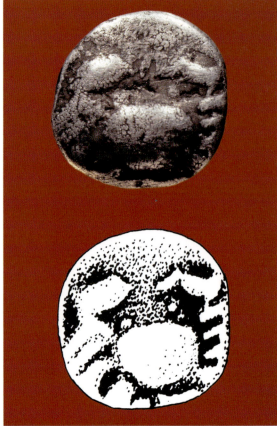

KOSHER CRAB. A faint and badly worn depiction of a crab decorates the obverse of this sixth-century B.C.E. silver coin, the earliest ever found in Israel. The coin was likely minted on the small Aegean island of Kos, where the crab served as a kind of local emblem. The coin's presence at Ketef Hinnom evidences commercial links between the Aegean and Judah in the sixth century B.C.E.

One of the more intriguing finds from the repository was a small brown limestone seal inscribed with the name "Palta" in ancient Hebrew script that dates to the seventh or early sixth century B.C.E. The name appears on the seal in mirror writing so that it would appear correctly when impressed into a lump of clay that sealed a document. Separating the seal into two fields is a lotus bud design, common in this period. The name appears in the upper field; a palm branch is depicted in the lower field.

The name is of more than passing interest. Like so many names of this kind, it is an abbreviation. The full name included a so-called theophoric element—the name of a deity. In this case the full Hebrew name would have been Pelatyah or Pelatyahu, the deity being Yahweh, the personal name of the Israelite God. Usually names on seals would include

the name of the father. That this seal does not may suggest it is a family name, perhaps the family that owned the burial cave. The prophet Ezekiel (Ezekiel 11:1,13) mentions a high governmental official (in the early sixth century B.C.E.) named Pelatiah son of Beniah (in English; Pelatyahu ben Benayahu in Hebrew). Is this his seal? Was he so well known that he didn't need the name of his father included on his seal? Or is this a family name? Or some other Palta? We are unlikely ever to know for sure.

Among the other finds in the repository were about 45 iron arrowheads and one bronze arrowhead. The bronze arrowhead is of the type known as Scytho-Iranian, used by the Babylonian army in 586 B.C.E. when the Babylonians attacked and conquered Jerusalem and destroyed the Temple that had stood on the Temple Mount for about 400 years since Solomon built it in the tenth century B.C.E. One cannot help wondering whether this bronze arrowhead killed a Judahite warrior who died defending the city.

Other metal objects in the repository included needles, cosmetic kohl sticks and bronze buttons, as well as a knife and an iron chisel. We also found a small alabaster cosmetic dish, four dome-shaped stone spindle whorls, as well as an array of bone and ivory inlays incised with concentric circles that probably once decorated wooden boxes.

An unusual find that at first puzzled us was a series of bone objects that looked like grooved cylinders with two holes drilled at each end. We finally figured out what they were: They were the bone handles from large bronze cooking pots and cauldrons. The bone handles allowed the metal vessels to be lifted when hot. The two holes were for rivets that attached the handles to the pots. Presumably the metal pots themselves were removed from the repository for remelting and so only the handles remained. This type of handle has not been found before in Israel, but a large group of them was found in excavations at the Temple of Hera on the island of Samos in the Aegean Sea. There the handles were found still attached with rivets to the bronze cauldrons.

Another interesting find from the repository was a small cream-colored glass *amphoriskos* (a small two-handled bottle) decorated with yellow and blue bands. The vessel was formed on a sand core and dates to the sixth–fifth centuries B.C.E. Glass vessels of this kind are quite rare in excavations in Israel. Glass-blowing was not invented until the first century B.C.E.

The large amount of pottery from the repository included more than 250 complete vessels. These consisted mainly of wine decanters, juglets, perfume bottles and oil lamps—no store jars or cooking pots. The pottery fell into two general assemblages—one from the late First Temple period (seventh–early sixth centuries B.C.E.) and the other from the Babylonian and early Persian periods (sixth–fifth centuries

COLLECTION OF THE ISRAEL ANTIQUITIES AUTHORITY/PHOTO © THE ISRAEL MUSEUM, JERUSALEM

CONTACT WITH THE BROADER MEDITERRANEAN world is evidenced by this delicately crafted glass vessel, or *amphoriskos*, from the sixth century B.C.E. The bottle (from Cave 34) was made by the core-formed technique, several centuries before the invention of glass-blowing. Core-formed vessels were crafted by dipping a "core" of sand and dung that had been modeled into the desired shape into a vat of molten glass. The intricate patterns of yellow and blue decoration were made from threads of heated glass that were applied while the basic vessel was still hot and molten. When the bottle had cooled, the sand core was removed, leaving a brilliant multicolored vessel.

B.C.E.)—in short, from both before and after the Babylonian conquest of Jerusalem in 586 B.C.E.

Some types persisted in both periods, whereas others are distinctive to one period or the other. Among the complete vessels is a group dating to the Babylonian period (586–538 B.C.E.). These include carrot-shaped bottles, oil lamps with flat bottoms, decanters with sack-shaped bodies and clay alabastra (pottery imitations of small alabaster perfume bottles) with two degenerated handles. Only a few of these vessels have previously been found in excavations in Judah. This is an important pottery assemblage because it shows that even after the Babylonian capture of Jerusalem, life in

GORDON FRANZ/COURTESY OF GABRIEL BARKAY

PIERCING DISCOVERY. Amid the scattered bones and artifacts in an undisturbed tomb repository, excavators discovered scores of iron arrowheads used by the Judahites and one bronze Scytho-Iranian arrowhead of the type that was used by Babylonian soldiers during the siege of Jerusalem in 586 B.C.E. The pointed tips from several of the iron arrowheads were found bent or broken, indicating they had actually been used in battle.

the city continued. Some of the Jerusalemites who remained during the Babylonian Exile were quite wealthy, despite the notice in Jeremiah 39:10 that only the "vinedressers and plowmen" remained in the land. This group of wealthy families continued to live—and bury their dead—in Jerusalem during the Babylonian and Persian periods.

I have not yet mentioned the jewelry found in the undisturbed repository. That deserves special notice. The treasure trove of jewelry from this repository is unequalled in Jerusalem excavations. It gives us our first glimpse of the jewelry worn by women (and perhaps also by men) in Jerusalem at the end

of the First Temple period. The repository yielded more than a hundred silver items and six gold items, including simple crescent-shaped earrings, 15 silver earrings, four silver finger rings, about 50 silver beads, a silver pendant and a scarab mounted in silver. The most common decoration on the earrings was a granulation technique, that is, the attachment of tiny silver balls to the body of the earrings. A large number of beads were made of semiprecious stones—agate, carnelian and rock-crystal—as well as more common materials like glass, faience and shell. Another especially fine piece is a silver signet ring bearing the figure of a galloping griffin with a feline

Jerusalem's Jewels

The Ketef Hinnom excavations revealed one of the largest collections of ancient jewelry ever found in Jerusalem. Countless pieces of gold, silver and precious stones worn by Jerusalem's wealthier residents from the Iron Age to the Roman period were recovered, including a remarkably well preserved pair of gold earrings in the shape of stylized animal heads from the Persian period (right) and an ornate gold earring inlaid with carnelian beads from the Roman era (at top, far left).

In the Chamber 25 repository, more than a hundred silver and gold objects were also found, as well as myriad beads of agate, carnelian, glass and faience (left). Many of the earrings are decorated with intricate patterns of applied silver granulation, a decorative technique also known from Phoenician and Etruscan jewelry. The beads would have been strung together as colorful necklaces (right) that were then placed around the neck of the deceased. Other deposits in the repository were silver rings, pendants and a signet ring engraved with the figure of a galloping griffin (at bottom, far left).

The Ketef Hinnom collection speaks to the cosmopolitan character of Jerusalem society during the final years of the Judahite monarchy, as well as, surprisingly, the decades following the Babylonian destruction of the Temple in 586 B.C.E. Jerusalem's wealthy adorned themselves with the same fashions and jewels found in any ancient Near Eastern capital of the seventh and sixth centuries B.C.E. Perhaps it was precisely such splendid displays of wealth that provoked the ire of the prophet Isaiah, who admonished Jerusalem's wealthy:

"In that day the Lord will take away the finery of the anklets, the headbands and the crescents, the pendants, the bracelets and the scarves, the headdresses, the armlets and sashes, the perfume boxes and the amulets, the signet rings and nose rings" (Isaiah 3:18–21).

COLLECTION OF THE ISRAEL ANTIQUITIES AUTHORITY/PHOTO © THE ISRAEL MUSEUM, JERUSALEM

---

body, the head and wings of an eagle and a coiled tail.

The Bible describes, somewhat hyperbolically, the wealth of Jerusalem during the monarchy: "[Solomon] made silver in Jerusalem as common as stones" (1 Kings 10:27). On numerous occasions Jerusalem's treasures were pillaged by invaders (e.g., 1 Kings 14:26; 2 Kings 25:15). The ladies of Jerusalem are castigated because of their ostentatious jewelry and luxurious attire: "In that day the Lord will take away the finery of the anklets, the headbands, and the crescents, the pendants, the bracelets, and the scarves, the headdresses, the armlets and the sashes, the perfume boxes and the amulets, the signet rings

and the nose rings" (Isaiah 3:18–21). The jewelry from Ketef Hinnom gives a startling reality to these passages and indicates that this same situation prevailed even after the Babylonian invasion among those who remained in the city.

The stars of the repository, however, were two tiny silver amulets. When we found them, they were rolled up like small scrolls with a hole down the middle through which a necklace or string could be threaded.

I vividly remember when the first one was found in 1979, our second season at the site. Area supervisor Gordon Franz (of the Institute of Holy Land

Ketef Hinnom I	**Ketef Hinnom I**
יהו . . .	...]YHW ...
. . .	...
גד[ל שמר]	THE GREA[T GOD WHO KEEPS]
הברית ו	THE COVENANT AND
[ה]חסד לאהב	[G]RACIOUSNESS TOWARDS THOSE
ו] ושמרי [מצ] (י]ו שמרי [מצ :ALT)	WHO LOVE [HIM] AND
[ותו] . . .	THOSE WHO KEEP [HIS COMMANDMENTS ...
ת העלם .[.] (תה על נ.[.] :ALT)	THE ETERNAL? [...].
[ה]ברכה מכל [פ]	[THE?] BLESSING MORE THAN ANY
ח ומהרע	[SNA]RE AND MORE THAN EVIL.
כי בו גאל	FOR REDEMPTION IS IN HIM.
ה כי יהוה	FOR YHWH
[מ]שיבנו [ו]	IS OUR RESTORER [AND]
צור יבר	ROCK. MAY YHWH BLES[S]
ך יהוה ו	YOU AND
י[שמרך [י]	[MAY HE] KEEP YOU.
[א]ר יהוה	[MAY] YHWH MAKE
פנ[יו] . . .	[HIS FACE] SHINE ...

The Blessings of YHWH

NEAR THE BOTTOM of the Chamber 25 repository lay a tiny silver plaque that had been rolled up like a miniature scroll (shown actual size at right) and deposited in the tomb as an amulet for the deceased. A second amulet was found while sifting the repository debris. Once researchers had painstakingly unrolled the delicate sheets of silver foil, they found that each plaque was faintly inscribed with multiple lines of ancient Hebrew script characteristic of the late Iron Age. These photographs of the unrolled plaques, taken by the West Semitic Research Project in 1994, were produced with special fiber-optic lighting techniques and time-exposure methods. The innovative techniques allowed scholars to discern numerous characters in the faintly inscribed plaques that had been previously overlooked or misread under normal lighting.

When deciphered, the inscriptions revealed one of the earliest extrabiblical references to the Israelite God Yahweh and the oldest-known reference to a passage from the Bible: the priestly blessing in Numbers 6:24–26, which beseeches the Lord to bless the children of Israel. Excavator Gabriel Barkay believes the inscribed amulets were likely meant to protect the owner from evil.

Ketef Hinnom II	**Ketef Hinnom II**
ה/ו ברך ה	[FOR PN, (THE SON/DAUGHTER OF) XXXX]H/HU.
[א] ליהו[ה]	MAY H[E]
העזר ו	SH[E] BE BLESSED BY YHWH,
הגער ב	THE WARRIOR AND
[ר]ע יברך	THE REBUKER
יהוה י	OF [E]VIL: MAY YHWH BLESS YOU,
שמרך	KEEP YOU.
יאר יה	MAY YHWH MAKE
[ו]ה פניו	HIS FACE SHINE
[אל]יך וי	UPON YOU AND
שם לך ש	GRANT YOU P[EA]CE
[ל]ם	

Studies, now the Jerusalem University College) and excavator Judith Hadley (now of Villanova University) called me into the repository and pointed toward a purplish object that looked like a cigarette butt lying in the soil. The second amulet was found only during our sifting operation—when all the soil from the repository was sifted through a fine mesh screen.

We immediately suspected the two rolled-up objects contained writing, but to find out, and to learn what they said, we would need to unroll them—no easy task. Fortunately, expert conservationists Marina Rosovsky, Joseph (Dodo) Shenhav and David Bigelajzen of the Israel Museum developed a unique method to unroll the objects.[12] A special acrylic glue was applied to the rolls that allowed the silver sheet to be gradually separated from the rest of the roll as the adhesive dried. After the amulets were unrolled, they were then covered with polyester Mylar film and placed between two thin layers of glass for protection. Finally, we were able to see that the sheets did indeed contain writing.

Both plaques are very thin and made of almost pure silver (99 percent silver, 1 percent copper). Both are damaged, mainly on their outer edges; they are very corroded and cracked. The larger plaque (Ketef Hinnom I) has traces of 18 lines of writing (though there were probably 19 originally), each line containing from five to seven letters. The smaller plaque (Ketef Hinnom II) probably originally had 18 lines of writing, of which the main parts of 12 are preserved. The decipherment of the second plaque has proved more difficult than the first.

The larger plaque is 97 millimeters long and 27 millimeters wide (less than 4 in. long and 1 in. wide). The second one, found in the sifting, is even smaller. When I was first called to the museum to look at them unrolled, I could immediately see that they were densely covered with writing in ancient Hebrew script. The first word I saw was *YHWH*, the tetragrammaton, the four-letter name of the Hebrew God, usually written "Yahweh" in Latin letters.

The task of deciphering the text was long and laborious. The letters themselves are almost microscopic—between 1.7 and 5 millimeters. They can barely be seen; they were scratched very shallowly with a sharp instrument, recalling the description in Jeremiah 17:1 of the message that was inscribed "with an iron pen with a diamond point." The individual letter strokes are approximately the width of a hair. The plaques themselves are thin sheets of beaten silver reminiscent of "the beaten silver brought from Tarshish" cited by the prophet Jeremiah (Jeremiah 10:9). It was not until 1989 that I felt confident enough to publish the texts in Hebrew.[13] (An English version was published in 1992.[14]) With the passage of time, new methods of examining the inscriptions using fiber-optic light and computer imaging, as well as advanced photography methods, were developed. Using these new methods, a revised version of the texts was published jointly with Andrew G. Vaughn, Marilyn J. Lundberg and Bruce Zuckerman in 2004.[15]

The texts of the two inscriptions are printed in the box on p. 416. Each contains slight variations of parts of the three blessings that appear in the famous priestly blessing from Numbers 6:24–26:

The Lord bless you and keep you.
The Lord make his face to shine upon you,
    and be gracious to you.
The Lord lift up his countenance upon you,
    and give you peace.

These are the words with which observant Jews still bless their children before the Sabbath meal on Friday night and that are also used in prayers in synagogues.

In the first amulet from Ketef Hinnom we have traces of the first two blessings of this tripartite Biblical text:

May YHWH bles[s]
you and
[may he] keep you
[May] YHWH make
[his face] shine ...

In the smaller plaque are traces of an abridged version of all three blessings:

May YHWH bless you, keep you.
May YHWH make
his face shine
upon you and
grant you p[ea]ce.

In addition, the middle part of the first plaque contains a variation of Deuteronomy 7:9: "Know, therefore, that only the Lord your God is God, the steadfast God who keeps his covenant faithfully to the thousandth generation of those who love him and keep his commandments."

From the larger plaque, we read:

...]YHW...

the grea[t God who keeps]
the covenant and
[G]raciousness towards those who love [him]
    and (alternate: those who love [hi]m)
those who keep [his commandments ...]. the
    Eternal(?) [...].

The tiny rolled-up scrolls were no doubt intended to be worn as amulets to safeguard their owners.

The prophylactic nature of our two tiny scrolls to prevent sickness and disease is evident from the words "bless" and "keep." But the amulets were also regarded as having an apotropaic effect, as a protection against evil. This point is emphasized in the smaller amulet by a reference to Yahweh as the "rebuker of evil": "May he/she be blessed by YHWH, the warrior and the rebuker of Evil."

The amulets can be securely dated on a combination of three grounds. Paleographically they can be dated by the shape and form of the letters to the late seventh century B.C.E., before the Babylonian conquest. Stratigraphically the first amulet was found only about 7 centimeters (less than 3 in.) above the repository floor, which testifies to its relative antiquity within the repository assemblages, which rose to about 2 feet total. The second plaque was found in the innermost part of the repository, far from the entrance, among the earliest deposits. Finally, the date suggested paleographically corresponds to the chronological horizon of the late Iron Age pottery found in the repository. The silver plaques thus come from the late seventh century B.C.E., or the time of the prophet Jeremiah and King Josiah.

The implications of this dating are startling. First of all, it means that these texts on our silver plaques are the oldest composition of words similar to Biblical verses in existence. The earliest Biblical texts among the Dead Sea Scrolls date to about 250 B.C.E. at the earliest. That means that our texts are older than the next oldest Biblical texts by nearly 400 years.

Moreover, these inscriptions are the only texts of the First Temple period with clear similarities to Biblical verses.

This has important implications for the Biblical text. The Pentateuch, or Five Books of Moses, is usually divided by text-critical scholars into four source strands, labeled J (for Yahwist, or Jahwist in German), E (for Elohist), D (for Deuteronomist) and P (for the Priestly Code). The priestly blessing from Numbers, which is quoted in our silver plaques, is generally considered part of P, the Priestly Code. (So, too, the passage from Deuteronomy 7:9, which has echoes in the larger silver amulet.)

There is a major scholarly disagreement as to the date of the Priestly Code. Some scholars contend it predates the Babylonian conquest. Others say it is later. Our two texts seem to support those who contend that the Priestly Code was already in existence, at least in rudimentary form, in the First Temple period.

The priestly blessing seems to have been widely used during the First Temple period. Its influence can be traced both in the Bible itself (see Psalm 67:1, for example) and in early Hebrew epigraphy. In addition to our references, an inscription painted on a large pithos at Kuntillet 'Ajrud in the Sinai Peninsula contains the Hebrew words *YBRK wYŠMRK wYHY 'M 'DNY*, which can be translated as "[may God] bless you and keep you and be with my Lord." This, too, dates to the First Temple period.

The Ketef Hinnom excavations have made an enormous contribution, not only to our understanding of life in Jerusalem more than 2,500 years ago, but also to our understanding of the development of the text of the Hebrew Bible.

Today the seven burial caves of Ketef Hinnom lie hidden behind the Menachem Begin Heritage Center, unmarked, unguarded and unprotected. They deserve better.

All uncredited photos courtesy of the author.

[1] The name Ketef Hinnom, "the shoulder of Hinnom," was coined by the author based on the geographic descriptions of Joshua 15:8, 18:15.

[2] Both Pompey's earlier camp and the siege wall of Titus are mentioned by Josephus. See Josephus, *War* 5.12 (504–507).

[3] The excavations were directed by the author under the auspices of the Institute of Archaeology of Tel Aviv University and the Israel Exploration Society. The work was carried out with financial support from the Yad Hanadiv Foundation, the B'nai Brith Organization and several other institutions. The 1994 season was financed by a generous donation of the late Leon D. Weindling through the Jerusalem Foundation. The 1996 season was conducted as a salvage dig under the auspices of the British School of Archaeology in Jerusalem. Many volunteers and students, groups and individuals, from Israel and abroad participated in the excavation. Of special importance was the contribution of the students of the American Institute of Holy Land Studies in Jerusalem (now the Jerusalem University College) and groups organized by the Biblical Archaeology Society.

[4] C.W.M. Van de Velde, *Narrative of a Journey through Syria and Palestine in 1851* (London: Blackwood, 1854).

[5] This named church is the first on a list of 35 churches beginning in the western part of the city. Until our discovery of this hitherto unknown church at Ketef Hinnom, St. George's Church was thought to be located far west of the city. That identification should now be reconsidered since the site of Ketef Hinnom is a much more suitable location for this church. Moreover the name of St. George, to whom the church was dedicated, is mentioned in one of the Greek inscriptions of the Byzantine period incised on the façades of burial caves in the nearby Hinnom Valley. The Byzantine Period church we uncovered should therefore be identified with the "Church of St. George outside the walls" mentioned by Thomas ("the undertaker"), who described the city's building and victims following the Persian conquest of 614.

[6] Rina Avner, "The Kathisma Church," *New Encyclopedia of Archaeological Excavations in the Holy Land* 5 (2008), pp. 1831–1833.

[7] Dan Barag, "Brick Stamp-Impressions of the Legio X Fretensis," *Bonner Jahrbücher* 167 (1967), pp. 244–267.

[8] A. Grossberg, "Cooking Pots with Holes Found in Jerusalem and the Customs of Haverim and Amei ha-Aretz," in E. Baruch and A. Faust, eds., *New Studies on Jerusalem*, vol. 8 (2002), pp. 59–71 (Hebrew) (English summary on p. 11).

[9] Large parts of the Herodian period quarry were unearthed in the excavations directed by Y. Zelinger and Rina Avner on behalf of the Israel Antiquities Authority in 1999–2003, prior to the construction of the building of the Menachem Begin Heritage Center at Ketef Hinnom. A report of this excavation is forthcoming in

'Atiqot, the bulletin of the Israel Antiquities Authority.

[10] The angular cornice at the meeting point of the walls and the ceiling is mentioned by the name *tephahot* in 1 Kings 7:9. The term means "hand breadth," which is 1/7 of a cubit (7.5 cm)—the exact height of the cornices discovered in the burial caves. In Jerusalem, there are about 35 burial chambers from the Iron Age which have the cornice preserved.

[11] I would like to express my thanks to Professor Patricia Smith of the Hebrew University's Medical School for this information.

[12] Marina Rosovsky, David Bigelajzen and Dodo Shenhav, "Cleaning and Unrolling the Silver Plaques," *Tel Aviv* 19 (1992), pp. 192–194.

[13] Gabriel Barkay, "The Priestly Benediction on the Ketef Hinnom Plaques," *Cathedra* 52 (1989), pp. 37–76 (Hebrew).

[14] Gabriel Barkay, "The Priestly Benediction on Silver Plaques from Ketef Hinnom in Jerusalem," *Tel Aviv* 19 (1992), pp. 139–192.

[15] Gabriel Barkay, Andrew G. Vaughn, Marilyn J. Lundberg and Bruce Zuckerman, "The Amulets from Ketef Hinnom: A New Edition and Evaluation," *Bulletin of the American Schools of Oriental Research* 334 (2004), pp. 41–71. See also Gabriel Barkay, Marilyn J. Lundberg, Andrew G. Vaughn, Bruce Zuckerman and Kenneth Zuckerman, "The Challenges of Ketef Hinnom: Using Advanced Technologies to Reclaim the Earliest Biblical Texts and Their Context," *Near Eastern Archaeology* 66 (2003), pp. 162–171.

Related Reading

Hershel Shanks, First Person: "Ketef Hinnom," BAR, January/February 2011.

Esther Eshel and Armin Lange, "'The Lord Is One': How Its Meaning Changed," BAR, May/June 2013.

9

Jerusalem in Flames; and the Dead Sea Scrolls

The first century C.E. brought horrific destruction to Jerusalem and its Temple, but it also saw the safe-keeping of the Dead Sea Scrolls in the caves of Qumran, where the Jewish texts would remain for nearly two millennia. When these Biblical texts were discovered in the late 1940s and 1950s, they were immediately hailed as "the greatest manuscript discovery of modern times."

Nearly every issue of BAR has an article about Jerusalem or the Dead Sea Scrolls. They are our two most popular subjects. In this chapter they are brought together by the Roman conquest of Judea: the capital city that fell in a fiery destruction, and the manuscripts that were hidden away in desert caves at Qumran before the Romans attacked the site two years prior to sacking Jerusalem.

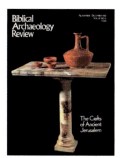

NOVEMBER/DECEMBER 1983
**Jerusalem in Flames—
The Burnt House
Captures a Moment
in Time**

The horrid reality of the Roman destruction of Jerusalem in 70 C.E. is portrayed nowhere more vividly than in the excavation photograph that opens Nahman Avigad's article. Avigad's excavation diary matches the emotion of the photograph. He was digging an area overlooking the Temple Mount, where once stood the Temple that the Roman legions destroyed when suddenly the past became real, as he observes in this chapter's first article.

Only adding to the immediacy of what the excavators were uncovering was a weight inscribed with the name "Bar Kathros"—perhaps the owner of the house—known from other sources as a family of high priests.

MARCH 1977
**The Dead Sea Scrolls
and the People Who
Wrote Them**

In an early BAR article, the second in this chapter, Frank Moore Cross, the towering Harvard epigrapher and Biblical scholar, provided an overview of the context of the scrolls. He also described the ruins of Qumran, the settlement adjacent to the caves where the scrolls were discovered. It was Qumran's residents who assembled the library we know as the Dead Sea Scrolls.

Much has happened since this article was published in 1977. The total number of scroll manuscripts now stands at close to 900. Controversies have been refined and developed, but this article remains relevant, incisive and, in its own special way, authoritative.

BAR has of course published much more about the scrolls, perhaps most notably of the struggle to free the scrolls from the small contingent of lagging scholars assigned to publish them.*

---

* A group of BAR articles was collected in a widely praised book published under the title *Understanding the Dead Sea Scrolls* (Random House, 1992). I also published an overview of the scrolls under the title *The Mystery and Meaning of the Dead Sea Scrolls* (Random House, 1998). The controversies involved in the struggle to release the scrolls are recounted in detail in my autobiography, *Freeing the Dead Sea Scrolls and Other Adventures of an Archaeology Outsider* (Continuum, 2010). See also my book titled *The Copper Scroll and the Search for the Temple Treasure* (Biblical Archaeology Society, 2007).

The Burnt House Captures a Moment in Time

NAHMAN AVIGAD

WE CAME UPON IT SUDDENLY, in the very first year of our excavations. At that time we had not yet excavated a single house that had witnessed the catastrophe of 70 A.D., when the Romans destroyed Jerusalem. We were still emotionally unprepared for the impressions and associations raised by the prospect before us. In subsequent years, after several other burnt houses had been discovered, our emotions became somewhat blunted to the sight of such stark violence. But not only was this Burnt House the first such discovery, its preservation of traces of destruction and fire and the quantity of objects found in it were never exceeded. In January 1970, after heaps of rubble and refuse had been cleared away, we removed a rather thick layer of fill and refuse containing nothing ancient. Then stone walls suddenly began sprouting out of the earth. We saw immediately that these were the walls of rooms. As a first step in stratigraphic excavation, we dug a trench the breadth of one of the rooms, in order to determine the sequence of the layers. At a depth of about a meter, we encountered a floor of beaten earth. Already, the sides of the trench were providing a clear and impressive cross section, which we were able to read like an open book.

The upper layer contained fallen building stones that had changed color as the result of a fire. The layer beneath was a mixture of earth, ashes, soot and charred wood; at the bottom of the cross section, overlying the floor, were pottery fragments and parts of scorched stone vessels. The plastered walls were also black with soot. The picture was clear to any trained eye. There was only one phase of occupation, and its composition was unambiguous: the building had been destroyed by fire, and the walls and ceiling had collapsed along with the burning beams, sealing over the various objects in the rooms.

When did this occur? The pottery indicated that it was sometime in the first century A.D.

Was the destruction of this building, so close to the Temple Mount, connected with the Roman destruction of Jerusalem in 70 A.D.? We seemed to have before us a unique picture of a house sacked by the Roman legions. The household effects were buried and left just as they had been, undisturbed by later activities.

In the excavation diary I wrote: "On the same day (13 January 1970) I was somewhat excited." But after the initial excitement came moments of doubt. My initial impression might merely have been wishful thinking, and the facts might not lend themselves to such far-reaching conclusions. My chief assistant at the time, Ami Mazar, was away, and Roni Reich, the area supervisor, was as carried away as I was. I therefore invited several of my fellow Jerusalem archaeologists to visit the site, each one separately, to see their reactions to the cross section. All of them arrived at the same conclusion as ours.

Systematic excavation of the entire area only served to increase our tension as well as our expectations. The salient question was whether the same phenomenon would be found in the other rooms as well. As we cleared each room, an identical picture emerged. First we would come across stone debris from the collapsed walls, which filled the rooms. The dressed blocks were of the soft, local *nari* limestone, which had been baked to various colors by the great heat of the fire. Some had become

CAUGHT IN THE FIRE when the Romans attacked, a young woman who was in the kitchen of the Burnt House sank to the floor and was reaching for a step near the doorway when she died. The fire had spread so fast, perhaps fed by oil used in this kitchen, that she could not escape and was buried by falling debris.

lime-white, while others were gray, red, and yellow, and mostly very crumbly. Among the debris filling the rooms were a mixture of ash and soot and large quantities of charred wood.

Soot reigned over all, clinging to everything. It covered the plastered walls. Even the faces of our workmen turned black. There was no doubt that the fire had rampaged here, apparently fed by some highly flammable material contained in the rooms. It may well have been some oil, which would account for the abundance of soot. The traces were so vivid that one could almost feel the heat and smell the fire.

When we reached the floor level, objects began appearing, scattered about or in heaps: pottery, stone vessels, broken glass, iron nails, and the like. The known types of pottery gave us a general dating in the first century A.D. for the destruction of the building. But the many coins strewn over the floor—partly from the Roman Procurators of Judea and mostly from the First Jewish Revolt against Rome—permitted a more precise dating. The coins of the revolt bear the legends "Year Two/The Freedom of Zion," "Year Three/The Freedom of Zion," and "Year Four/Of the Redemption of Zion." The latest, from the fourth year of the revolt, date to 69 A.D.

It was now quite clear that this building was burnt by the Romans in 70 A.D., during the destruction of Jerusalem. For the first time in the history of excavations in the city, vivid and clear archaeological evidence of the burning of the city had come to light. We refrained from publicizing this fact immediately, in order to keep from being disturbed by visitors. But word of the discovery soon spread and people began thronging to the site to see the finds on the spot.

The already considerable excitement upon seeing the scorched objects being recovered from the ashes increased with the discovery of a spear leaning against the corner of a room. Beyond the image of the destruction, each of us pictured in his mind the scene so vividly described by the first-century Jewish

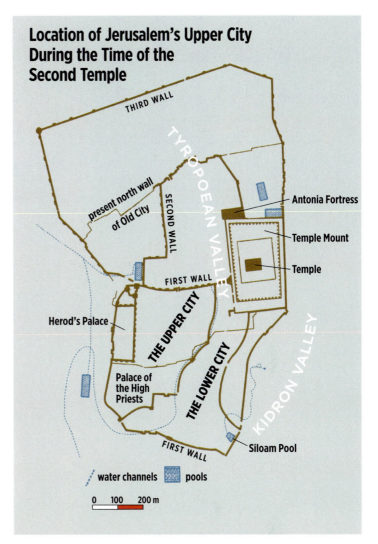

Location of Jerusalem's Upper City During the Time of the Second Temple

THIRD WALL

present north wall of Old City

SECOND WALL

TYROPOEAN VALLEY

Antonia Fortress

Temple Mount

Temple

FIRST WALL

Herod's Palace

THE UPPER CITY

THE LOWER CITY

KIDRON VALLEY

Palace of the High Priests

FIRST WALL

Siloam Pool

water channels   pools

0   100   200 m

LOOKING TOWARD THE TEMPLE MOUNT, excavators pause in their work of uncovering a building in Jerusalem's Upper City.

During Second Temple times, a priest would stand at the pinnacle of the southwest corner of the Temple Mount, the wall angle in front of the silver dome, and blow the shofar, or ram's horn, to herald the Sabbath and important festivals. But on August 28, 70 A.D., the Jews of the Upper City who looked toward the Temple Mount saw not the trumpeter but their Temple in flames. Perhaps the sight gave them courage because, according to Josephus, they held out against the Roman assault for nearly a month after the destruction of the Temple. Finally, on September 20, the Romans overran the city, slaughtering the inhabitants and putting the entire city to the torch.

historian Josephus: the Roman soldiers spreading out over the Upper City, looting and setting the houses alight as they slaughtered all in their path. The owner of this house, or one of its inhabitants, had managed to place his spear so it would be readily accessible, but he never got to use it.

Something amazing occurred in the hearts of all who witnessed the progress of excavations here. The burning of the Temple and the destruction of Jerusalem—fateful events in the history of the Jewish People—suddenly took on a new and horrible significance. Persons who had previously regarded this catastrophe as stirring but abstract and remote, having occurred two millennia ago, were so visibly moved by the sight that they occasionally would beg permission to take a fistful of soil or a bit of charred wood "in memory of the destruction." Others volunteered to take part in uncovering the remains, regarding such labor as sacred. The latent sentiment released—by people normally quite composed and immune to showing their emotions—was unbelievable.

The series of rooms uncovered was from the basement level of a large house whose continuation lies under a new dwelling on the north, so it could not be excavated. On the west, the building is abutted by an earth fill and building remains from the Israelite period. This is a good example of how a house from the days of the Second Temple was built over a site from the First Temple period.

The plan of the Burnt House, as far as it could be recovered, included a small courtyard paved with stones (1), three medium-sized rooms (2, 3, 4), a small room (5) that was the only one not burnt and that contained no finds, a small kitchen (6), and a small, stepped ritual bath (7). The walls of the rooms were generally preserved to the height of about one meter; they were coated with a thin white lime plaster, while the floors were of beaten earth. The ovens sunk into the floors of these rooms are evidence that these were not dwelling quarters but probably a workshop. Although a variety of small objects were scattered in disarray throughout the rooms, the outstanding feature in each room was a heap of broken objects, including stone vessels, stone tables, and pottery. Before the building collapsed, the violent hand of man had cast unwanted belongings into heaps on the floor—seeing this, we recalled Josephus's description of the Roman soldiers looting the houses after the city had been conquered.

One fine day in January 1970, while we were still excavating the Burnt House, our registrar of finds, Sara Hofri, came running over from our expedition office with a stone weight in her hands, shouting "Inscription"—a word that electrifies any archaeologist working on a dig. This weight, one of the many found in the Burnt House had been washed and was then found to bear letters incised in thin lines. The inscription was not in the Greek script so often found on such weights but rather in Hebrew (to be more precise, in the "square" Aramaic script). Except for the first letter in the upper line, of which only the tip remains, and the first letter in the lower line, which was partly blurred, the inscription was intact could clearly be read: "(of) Bar Kathros,"or "(of) the Son of Kathros."

Brief inscriptions of this sort which lend a personal touch to the silent finds, are invaluable to the excavator. They bring bone-dry discoveries to life by adding the historical dimension of the material

AT THE READY, this spear was propped against a wall in the Burnt House where its owner could quickly grab it to defend himself against the invading Romans. But the Romans burned this house so quickly that the spear was never touched; instead it was buried in place by the fiery debris of collapsed walls and ceiling, preserving for 2,000 years this image of resistance and tragedy.

"OF BAR KATHROS," proclaims the Hebrew inscription on this stone weight found in the Burnt House. An artist's drawing of the weight (right) shows the partially broken letter *dalet* (the first letter, reading right to left) which means "of." Now archaeologists can give a name and even a family history to the owners of this workshop. The Bar Kathros family was infamous—as High Priests, they served as overlords of their fellow Jews during Roman rule and abused their power through nepotism and libel.

itself. This inscription opened up the possibility of identifying the owner of the house and ascertaining the sort of people who lived there. Did the name Bar Kathros fit into the picture of the period, the locale and the events being revealed before us through the archaeological discoveries? The "House of Kathros" is known as one of the families of High Priests who, in practical terms, ruled the Jews of Palestine in the days of the Roman procurators. They had taken over important offices in the Temple and abused their position there through nepotism and oppression. A folksong preserved in Talmudic literature relates the corruption of these priests:

> Woe is me because of the House of Boethus,
>   woe is me because of their slaves.
> Woe is me because of the House of Hanan,
>   woe is me because of their incantation.
> Woe is me because of the *House of Kathros*,
>   woe is me because of their pens.
> Woe is me because of the House of Ishmael,
>   son of Phiabi,
>   woe is me because of their fists.
> For they are the High Priests, and their
>   sons are treasurers, and their sons-in-law are
>   trustees, and their servants beat the people
>   with staves."
>   (Babylonian Talmud, Pesahim 57, 1 =
>   Tosefta, Minhot 13, 21)

This refrain gives vent to the groanings of a people under the oligarchic rule of a priesthood that used any means to further its own interests. Apparently, each of the priestly families mentioned here practiced its own form of oppression: the one through a sharp tongue, the next through a sharp pen, and most of them, through simple brute force. The members of the "House of Kathros," who are accused of misusing the written word, were infamous for their libelous slander.

It can be assumed that our Bar Kathros was a scion of this same Kathros family. He lived in the

same period, and his name—not a common one—was unknown outside that family. (The word *bar*, literally "son of" without a personal name before it, indicates that the name here is a family rather than that of an actual father.) The house in which his inscription was found is situated opposite the Temple Mount, in a neighborhood that was populated by the nobility of Jerusalem.

We have defined a small room (6) at the northern edge of the Burnt House as a kitchen. This room, too, was entirely burnt out during the fire. Near its northern wall was a crude hearth of small fieldstones, built in two parts. The left-hand section contained a round pottery oven.

A unique find came to light near the doorway on the east, where more of the wall was destroyed than at any other spot. Leaning against the preserved fragment of the wall were the skeletal remains of the lower arm and hand of a human being, with the fingers still attached. The hand was spread out, grasping at a step. Dr. B. Ahrensburg, who examined these remains, determined that they were of a woman in her early twenties. The associations conjured up by this spectacle were rather frightful. We could visualize a young woman working in the kitchen when the Roman soldiers burst into the house and put it to the torch. She tried to flee but collapsed near the doorway, only to perish in the flames. This arm seems to be the first and only human remains discovered so far that can definitely be associated with the great human tragedy that accompanied the destruction of Jerusalem in 70 A.D. This tangible evidence, surprising in its freshness and shocking in its realism, gave us the feeling that it had all happened only yesterday.

We are well aware of the events of this tragedy: The Romans captured the Temple and burnt it on the ninth of Ab (28 August, 70 A.D.), taking the Lower City at the same time. But the Upper City on the Western Hill, above the scarp facing the Temple Mount, held out stubbornly. On the eighth of Elul, a

The Burnt House

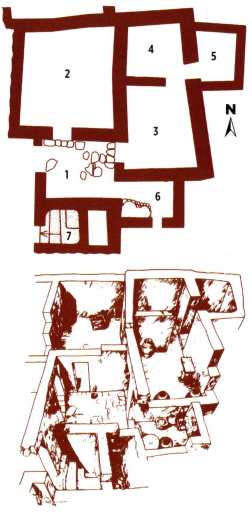

and burnt the houses with all who had taken refuge within. Often in the course of their raids, on entering the houses for loot, they would find whole families dead and the rooms filled with the victims of the famine...Running everyone through who fell in their way, they choked the alleys with corpses and deluged the whole city with blood, insomuch that many of the fires were extinguished by the gory stream. Towards evening they ceased slaughtering, but when night fell the fire gained the mastery, *and the dawn of the eighth day of the month Gorpiaeus [Elul] broke upon Jerusalem in flames*—a city which had suffered such calamities...The Romans now set fire to the outlying quarters of the town and razed the walls to the ground. Thus was Jerusalem taken in the second year of the reign of Vespasian, on the eighth of the month Gorpiaeus [20 September, 70 A.D.].

(*The Jewish War* VI, 8–10)

The story of the Burnt House, which so dramatically and vividly illustrates a most tragic and fateful chapter in the history of Jerusalem, thus comes to an end. But although the house met its end, the story itself is actually not yet complete, for in our own days, two thousand years later, when the descendants of the slaughtered returned to the site, they uncovered the physical traces of the destruction and rebuilt their homes over the ruins. Now they too, like Bar Kathros, can look out through their windows and see the Temple Mount, where the "previous tenant" had apparently worshipped. History has repeated itself. We hope that no other folksong beginning with the refrain "woe is me" will ever be heard here again. ◳

This article has been adapted from Chapter Three, section 5, of Discovering Jerusalem: Recent Archaeological Excavations in the Upper City *by Nahman Avigad (Thomas Nelson Publishers: Nashville, 1983). Printed by permission of Thomas Nelson Publishers.*

Related Reading

Nahman Avigad, "The Ancient Cardo Is Discovered in Jerusalem," BAR, December 1976.

Nahman Avigad, "Jerusalem Flourishing—A Craft Center for Stone, Pottery and Glass," BAR, November/December 1983.

Nitza Rosovsky, "A Thousan d Years of History in Jerusalem's Jewish Quarter," BAR, May/June 1992.

Shua Kisilevitz, Alexander Onn, Brigitte Ouahnouna and Shlomit Weksler-Bdolah, "Layers of Ancient Jerusalem," BAR, January/February 2012.

month after the Temple had been burnt, the Romans attacked the Upper City with full fury, taking it, setting the houses afire and slaughtering the inhabitants. Josephus describes the fighting in detail:

Caesar, finding it impracticable to reduce the upper city without earthworks, owing to the precipitous nature of the site, on the twentieth of the month Lous [Ab] apportioned the task among his forces. The conveyance of timber was, however, arduous, all the environs of the city to a distance of a hundred furlongs having, as I said, been stripped bare...The earthworks having now been completed after eighteen days' labor, on the seventh of the month Gorpiaeus [Elul], the Romans brought up the engines. Of the rebels, some already despairing of the city retired from the ramparts to the citadel, others slunk down into the tunnels. Pouring into the alleys, sword in hand, they [the Romans] massacred indiscriminately all whom they met,

The Dead Sea Scrolls and the People Who Wrote Them

FRANK MOORE CROSS

AFTER A QUARTER CENTURY OF discovery and publication, the study of the manuscripts from the desert of Judah has entered a new, more mature phase. True, the heat and noise of the early controversies have not wholly dissipated. One occasionally hears the agonized cry of a scholar pinned beneath a collapsed theory. And in the popular press, no doubt, the so-called battle of the scrolls will continue to be fought with mercenaries for some time to come. However, the initial period of confusion is past. From the burgeoning field of scroll research and the new disciplines it has created, certain coherent patterns of fact and meaning have emerged.

The scrolls and the people who wrote them can be placed within a broad historical framework with relative certainty by virtue of external controls provided by the archaeologist and the palaeographer. At that point, the historian must begin his difficult task—difficult because internal data from the scrolls pose special historiographic problems resulting from their esoteric language. The usual methods of historical criticism are difficult to apply without excessive subjectivity.

The archaeological context of the community of the Dead Sea—its caves, community center, and agricultural adjunct at 'En Feshkhah—has been established by six major seasons of excavations. The ancient center has yielded a clear stratification, and

in turn the strata are closely dated by their yield of artifacts, notably coins. For the era in which we are especially interested, the site exhibits three phases. The first of these, so-called Period Ia, consists of the remains of the earliest communal structures. In Period Ib the settlement was almost completely rebuilt and enlarged. The coins suggest that the buildings of the second phase were constructed no later than the time of Alexander Jannaeus (103–76 B.C.). The dating of the first phase is more difficult. So thoroughly were the structures of the first phase rebuilt that only the barest foundations were left. The problem is further complicated by the relatively short life and small size of the first phase; few coins accumulate in foundations in the first years of occupation. Moreover, coins have a considerable period of currency. When Alexander Jannaeus introduced the new Jewish coinage, coins of the Seleucid kings continued to circulate. The earliest coins of Period Ia appear to be five Seleucid coppers of imprecise date from the reign of Antiochus VII Sidetes (138–129 B.C.). This and other coin evidence indicates that the first buildings were probably constructed at the site in the desert of Qumran sometime in the interval between 140 and 100 B.C.

In the second phase, Period Ib, the community center took its permanent form, though extensions or repairs of a minor sort were introduced before

THE CAVES in which the
Dead Sea Scrolls were found.

THE CAVES in which the scrolls were found. The Dead Sea Scroll caves in the foreground. Across the wadi, on a plateau, are the remains now excavated, of the desert community that secreted the scrolls in the caves. None of the rooms appears to have been occupied as living quarters. In the background is the Judean wilderness.

the destruction of its buildings in the earthquake of 31 B.C., reported by the first century historian Josephus. After a short, but indeterminate period of abandonment, the site was reoccupied, rebuilt, and repaired precisely on the plan of the old communal complex. It flourished until 68 A.D., when it was stormed and occupied by the forces of the Roman Emperor Vespasian in the course of his raid on Jericho.

Theoretically, I suppose, the communities occupying the ruins in each of these phases need not have been related.* In fact, the community of the second and third, and no doubt the little known first phase, was one continuing community. It takes more than the historian's normally vivacious imagination to conceive of two communities, following one upon another and leading the peculiar life reflected at Qumran without having a relationship to one another. The very setting of the community requires a special explanation. Only powerful motivations would send a large group of persons into this wasteland. But more difficult to explain than the desolate environment chosen by the desert folk is the special character of the community center. The center was composed of communal facilities for study, writing, eating, domestic industries, and common stores. The members of the community did not live in the buildings (for the most part at any rate) but in caves and shelters radiating out from the central buildings. Thus, the architectural functions of the rooms and structures require a special mode of religious and communistic life. We can conclude

* As claimed by G. R. Driver, for example, in his erratic and arbitrary study, *The Judaean Scrolls* (Oxford, Blackwell, 1965).

only that the people of the scrolls founded the community in the second half of the century B.C. and occupied it, with a brief interruption in the reign of Herod the Great, until the dreadful days of the Jewish Revolt which culminated in the Roman destruction of the Jewish State.

Corroboration of this dating of the archaeological evidence is immediately furnished by the palaeographical analysis of some six hundred manuscripts recovered from Qumran. The main lines of the evolution of the late Aramaic and early Jewish bookhands had already been fixed on the basis of documents and inscriptions analyzed between the two World Wars.* Now, thanks to the discoveries in the Judean desert, the science of early Jewish palaeography has grown rich in materials for the typology of scripts.** These discoveries include not only the manuscripts of Qumran in Palaeo-Hebrew, Jewish, and Greek bookhands, but also the important discoveries from the Wadi Murabba'at and the Nahal Hever, written in both formal and cursive Jewish hands, as well as in Greek, Latin and Nabataean. While these discoveries have occupied the center of the stage, other discoveries from the Wadi ed-Daliyeh north of Jericho, from the excavations of Khirbet Qumran, from the tombs of Jerusalem, from Khirbet el-Kom, and from the excavations at Masada, to mention only the most important, have steadily expanded, extending our knowledge of the evolution and relative dating of early Jewish scripts.

Not only do we now possess ample materials for precise typological analysis of the scripts of the Qumran manuscripts, we have also accumulated a series of externally dated scripts by which the relative dates gained by typological study can be turned into absolute dates. Most striking no doubt are the documents bearing date formulae of the late fourth century B.C. (Daliyeh), of the third century (el-Kom), and of the first century and second century of the Christian era (Qumran, Murabba'at and Hever), which overlap in part and extend the Qumran series backward and forward in time. To these may be added documents from excavations, notably from Qumran itself and Masada, dated by archaeological context to the first century B.C. and later.

The scripts from Qumran belong to three periods of palaeographical development. A very small group of Biblical manuscripts belong to an archaic style

whose limits are about 250–150 B.C. Next, a large number of Qumran manuscripts, Biblical and non-Biblical, were written in a style reflecting the Hasmonean period, that is, between 150 and 30 B.C. However, scrolls of specifically sectarian content, many composed and copied at Qumran, begin only about the middle of the Hasmonean period, that is, about 100 B.C. Finally, there is a relatively large corpus of Herodian manuscripts dating between 30 B.C. and 70 A.D.

The termination of the series with late Herodian hands correlates precisely with the archaeological data. The library was abandoned at the time of the destruction of the community in 68 A.D. We must in turn establish the origins of the community no later than the date of the earliest sectarian compositions, that is, somewhat before 100 B.C. Nonsectarian scrolls, especially the Biblical manuscripts, begin in quantity about 150 B.C. Scrolls of the Archaic Period are exceedingly rare and were probably master scrolls brought into the community at the time of its founding. Extant copies of such characteristic sectarian scrolls as the Rule of the Community and the Damascus Document go back to the beginning of the first century B.C. Sectarian commentaries on Habakkuk, Nahum, and other Biblical works date mostly from the second half of the first century B.C. and contain traditional lore of Biblical interpretation developed in the community in its earlier history and precipitated into writing relatively late in the life of the sect.

Extant classical tests which treat the second century B.C. mention four Jewish movements in Judea; the Hasidim, a pious "congregation" which disappeared in the Maccabean era, and three orders which emerge no later than the early Hasmonean era and presumably have their roots in the Maccabean period. These are the Essenes, the Pharisees, and the Saducees. Of these three, only the Essene order can be described as separatist, in the radical sense that they regarded themselves as the only true Israel and separated themselves fully from contact with their fellow Jews. Josephus informs us that the Essenes rejected even the sacrificial service of the Temple as unclean and "offered their sacrifices by themselves." Pliny (or rather his sources) tells us of their "city" in the wilderness between Jericho and 'En Gedi near the shore of the Dead Sea—where the Qumran ruins are located.

This reference in Pliny is decisive in identifying the sectarians of Qumran with the Essenes, in the absence of strong counter-arguments. We know of no other sect arising in the second century B.C. which can be associated with the wilderness community. Surface exploration has turned up no

---

* See W. F. Albright, "A Biblical Fragment from the Maccabean Age: The Nash Papyrus," *Journal of Biblical Literature*, Vol. 56 (1937), pp. 145–176.

** See F. M. Cross, "The Development of Jewish Scripts," in G. Ernest Wright (Ed.), *The Bible and the Ancient Near East*, pp. 133–202.

rival settlement in the crucial era. Further, the community at Qumran was organized precisely as a new Israel, a true sect which repudiated the priesthood and cultus of Jerusalem. Neither the Pharisees nor the Saducees can qualify. The Essenes qualify perfectly. There is no reason to belabor the point. A careful examination of the classical references side by side with the texts of Qumran establishes the identification, in my opinion, beyond cavil. The strongest argument which has been raised against the identification of the Qumran sect with the Essenes is as follows: Since Palestine "swarmed" with obscure sects in the first century of the Christian era, one must exercise caution in assigning the Dead Sea sect to a known group. The argument had plausibility only when a few manuscripts of uncertain date were known.

The Qumran sect was not one of the small, ephemeral groups of the first century of the common era. Its substantial community at Qumran was established in the second century B.C. and flourished some two centuries or more. Moreover, it was not restricted to Qumran, but, like the Essenes of the classical sources, counted its camps and settlements throughout the villages of Judah.

Its own sectarian literature was enormous, exercising a considerable influence upon later sectarian, including Christian, literature. The task, therefore, is to identify a major sect in Judaism. To suppose that a major group in Judaism in this period went unnoticed in our sources is simply incredible.

The scholar who would "exercise caution" in identifying the sect of Qumran with the Essenes places himself in an astonishing position: he must suggest seriously that *two* major parties formed communistic religious communities in the same district of the desert of the Dead Sea and lived together in effect for two centuries, holding similar bizarre views, performing similar or rather identical lustrations, ritual meals, and ceremonies. He must suppose that one carefully described by classical authors, disappeared without leaving building remains or even potsherds behind; the other, systematically ignored by the classical sources, left extensive ruins, and indeed a great library. I prefer to be reckless and flatly identify the men of Qumran with their perennial houseguests, the Essenes. At all events, in the remainder of this article, I shall assume the identification and draw freely upon both classical and Qumran texts.

The Essenes of Qumran were a priestly party. Their leader was a priest. The archenemy of the sect was a priest, usually designated the Wicked Priest. In protocols of their community, the priests took precedence, and in the age-to-come, a messiah priest ranked above the traditional Davidic or royal messiah. There is some reason to believe that the sect conducted a sacrificial system in its community at Qumran. At any rate, the community was preoccupied with priestly lore, ceremonial law, the orders of the priests, and the liturgical calendar; many of their sectarian compositions reflect their almost obsessive interest in priestly orthopraxy (i.e., correct orthodox practice and observance).

The community referred to its priesthood as "sons of Zadok," that is, members of the ancient line of high priests established in Scripture. At the same time, they heaped scorn and bitter condemnation upon the ungodly priests of Jerusalem, who, they argued, were illegitimate. This animosity toward the priests in power in Judah on the part of the priests at Qumran did not stem merely from doctrinal differences. Our texts rather reflect a historical struggle for power between high priestly families. The Essenes withdrew in defeat and formed their community in exile which was organized as a counter-Israel led by a counter-priesthood or, viewed with Essene eyes, as the true Israel of God led by the legitimate priesthood. The theocrat of Jerusalem, the so-called Wicked Priest, attacked the Essene priesthood, even in exile, and made an attempt on the life of the Righteous Teacher, the Essene priestly leader. For their part, the Essene priests confidently expected divine intervention to establish their cause. They predicted that the Wicked Priest and his cronies would meet violent death at the hand of God and their enemies; and they searched Scripture for prophecies of the end of days when they, the poor of the desert would be reestablished in a new, transfigured Jerusalem.

Mention of the Essene hopes of a New Age of glory leads us naturally to some comments on the special theological views of the Essenes which informed their understanding of history and gave to their community its peculiar institutions. The Essenes belong in the center of that movement which goes under the designation *apocalypticism*. The late visionaries of the Old Testament, notably the author of Daniel, as well as the later Baptist and Christian communities, discovered themselves to be living in the last days of the Old Age, or rather in the days when the Old Age was passing away and the Kingdom of God was dawning. According to apocalypticism, the upsurge of evil powers in history reflected the last defiant outbreak of cosmic Satanic powers, and the gifts of the Holy Spirit, manifest in the community of the faithful, adumbrated the age of the Spirit to follow the final war in which the Spirit of Truth and his heavenly armies would put an end to the rule of the powers of darkness.

The constitution of the Essene community was a

crystallized apocalyptic vision. Each institution and practice of the community was a preparation for or, by anticipation, a realization of, life in the New Age of God's rule. On the one hand, their communal life was a reenactment of the events of the end-time, both the final days of the Old Age and the era of Armageddon. On the other hand, their community, being heirs of the kingdom, participated already in the gifts and glories which were the first fruits of the age-to-come.

For the apocalyptist of Qumran, the key to these future mysteries was at hand. One had only to read Biblical prophecies with the understanding given the inspired interpreter (that is, one who reads under the power of the Holy Spirit), because the secrets of events to come in the last days were foretold by God through the mouth of his holy prophets. So the Essenes searched the Scriptures. They developed a body of traditional exegesis, no doubt inspired by patterns laid down by their founder, which is reflected in most of their works, above all in their Biblical commentaries, *pesharim*, in which their common tradition was fixed in writing.

In apocalyptic exegesis, three principles should be kept in mind. Prophecy openly or cryptically refers to the last days. Second, the so-called last days are in fact the present, the days of the sect's life. And, finally, the history of ancient Israel's redemption, her offices and institutions, are prototypes of the events and figures of the new Israel.

On this basis, the Essene camp in the wilderness found its prototype in the Mosaic camp of Numbers (see Numbers 2–4; Numbers 9:15–10:28). The Essenes retired to Qumran to "prepare the way of the Lord" in the wilderness. As God established his ancient covenant in the desert, so the Essenes entered into the new covenant on their return to the desert. As Israel in the desert was mustered into army ranks in preparation for the Holy War of conquest, so the Essenes marshaled their community in battle array and wrote liturgies of the Holy Warfare of Armageddon, living for the day of the second conquest when they would march with their Messianic leaders to Zion. Meanwhile, they kept the laws of purity laid down in Scripture for soldiers in Holy Warfare, an ascetic regimen which at the same time anticipated life with the holy angels before the throne of God, a situation requiring similar ritual purity.

The offices of the sect reveal this apocalyptic typology. The council of the community was numbered after the princes of Israel and Levi in the desert; at the same time, they prefigured the judges who would rule the tribes of Israel in the New Age. As God sent Moses, Aaron, and David,

so they looked for three messiahs—prophet, priest and prince. The founder of their community bore a Biblical sobriquet, the "Righteous Teacher" (from Hosea 10:12 and Joel 2:23), apparently understood as the title of a priestly forerunner of the Messianic age. And even the enemies of the sect, the False Oracle, the Wrathful Lion, and so on, all bore designations culled ingeniously from prophecy.

The great external events of history of their times were discovered in the Scriptures, predicted as signs of the last days: The Seleucid rule, the wars of the Hasmoneans, the rise of the Romans, and the conquest of Palestine by Pompey. And the internal events of sectarian life and history were rehearsed even more dramatically in the sayings of the prophets. Here we come upon one of the major difficulties in writing Essene history. Major political events and, from our point of view, minor or private events in the life of the sect are mixed in their expositions of Scripture in dizzying fashion, and, as if this were not bad enough, the whole is veiled in the esoteric language of apocalyptic.

To sum up. The Essenes of Qumran were a community formed and guided by a party of Zadokite priests. In the latter half of the second century B.C., having lost hope of regaining their ancient authority in the theocracy of Jerusalem and under active persecution by a new house of reigning priests, they fled to the desert and, finding new hope in apocalyptic dreams, readied themselves for the imminent judgment when their enemies would be vanquished and they, God's elect, would be given final victory in accordance with the predictions of the prophets.

It is not difficult to identify the priestly conflict out of which the dissident Essene party emerged. In the days of Antiochus Epiphanes (175–163 B.C.), the orderly succession of Zadokite high priests failed. The high priestly office became a prize dispensed by the Seleucid overlord Antiochus, to be purchased by the highest bidder. The strife between rivals for the theocratic office soon developed into civil war, and in the resulting chaos divine Antiochus found opportunity to carry out his fearful massacres, terminating in the notorious desecration of the Temple and the Hellenization of Holy Jerusalem. The stage was set for the rise of Maccabees, whose destiny it was to lead the Jews in a heroic war of independence, and who, having won popularity by freeing Judah from foreign suzerains, themselves usurped the high priestly office. In this way, the ancient Zadokite house gave way to the lusty, if illegitimate, Hasmonean dynasty. Essene origins are to be discovered precisely in the struggle between these priestly houses and their adherents.

Perhaps the historian should say no more.

However, historical allusions in Essene Biblical commentaries tempt one to reconstruct the origins of the Qumran sect more precisely. We should like to know the identity of the Wicked Priest of Jerusalem and to fix more exactly the occasion for the flight and persecution of the sectarians; and we should like, if possible, to relate the Essene sect to the other Jewish parties, especially to the Pharisees who came into being in the same historical milieu. Perhaps it is too much to ask the identity of the Essene Teacher or of other sectarian figures who, from the standpoint of general history, played insignificant roles.

COLUMN 10 OF THE HABAKKUK COMMENTARY found in cave 1, which contains two quotations from Habakkuk (2:13 and 2:14). Note especially line 7 and line 14 (the last line) in which a single word appears in a different script. The word is the ineffable name of God, Yahweh, known as the tetragrammaton because it contains four letters, yod, heh, vov, heh. The tetragrammaton is written in archaic Hebrew script, while the remainder of the scroll is written in the newer square Hebrew script which has persisted in Hebrew to the present day. The archaic Hebrew script was in general use until about the 6th–5th century B.C. when it was replaced by the square script. However, the Dead Sea Scrolls often retain the archaic Hebrew script for the tetragrammaton, as in the examples here.

Scholarly debate on these more precise details of Essene history continue. No consensus has fully emerged. My own views underwent a major change as the archaeological and palaeographical data piled up and narrowed options. Nevertheless, I think it is very likely that the Wicked Priest of Jerusalem can be identified with the High Priest Simon Maccabeus, the last and perhaps the greatest of the five Maccabean brothers. In February of 134 B.C., Simon together with Judas (probably his eldest son) and Mattathias his youngest toured the cities of Judah, evidently reviewing fortifications which he had built or which were in the process of construction. On their tour, Simon and his sons descended to Jericho. Jericho was administered under Simon by one Ptolemy son of Abubos. Ptolemy had ambitions to rule Judea and he organized a plot of considerable proportions.

Ptolemy's opportunity came upon the occasion of Simon's visit to Jericho. Ptolemy held a banquet for his victims in a newly completed fortress guarding Jericho. When Simon and his sons were drunk, Ptolemy's men murdered Simon, and later his two sons. Ultimately Ptolemy's plot failed. John Hyrcanus, Simon's remaining son, who was then in Gezer, eluded assassins sent to slay him and escaped to Jerusalem in time to rally loyal Jews against the forces sent by Ptolemy to take the city. Ptolemy sent to Antiochus VII Sidetes for immediate aid. Antiochus arrived too late to succor Ptolemy, but Antiochus was successful in reducing the country and in forcing Jerusalem to surrender.

These events comport well with certain historical allusions found in so-called List of Testimonia from Cave 4 at Qumran. One of the Testimonia (the fourth) refers to a "Cursed One", predicted in Joshua 6:26. The passage in Joshua follows the account of the ancient destruction of Jericho and reads this way:

"May the Lord's curse light on the man who comes forward to rebuild this city of Jericho: The laying of its foundations shall cost him his eldest son, the setting up of its gates shall cost him his youngest."

The curse was once fulfilled when in the ninth century B.C. Jericho was rebuilt by a certain Hiel with the loss of his sons (see 1 Kings 16:34). The Essenes chose this particular text, once fulfilled, and reapplied it to their own time. The Testimonia, partly reconstructed, reads in part as follows:

"And behold, a cursed man, a man of Belial, shall come to power to be a trapper's snare and ruin to all his neighbors, and he shall come to power and [his sons] ... [with him], the two of

them becoming violent instruments, and they shall rebuild again the [city ... and shall set] up a wall and towers for it, to make a stronghold of wickedness [in the land and a great evil] in Israel and horrors in Ephraim and in Judah ... [and they shall commit sacrilege in the land and great contumely among the children of [Jacob and blo]od [shall be poured out] like water on the battlement of the daughter of Zion and in the district of Jerusalem."

If we follow the pattern of close apocalyptic exegesis which normally obtains in sectarian exposition of Scripture, we must look for an event connected with the fortification of Jericho by a major enemy of the sect when the dreadful curse of Joshua repeated itself. And properly, we must look for a high priest of Jerusalem who associated his sons with him in his rule.

The events concerning the murder of Simon and his two sons in Jericho when they came to inspect the new fortifications at Jericho, as well as the bloody aftermath of their triple assassination, seem to explain adequately the resurrection of the old curse on Jericho by the Essenes. Most of the elements of the prophecy fit strikingly; the association of the cursed man with two sons in the fortification overlooking Jericho their death at the hands of Ptolemy's henchmen as evidence of the effectiveness of the curse, and the subsequent devastation and bloodshed in Judah and Jerusalem. I find it very difficult not to conclude that Simon is established as the Cursed Man of the Testimonia.

Is this "Cursed Man" identical with the Wicked Priest? The other Testimonia relate to the messianic prophet, priest, and king, as well as to the priestly forerunner of the New Age who founded the sect. The juxtaposition of the "Cursed Man" with the other central figures of the sect strongly suggests that the "Cursed Man" is in fact the Wicked Priest.

Jonathan (162–142 B.C.), the second of the Maccabean brothers, not Simon, was the first to usurp the high priestly office and some have suggested that it is he who should be identified with the Wicked Priest. Several historical factors, however, make this choice unlikely. Jonathan's position was tenuous throughout his term in the office. Jewish independence was not to be fully won until the reign of Simon. To the end of his days Jonathan struggled to maintain himself against foreign foes. It seems unlikely that he was sufficiently secure to turn upon his fellow Jews and persecute the Zadokites (Essenes); moreover, in view of the de facto nature of his theocratic rule and the uncertainty of the times, the Zadokite priests would not have abandoned hope and fled Jerusalem upon the occasion of Jonathan's donning the high priestly robes. On the contrary, we should expect that move only to *initiate* hostilities between the orthodox and the Maccabean nationalists.

Simon, Jonathan's successor, brought to fulfillment his brothers' national dreams. In the second year of his rule he succeeded in driving out the Syrian garrison from the citadel in Jerusalem. Judea only then became fully free of the Seleucid yoke. Simon ruled in peace and was at liberty to consolidate his realm. In 140 B.C., the third year of his reign, a great assembly was held "of the priests and people and heads of the nation and the elders of the country." The work of the assembly and the significance of its decree for the history of the high priesthood cannot be overestimated. The decree of the assembly was engraved in bronze and set up on stelae on Mount Zion. Simon was made high priest de jure and the high priesthood was given to Simon's house forever, "until a faithful prophet should arise" (1 Maccabees 14:30–39). The claim is here made to a legal transference of the high priesthood from the Zadokite dynasty (appointed by David!) to the Hasmonean dynasty. The illegitimacy of Simon's house is admitted tacitly in the phrase "until a faithful prophet arise," that is, until a final arbiter between the rival houses appears in the age-to-come. Further, the decree warned against any opposition to Simon by layman or priest, prohibited private assembly, and threatened punishment to anyone who acted contrary to the stipulations of the decree.

In this decree we can clearly discern the new high priest's determination to stamp out opposition, to persecute those who refused to recognize the full legitimacy of his office. This program, falling in the early years of Simon, seems to give the appropriate occasion for the crystallization of the Essene sect, its persecution and the persecution of the Righteous Teacher, and the exile in the wilderness of Judah. Simon had the leisure, power, popularity, and inclination to root out Jewish opposition to the ascendancy of his party and his house. Certain texts, especially the Testimonia, give evidence in support of our identification of the Wicked Priest with Simon. Finally, it should not be overlooked that the archaeological evidence for the dating of the foundation of the community fits more easily with a date in Simon's reign than with a date in Jonathan's reign.

I have not dealt, of course, with a large number of texts relating to the Wicked Priest and his relations with the Righteous Teacher and the exiled community. Most fit equally well with Jonathan or Simon, or indeed with a number of other priests. In this era one cannot complain of a shortage of wicked priests. One final text, however, deserves mention. In a passage of the Commentary on Habakkuk, the expositor comments, "This means the priest whose dishonor was greater than his honor. For he...walked in the ways of drunkednes in order to quench his thirst. But the cup of God's wrath will swallow him up...!" The high priest caroused once too often. In Jericho, at the hands of Ptolemy, the cup of pleasure turned into the cup of wrath and swallowed Simon. So I should interpret the text.

I have been able to fix the general framework of the Essene community's life in the desert. Perhaps I have succeeded also in identifying the villain of the esoteric commentaries. No doubt, I have also illustrated the complexities and frustrations which face the student of the Essene library from Qumran.

(For further details and bibliographic references, see F. M. Cross, *Canaanite Myth and Hebrew Epic* [Harvard University Press, 1973], Chap. 12.)

Related Reading

Hershel Shanks, "The Enigma of the Scrolls," January/February 1998.

Frank Moore Cross and Esther Eshel, "The Missing Link," BAR, March/April 1998; Ada Yardeni, "Breaking the Missing Link," BAR, May/June 1998.

Hershel Shanks, "Chief Scroll Editor Opens Up—An Interview with Emanuel Tov," BAR, May/June 2002.

Martin Abegg, Jr., Michael Phelps and Hershel Shanks, "'Will Marty Abegg Ever Find a Job?'" BAR, January/February 2003.

Hershel Shanks, "Qumran—The Pottery Factory," BAR, September/October 2006.

Hershel Shanks, "60 Years with the Dead Sea Scrolls," BAR, May/June 2007, and other coverage of the 60th anniversary of the scrolls' discovery in that issue and in July/August 2007 and September/October 2007.

Steve Mason, "Did the Essenes Write the Dead Sea Scrolls?" BAR, November/December 2008; Kenneth Atkinson, Hanan Eshel and Jodi Magness, Another View: "Do Josephus's Writings Support the 'Essene Hypothesis'?" BAR, March/April 2009.

"BAR's Crusades," BAR, July/August/September/October 2009.

Hershel Shanks, "Isaiah Among the Scrolls," BAR, July/August 2011.

Sidnie White Crawford, "A View from the Caves," BAR, September/October 2011.

Sidnie White Crawford, "Scribe Links Qumran and Masada," BAR, November/December 2012.

For more of BAR's coverage about the Dead Sea Scrolls, visit us online at biblicalarchaeology.org/deadseascrolls

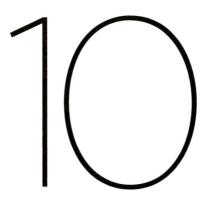

Where Jesus Walked (and Sailed)

For as long as there have been Christians, there have been Christian pilgrims who wanted to follow in Christ's footsteps. These four articles helped illuminate the earthly life of the man Jesus and the world in which he lived.

For almost 2,000 years devoted Christians have sought the landmarks of Jesus' life—to stand where he stood, touch what he touched and see what he saw. A pilgrimage to the Holy Land is a moving experience for those who are able. But for those who cannot make the journey, BAR brings the sights—and sites—of Jesus' world to life in richly illustrated articles that are the next-best thing to being there.

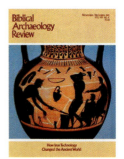

NOVEMBER/DECEMBER 1982
Has the House Where Jesus Stayed in Capernaum Been Found?

In this chapter's first article, American archaeologist James F. Strange analyzed a complicated structure in Capernaum that Italian archaeologists believe was originally the house of St. Peter where Jesus lived for a time. (I am listed as Strange's co-author only at his insistence, based on my editing of his manuscript, not because of any substantive contribution to the article.)

The article begins with an overview of Capernaum and the remains of its famous synagogue. Today it is recognized by all that this cannot be the synagogue in which Jesus preached. But, intriguingly, there is another, still-unexcavated building below this synagogue that may well be.

In the late 1960s and 1970s, Italian archaeologists and Franciscan Fathers Virgilio Corbo and Stanislao Lofredda turned their attention to an unusually shaped building nearby consisting of three concentric octagons. This is traditionally the shape of a memorial church—but a memorial of what? At an earlier stage a private

house that could be dated to the Roman period—that included the time of Jesus—had existed on the site. The house was typical of houses at Capernaum except in one respect: The walls had been subsequently plastered and then covered with graffiti by Christian pilgrims. The Franciscan epigrapher to the excavation, Emmanuele Testa, read one of the graffiti as including "Peter, the helper of Rome." Other graffiti referred to Jesus. The evidence may not be absolute proof, but there is "a considerable body of circumstantial evidence" suggesting that this was St. Peter's house where Jesus stayed in Capernaum.

NOVEMBER/DECEMBER 1993
Cast Your Net Upon the Water—Fish and Fisherman in Jesus' Time

Our next article is by Mendel Nun, a *kibbutznik* who lived on the shore of the Sea of Galilee for more than 50 years. Although he was not a trained academician, it was generally agreed that he understood the sea and the life around it and in it better than almost anyone. He immigrated to Palestine in 1939 and took the name Nun, which means fish in Aramaic, the common tongue in Jesus' time. He died in 2010.

Nun reminds us that fishermen were Jesus' earliest disciples and that understanding the fisherman's world helps us to understand the New Testament text in very specific ways.

Perhaps it was inevitable. It is now universally called the "Jesus Boat." Of course, it isn't. But it *is* from Jesus' time. And it is the kind of boat in which he

SEPTEMBER/OCTOBER 1988
The Galilee Boat—
2,000-Year-Old Hull
Recovered Intact

sailed. And it does come from the Sea of Galilee. In the next article, Israeli marine archaeologist Shelley Wachsmann (now teaching at Texas A&M University) described the extraordinary recovery of this boat from its watery grave. Half accidental, half improvised, but always imaginative, the recovery and preservation of this vessel is one of the most unusual stories in maritime archaeology. The "Jesus Boat" is now one of Israel's most popular tourist attractions.

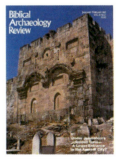

JANUARY/FEBRUARY 1983
The Undiscovered Gate
Beneath Jerusalem's
Golden Gate

Jim Fleming fell into a great discovery. In 1969, he was a graduate student in Jerusalem. One spring morning, while exploring the Old City wall outside the Golden Gate (where Jesus is said to have entered the city), he suddenly fell into a hole 8 feet deep. Disoriented but uninjured, in the dim light that reached into a mass grave full of human bones, he focused on the wall in front of him. There, directly below the Golden Gate, he was able to discern five wedge-shaped stones set in a massive arch. Here were the remains of a hitherto-unknown earlier entrance to Jerusalem! But when and by whom? These questions are explored in his article, which also explored several related aspects of this ever-fascinating wall. Dr. James Fleming is

now head of the Explorations in Antiquity Center in LaGrange, Georgia.

SEPTEMBER/OCTOBER 2005
The Siloam Pool—
Where Jesus Cured the
Blind Man

Some great finds are discovered accidentally. That is the case with the gate discussed in the previous article. In its own way that is also true of the pool described in the next article. But it was found only after long years of excavation. It was discovered in the long-term, continuing excavation in Jerusalem's City of David, the most ancient part of the city. During an Israel Antiquities Authority excavation then headed by archaeologists Ronny Reich and Eli Shukron, they had to make room for city workers to repair or replace an old sewer pipe. As the city's heavy equipment sought to expose the pipe, two ancient steps suddenly appeared. The archaeologists immediately stopped the repair work. An archaeological excavation of the area soon brought to light the hitherto lost but famous Pool of Siloam from Jesus' time. It was here that Jesus was said to have cured the blind man (John 9:1–11).

Until this discovery, the "Siloam Pool" could only be visited at a small pool from a much later time. Nothing more was known, except that this wasn't the famous Pool of Siloam referred to in the Hebrew Bible or in the New Testament. Now we can see the imposing remains from the turn of the era—at a slightly different location from the later pool. But we still haven't found the pool referred to in the Hebrew Bible.

Has the House Where Jesus Stayed in Capernaum Been Found?

Italian archaeologists believe they have uncovered St. Peter's home

JAMES F. STRANGE AND
HERSHEL SHANKS

ITALIAN ARCHAEOLOGISTS CLAIM to have discovered the house were Jesus stayed in Capernaum. Proof positive is still lacking and may never be found, but all signs point to the likelihood that the house of St. Peter where Jesus stayed, near Capernaum's famous synagogue, is an authentic relic.

Nestled on the northwest shore of the Sea of Galilee, the ruins of Capernaum slumbered peacefully for hundreds of years; indeed, some of its remains went undisturbed for thousands of years. Modern investigation of this site began in the mid–19th century, but even now the earth is still yielding new secrets. What the future holds, no one knows.

An American explorer and orientalist, Edward Robinson, first surveyed the site in 1838. Robinson correctly identified some exposed architectural remains as an ancient synagogue, but he did not connect the site with ancient Capernaum.

In 1866, Captain Charles Wilson conducted limited excavations on behalf of the London-based Palestine Exploration Fund. Wilson correctly identified the site as Capernaum and concluded that the synagogue was the one referred to in Luke 7:5, which was built by a Roman centurion who had admired the Jews of Kfar Nahum (Capernaum*).

*Capernaum is the Latinization of the Hebrew Kfar Nahum which means the village of Nahum.

THE CAPERNAUM SYNAGOGUE, residential area and octagonal church, clustered on the northwest shore of the Sea of Galilee. Beyond the trees is the red brick convent of the Franciscan Fathers.

The synagogue was built on a platform, mounted by steps at its southeast and southwest corners; the southwest steps are visible in this photo. The steps lead to a courtyard, or room, with an intact flagstone floor. This auxiliary room probably served as the synagogue's school room. The interior of the main prayer room was divided by two parallel rows of columns forming a nave and two aisles.

Recent excavations uncovered more ancient buildings beneath this synagogue. Since we know that, historically, the site of a town's synagogue rarely changes, one of these earlier buildings was very likely the Capernaum synagogue in which Jesus preached.

South of the synagogue is a residential area, the remains of private homes. Beyond that (84 feet south of the synagogue) is the octagonal church built over St. Peter's house.

As a result of the British interest in the site, local Bedouin began their own search for treasure. They smashed and overturned ancient architectural members looking for small finds to sell on the local antiquities markets. The Bedouin were soon followed by local Arab contractors who appropriated overturned and broken stones for use in new construction projects.

At last in 1894, the Franciscan Fathers acquired the site in order to protect its precious remains. To ensure that the exposed remains would not be carried away, the Franciscans reburied some of them and built a high stone wall around the property.

Naturally, special Christian interest in the site stemmed from Capernaum's importance in Jesus's life and ministry. According to the Gospel of Matthew, Jesus left Nazareth and "settled" in Capernaum (to render the verb literally) (Matthew 4:13). In and around Capernaum Jesus recruited several of his disciples including Peter, who was to become his spiritual fisherman (Mark 1:16–20). Jesus performed a number of miracles in Capernaum—for example, curing the man with the withered hand

A CORINTHIAN COLUMN CAPITAL from the Capernaum synagogue. A seven-branched candelabrum (menorah) decorates this elaborately carved capital. To the right of the menorah's base is a ram's horn (shofar) and, to the left, an incense shovel; both are ritual objects once used in the Temple in Jerusalem. This capital may have stood atop one of the columns separating the nave from an aisle inside the synagogue.

(Mark 3:1–5). Jesus frequently preached and taught at the Capernaum synagogue (Mark 1:21). In the Capernaum synagogue, Jesus first uttered those mystical words:

"Whoever eats my flesh and drinks my blood possesses eternal life, and I will raise him up on the last day...As the living Father sent me...he who eats shall live because of me. This is the bread which came down from heaven."
(John 6:54–58)

The word of Jesus went forth first from Capernaum. Capernaum was not only the center of Jesus's Galilean ministry, but it was also the place of his longest residence.

Where did Jesus live in Capernaum? While we are not told specifically, the fair inference seems to be that he lived at Peter's house. We are told that Jesus "entered Peter's house, [and] saw his mother-in-law lying sick with a fever..." (Matthew 8:14). That evening he was still at Peter's house (Matthew 8:16). Apparently Jesus lived there. In Mark we read that "when he [Jesus] returned to Capernaum after a few days, someone reported that he was at home" (Mark 2:1). The home referred to, it seems, is Peter's house. This same passage from Mark speaks of four men digging through the roof of the house to lower a paralytic on a pallet so that Jesus could heal him:

"And when he returned to Capernaum after a few days, someone reported that he was at home. And many were gathered, so many that they did not have any room, even about the door. And he was speaking the word to them. And they came bringing to him a paralytic, carried by four men. And since they could not get to him because of the crowd, they took apart the roof where he was. And when they had dug out a hole, they lowered the pallet on which the paralytic lay.

And when Jesus saw their faith, he said, 'My son, your sins are forgiven.'" (Mark 2:1–5).

Until 1968, the primary focus of excavations at Capernaum was the synagogue. This is understandable. It is indeed a magnificent building of shimmering white limestone that stands out in stark contrast to the rough black basalt of the surrounding houses. The synagogue was constructed on a platform to conform with the rabbinic injunction to build the synagogue on the highest point in the town.* The synagogue is entered by a flight of steps on either side of the platform. The entrance facade contains

*Tosephta Megillah IV.23.

three doors facing Jerusalem.

Inside the synagogue, two rows of stone benches, probably for elders who governed the synagogue, line the two long walls. The other congregants sat eastern fashion on mats on the floor.

Two rows of columns divide the main prayer room into a central nave and two side aisles. Parallel to the back wall, a third row of columns creates a third aisle in the rear of the main room. Adjoining the main room was a side room that was no doubt used for a variety of community functions—as a school, a court, a hostel for visitors, a dining hall, a meeting place. In antiquity, the synagogue served all these functions.

When this synagogue was first excavated by the Franciscan Friar Gaudentius Orfali in the 1920s, Friar Orfali identified it as the synagogue in which Jesus had preached and performed miracles. Today, however, all competent scholars reject this dating of the Capernaum synagogue. In 1968, the Franciscans renewed their excavations in the synagogue under the direction of two Franciscan fathers, Virgilio Corbo and Stanislao Loffreda. This pair of Italian scholars concluded that the synagogue dated to the fourth or fifth century A.D. Their dating was based primarily on a hoard of 10,000 coins they found under the synagogue floor. This new conclusion set off a lively debate, still unresolved, among scholars who had previously contended that the building should be dated to the late second or third century A.D.

Whatever the date of the surviving Capernaum synagogue, it is likely that the Capernaum synagogue in which Jesus preached stood on this same spot—although this cannot be proved. As we know from other communities, synagogue sites rarely change within a town. A new synagogue is simply reconstructed on the site of the old one. Recently, traces of earlier buildings have been found below the extant Capernaum synagogue. Judging from the size of these earlier buildings and the paving on their floors, they were probably private homes. One of these earlier remains may well be of a home converted into a synagogue in which Jesus preached.

The excavations undertaken by the Franciscans beginning in 1968 went far beyond the synagogue, however. The Franciscans also worked to uncover the town of which the synagogue was a part. It was in this connection that they discovered what was probably St. Peter's house where Jesus stayed when he lived in Capernaum.

Indeed, it was while investigating the context of the synagogue that they became especially interested in the remains of an unusual octagonal-shaped building 84 feet south of the synagogue, opposite the synagogue facade facing Jerusalem. This

GARO NALBANDIAN

THE INTERIOR OF THE CAPERNAUM SYNAGOGUE. Although this impressive row of white limestone columns looks like a facade, it is actually the narrow north end of the synagogue nave, 27 feet across. On either side of the nave, parallel to its length, is an aisle formed by rows of columns. The intact column in the left foreground and the broken one in the right foreground are two of the columns that separated the nave from the west aisle. The broken column in the rear of the photo is on the east aisle. The columns rest on pedestals, each carved from one stone. Originally, a second story of columns above the aisle ceilings formed an open gallery or balcony overlooking the nave. In the opening aerial photograph one may clearly see the nave with its two flanking side aisles perpendicular to the row of standing columns.

octagonal building had long been known and, along with the synagogue, it was frequently mentioned in medieval travelers' accounts.

Friar Orfali had done some work on the octagonal building in the 1920s. His plan showed the building as consisting of three concentric octagons. He found only four sides of the largest octagon, which was about 75 feet across; he assumed the other sides had been replaced by later construction. The second octagon was about 57 feet across; and the smallest 26 feet. The smallest octagon had rested on eight square pillars crowned by arches to hold the roof. The building had been paved with mosaics, traces of which remained. Inside the smallest octagon was an octagonal mosaic band of lotus flowers in the form of a chalice; in the center of this mosaic was

a beautiful peacock, an early Christian symbol of immortality. Unfortunately, the head and feet of the peacock had been destroyed.

Opinion regarding the octagonal building varied. Local guides invariably pointed it out to gullible tourists as the house of St. Peter, although its identification even as a private residence was not accepted by most scholars. Some suggested the concentric octagons were the public fountains of ancient Capernaum. The best scholarly view, however, was that it was an ancient church. Friar Orfali identified the building as a Byzantine baptistry, citing similar octagonal structures in Europe, such as San Giovanni in Fonte of Ravenna.

When Corbo and Loffreda renewed excavations in 1968, they discovered an apse together with a baptistry on the east side of the middle octagon—which was why the third or outer octagon did not close. The building was oriented by the apse to the east, the orientation of most ancient churches. The discovery of the eastward-oriented apse and the baptistry removed any doubt that the structure was in fact an ancient church. The Franciscans dated it

BLACK BASALT WALLS remain from houses at Capernaum in which Peter's contemporaries may have lived. The rough black basalt contrasts strikingly with the synagogue's finished white limestone.

The synagogue was built on a platform—which runs to the end of the photo at right—in order to conform to the rabbinic injunction (Tosephta. Megillah IV 23) to erect the synagogue at the town's highest point.

The construction of the basalt houses is identical to that of the house of St. Peter found beneath the octagonal church. Small stones were pounded between the large ones to strengthen the walls, but no mortar was used. The floors were also made of these rough basalt stones, often obtained from nearby wadis.

to the middle of the fifth century A.D. In its first phase, the church consisted of but two concentric octagons. The outer partial octagon was added later to form a portico on five of the eight sides—on the north, west, and south. The other three sides were occupied with the apse and two sacristies* on either side of the apse. The precise date of these additions has not been determined.

But why was the church built in the shape of an

* A sacristy is a room or building connected with a religious house, in which the sacred vessels, vestments, etc., are kept.

octagon? The answer is that octagonal churches were built to commemorate special events in Christian history which supposedly occurred at the site. For example, the Church of the Nativity in Bethlehem was built in an octagonal form by the Emperor Constantine in the fourth century A.D., supposedly directly over the cave where Jesus was born. The octagon in the Bethlehem church was intended to mark this spot. Presumably the octagonal church at Capernaum was intended to mark some other site of special importance in Christian history.

It is reasonable to assume, therefore, that this octagonal church at Capernaum was a memorial church. Some scholars believed that the octagonal church was built to memorialize Jesus's temporary residence in Capernaum and may well have been connected with ancient memories or traditions regarding the location of St. Peter's house, also called "the house of Simon and Andrew" in Mark 1:29.

When the Franciscan archaeologists, in their renewed excavations, dug beneath the mosaic floor

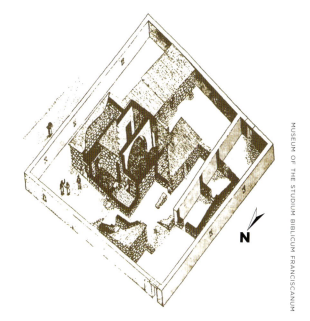

MUSEUM OF THE STUDIUM BIBLICUM FRANCISCANUM

HOUSE-CHURCH FROM THE FOURTH CENTURY. In this artist's reconstruction, we can see that the main room of St. Peter's first-century house has been renovated. Entrances have been added and an arch built over the center of the room supports a two-story high masonry roof. The original black basalt walls remain but they have been plastered, the room is now the central hall of a church. On the east side of this now venerated room is an atrium, or entryway, 10 feet wide and 27 feet long. Surrounding the house-church compound is a wall about 88 feet square.

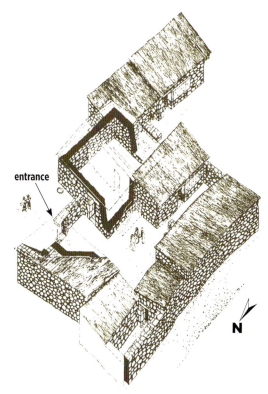

entrance

MUSEUM OF THE STUDIUM BIBLICUM FRANCISCANUM

AN ARTIST'S RECONSTRUCTION of the first century house that may have belonged to St. Peter. Like most houses of the early Roman period, it was a cluster of rooms structured around two courtyards. The center courtyard served as the family kitchen. Animals may have been kept in the other courtyard. The largest room of the house, delineated in black, later became the central hall of a house-church. At that time, a two-story arch was built inside the room to support an impressively high roof.

of the church they found some hard evidence to support this speculation.

Directly beneath the octagonal church they found the remains of another building which was almost certainly a church, judging from the graffiti on the walls left by Christian pilgrims. For example, a graffito scratched on one wall reads, "Lord Jesus Christ help thy servant..." A proper name followed in the original but is no longer readable. Another graffito reads, "Christ have mercy." Elsewhere on the walls crosses are depicted. The graffiti are predominantly in Greek, but some are also in Syriac and Hebrew. The presence of Hebrew graffiti suggests that the community may have been composed of Jewish-Christians at this time.

The central hall of this lower church is 27 feet long and 25 feet wide. The roof was supported by a large two-story-high arch over the center of the room. Two masonry piers made of worked basalt blocks, found against the north and south walls of the room, supported the arch. In addition to the bases of the piers, the excavators found two voussoirs, or wedge-shaped stones, from the arch that once supported the roof. The voussoirs were still covered with plaster and paint.

Two doors on the south and one on the north

St. Peter's house at Capernaum
(1st century A.D.)

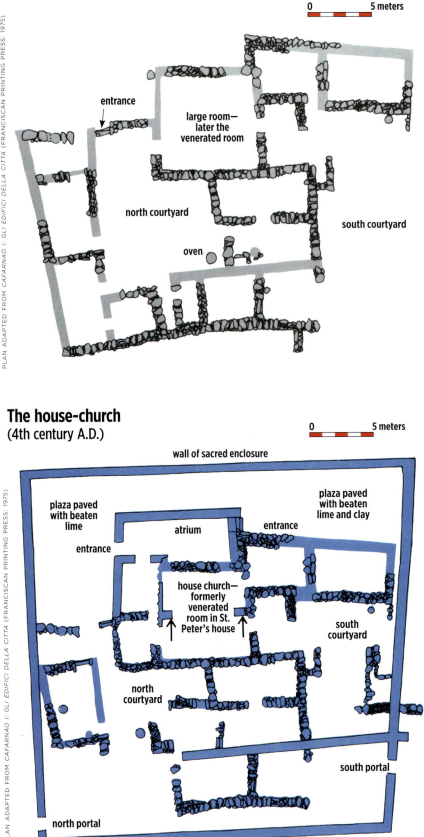

0   5 meters

PLAN ADAPTED FROM *CAFARNAO I: GLI EDIFICI DELLA CITTA* (FRANCISCAN PRINTING PRESS: 1975)

entrance

large room—
later the
venerated room

north courtyard

south courtyard

oven

The house-church
(4th century A.D.)

0   5 meters

PLAN ADAPTED FROM *CAFARNAO I: GLI EDIFICI DELLA CITTA* (FRANCISCAN PRINTING PRESS: 1975)

wall of sacred enclosure

plaza paved
with beaten
lime

plaza paved
with beaten
lime and clay

atrium

entrance

entrance

house church—
formerly
venerated
room in St.
Peter's house

south
courtyard

north
courtyard

south portal

north portal

How to Read the Plans

These plans show the archaeological remains of structures from the first to the fifth centuries found at the site of St. Peter's House at Capernaum.

In the first century the simple house of Peter occupied the site. Later in the first century the central room of Peter's house became the venerated room of a house-church. In the fourth century, an arch-supported roof was constructed over the room and a wall was built around the entire complex. In the fifth century, the foundations of the venerated room lay beneath the center of a church composed of two complete concentric octagons and a third incomplete octagon; the innermost octagon included eight square pillars supporting arches which, in turn, supported a domed roof.

In the gray plan (top) we see the remains of the first century house of Peter. The dark blue plan (below, left) shows the remains of the fourth century house-church. The arrows in this plan point to the basalt piers on which rested a two-story arch supporting the roof over the venerated room. Many of the walls used in the first century continued in use in the fourth and, therefore, are visible in both plans.

In the plan at right we see three layers of superimposed remains: gray is again used for structures from the first century; dark blue for structures added in the fourth century; and light blue for structures *added* in the fifth century. In order to see *all* the remains in use at each period it is necessary to look at the top plan for the first century, the second plan for the fourth century, and all walls enclosed in black lines in the plan at right for the fifth century. The enclosure wall of the entire complex, although built in the fourth century, was also used in the fifth century. The plan at right shows certain walls in gray which, although built in the first century, were also used in the fourth century (as can be seen in the second plan).

allowed easy access to the central hall. Smaller rooms (9 feet x 12 feet) adjoined the hall on the north. A long narrow room (10 feet x 27 feet) on the east is called the atrium by the excavators. Outside the atrium, which probably served as an entryway into the central hall, is a thoroughfare paved with hard-packed beaten earth and lime, providing a good solid surface for heavy foot traffic.

The central hall was plastered all over and then painted in reds, yellows, greens, blues, browns, white and black, with pomegranates, flowers, figs and geometric designs. Other objects almost surely appeared, but the fragmentary nature of the plaster makes interpretation difficult. The entire church

complex was surrounded by a wall about 88 feet long on each of its four sides.

This church complex we have just described was its final phase only, just before the octagonal church was built directly above it. This was how it existed in the late fourth century However, the origins of this fourth century church are of a far earlier time.

According to the excavators, the central hall of this church was originally built as part of a house about the beginning of the Early Roman period, around 63 B.C. Not all the house has been excavated, but almost 100 feet north to south and almost 75 feet east and west have been uncovered. This house was originally built of large, rounded wadi stones of the

The octagonal church
(5th century A.D., superimposed on
4th and 1st century remains)

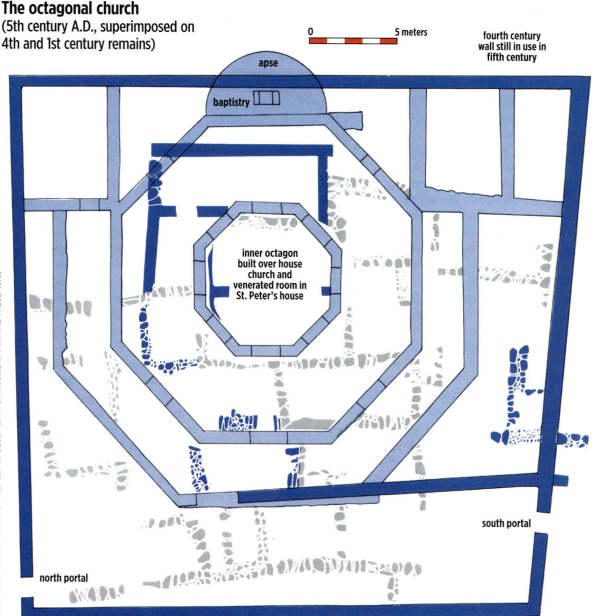

0   5 meters

fourth century
wall still in use in
fifth century

apse

baptistry

inner octagon
built over house
church and
venerated room in
St. Peter's house

south portal

north portal

PLAN ADAPTED FROM *CAFARNAO I: GLI EDIFICI DELLA CITTA* (FRANCISCAN PRINTING PRESS: 1975)

rough black basalt that abounds in the area. Only the stones of the thresholds and jambs of the doors had been worked or dressed. Smaller stones were pounded between the larger ones to make the wall more secure, but no mortar was used in the original house. Walls so constructed could not have held a second story, nor could the original roof have been masonry; no doubt it was made from beams and branches of trees covered with a mixture of earth and straw. (This is consistent with the tale of the paralytic let down through a hole in the roof). The archway was probably built inside the central room of the house in order to support a high roof when the house was later converted to a church.

The original pavement of the room also consisted of unworked black basalt stones with large spaces between. Here the excavators found pottery sherds and coins that helped date the original construction. (Such a floor of ill-fitting stones enables us easily to understand the parable of the lost drachma in Luke 15:8.)

The original house was organized around two interior courtyards, as was customary in the Roman period. The outside entrance on the east side opens directly into the north courtyard. This courtyard was probably the main work area for the family that lived here. A round oven, where the family's food was no doubt prepared, was found in the southwest corner of this courtyard.

This courtyard was surrounded by small rooms on the north and west. On the south was the largest room of the house. It was this room that later had the arch built into it so that its roof could be raised after the room became the central hall of the house-church. As originally built, the room had two entrances, one on the south and a second on the north. The room originally measured about 21 feet by 20 feet, a large room by ancient standards.

The southern door of this room led into the house's second courtyard. This courtyard may have been used for animals or for work areas associated with whatever house industry was engaged in by the owners. Curiously enough, several fishhooks were found beneath one of the upper pavements from the later house-church, although this does not prove that the inhabitants of the original house were fishermen.

For all intents and purposes, this house as originally built is indistinguishable from all other houses of ancient Capernaum. Its indoor living area is somewhat larger than usual, but overall it is about the same size as other houses. Its building materials are the usual ones. It was built with no more sophistication than the others in the region. In short, there is nothing to distinguish this house from its neighbors, except perhaps the events that transpired there and what happened to it later.

During the second half of the first century A.D., someone did mark this house off from its neighbors. Perhaps as early as the middle of the first century A.D. the floor, walls, and ceiling of the single large room of the house were plastered. This was unusual in ancient Capernaum. Thus far, this is the only excavated house in the city with plastered walls. In the centuries that followed, the walls were re-plastered at least twice. The floor too was replastered a number of times.

The pottery used in the room also changed when the walls were plastered. The pottery that dates to the period before the walls were plastered is much like the pottery found in other houses designed for domestic use—a large number of cooking pots, bowls, pitchers, juglets, and a few storage jars. Once the room was plastered, however, we find only storage jars and the remains of some oil lamps.

The activities associated with the building obviously changed. No longer was the preparing and serving of food a major activity. Judging from the absence of bowls, people were no longer eating on the premises. The only activity that persisted was the storage of something in the large, two-handled storage jars of the period. Unfortunately, we cannot be sure what was stored. Within the thin layers of lime with which the floor was plastered and re-plastered, the excavators found many pieces of broken lamps.

At this time in early Roman history the only rooms that were plastered in such poor houses were important ones in which groups of people regularly gathered. Plaster provides a reflective surface and aids illumination. Both the plastering and the absence of pottery characteristic of family use combine to suggest that the room, previously part of a private home, was now devoted to some kind of public use. In view of the graffiti that mention Jesus as "Lord" and "Christ" (in Greek), it is reasonable to conclude, though cautiously, that this may be the earliest evidence for Christian gatherings that has ever come to light.

We have already referred to the fact that during the approximately 300 years that the building served as a so-called house-church, over a hundred graffiti were scratched on the plastered walls. These include, by our count, 111 Greek inscriptions, 9 Aramaic, 6 or perhaps as many as 9 Syriac in the Estrangelo alphabet,* 2 Latin, and at least 1 Hebrew inscription. Various forms of crosses, a

---

*The Estrangelo alphabet is one of the most common of the Syriac alphabets. It probably first came into use in the first or second century A.D. and was most common in the third and fourth centuries A.D. Although its frequency then declined, it is still in use today.

RECONSTRUCTION of a first-century Capernaum house. This bird's-eye view shows a model of a house whose size, number of rooms, and building materials are all typical of houses built in Capernaum about 60 B.C. The simple stone walls of the one-story residence could not support a masonry roof. Instead, a crisscross of tree branches was used, augmented for some rooms with a mixture of earth and straw.

GARO NALBANDIAN, COURTESY MUSEUM OF THE STUDIUM BIBLICUM FRANCISCANUM

boat, and perhaps a monogram, composed of the letters from the name Jesus, also appeared.

According to the Franciscan excavators, the name of St. Peter appears at least twice in these inscriptions. Many scholars are highly skeptical of these readings—and with good reason. Unfortunately, the scholarly publication of these very difficult inscriptions does not allow completely independent verification of the excavators' conclusions because of the poor quality of the photographs. But even accepting the Franciscan expedition's drawings of what they see on these plaster fragments, there are still problems.**

Let us look more closely at these inscriptions allegedly referring to St. Peter. One, according to the excavators, is a Latin and Greek inscription that refers to "Peter, the helper of Rome." This of course would be astounding, if this is what it actually said. If we look at the photograph of the inscription, it is difficult to see anything more than a "mare's nest" of jumbled lines.

However, the epigrapher of the expedition, Emmanuele Testa, provides us with a drawing of the scratchings on the plaster fragment, which

appears to be a faithful reproduction of what we called the "mare's nest."

From this, the epigrapher extracted in another line drawing what the excavators see—letters in an inscription.

The excavators see XV scratched over the underlying inscription. We see instead two large XX's apparently scratched over the inscription in an effort to deface it, but this is a small point.

The excavators read the underlying inscription:

RO M AE BO ...
PETR US

The first four letters of the name Peter (PETR), we are told, are in the form of a monogram—a cluster of letters. "Rome" is in Latin, as is "Petrus." BO is taken as a Greek word BO[HΘDC] or some other Greek word from that root, meaning helper.

To the senior author of this article, the strokes which compose two of the letters of the name Peter, T (cocked to the right) and U (appearing as V in the drawing) are rather clearly part of the two XX's incised over the underlying inscription. So we are really left with pure ambiguity.

The word ROMAE is possible, but the MA does not look like anything at all to our eyes. Other readings are possible, especially because horizontal lines appear above the three groups of letters in

**See *Cafarnao, Vol. IV (I graffiti della casa di S. Pietro)* by Emmanuele Testa (Jerusalem: Franciscan Printing Press, 1972); and James F. Strange, "The Capernaum and Herodium Publications, Part 2," *Bulletin of the American Schools of Oriental Research*, No. 233 (1979), pp. 68–69.

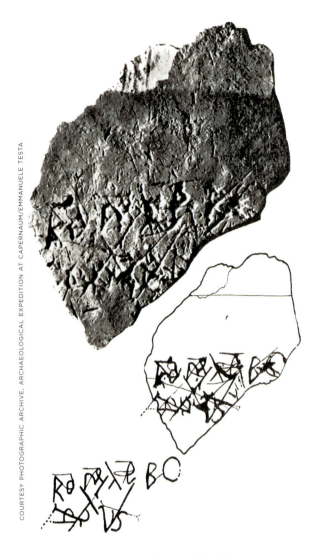

A "ST. PETER" GRAFFITO? The name "Peter" may appear in this "mare's nest" of lines (top) scratched on a wall of the Capernaum house-church.

The drawing (center) is an exact reproduction of the inscription. It was made by Emmanuele Testa, epigrapher for the Franciscan expedition that excavated the building in the late 1960s. To the Franciscan excavators, the lines form the words "Peter, the helper of Rome," but many scholars dispute this reading.

At bottom is another drawing made by Testa, this one an interpretation of the drawing of the "mare's nest" of lines. The excavators read:

RO M AE BO…

PETR US

ROMAE is Latin for Rome; PETRUS, Latin for Peter; and BO(HΘDC), Greek for helper.

Some scholars see two large X's scratched over the inscription in an apparent effort to deface it. The strokes the excavators claim for "T" and "U" in the so-called "Peter" are, in fact, part of the two XX's incised over the inscription. Also, the graffito shows horizontal marks above the groups of letters in the first line, indicating that these letter groups are Greek abbreviations. Thus, the meaning of the entire inscription is still a mystery.

COURTESY PHOTOGRAPHIC ARCHIVE, ARCHAEOLOGICAL EXPEDITION AT CAPERNAUM/EMMANUELE TESTA

the first line, which suggests that each of the three groups is a Greek abbreviation.

The excavators see a second reference to St. Peter in another graffito on a plaster fragment, this time in Latin but in Greek letters.

Π   Ε   Τ   Ρ   V   C
(Pi) (Epsilon) (Tau) (Rho) (Upsilon) (Lunate Sigma)

The excavators' photograph and drawing of the fragment are printed on page 457.

The first letter (Pi) seems clear on the left. The last letter (C) is broken off at the end of the fragment. According to the excavators, the third, fourth, and fifth letters (Tau, Rho and Upsilon) are combined in a monogram to form a cross, with another cross to the right. To the senior author of this article, however, critical elements in the putative monogram are part of two XX's defacing the underlying inscription, XX's similar to those in the other "Peter" inscription. Moreover, what the excavators see as a sigma appears rather clearly to be an omicron.

Even if these were references to the name Peter, they could well be references to pilgrims named Peter who wrote on these walls, rather than invocations of the name of St. Peter. For these reasons, we are skeptical of this alleged inscriptional support for identifying the original house as St. Peter's.

With what, then, are we left?

Was this originally St. Peter's house where Jesus stayed in Capernaum?

Reviewing the evidence, we can say with certainty that the site is ancient Capernaum. The house in question was located 84 feet south of the synagogue. Although the extant synagogue dates somewhere between the late second century and early fifth century, it is likely that an earlier synagogue stood on this same site.

The house in question was originally built in the late Hellenistic or early Roman period (about 60 B.C.). It was constructed of abundantly available, rough, black basalt boulders. It had a number of small rooms, two courtyards and one large room. When it was built, it was indistinguishable from all the other houses in the ancient seaside town.

Sometime about the middle of the first century A.D. the function of the building changed. It was no longer used as a house. Domestic pottery disappeared. The center room, including the floor, was plastered and replastered. The walls were covered with pictures. Only this center room was treated in this way. Christian inscriptions, including the name of Jesus and crosses, were scratched on the walls; some may possibly refer to Peter. Remnants of oil lamps and storage jars have been recovered. Fishing hooks have been found in between layers on the floor.

now become a house-church, an atrium was constructed in the fourth century about 27 feet long and 10 feet wide. Finally, a wall was built around the sacred compound.

This house-church survived into the mid-fifth century. Then precisely over the now plastered central room, an octagonal church was built, covering the same area and with the same dimensions. This was the kind of structure used to commemorate a special place in Christian history.

In addition, we know that as early as the fourth century, Christian pilgrims on visits to the site saw what they believed to be St. Peter's house. Sometime between 381 A.D. and 395 A.D. a Spanish nun named Egeria (Etheria) visited the site and reported in her diary that she had seen the house of St. Peter which had been turned into a church: "In Capernaum a house-church (*domus ecclesia*) was made out of the home of the prince of the apostles, whose walls still stand today as they were." A similar report appears in the diary of the anonymous sixth-century A.D. Italian traveler known as the Pilgrim of Piacenza. However, by this time the octagonal church had been constructed, so he refers to a church that had been built on the site: "We came to Capernaum to the house of St. Peter, which is now a basilica." Thus, even from this very early period, the site was associated with St. Peter's house.

Is this then the house of St. Peter? It cannot be confirmed—certainly not by inscriptions referring to St. Peter. But a considerable body of circumstantial evidence does point to its identification as St. Peter's house. Though we moderns search for proof, that hardly mattered to those ancient pilgrims who scratched their prayers on the walls of the house-church in the belief that this was, indeed, St. Peter's house. So, for that matter, what "proof" does a modern pilgrim need? ◪

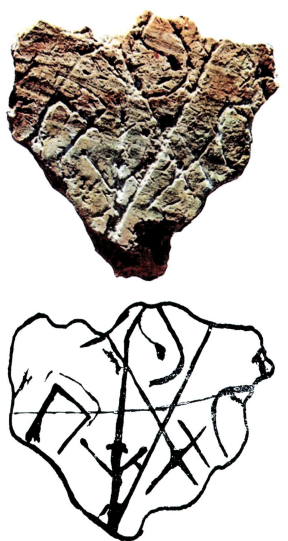

GREEK LETTERS FOR "PETER." This inscription is one of a hundred scratched on the walls of the Capernaum building that served as a church from about the mid-first century through the fourth century A.D.

A drawing shows the various marks on the plaster. The first letter on the left is clearly *pi*. The excavators also see the following letters: *epsilon* (E), *tau* (T), *rho* (R), *upsilon* (V) and *lunate sigma* (C). However, another interpretation is that the key strokes of these letters are really part of two XX's incised over the inscription, similar to the XX's in the other "Peter" graffito.

Even if one accepts the reading of "Peter," perhaps the inscription refers not to St. Peter, but to a pilgrim named Peter who visited the site sometime during these 300 years.

In a later century, two pilasters were erected on the north and south walls of this room; the lower parts of the pilasters have been found in the excavations. These pilasters supported a stone arch which in turn supported a new roof, no longer a light roof of branches, mud and straw, but a high masonry roof. On the eastern side of what had

Our always-astute readers noted minor errors in a couple of the picture captions in this article. They are corrected in the Queries and Comments section of the March/April 1983 issue of BAR.

Related Reading

Hershel Shanks and James F. Strange, "Synagogue Where Jesus Preached Found at Capernaum," BAR, November/December 1983.

John C.H. Laughlin, "Capernaum: From Jesus' Time and After," BAR, September/October 1993.

Hershel Shanks, "Where Mary Rested," BAR, November/December 2006.

Yitzhak Magen, "Bells, Pendants, Snakes and Stones," BAR, November/December 2010.

Cast Your Net

Upon the Waters

Fish and Fishermen in Jesus' Time

MENDEL NUN

FOR MORE THAN 50 YEARS, I have lived at Kibbutz Ein Gev on the shore of the Kinneret, the Sea of Galilee. For much of that time, I have been a fisherman. The Hebrew letter *nun* (N) means fish in Aramaic. My former name—I was born in Latvia—began with an *N*. When I became a fisherman, I simply took that first letter as my new surname.

I am continually surprised at how accurately the New Testament writers reflect natural phenomena on the lake. But we should not expect to find clear professional accounts of early fishing experiences in Biblical parables and vignettes, for several reasons.

First, the Gospel writers were already chronologically quite distant from Jesus' life on the lakeshore; and they did not intend to write historical texts, but rather stories with a religious message. The problem of translation from the original—a question that has long occupied scholars—creates additional difficulties. But if we look closely at ancient life on the lake, we can better understand the stories about the sea of Galilee, the scene of most of Jesus' ministry.

Fishermen and sailors were Jesus' earliest disciples and followers. It was to them that he first preached, standing on the shore of the lake. As his audience grew, he began to preach from fishing boats, and especially from a small boat that his disciples kept ready for him (Mark 3:9). For longer trips, to teach in the towns and villages of the region, Jesus sailed in the boats of the fishermen.

The name "Sea of Galilee" appears for the first

"CAST NETS AND MUSHT" could be the title of Duccio di Buoninsegna's painting, "The Calling of the Apostles Peter and Andrew," pictured here. Several clues in the Gospels indicate to Mendel Nun, chronicler of the ancient history of the Sea of Galilee, that a great draught of musht (known popularly as St. Peter's fish) filled the apostles' cast nets when they fished on the Sea of Galilee. But the Sienese artist (active 1278–1318/19) clearly did not glean the evidence from the Gospels that would have allowed him accurately to depict the fish, nets, place and time of the day.

time in the New Testament, but it is also called the Sea of Tiberias and the Sea, or Lake, of Gennesar or Gennesaret. (Tiberias is a city on the western shore of the lake; Gennesar or Gennesaret was a city and a plain on the western shore. Galilee is the region of the country in which the lake is situated.) In the Hebrew Bible, the lake is called by an older name: Yam Kinneret, or Sea of Kinneret. Kinneret (the name of an early pagan deity) is the name by which it is known in Israel today. In the Hebrew Bible, it is mentioned only four times, all in connection with the borders of the tribal allotments in the Promised Land (Numbers 34:11; Joshua 12:3, 13:27; and Deuteronomy 3:17).

For more than 5,000 years, fishing methods on the Sea of Galilee remained the same. Arab and Jewish fishermen from Tiberias preserved the ancient traditions until the middle of this century. Then things began to change: Invisible synthetic fibers replaced cotton thread, making it possible to fish in the daytime with the same nets used at night. New species of fish were introduced and indigenous species declined. Motors replaced oars and sails; electronic fish detectors were used to locate schools of fish. All this changed the face of the Sea of Galilee.

But there are still those of us who remember how it was done in an earlier time, and those traditions help us understand the Bible better.

Perhaps one of the best-known Biblical fishing references to the Sea of Galilee is in the Gospel of Luke (Luke 5:1–7). Jesus saw two empty boats on the shore of Tabgha, where fishermen from Capernaum stayed in the winter. The fishermen nearby were washing their nets. Jesus went into Simon's boat and preached. When he finished, he told Simon to put his nets back into the water. Simon answered that this would be useless; they had fished all night and caught nothing. But he and his men nevertheless got back into the boat and lowered their nets, as Jesus had told them. The nets enclosed a whole school of fish! The fishermen in Simon's boat called their partners in the other boat to help them. They filled both boats with fish. The fishermen became frightened by this miracle. Jesus told them not to be afraid: "Henceforth you will be catching men." When they returned, they left everything and followed Jesus.

I think we can identify the kind of fish caught, the kind of net Simon and his co-workers used and their fishing technique.

The previous night's fishing, which had produced nothing, involved a partnership of two boats. Indeed, until very recently, this was exactly how fishing was organized in the limited fishing area at Tabgha;

NAPHTALI

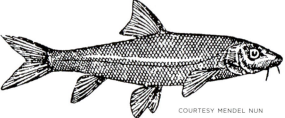

COURTESY MENDEL NUN

THE *BARBUS LONGICEPS*, or Long-Headed Barbel, named for the barbs at the corners of its mouth, is a popular Sabbath meal. The sleek, silvery fish can reach a length of 30 inches and can weigh up to 15 pounds—a big haul for a small fry.

without a partnership, conflict could easily arise.

Although the indigenous fish population of the Sea of Galilee consists of 18 species, only 10 are commercially important. The remainder are small inshore species, insignificant in number and quality. The commercially important fish can be divided into three groups, the last of which, I believe, is the one referred to in the story from Luke; but the other fish are no less interesting and sometimes have their own Biblical connections.

First, and quite outside of these three groups and of no economic importance locally, is the catfish

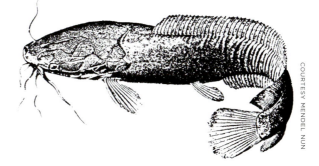

COURTESY MENDEL NUN

THE MUSTACHED FISH, or catfish, may not be eaten by Jews because it lacks scales, and "everything in the water that has not fins and scales is an abomination" (Leviticus 11:9–11). Because of this, the fish had diminished local commercial appeal.

(*Clarias lazera*), whose Hebrew name, *Sfamnun*, means mustached fish. It has no scales, so it may not be eaten by Jews (see Leviticus 11:9–12). This of course reduces its economic importance and excludes it as a candidate for the fish referred to in Luke. Nevertheless, it is the largest of the indigenous fish in the lake, sometimes growing to a length of 4 feet and weighing 25 pounds. It is the sole representative of the African family of catfish in Israel. The first-century A.D. Jewish historian Flavius Josephus noted that the same fish was found in the Nile, and on this basis supported the then-popular belief that there was an underground connection between the Nile and the Sea of Galilee, and that it emerged from the ground at the largest spring at Tabgha.

The first important group of indigenous fish in the lake is the Kinneret sardine, *Acanthobrama terrae sanctae*. It is the smallest of the commercial fish in the lake. Nevertheless, it is economically important; it constitutes more than half of the yearly catch from the lake—about 1,000 tons. At the height of the sardine season, tens of tons of sardines are caught every night. This is why, already in antiquity, they were conserved by pickling. The center of this industry was the town of Magdala, hence its name *Migdal Nunia*, or Migdal of the fish, and *Tarichea* in Greek, meaning the place where fish are salted. In ancient times, pickled sardines were an important element of diet throughout the country—especially for those who lived near the lake.

The second group of important indigenous fish in the lake is the biny group (Barbels), which consists of three species of the Carp family (*Cyprinideae*). The identifying characteristics of this family are the barbs at the corners of the mouth; from these comes the Semitic name "Biny," which means hair (in the Babylonian Talmud the fish are called "Binita"). Of the three members of the group, only two have major economic importance—the Long-Headed Barbel (*Barbus longiceps*), a handsome troutlike fish with a narrow silvery body and pointed head that feeds on mollusks and snails at the lake bottom and on small fish, especially sardines, and the *Barbus Canis*, "Kishri" in Arabic, meaning "scaley." The Kishri is a predatory fish, feeding on small fry, and is therefore always found near schools of sardines, which are caught together with this fish. Both barbels are well fleshed and popular as the fish dish for the Sabbath and feasts. The Talmud describes how Tiberias fishermen brought seven barbels as a gift to the Patriarch Yehuda haNasi (2nd–3rd century A.D.) during his stay in the city. The third species of Barbel, the Hafafi (*Varicorhinus damascinus*), feeds on decaying matter found in mud, which affects the flavor; therefore its value is not great.

The third and largest category of indigenous fish is the musht, which means "comb" in Arabic, because the five species of this group have a long dorsal fin that looks like a comb. The biggest, the most common and the most important of these is the *Tilapia Galilea*, which can reach a length of 1.5 feet and weigh about 4.5 pounds. The body has a silvery color, which gives it the Arabic nickname *musht abiad*, meaning white musht. With the cooling of the waters of the lake as winter starts, the musht congregate and move in shoals, especially toward the northern part of the lake and the warm springs. When the water warms up in the spring, they disperse and we find pairs of these fish living together for as long as two months—a phenomenon unusual for fish. After a prolonged courtship, the pair digs a hollow in the soft bottom of the lake near the shore or in a lagoon and deposits its eggs. After fertilization, the parents take the eggs into their mouths for two or three weeks, until they hatch. Even after the young are hatched, the parents keep

FROM THE PICTORIAL ENCYCLOPEDIA OF FISHES

DOMESTIC LIFE ON THE LAKE BOTTOM. A musht "couple" spend up to two months together—an unusually long time for fish—before digging a hole for their eggs. After the eggs are fertilized, the musht, popularly known as St. Peter's fish, carry the eggs in their mouths until they hatch.

watch over the young fry for a few days; this is the source of its modern Hebrew name *ammun—am* in Hebrew meaning nurse, and *nun* meaning fish.

The musht is the only large fish in the lake that moves in shoals, which of course is a key to the identification of the fish in the story in Luke, although not the only one.

The flat shape of the musht makes it especially suitable for frying. The skeleton consists of an easily detachable backbone and relatively few small bones, and thus it is easy to eat. It has long been known as St. Peter's fish. Recently, it has even been exported under this name. But, alas, the name is a misnomer.

Presumably the fish got its name because of an incident recorded in the Gospel of Matthew (Matthew 17:24–27). In this episode, the tax collectors come to Capernaum to collect the half-shekel Temple tax that each Jew was required to pay annually. Jesus tells Peter, "Go to the sea and cast a hook, and take the first fish that comes up, and when you open its mouth you will find a shekel; take that and give it to them for me and yourself."

The musht was probably given the name St. Peter's fish because of this miracle. However, this cannot have been the fish Peter caught with a hook and line. The reason is simple: Musht feeds on plankton and is not attracted by other food. It is therefore caught with nets, and not with hook and line. The fishermen on the lake have, since time immemorial, used a hook baited with sardine to fish for barbels, which are predators and bottom feeders. Peter almost surely caught a barbel. There can be only one explanation for the confusing change of name. It was good for tourism! The Sea of Galilee has always attracted pilgrims; musht (today raised mostly in ponds) is part of the unique local cuisine. It is delicious, especially when freshly fried. In ancient times, just as today, the fishing boats delivered their catch to the eating places on shore. Indeed, the proverbial metaphor for speed in the Talmud is "as from

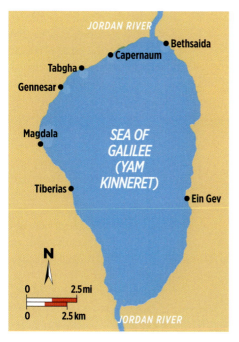

the sea into the frying pan." This expression was part of daily speech in Tiberias and clearly refers to musht and not barbels; the latter are best when boiled.

The first Christians were local people and were therefore familiar with the various fish. They of course knew that the fish Peter caught could only have been a barbel and not a musht. However, as pilgrims began to come from distant regions, it no doubt seemed good for business to give the name "St. Peter's fish" to the musht being served by the early lakeside eating houses. The most popular and easily prepared fish acquired the most marketable name! But even if Peter did not catch a musht, he deserves to have his name associated with the best fish in the lake.

Returning to the miracle of the fish caught in Luke (5:1–7), additional clues that the fish were musht are the kind of net referred to and the place and the time of the event. Several kinds of nets were used in the Sea of Galilee. The most important were the seine, the cast net and the trammel net.

The seine, or dragnet, is the oldest type of net. Until recently, it was the most important fishing method on the lake. The seine net is referred to in both the Hebrew Bible and the Talmud (*herem*).

The seine is essentially a dragnet made of netting shaped like a long wall, 750 to 1,000 feet long, about 5 feet high at its "wings" and 25 feet high at the center. Its footrope is weighted with sinkers, while the head-rope has cork floats. The dragnet is spread 100 yards or more from shore and parallel to it. It is then hauled toward the shore with towing lines attached to each end by a team of 16 men for large nets, or a smaller team for smaller nets. From Egyptian tomb paintings from the third millennium B.C., as well as other sources, we know that this fishing method was widely used in ancient times.

I remember in the 1940s and 1950s sailing out in the early morning and arranging the heavy seine on the "table" of the stern of the boat. When we arrived at the shore of the fishing ground, half the crew would alight and take the first rope. We would then sail out with the trailing line until it was pulled straight. The boat would then turn and sail parallel to the shore until the net was "spread," and then

TO MARKET, TO MARKET, fishermen bring their haul of Kinneret sardines, the smallest commercially important fish in the Sea of Galilee. The sardine accounts for more than half of the yearly catch from the lake. Pickled, this fish constituted an important part of the diet of those who lived by the sea in ancient times. The pickling industry was located in Magdala, the home of Mary Magdalene, on the western shore of the sea.

NAPHTALI

THE SEINE NET, or dragnet, up to 1000 feet long and 5 to 25 feet high, is dropped by fishermen about 100 to 300 yards from shore and stretched parallel to the land. Cork on the net's head-rope keeps it upright while sinkers pull down the footrope, creating a wall of mesh under water—sure to trap any fish in its path. Fishermen on the shore haul in the net by pulling on tow ropes attached to each end of the net. A good catch can bring a few hundred pounds of fish.

turn back to the shore trailing the second set of ropes. On reaching the shore, the remaining half of the crew would alight and take the end of the other towing line, leaving the boat on the shore.

The whole team would then harness themselves to the ropes and pull the net to the shore. The sinkers had dragged the net to the bottom, the floats had lifted the head-rope, and the net formed a rectangular wall that advanced to the shore with its lower edge at the bottom of the lake. The two groups would climb up the beach, moving toward each other.

The whole operation took an hour or more. A good catch could bring in hundreds of pounds of fish. After the fish were sorted, the net was again arranged on the stern, the ropes were coiled and placed in the boat, and the work started all over again at another location. This would be repeated as often as eight times during a day's fishing.

An ancient tradition preserved in the Talmud* relates that the Biblical hero Joshua bin Nun granted exclusive fishing rights in the Kinneret to the tribe of Naphtali, entitling that tribe to set seines (*herem*) around the entire shoreline of the lake. To enable them to exercise this right, a strip of land at the southern tip of the lake belonging to the tribe of Gad was added to the lot of Naphtali. In width it was equal to "the full seine rope," about 150 feet.

The prophet Habakkuk says that God sometimes treats men as the fisherman catches fish. "He drags them out with his seine, he gathers them in his trapnet" (Habakkuk 1:15). The prophet Ezekiel mentions three times the "place of the spreading of

*Babylonian Talmud, Bava Kama 81a, 81b; Tosefta Bava Kama 8.17.

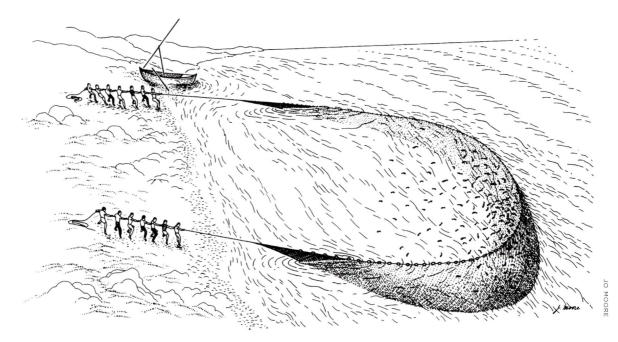

JO MOORE

FROM F. W. FARRAR, *THE LIFE OF CHRIST*

WARY OF HIS SHADOW alerting the fish, a fisherman throws a cast net. The circular net (its diameter measures about 20 to 25 feet) is tossed from shallow water, as shown at left in this 19th-century etching, or from a boat, as in the photo below. Lead sinkers plunge the net to the bottom of the sea. Fishermen then dive down after the net and either remove the trapped fish individually through the mesh or carefully pull together the edges of the net and carry up the net to the surface with the catch inside.

seines," referring to the practice of drying seines by laying them flat on the ground (Ezekiel 26:5, 26:14, and 47:10).

The seine net is referred to metaphorically in the Gospel of Matthew when Jesus explains the kingdom of heaven:

> "The kingdom of heaven is like a seine net [Greek, *sagene*]** which was spread into the sea and gathered fish of every kind; when it was full, men drew it ashore and sat down, and sorted the good into vessels but threw away the bad" (Matthew 13:47–48).

This exactly fits the function of the seine. It is spread into the sea, then dragged to the shore; in the process all kinds of fish are caught, which the fishermen sitting on the shore sort out. The "bad" ones refer to the scaleless catfish, forbidden by Jewish law and not even offered for sale.

There is one inaccuracy in the Biblical description, however. The words "when it was full" seem to indicate that there was a waiting period for the net to fill. The basic feature of seine fishing is to start hauling immediately, as soon as the net is spread. If this is not done, the fish will escape and the whole operation fails. We may assume this slight inaccuracy is due to a desire to emphasize the theological message of the parable.

A second kind of net, a cast net, is used by a single fisherman. It is circular, about 20 to 25 feet

**The Greek word is *sagene*, from which seine is derived. It would be more accurate to translate it as seine net, rather than simply net.

COURTESY MENDEL NUN

in diameter, with lead sinkers attached to the edge. The fisherman arranges the net on his right arm and, standing in shallow water or in a boat, throws it on the water, where it is pulled down like a parachute by the lead, finally sinking to the bottom. There are two ways of retrieving the catch. The fisherman may dive down to the net, pull the fish through the meshing one by one and put them into a pouch. Or he may gather all the lead sinkers together, lifting the edges carefully over the bottom. He then takes the net up into the boat with the catch inside. When cast from shallow water, and especially if the

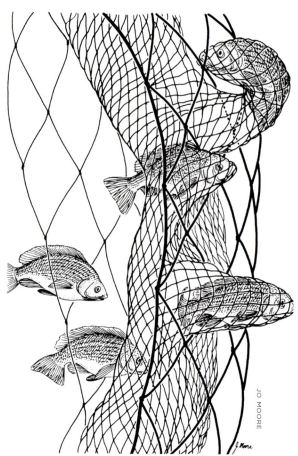

THE MORNING AFTER a night of fishing, fishermen disentangle their catch from the trammel net, wash out the net and then hang it up to dry, as shown in the photograph from Kibbutz Ein Gev around 1940.

The trammel net is the only net used in ancient times that still today is common on the Sea of Galilee. The net has three walls, with mesh of increasing density, as in the drawing. Fish pass easily through the outer walls, with their looser netting, only to find themselves caught in the inner, tightly woven wall. Attempts to push through or retreat entangle them further.

catch is heavy, the net is dragged to the shore.

Like the seine, the cast net is an ancient device. Complete cast nets have been found in Egyptian tombs dating to the second millennium B.C. Two kinds were used in the Sea of Galilee, one for large fish and the other for sardines. The sardine cast net had a small mesh and a system of cords for retrieving it. The cast net for bigger fish had a larger mesh and heavier sinkers to prevent the fish from escaping before the net reached the bottom. In using the cast net, the fisherman must approach his prey silently and without casting a shadow.

The cast net, too, is referred to in the prophecy of Ezekiel, in which the Lord says: "I will therefore spread out my net [cast net] over you with a company of many people; and they shall bring you up in my seine" (Ezekiel 32:3).

The cast net is mentioned by name (the Greek word *amphiblestron* means "to throw around") in Mark's Gospel (and its parallel in Matthew). Jesus sees Simon and his brother Andrew throwing cast nets and says to them: "'Follow me and I will make you fishers of men.' And immediately they left their nets and followed him" (Mark 1:16–18/Matthew 4:19–20).

The third type of net is the trammel net, the only one used in ancient times that is widely used on the lake today. Unlike other nets that have only one "wall," this is a compound net consisting of three layers held together by a single corked head-rope and a single leaded footrope. The identical outermost and innermost walls are 6 feet high with large meshes measuring 5 inches from knot to knot. The middle layer is made up of a fine meshed net. It is higher than the other two walls and hangs loosely between them. It can slip in and out between the other two walls. The trammel net has another special characteristic: It is always used with at least five such units attached to each other. Each unit is over 100 feet long, so the total assemblage is at least 500 feet long.

One type of trammel net was used for catching musht and another for barbels; they differed in thickness of thread and size of mesh. In the Roman period, fishing nets were made of linen thread; a section of linen net from the time of the Second Jewish Revolt against Rome (132–135 A.D.) was found in a cave near Ein Gedi.

When I used to fish with a trammel net, we would meet on shore in early evening, mending our nets and tying them together while arranging them on the stern of the boat. Sailing or rowing to the fishing grounds, we would quietly lower the net into the water so that it formed a wide curve, with the open side parallel to the shore. The leaded footrope pulled the net to the floor of the lake, and the floating line kept the net upright. In deep water, the net could be spread in different shapes, even in spiral form. After the net had settled, it would stand like a wall on the lake floor. Gourds, and later empty tin cans, were used as floats, tied to the two ends of the net, serving as signs in the dark to mark the position of the net.

Then the boat would enter the area between the net and the shore. We would make noise and turbulence by splashing with our oars and stamping on the bottom of the boat. The frightened fish would dive to the bottom and, in their flight toward deep water, find themselves facing the net. The fish would pass easily through the large mesh of the first layer, but immediately come to the narrow meshing of the middle layer. Pushing against it takes the fish through the third wall. Trying to retreat, he finds himself hopelessly entangled in a kind of net bag. The net was hauled out and the fish disentangled by hand, one by one. The net would then be prepared for the next operation, and the boat would move on.

Usually a trammel net is lowered and hauled up 10 to 15 times during a night's work. A good night's catch can bring 100 to 200 pounds of fish. When a trammel net is lowered around a school of fish during the musht season, hundred of pounds may be caught. Veteran fishermen speak of memorable single hauls of as much as half a ton.

When the catch is large, the fish are not extracted one by one; instead the net is hauled into the boat like a bundle with the fish entangled inside, and the

ANCIENT LINEN NET. This net from the second century A.D., found in a cave near Ein Gedi on the shore of the Dead Sea, closely resembles modern nets.

fishermen spend considerable time disentangling them.

When the night's work is finished, the sections of the net are separated, and each part is washed and rinsed in the lake so that it will be free of silt. Then it is hung up to dry on poles or on a wall. The process of washing a net in the morning is specific only to the trammel net.

Traditionally, fishing with the trammel net has been done at night or at dusk, when the fish cannot see the threads of the net; during the day, they would avoid it.

The Hebrew Bible refers to entangling nets as *metzuda*, or *matzod* ("trap" in Hebrew). The writer of the Book of Ecclesiastes uses nets to express his pessimistic view of the fate of mankind. "For man does not know his time. Like fish that are taken ["entangled," in the Hebrew text] in an evil net…so the sons of men are snared" (Ecclesiastes 9:12).

In Job these nets symbolize a situation from which there is no escape: "Know then that God has put me in the wrong, and encompassed me with his [entangling] net" (Job 19:6).

When the trammel net is used in a particular way in combination with another net it is called a veranda net. This net was used by day to catch wily leaping fish like musht. (In the Mediterranean, it is used to catch grey mullet, another leaping fish.) The veranda technique is effective with fish that move in shoals, another characteristic of the musht (and grey mullet).

Here is how the veranda net works: As soon as a

COURTESY MENDEL NUN

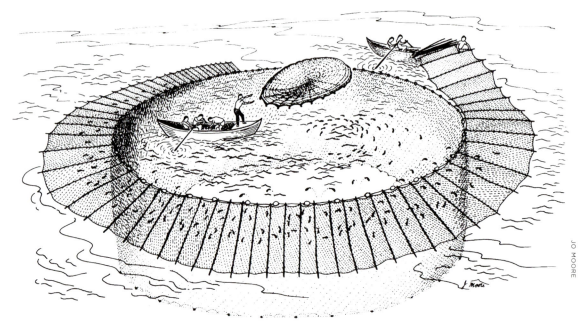

JO MOORE

THE VERANDA METHOD, depicted in the photo and drawing above, catches even the wiliest leaping fish. One net encircles a shoal of fish in a barrel of mesh while a second net, a trammel net, is spread on the water's surface and kept afloat with reeds, creating a kind of ledge around the net barrel. Fish that jump over the barrel's rim are trapped in the floating trammel net while fish remaining in the barrel are caught in cast nets that are thrown from a boat into the barrel, as shown in the drawing, and retrieved by divers.

school of musht is detected, usually with the help of an observer on shore, the school is surrounded by a net and enclosed in a kind of barrel extending from the lake bottom to the surface. As soon as the school is thus contained, a second boat comes to spread a trammel net horizontally around the "barrel." The horizontal trammel net, attached to reeds, floats on the surface around the edge of the barrel. When the musht try to escape by jumping over the rim, they become entangled in the floating horizontal trammel net. In order to startle the fish and make them jump, more trammel nets are spread out in a spiral within the barrel. Finally, those brave and cautious fish that do not jump over the barrel rim are caught by cast nets thrown into the center of the barrel. These nets, as we have seen, must be retrieved by divers.

Now we can appreciate more fully what happened in the story described at the beginning of this article in Luke.

While Jesus is preaching from the boat, he sees a school of musht nearing the shore, as often happens during the morning hours of the winter. Following Jesus' instruction, Simon's boat immediately takes off. The trammel nets, having been already washed, are lowered at the spot indicated by Jesus. The catch is enormously successful! In fact, the nets are so full that they begin to tear as they are hauled into the boats (Luke 5:6). There isn't room for the overflowing nets on the one boat.

Simon's crew calls to their partners' boat for assistance. The boat swiftly arrives and takes some sections of the nets on board.

It is clear that a trammel net was used, for the text uses the plural "nets." Only the trammel net consists of more than one net.

The miracle in Luke is not unlike the recollections of many veteran Kinneret fishermen who even today recall extraordinary catches of musht with a single haul of a trammel. It is an experience that cannot be repeated today: The musht population has been decimated by the extreme efficiency of modern fishing.

The story in Luke continues:

"When Simon Peter saw [the enormous catch], he fell down at Jesus' knees, saying, 'Depart from me, for I am a sinful man, O Lord.' For he was astonished, and all that were with him, at the catch of fish which they had taken; and so also were James and John, sons of Zebedee, who were partners with Simon. And Jesus said unto Simon, 'Do not be afraid; henceforth you will be catching men.' And when they had brought their boats to land, they left everything and followed him" (Luke 5:8–11).

A parallel to this miracle story is told in John 21:1–9, with some slight variations. Again it occurred "just as day was breaking." The night before, the fishermen had caught nothing. In the morning Jesus told them to "cast the net on the right side of the boat." When they did, they could not haul in the net for the quantity of fish in it. Then, "when Simon Peter heard that it was the Lord, he put on his clothes, for he was stripped for work, and sprang into the sea. But the other disciples came in a [small] boat, dragging the net full of fish, for they were not far from the land, but about a hundred yards off.'"

This is a new element: Peter's dive into the water implies that the trammel net was used here by the veranda method. As we know, in this method two boats work together. In the final stage of this strategy a cast net is thrown over the "barrel" to catch those cautious fish that have not jumped over the rim of the barrel onto the floating trammel net that surrounds it, veranda fashion. The cast net, after being thrown into the bottom of the barrel, must be retrieved by a diving fisherman. That is what Peter is doing here—retrieving the parachutelike cast net after it has fallen to the bottom. Incidentally, the distance—"about a hundred yards off" the shore—also fits with the use of the veranda method.

But this is not the end of the story in John. Jesus asks Simon to bring a few fish. Simon obeys, but instead of bringing fish from the full load in the boats, he hauls a new net up to the shore (John 21:11). It is clear that the reference is not to the nets already in the boat. This new net that Simon hauls alone could be only a cast net, which can be cast and hauled in by just one man. A seine, like a trammel net, requires a crew; furthermore, the seine cannot be used on the rocky shore of Tabgha, where, according to Christian tradition, the story takes place.

Hauling up his cast net, Simon finds a catch of 153 large fish—musht, of course, because no other fish could be caught in this time and place. This is the area where musht schools concentrate in the winter. Such a catch is seen as a miracle. But of course, 153 fish would be a minor miracle compared to the exploit of the two fully loaded boats, previously recounted. Apparently John added another tale, not mentioned in Luke—the tale of a miraculous catch with a cast net.

The study of these Biblical excerpts about fishing on the Sea of Galilee and the details of the craft reveals to us a hitherto unknown world—one not found in any ether source. This is the world of Jewish fishermen, living and working on the lake during the crucial period toward the end of the time of the Second Temple. The picture that emerges is rich in its simplicity, and is centered on a search for answers to life's basic questions. 🦐

We received a number of interesting letters in response to this article. Read them in Queries and Comments in the March/April 1994 issue.

Related Reading
Mendel Nun, "Ports of Galilee," BAR, July/August 1999.

The Galilee

Boat 2,000-Year-Old Hull Recovered Intact

SHELLEY WACHSMANN

A SEVERE DROUGHT GRIPPED ISRAEL in 1985 and 1986. The winter rains barely came. Water was pumped from the Sea of Galilee to irrigate parched fields throughout the country. Predictably, the Kinneret (the Hebrew name of the freshwater inland lake also known as the Sea of Galilee) shrank. Wide expanses of lakebed, normally covered with water, were exposed.

Moshe and Yuval Lufan live with their families on Kibbutz Ginnosar on the northwest shore of the lake. Avid amateur archaeologists, Moshe and Yuval frequently explored the newly exposed lakebed for ancient remains.

In January 1986 they were examining an area south of the kibbutz, where a tractor stuck in the mud had churned up some ancient bronze coins. Nearby they found a few ancient iron nails, and shortly afterwards they saw the oval outline of a boat, entirely buried in the mud.

Of course it could have been a 19th or 20th-century boat as easily as an ancient one. The brothers asked their father, a fisherman of 20 years, whether he had ever heard of a modern boat sinking anywhere near this site. "No" was his reply. Besides, he pointed out, the boat was buried so deeply in the mud that it must have been there for a very long time.

"Ask Mendel," was the father's advice.

Mendel Nun is unique. A member of Kibbutz Ein Gev, on the east side of the lake, Mendel has made

THE GALILEE BOAT, resurrected after being buried in lake mud for some 2,000 years, makes its 550-yard voyage to the Yigal Allon Museum at Kibbutz Ginnosar. Subsequently, a crane lifted the boat ashore. The conservator, Orna Cohen, had decided that the sea provided the best means for transporting the 26-foot-long boat from the excavation site to the museum. The boat was wrapped in buoyant polyurethane for protection.

Based upon the boat's construction techniques, associated artifacts and radiocarbon dates, the boat has been dated to between the first century B.C. and the late first century A.D. It is probably the type of boat that was used by Jesus and his disciples in their many travels upon the Sea of Galilee and by the Jesus in the nautical battle of Migdal.

the Kinneret—in all its aspects from archaeology to zoology—his specialty. He is widely known as Israel's number one "Kinneretologist."

Mendel visited the site, but could offer no opinion as to whether the buried boat was ancient or modern. However, he notified Yossi Stefanski, the local inspector for the Department of Antiquities, of the discovery, and Stefanski in turn notified me as the Department's Inspector of Underwater Antiquities.

On Tuesday, February 4, 1986, I returned from a coastal survey on the Mediterranean to find a note on my desk—something about a boat, possibly ancient, in the Kinneret. The next day I drove to Ein Gev with my colleague Kurt Raveh to pick up Mendel; from there we went to meet the Lufan brothers at Ginnosar.

Over coffee and cake, Yuval and Moshe told us about their discovery. Everyone wanted to know whether the boat was ancient.

I explained that ancient boats found in the Mediterranean were built in an unusual way. The planks of the hull were edge-joined with

WHERE'S THE BOAT? Buried in the mud beneath Yuval Lufan's feet, the Galilee boat revealed its presence by a faint oval outline. Lufan and his brother Moshe, both residents of Kibbutz Ginnosar, discovered the boat while combing the Sea of Galilee's newly exposed lakebed for remains of ancient craft. Consecutive winters of below average rainfall had caused a dramatic drop in the sea's water level. The mudbed in which the boat was discovered is normally well under water, beyond the reach of amateur archaeologists. Even as the excavation proceeded, the lake returned and threatened to engulf the site. Only the rapid construction of a temporary dike enabled the archaeologists to finish their work.

"mortise-and-tenon" joints that were held in place with wooden pegs. This form of construction has been found as early as the 14th–13th centuries B.C. (it was used in the famous Ulu Burun [Kas] wreck, now being excavated off the coast of Turkey) and continued to be used through the Roman period. All we had to do was scrape away the mud from the top of the uppermost strake (as the continuous lines of planks extending from bow to stern are called) to see whether we could find the dark rectangular remains of the "mortise-and-tenon" joints with round dot-like heads of wooden pegs. This would be the telltale sign that the boat was ancient—assuming, of course, that Kinneret boats developed in a parallel fashion to Mediterranean craft.

The five of us bundled into our jeep and drove to the site. Kurt and I quickly excavated a small section at midship. As we carefully removed the mud, "mortise-and-tenon" joints appeared. They were locked with wooden pegs, the round heads easily visible.

The boat was ancient! This was the first time an ancient boat had been discovered in the Kinneret.

In our excitement, we hardly noticed that it had begun to rain. Suddenly, a torrent of water descended on us. We ran for the jeep. It rained for perhaps a minute and then stopped as suddenly as it had begun. We got out of the jeep and saw a beautiful double rainbow cascading into the Kinneret—straight out of Central Casting, a portent of things to come.

We stood on the shore speculating about the date of the wreck and how it had sunk. Our initial thought was that the boat might have been used by Jews in the First Jewish Revolt against Rome (67–70 A.D.) and sunk by the Romans in the famous Battle of Migdal.

As we stood on the shore watching the rainbows fade, Mendel recounted the story as it was told by the first-century Jewish historian Josephus.

At the outbreak of the revolt in 67 A.D., the Jews prepared a war fleet at Migdal (the home of Mary Magdalene, about a mile south of the site where the boat was discovered). This fleet consisted of fishing boats provisioned for battle. Tiberias, a large town at the southern end of the lake, soon surrendered

COURTESY ISRAEL DEPT. OF ANTIQUITIES AND MUSEUMS/PHOTO: SHELLEY WACHSMANN

A BRILLIANT RAINBOW arcs across the Galilee sky. Like a favorable portent, the rainbow appeared shortly after the archaeologists verified that the buried boat was ancient.

to Vespasian. The Romans then built a large fortified camp between Tiberias and Migdal.

The Jews from Migdal, under Jeshua Ben Shafat, carried out a daring raid on the camp that caught the Romans by surprise. When the Romans managed to organize themselves, the Jews effected an orderly retreat, and taking to their boats, rowed out into the lake. When they reached bowshot range, they anchored "phalanx-like" opposite the Romans and engaged them in an archery battle.

The Romans then attacked Migdal, massacring the Jews in the city. Many of the Jews sought to escape by boat. Those who managed to do so took refuge on the lake, keeping as far out of range of the Romans as they could.

The next day, Vespasian ordered craft to be built to pursue the Jews in their boats. These were quickly

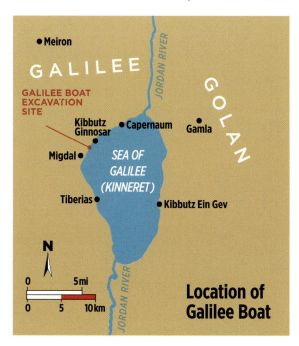

Meiron

GALILEE

GALILEE BOAT EXCAVATION SITE

JORDAN RIVER

Kibbutz Ginnosar

Capernaum

Gamla

GOLAN

Migdal

SEA OF GALILEE (KINNERET)

Tiberias

Kibbutz Ein Gev

N

0   5mi
0   5   10km

JORDAN RIVER

Location of Galilee Boat

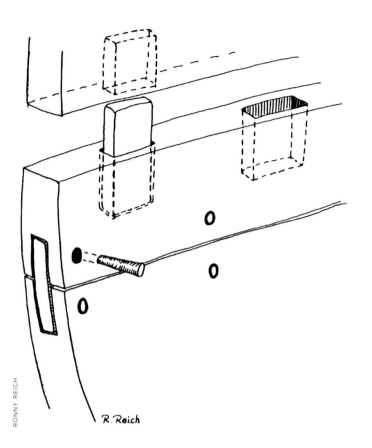

RONNY REICH

R. Reich

WHEN TELLTALE SIGNS of mortise-and-tenon joints appeared, the excavators knew they had found an ancient boat. Two round-headed wooden nails, right and left of center (below), peek out of a small section of the uppermost plank. In antiquity, Mediterranean shipbuilders devised the mortise-and-tenon method of joining the hull planks to one another (drawing, above). Instead of overlapping adjacent planks and fastening them together, shipbuilders placed the planks in an edge-to-edge position and joined them by means of wooden links (tenons) inserted in slots (mortises) carved in the two planks. The tenons were then firmly secured within the mortises by pegs through the plank and its tenon. When the craft was placed in water, the wood swelled, forming a watertight fit. This joining technique has been discovered in vessels dated as early as the 14th–13th centuries B.C.; it went out of use in the Byzantine period.

prepared. Roman archers and infantry armed with swords and javelins were stationed on the Roman vessels, and battle was soon joined with the refugees on the lake.

In the ensuing battle the Jews "were sent to the bottom, boats and all." Some tried to escape by breaking through the line of Roman vessels, but to no avail. The Romans reached them with their lances or jumped into their boats and killed them with their swords. Those who fell into the water were dispatched with arrows, while any who tried to climb on to the Roman vessels were beheaded or had their arms cut off by the Romans.

The remaining Jewish boats were driven to land, and the shore became a killing field. Describing the aftermath of the battle, Josephus wrote:

> "During the days that followed, a horrible stench hung over the region, and it presented an equally horrifying spectacle. The beaches were strewn with *wrecks* and swollen bodies, which, hot and clammy with decay, made the air so foul that the catastrophe that plunged the Jews in mourning revolted even those who had brought it about. Such was the outcome of this naval engagement. The dead, including those who earlier fell in the defense of the town (Migdal), numbered 6,700."

I remember thinking that the battle of Migdal was the nautical equivalent of Masada. Was the buried boat we were looking at a wreck that had washed up on that vermillion beach?

During the next two days we carried out a probe excavation around the boat. We opened a few small sections along its length to determine its state of preservation and to try to date it more accurately. During this excavation, we found two pottery

COURTESY ISRAEL DEPT. OF ANTIQUITIES AND MUSEUMS/PHOTO: SHELLEY WACHSMANN

COURTESY ISRAEL DEPT. OF ANTIQUITIES AND MUSEUMS/PHOTO: TSILA SAGIV

COOKING POT, left, and oil lamp. These beautifully preserved pottery vessels date respectively from the mid-first century B.C. to the mid-second century A.D. and from the first to the second centuries A.D. The oil lamp was found inside the boat, and the cooking pot was unearthed just outside the boat.

COURTESY ISRAEL DEPT. OF ANTIQUITIES AND MUSEUMS/PHOTO: DANNY FRIEDMAN

THE BOAT EMERGES from the muck, on the first night of digging. The drought had broken, and forecasts were calling for more rain. Racing the rising lake waters, the team of experts and local volunteers was forced to work day and night. By digging at night, however, they risked damaging or losing smaller artifacts not visible in the warm yellow glow of gas lanterns, their only light source. To avoid any oversights, they removed mud by hand and placed it in plastic boxes precisely labeled according to location. Then, by daylight, they could examine the earth for artifacts.

vessels: a cooking pot (or casserole) outside the boat and an oil lamp inside it. Both dated to the early Roman Period (mid-first century B.C. to mid-second century A.D.). The link between this pottery and the wreck was illusive because the pottery was not part of the boat's cargo. Still, these finds did indicate a period of human activity in the immediate vicinity of the boat.

To protect the boat at the conclusion of the probe, we reburied it. Moshe and Yuval brought a tractor from the kibbutz and pushed pieces of jetsam, old pipes and heavy tree trunks around the site so that no one would drive over it accidentally. As an added precaution, they dug two "decoy" excavations farther down the beach to mislead looters and the just plain curious.

The discovery was to be kept secret until the

rising waters of the Kinneret safely covered the boat. At that time it would be possible to reveal its discovery and, hopefully, organize a proper excavation.

That was Friday, February 7th. On Sunday, we were startled to read newspaper reports of a wreck from Jesus' time that had been discovered in the Sea of Galilee. Somehow the news had leaked. By Monday the press was writing in front page stories about the discovery of the "boat of Jesus."

The media hype was soon overwhelming. The Ministry of Tourism actively promoted the "Jesus connection" in the hope of drawing pilgrims to Israel. In Tiberias, Ultra-Orthodox Jews, fearful that excavation of the boat would promote Christian missionary work, demonstrated against it.

Soon rumors were circulating that the wreck was full of gold coins. Stories had been making the rounds for years of a ship that sank in the Kinneret during World War I, while carrying payment for the Turkish army. Now our wreck was becoming entwined with these stories, and people began searching for the non-existent treasure.

In Israel it is extraordinarily difficult to keep new archaeological finds hidden. Our boat proved to be no exception. Tuesday night, Moshe and Yuval were watching the site, through field glasses, from

Dating the Pottery from the Galilee Boat Excavation

Seventeen identifiable pieces of ancient pottery—including a complete lamp and cooking pot, as well as fragments of cooking pots, storage jars, a jug and juglets—were recovered from the Galilee boat and from the surrounding area during the excavation. The pottery was not significantly water-worn, so we assume that the pieces were deposited near the places where they were found.

The pottery types recovered are all known from other Galilee excavation sites. Several of the more common types were made at Kefar Hananya, a Galilean pottery manufacturing center of the Roman period, located about 8½ miles northwest of the boat site.[1]

None of the pottery is necessarily related to the hull itself; hence it cannot be used to date the boat. To date the boat, only intrinsic evidence may be used: evidence such as the carbon-14 dates obtained for the wood, and the method of vessel construction. However, the pottery recovered during the excavation is significant for estimating when there was activity in the vicinity of the boat.

The pottery pieces found near the Galilee boat were the same types as pottery recovered in excavations at Capernaum and Migdal (also known as Magdala), two ancient settlements on the coast of the Sea of Galilee; at Meiron, in the Upper Galilee; and at Gamla, in the western Golan.

The pottery at Capernaum, Migdal and Meiron was dated by its association with datable coins and artifacts and by its location in a dated stratum of remains. By these means, six pottery assemblages from these sites, which were similar to the boat pottery, could be assigned to the period from late first century B.C. to about mid-first century A.D., with one Capernaum assemblage continuing a few decades later. A seventh, similar pottery collection, also from Capernaum, could be dated by three coins in its context to the middle decades of the first century A.D. until about the year 70. One of those coins was from 54 A.D. and two others were from 67–68 A.D.—the former minted at Sepphoris in the 14th year of Nero's reign, and the others from the second year of the Jewish Revolt against Rome. The pottery found at Gamla was all in use before the city was taken by the Romans in 67 A.D., never to be resettled.

By comparing the pottery found near the Galilee boat with these well-dated assemblages from nearby sites, we may conclude that the boat pottery is typical of the period from the late first century B.C. to the decades following the mid-first century A.D., or until about the year 70 A.D. Moreover, later, common Galilean pottery types, first occurring in late first- and early second-century A.D. contexts, are notably absent. The ceramic evidence thus suggests a marked decline or cessation of activity in the vicinity of the boat in the late first century A.D., a conclusion consistent with the Roman victory in 67 A.D. that destroyed the boats of Migdal and left many of its people dead. —DR. DAVID ADAN-BAYEWITZ, BAR-ILAN UNIVERSITY, RAMAT GAN, ISRAEL

[1]David Adan-Bayewitz and Isadore Perlman, "Local Pottery Provenience Studies: A Role for Clay Analysis," *Archaeometry* 27 (1985), pp. 203–217; Adan-Bayowitz, *Common Kitchen Ware in Roman Galilee: A Study of Local Trade* (Ramat-Gan, Israel: Bar-Ilan University Press, in press).

Ginnosar. They saw some people with flashlights in the area of the boat. Yuval immediately called me, and I drove to Ginnosar, arriving about midnight. The people had left without finding the boat. The three of us sat in a grove of trees watching the site until 3 a.m. The coast remained deserted. We knew that if we did not excavate the boat soon, there might be no boat to excavate. It was only a matter of time until someone would find and destroy the boat in search of nonexistent treasure.

Archaeology throughout the world is dotted with cases of important discoveries destroyed because looters reached them before the archaeologists. We decided we had to excavate the boat immediately despite the fact that the archaeological and organizational logistics were mind-boggling.

A proper excavation takes time to prepare. Funds must be raised, team members recruited and a myriad of details worked out. Months, and sometimes years, go by before a planned excavation goes into the field. We would go into the field in *three days*.

The next day, February 12, I spent preparing a detailed excavation proposal for the Director of the Department of Antiquities, Avraham (Avi) Gitan. I made one condition concerning the excavation. We could assemble a local team for the archaeological excavation and conservation, but we were lacking someone who could make sense of the boat's construction once it was excavated. For this we would have to bring in someone from outside the country. We contacted Professor J. Richard (Dick) Steffy of the Institute of Nautical Archaeology, Texas A&M University, the world's leading expert on ancient ship construction.

Would he be able to come over on such short notice? If so, how were we going to pay for his trip? We called Dick from Ginnosar. He had already heard about the boat from the newspaper accounts and agreed to spend a week with us from February 20 to 25. Getting a ticket for Dick through governmental channels would be difficult on such short notice. However, the new American ambassador to Israel, Thomas Pickering, was a keen amateur archaeologist, and we wondered out loud whether the embassy might have a cultural grant program that could help in such situations. We contacted the American Embassy, and within 14 hours we had an OK on Dick's flight.

The excavation was on. Its purpose was to excavate the boat, study it *in situ* and move it to the

COURTESY ISRAEL DEPT. OF ANTIQUITIES AND MUSEUMS/PHOTO: DANNY FRIEDMAN

Yigal Allan Museum at Kibbutz Ginnosar for conservation—if possible, in one piece. We were to start on Sunday, February 16.

Before we could begin excavating, however, a new problem arose—literally arose. The lake was threatening to cover the boat again.

Moshe and I walked out to the site on Saturday night. When I had first seen the boat, less than two weeks before, the waterline was about 100 feet east of the site. Now it had advanced to within about 30 feet of the boat—and the forecast was for more rain. If the rain continued, the site would soon be inundated.

On the way back to Ginnosar, Moshe tried to cheer me up by saying that perhaps water was being pumped out of the lake for irrigation purposes. The Kinneret serves as the main reservoir of Israel's fresh water. There are three huge pumps that take water from it to the National Water Carrier.

This gave me an idea that was definitely on the "Far Side." Perhaps it might be possible to lower the level of the lake by pumping water out of it. I knew that Avi Eitan was meeting with the Minister of Education the next day concerning the boat. I phoned him and asked him to pass on a plea to

BIRD'S-EYE VIEW of the boat on the second day of excavation. Between the two excavators, at midship line on the far side of the boat, a narrow section of mud was cut out, down to the wooden hull.

the Minister of Education to ask the Minister of Agriculture to pump water out of the Kinneret into subsidiary reservoirs that would keep the water level steady until we could finish excavating the boat. In a country where *raising* the level of the Kinneret is a national passion, I doubted that this would be politically feasible, but it was worth a try.

On the day the excavation was to start, we were delayed by an armed band from a nearby settlement that laid claim to the boat. This matter was settled by the police and by a diplomatic effort on the part of the Director of the Department of Antiquities, who quietly explained that all antiquities belong to the state. We had lost half a day.

As we began excavating in the late afternoon, curiosity seekers crowded around, waiting for us to find the "treasure." For the next four hours, we excavated *next to* the boat. It became dark, and the crowd dispersed.

Then we began digging in earnest. With the lake

COURTESY ISRAEL DEPT. OF ANTIQUITIES AND MUSEUMS/PHOTO: DANNY FRIEDMAN

SUSPENDED ABOVE THE BOAT from two bridges of metal poles, wooden planks provided a useful, if uncomfortable, platform from which workers could excavate without touching the fragile, waterlogged timbers. The bridges also supported a white tarpaulin that shielded the boat from direct sunlight, which might otherwise cause the wood to dehydrate and disintegrate.

rising steadily, we decided to work around the clock. Gas fishing-lamps lit up the area with an eerie, warm yellow glow. Work went slowly as we removed the mud from inside the boat, being careful to leave a 6-inch layer of mud covering the wood.

The excavation team slowly formed. Orna Cohen was to be our conservationist; Danny Friedman joined as our photographer. Edna Amos, an archaeologist who had worked previously with Kurt and me in the Mediterranean, heard about the project during that first afternoon of excavation and dropped by to say hello. I immediately drafted her as our recorder. Edna worked through that night till 6 o'clock the next morning and returned the next day to become our permanent recorder.

During the evening we received a visit from members of the Kinneret Authority, the governmental body responsible for the lake. They had received a strange message from the Minister of Agriculture—to lower the level of the lake. They assumed that the message had been scrambled—no one in his right mind would want to *lower* the level of the lake.

I laughed and explained our predicament. They came up with a way to save the site, however, without lowering the level of the lake: Build a massive dike around the site to protect it from the encroaching lake. They promised to return the next morning with workers and supplies.

During the night we cut a narrow section down to the wooden hull at midship. Lying on our stomachs in the cold, wet mud, we excavated it by hand to avoid any possibility of damage to the boat from instruments. The wood slowly appeared; it was beautifully intact.

It was obvious, however, that in excavating clumps of mud in the dark we might miss artifacts. For that reason, all the mud excavated inside and next to the boat was placed in plastic boxes, which were given basket numbers and their positions recorded. The boxes were dumped in numbered piles that were later examined for artifacts. Moshe found an ancient pyramidal arrowhead in this way. More about this later.

Shortly after 6 a.m. Monday morning, the wind suddenly shifted to an easterly. It began pushing the water toward the boat. But it was not long thereafter that the Kinneret Authority team arrived, like the proverbial cavalry, and began building a dike of earthworks and sandbags around the site to protect it from the rising water. The site was saved from the encroaching water. Although the lake continued to rise, there was no longer a problem of water.

It is impossible to describe the effect the excavation had on everyone involved. Kibbutz Ginnosar "adopted" the excavation, supplying volunteers and logistics. The kibbutzniks would finish their own day's work and then join us for another eight or ten hours at night. Volunteers arrived from all over the country. The excitement was infectious. By the second afternoon, members of Moshav Migdal had also joined us. Previous arguments about where the boat would be exhibited were laid aside as we all pulled together in a concerted effort to save the boat. Because of this new-found harmony, we nicknamed it "the Love Boat."

On the second day of the excavation, as we were widening the excavation pit with a backhoe (lent by a moshavnik from Migdal), Zvika Melech, another moshavnik, showed me some pieces of water-logged wood. We could not stop using the backhoe because enlarging the pit was our top priority, but now each shovel load had to be dumped in front of us and examined. We removed the loose pieces

DOTTED WITH NUMBERED TAGS, all the wooden sections were meticulously labeled to record their correct locations. Running lengthwise across the boat, white plastic strings outline the planking structure. A dangling sprinkler, brought from Kibbutz Ginnosar, sprayed the boat continually to prevent it from drying out. The wood's micro-structure was supported mainly by water. Any evaporation would lead to the wood's collapse.

ZVI MAOZ

LUSH PLANTED FIELDS meet the shore of the Sea of Galilee. At upper left stands the Yigal Allon Museum—a tall white building at the water's edge—where the Galilee Boat is now housed. When this photo was taken, the boat still lay on shore under a tarpaulin, the white speck at center, 550 yards to the right of the museum.

Throughout the complex excavation and transportation of the boat, the two nearby agricultural communities, Kibbutz Ginnosar and Moshav Migdal, enthusiastically volunteered both workers and equipment.

COURTESY ISRAEL DEPT. OF ANTIQUITIES AND MUSEUMS/PHOTO: DANNY FRIEDMAN

PROTECTED BY A POLYURETHANE COCOON, the Galilee Boat floats again, for the first time in 2,000 years. The 550-yard voyage to the Yigal Allon Museum required extensive preparation. Conservator Orna Cohen of Hebrew University planned and supervised the construction of fiberglass and polyester resin frames, fitted inside and outside the boat's hull. The boat was then wrapped in thin plastic sheeting and sprayed with polyurethane liquid, which hardened into a protective shell. Completely encased, the boat was ready to float.

After a steam shovel, right, cut a channel through the dam that had been built to protect the excavation site from rising water, the Galilee boat sets out on its last voyage.

of waterlogged wood. The shovel load was then dumped on the side of the pit where Moshe, using a metal detector, removed iron nails. Suddenly sticking his hand into the pool of water, Zvika yelled, "This wood is connected to something!" Zvika had found what Dick Steffy later identified as fragments of *two* additional boats. The boat fragments were sandbagged, and we began excavating there by hand. Zvika, of course, was put in charge of the area.

On the second evening of excavation, the upper part of the partially excavated stern on the starboard quarter of the boat buckled. We had dug too far on either side without supporting it sufficiently. Someday, when the boat is reconstructed, those timbers will be refitted to the boat. But that evening was one of the worst I can remember. We all felt that despite our best efforts the boat was falling apart.

In order to avoid touching the fragile wood while

archaeologist turned conservator, who had just returned from a year of studies in England to take charge of this problem. By the eighth day of excavation, the archaeological aspects of the excavation had been completed. Now the question was how to move the boat. It was Orna's ball game.

The craft's wooden timbers were thoroughly water-logged. This meant that the cellular material inside the wood cells had been replaced with water to the degree that the wood, according to Orna's study, was now 80 percent water and had the consistency of wet cardboard. Any evaporation of water from such wood is extremely dangerous, causing the cell walls to collapse. This process is irreversible; the wood shrinks and fragments, and it cannot be restored to its former structure. Because of such dangers during the excavation, we sprayed the boat with water day and night, and even covered it with wet sponges and polyethylene sheets, in addition to shading it from direct sunlight.

Moving an entire boat of such soft material was a nearly impossible mission—and yet we had to move it approximately 1,600 feet to the Yigal Allon Museum at Kibbutz Ginnosar.

Orna consulted experts on the transport of large objects. It seemed that it was impossible to move a 26-foot-long boat of such fragile wood without seriously damaging it.

But Orna devised a method that had never been tried before. She decided to strengthen the boat inside and out with a fiberglass-and-polyester resin frame molded to the shape of the hull. The entire boat would then be encased in a polyurethane foam "straitjacket" to hold it together. We were-going to attempt to move the boat intact.

First, frames of fiberglass/polyester (strengthened with old pieces of PVC irrigation hose) were laid down inside the boat. Then the entire hull was covered with fine plastic sheeting, and polyurethane foam was sprayed into the hull. This material sprays on as a dark orange liquid and quickly bubbles up and solidifies, looking every bit like a living entity engulfing the boat.

Next we excavated narrow tunnels under the boat. External fiberglass frames were then molded to the outside of the hull and the tunnels were filled with polyurethane. These polyurethane strips hardened into external supports for the boat. This allowed the remaining clay and mud beneath the boat to be excavated. Fiberglass trusses were again added and the remaining areas were filled with polyurethane. By the end of the process, the entire boat—without having been moved or shifted—had been wrapped in a protective cocoon that looked somewhat like an overgrown, melted marshmallow.

excavating, Moshe built a series of metal bridges, on which the excavators could lie, over the boat. As the excavation progressed, the bridges were raised, and a platform suspended on ropes was lowered from it. Excavators lay prone on this platform for hours as they dug out the remaining mud by hand.

Each part of the boat was tagged and numbered. White plastic tubing was used to outline the strakes to enhance photographic recording. By the time Dick Steffy arrived on the fifth day of excavation, much of the hull had been exposed. Dick's presence at the excavation site gave us all a feeling of security. His vast knowledge and good common sense were invaluable.

At the conclusion of a *normal* excavation, the excavator gives a few boxes of artifacts to the conservationist. But in our case, the boat itself was one big conservation problem. At the beginning of the excavation I had called in Orna Cohen, an

How Old Is the Galilee Boat?

The Galilee boat has been dated by a method called radiocarbon dating. This method could be used because the boat was made of wood, a carbon-containing material.

To understand radiocarbon dating, it's important to understand some basic facts about the world of nature. Carbon in the atmosphere exists in three forms—called isotopes—that differ in the weight of their atoms but not in their chemical behavior, so organisms use them as if they were exactly the same. The most abundant form is carbon 12, but for every 10^{12} atoms of carbon 12 there is one atom of the heaviest form, radioactive carbon 14. Carbon 14 is constantly being produced in the atmosphere.

To say that carbon 14 is radioactive means that it decays to the stable, non-radioactive nitrogen at a constant rate. This decay accounts for the fact that the number of carbon-14 atoms in the atmosphere and in living organisms, which continuously exchange carbon with the atmosphere as part of the biological processes of life, does not increase without limit but remains approximately constant.

As long as an organism is alive, the carbon within it is composed of the same proportion of carbon 12 and carbon 14 as the carbon in the atmosphere. But when an organism dies, such as a tree cut for use of its wood, the exchange process stops and decay of carbon 14 proceeds without any replenishment of the supply from the atmosphere.

For any particular radioactive isotope, it is possible to measure its half-life, or the time it would take for one-half of the original radioactive atoms in a sample to decay to a stable form. For carbon 14 the half-life is 5,568 years. This half-life makes it useful for archaeology because the changes are large enough for meaningful measurement in the time periods archaeologists care about.

In the case of the Galilee boat, we assume that the wood used to make it was cut within a short time of the boat's construction. Therefore, the radiocarbon age of the wood represents the true age of the boat.

Samples of the Galilee boat's wood, each weighing several grams, were removed and sent to a laboratory. Using gas proportional counters, which count the radioactive decay events that occur within the carbon 14, the amount of radioactive carbon 14 in the sample relative to the amount of stable carbon 12 was measured. Knowing how long it takes for half the atoms of carbon 14 to decay—namely 5,568 years—it was possible to calculate, based on the current proportion of isotopes present, how old the boat was when it was made (that is, when the living trees used for it were cut). Ten samples from different parts of the boat were counted. The result was that the boat began its life as a fishing vessel on the Sea of Galilee in 40 B.C., plus or minus 80 years, or between 120 B.C. and 40 A.D.

—DR. ISRAEL CARMI, WEIZMANN INSTITUTE OF SCIENCE, REHOVOT, ISRAEL

Now that it was packaged, how would we move it? We considered carrying it overland by truck or helicoptering it out, but the related movement and vibrations were likely to destroy the boat. In the end, Orna opted for the obvious solution.

Once the boat was "packaged," we pumped water back into the excavation pit. Buoyed by the polyurethane, the boat floated at lake level. With a steam shovel, a channel through our precious dike was opened to the lake. The boat was floated through this channel out into the lake. For the first time in two millennia, the boat "sailed" again to the cheers of an onlooking crowd.

The entire excavation had taken eleven exhausting days and nights.

The next day, the boat was lifted onto the shore by a huge crane. Within ten days thereafter, a reinforced concrete pool with white tiles was constructed to serve as the boat's conservation tank. The boat was then raised once again by crane and placed inside the empty conservation pool.

Now began the long and laborious task of removing the polyurethane casing—tantamount to re-excavating the boat. We had not thought of putting trip-wires inside the polyurethane casing; we paid dearly for this mistake. In the tight confines of the conservation pool, the re-excavation was doubly difficult.

We could not fill the conservation pool with water and submerge the boat until all the polyurethane had been removed; otherwise, some parts of the boat would strain to float and the stress would cause breakage. But the boat was now drying out at an alarming rate, no matter how much we sprayed it with water. As time passed, it seemed we were losing the battle. Hairline cracks began to appear. I felt like a doctor about to lose his patient at the end of an extensive operation.

In what was surely the 11th hour, we finally finished the re-excavation of the boat and submerged it in water—and we ourselves nearly dropped from exhaustion.

The boat will now be treated for a period of five to seven years. A synthetic wax called PEG (polyethylene glycol) will be added to the water in slowly increasing concentrations. Simultaneously, the temperature of the water will be gradually raised. In this way, the PEG will penetrate the cellular cavities of the deteriorated wood and replace the water in the cells. At the conclusion of this years-long process, we will be able to exhibit the boat outside the conservation pool and study it in a dry environment. In the meantime, entrepreneurs from Kibbutz Ein Gev and from Tiberias are ferrying tourists across the lake to see "the boat from Jesus' time."

It does seem that the boat fits this time range

PROTRUDING FROM THE MUD, the stern end of the boat's keel terminates in a notch, called a hook scarf, left. Missing is the sternpost, which originally attached to this wooden locking connection. The sternpost was carefully removed in antiquity for reuse in another boat, just as spare parts today are scavenged from old cars.

and is of the type that would have been used by Jesus and his disciples.

I have already mentioned the pottery that gave us a general idea of the date of the boat. Dr. David Adan-Bayewitz of Bar-Ilan University, who studied this pottery, considerably narrowed the time range.

By comparing the datable pot sherds found in the excavation to nearby stratified assemblages, he concluded that the pottery found with the boat is typical of the latter part of the first century B.C. to the decades following the mid-first century A.D., or until about the year 70 A.D. As noted previously, this pottery does not date the boat directly; however, it does indicate a period of human activity in the immediate area of the boat. This period appears to end at the time of the First Jewish Revolt against Rome and may be related to the decimation of the population of Migdal at that time.

It therefore seems likely that the boat arrived at the site prior to the battle of Migdal.

Wood from the boat itself was dated by the carbon-14 method.* Dr. Israel Carmi of the Depart ment of Isotope Research of the Weizmann Institute carried out analysis on ten samples of wood from the boat and arrived at an average date of 40 B.C., plus or minus 80 years; that is, from 120 B.C. to 40 A.D.**

Dick Steffy independently came to about the same conclusion based on his knowledge of ancient boats. In his hand-written report to the Director of the Department of Antiquities, Dick wrote: "If this were a hull found in the Mediterranean I would date

* For an explanation of the carbon-14 method of dating, see the box opposite.

**However, the carbon-14 test tells us when the wood was cut. Some of the wood on this boat may have been reused from hulls of earlier boats.

it between the first century B.C. and the second century A.D." He noted, however, that building tra ditions may have continued in the Kinneret after they had gone out of use in the Mediterranean.

Admittedly, each of the dating methods is insuf ficient in itself; however, taken together, these different dating techniques suggest a date between the first century B.C. and the late first century A.D.

Dr. Ella Werker of the Department of Botany at Hebrew University examined the wood from which the boat was made. This examination revealed that while most of the boat was constructed of cedar planking and oak frames, there are five other woods represented by single examples. These are: sidar, Aleppo pine, hawthorn, willow and redbud.

The boat is 26.5 feet long, 7.5 feet wide and 4.5 feet high. It has a rounded stern and a fine bow. Both the fore and aft sections were probably decked in, although the boat was not preserved to this height.

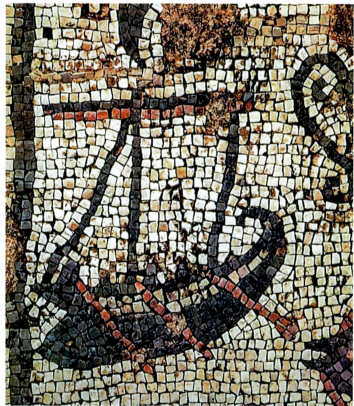

OARS POISED, a boat in a first-century A.D. mosaic remains forever at sea. Decorating a house in the Galilee seaside town of Migdal, only a mile from the discovery site of the Galilee boat, the mosaic boat appears to be propelled by six oars, three on each side. However, the sternmost oar widens at its base and therefore should be interpreted as a steering oar, or quarter rudder. Thus, this mosaic boat may resemble the Galilee boat, which probably had four rowers (two on each side) and a helmsman who steered with the quarter rudder.

COURTESY ISRAEL DEPT. OF ANTIQUITIES AND MUSEUMS/PHOTO: DANNY FRIEDMAN

RIBS OF WOOD lie bare in the boat's specially built concrete conservation pool. Once inside the pool, the boat had to be stripped of its casing—an excavation in itself. Having outsmarted the Sea of Galilee's encroaching waters, the team now had to work furiously to remove the protective shell before the wood dried out. The boat could be re-immersed only after every shred of polyurethane had been taken off, because the buoyancy of the polyurethane would cause the parts of the boat underwater to rise. This would dangerously strain the boat's fragile frame.

Dick Steffy's study of the boat suggests that it had been built by a master craftsman who probably learned his craft in the Mediterranean or had been apprenticed to someone who had. But he had to use timber that was far inferior to what was used on Mediterranean vessels. Perhaps better materials were beyond the financial reach of the owner. Many of the timbers in our boat, including the forward portion of the keel, were apparently in secondary use, having been removed from older boats.

The boat must have had a long life, for it had been repeatedly repaired. It ended its life on the scrap heap. Its usable timbers—including the stempost and sternpost—were removed; the remaining hull, old and now useless, was then pushed out into the lake where it quickly sank into the silt.

Did the boat have a mast? Steffy's careful detective work demonstrated that it did. A mast cannot be placed directly on a hull. It normally sits on a construction of wood called a mast step. This may be a simple block of wood or a complicated construction. Steffy found four nail holes where the mast block had been connected to the keel. The impression of the mast block was still visible on the top side of the keel. The mast block, like so many other reusable parts of the boat, had been removed in antiquity.

The boat could thus be both sailed and rowed. It was probably used primarily for fishing, but could also serve for transportation of goods and passengers. During times of arm ed conflict, it could serve as a transport.

The recovery of an ancient arrowhead in the excavation may indicate that a battle took place in this area. Arrowheads of the same pyramidal design have been recovered outside and next to the walls of Gamla on the Golan heights, another site where, despite an initial Jewish military success, the Romans successfully routed Jewish defenders, after a battle that ended in bloody disaster.* Danny Friedman, our photographer, who also works at Gamla, studied the pyramidal arrowhead found at

* See "Gamla: The Masada of the North," and Flavius Josephus, "The Fall of Gamla," BAR, January/February 1979.

our site. This type of arrowhead is apparently of foreign origin and was probably a specialty of a foreign auxiliary archer unit attached to the Roman legions. (Only 14 of approximately 1,600 arrowheads found at Gamla are of this type.)

The fact that fragments of two other boats and other wooden debris were found during the excavation suggests to Dick that the area was used for building and repairing boats. This conclusion is also supported by the circumstance that, before our boat was sunk, parts that might be used in other boats were removed—much like an old car today might be kept near a garage to serve as a source for used parts.

Was our boat typical of the kind referred to so often in connection with Jesus and his disciples in the Gospels and in Josephus' description of the battle of Migdal?

During the excavation, Dick had suggested that there were probably four rowers on a boat like ours.

At first this seemed to be contradicted by a mosaic picture of a boat found at Migdal. The mosaic shows a boat that apparently had three oars on each side. But when I examined the Migdal mosaic boat more closely I discovered that the two forward oars were represented as a single line of red tesserae (mosaic stones) that stood out against the black and white hull; but the sternmost oar widened at the bottom—it was a steering oar. The boat in the mosaic must have had four rowers, as Dick had predicted for our boat, and a helmsman—a crew of five.

Then I reexamined some passages in Josephus in which he describes how, when he was commander of the Jewish rebel forces in Galilee, he put four sailors in each of the boats; elsewhere he talks of a helmsman—thus each boat again had a crew of five.

How many people could our boat hold? In one passage in Josephus he refers to himself, some friends, and seven combatants in a boat, which, with a crew of five, would total at least 15. In another passage, he tells of ten men of Tiberias who were transported in a single "fishing boat." With a crew of five, this too would total 15 men.

Based on skeletons he has examined, Joe Zias, a physical anthropologist at the Department of Antiquities, estimates that, in the Roman-Byzantine period, Galilean males were about 5 feet, 5 inches tall and averaged about 140 pounds. Fifteen such men would weigh just over a ton and could fit into our boat.

A boat like this could easily accommodate Jesus and his disciples, who regularly used boats on the Sea of Galilee. (See Matthew 8:18, 23–27, 9:1, 14:13–14, 22–32, 15:39, 16:5; Mark 4:35–41, 5:18, 21, 6:32–34, 45–51, 8:9–10, 13–14; Luke 6:1, 8:22–25, 37, 40; John 6:16–21.) The gospel passages do not

indicate precisely, however, how many disciples were in the boat with Jesus during the recorded boat trips on the Sea of Galilee.

While the Gospels do not help in defining passenger capacities, there are two references to crew sizes.

Jesus called James and John, the sons of Zebedee, while they were in their boat tending their nets "and they left their father Zebedee in the boat with the hired servants, and followed him" (Mark 1:20). Thus, the boat of the Zebedee family was crewed by at least five men (Zebedee, James, John and two or more hired servants).

In mid-April 1987, over a year after the conclusion of the excavation, I wrote to Dick, suggesting this working hypothesis: The Kinneret Boat represents a class used on the lake during the Second Temple period. This is apparently the same class described by Josephus and in the Gospels and represented in the Migdal Mosaic.

Dick replied:

"Your working hypothesis sounds okay, but may I make a further suggestion? Shell construction limited design possibilities, so there probably were not as many different boat designs on the Kinneret in antiquity as there are today. I suspect there were small boats—rowboats for one or two fisherman—and big boats such as ours. They may have varied somewhat in appearance and size, but basically they must have been limited to a couple of different hull forms in any given period. Without propellers to push them along, it seems unlikely that boats much larger than ours would have been practical on such a small body of water."

Is there any historical evidence for the smaller boat types that Dick postulated? Perhaps. Small boats may be inferred from another story Josephus tells about his adventures in Tiberias.

Pursued by an angry crowd, Josephus and two of his bodyguards "advanced to the rear" by commandeering a boat moored nearby and making a dash for it. Considering the speedy exit, it seems likely that they had taken a smaller type of boat.

Mendel Nun explained to me that boats of similar size to our boat were still in use on the Kinneret at the beginning of the 20th century—prior to the introduction of the motor. Known as *Arabiye*, they were used with a seine net. This type of net, used for catching shoals of fish near shore requires a boat 20 to 25 feet long. The net is spread out with its ropes as the boat advances. The net varies in size from about 500 to 1,500 feet long, and requires a large stern platform to handle. Known as a *sagene* in

Greek, this type of net is referred to by Jesus in the parable in which he compares heaven to a net:

> "Again, the kingdom of heaven is like a net which was thrown into the sea and gathered fish of every kind; when it was full, men drew it ashore and sat down and sorted the good into vessels but threw away the bad. So it will be at the close of the age. The angels will come out and separate the evil from the righteous" (Matthew 13:47–50).

Because a boat that uses this kind of net requires a large stern platform, this might enable us to picture more accurately the episode in which Jesus stilled the waters of the Sea of Galilee. A storm arose while Jesus with some of his disciples was crossing from one side of the lake to the other. In Mark's version of the story, Jesus was "in the stern, asleep on the pillow" (Mark 4:37). The large stern deck may explain why Jesus chose the stern in which to sleep. The stern deck was the station of the helmsman. While it would have been exposed to the elements, the area under the stern platform would have been the most protected area of the boat. Jesus probably slept beneath the stern platform. There he would have had the greatest protection from the elements and been out of the way of the other people on board:

> "And a great storm of wind arose, and the waves beat into the boat, so that the boat was already filling. But he was *in the stern*, asleep on *the pillow*; and they woke him and said to him, 'Master, do you not care if we perish?' And he awoke and rebuked the wind and said to the sea, 'Peace! Be still!' And the wind ceased, and there was a great calm" (Mark 4:37–39).

More than a century ago, it was noted that the definite article used in relation to the pillow indicates that this was part of the boat's equipment. This may have been a sandbag used for ballast. Such ballast sacks were used on sailboats in the Mediterranean that used the seine net. There were two types of these: one, weighing 110–130 pounds, called in Arabic *kîs ṣābûra*, which means "balance (or ballast) sack"; or two sandbags of about 55 pounds each, used together. The latter was called a "balance (or ballast) pillow" (Arabic: *meḥadet ṣābûra*).

These sandbags were used to trim the boat when under sail; when not in use, they were stored beneath the stern deck where they could be used as pillows by crews resting there.

In conclusion, the Kinneret Boat is *of the class* referred to both in the Gospels in relation to Jesus' ministry in the Sea of Galilee region, and by Josephus in his description of nautical warfare on the lake during the First Jewish Revolt against Rome.

At present we have no proof that our boat played any part in these momentous events. But it does allow us better to understand them and seafaring on the Kinneret nearly 2,000 years ago.

Related Reading

Mendel Nun, "Cast Your Net Upon the Waters: Fish and Fishermen in Jesus' Time," BAR, November/December 1993 (see p. 458 of this book).

Mendel Nun, "Ports of Galilee," BAR, July/August 1999.

Strata: "New 'Harbor' for the Galilee Boat," BAR, May/June 2000.

Shelley Wachsmann, Archaeological Views: "Archaeology Under the Sea," BAR, November/December 2006.

Nili Liphschitz, "Cedars of Lebanon: Exploring the Roots," BAR, May/June 2013.

The Undiscovered Gate Beneath Jerusalem's Golden Gate

JAMES FLEMING

THE SKY WAS CLEAR AND blue that spring day in April 1969. The early morning sun glanced off the mauve-colored Mount of Olives. Tiny wild flowers dotted the hillside. The air was fresh and fragrant after an unusually heavy rain the night before.

It was a perfect time to explore the walls and gates of Jerusalem. I was then a graduate student at the American Institute of Holy Land Studies and was studying Biblical archaeology under Professor Moshe Kochavi of Tel Aviv University. I had taken a special interest in the topography of Jerusalem.

I slung my camera over my shoulder and headed for the outside of the eastern wall of the Old City. I would follow this wall through the Moslem cemetery to the Golden Gate, which was easily worth a morning's exploration. As I breathed the spring air deeply, I had no idea that I would soon be knee-deep in human bones!

The Golden Gate is one of the most beautiful of Jerusalem's eight Old City gates. Today the two arches of the gate are sealed shut and stand in silent contrast to the hubbub of the Jaffa Gate on the west and the Damascus Gate on the north. Scholars are not sure when the Golden Gate was mortared in. It may have been blocked for security reasons during the various Arab-Crusader conflicts from the 11th to the 13th centuries. Or it may have been closed by the Ottoman Turks after Suleiman the Magnificent rebuilt the walls of Jerusalem from 1539 to 1542. The most recent clearing and strengthening of the gate was done by the Turkish authorities in 1891.

Though security probably was the main reason for the gate's closure, some historians wonder if the gate's Biblical associations may also have been an influence. The final judgment of mankind and the messianic associations of Jewish, Christian and Moslem traditions are linked with this gate. In the Middle Ages, religious Jews prayed there as they do now at the Western or Wailing Wall. Christians have always associated the Golden Gate with Palm Sunday as well as with the second coming of Jesus. Moslems wanted to be buried near it because the Koran connects Allah's final judgment with this gate. Over the centuries, as the political climate changed, the Jewish and Christian presence near the gate shrank, while the Moslem cemetery enlarged along the city's eastern wall to the gate's very portals.

Most of the last judgment and messianic associations with the Golden Gate stem from the Bible. In Zechariah 14:4–5, the prophet delivers an oracle on the day of the Lord's coming. "On that day his feet shall stand on the Mount of Olives which lies before Jerusalem on the east;...Then the Lord your God will come, and all the holy ones with him." From this passage, it would seem that the Lord's entrance into the city would be from the east, perhaps through this gate.

The prophet Joel also delivers an oracle on the "Day of the Lord." It begins with this famous passage: "And I will give portents in the heavens and

TWIN ARCHES OF THE GOLDEN GATE, one called the Gate of Mercy and the other the Gate of Repentance in ancient traditions, stand silent watch over a Moslem cemetery outside the eastern wall of Jerusalem's Old City.

Just behind the crenelated wall is the paved platform of the Temple Mount on which—unseen to the left—stand the golden Dome of the Rock and the silver-domed Mosque of El Aksa. Beyond the Temple Mount, houses, shops, schools, mosques, synagogues and churches cling tightly to the dense network of streets in Jerusalem's walled Old City.

JAMES FLEMING

JAMES FLEMING

UNDERGROUND ARCH. Formed by five smooth wedge-shaped stones, the arch marks the top of an earlier unexcavated gateway directly beneath the Golden Gate. This arch had not been seen in recent times until the author fell into a Moslem tomb just outside the Golden Gate. Bones of a mass burial in this tomb partially obscure the ancient arch.

on the earth, blood and fire and columns of smoke. The sun shall be turned to darkness, and the moon to blood, before the great and terrible day of the Lord comes." (Joel 2:30–31) The oracle goes on: "I will gather all the nations and bring them down to the Valley of Jehosaphat, for there I will sit to judge all the nations round about." (Joel 3).

Jehosaphat is not only the name of an Israelite

king; it also means "judgment," and therefore the Valley of Judgment is probably another name for the Kidron Valley, which lies east of Jerusalem between the city itself and the Mount of Olives. Accordingly, on the day of the Lord forecast in Joel, the nations may be gathered in the valley east of Jerusalem and be judged by God. Judgments were customarily rendered in the gates of a city (see Genesis 19:1, 23:10), so presumably the Lord would render His judgments at the eastern gate of Jerusalem, near the Temple. Thus the association of Judgment Day with the Golden Gate.

Jesus's triumphal entry into Jerusalem on Palm Sunday (the Sunday before Passover and the last week of his ministry) was probably through the city's eastern gate. Jesus's entry into Jerusalem is recorded in all four Gospels. According to Luke 19:37, "As he was now drawing near, at the descent of the Mount of Olives [east of Jerusalem], the whole multitude of the disciples began to rejoice and praise God with a loud voice for all the mighty works that they had seen, saying, 'Blessed is the King who comes in the name of the Lord!'" Mark adds that Jesus entered the city and went directly to the Temple (Mark 11:11), possibly through the eastern gate. (Some of the crowd assembled along the road may have been looking for the fulfillment of the prophecies in Zechariah and Joel.)

In 614 A.D., the Persians invaded and destroyed Byzantine Jerusalem. The Christians recaptured the city under Emperor Heraclius and rescued "the true cross" from the Persian invaders. On March 21, 629 A.D., the cross was returned to the Church of the Holy Sepulchre in a regal procession through the Golden Gate, similar to that of the first Palm Sunday 600 years earlier.

With the coming of Islam, Moslems too began to associate the Golden Gate with messianic expectations. The *sura*, traditions of the Prophet Mohammed, likens the last judgment to a narrow path on the blade of a knife stretched from a mountain to the gate of heaven. Many Moslems understood this symbolic knife blade to span the Kidron Valley from the Mount of Olives to the Golden Gate. The two arches of the Golden Gate therefore have Arabic names associated with the final judgment: the northern arch is called the Gate of Repentance and the southern arch is called the Gate of Mercy. (Jews also refer to this gate as the Mercy Gate.)

These ancient prophetic and apocalyptic associations with the eastern gate of Jerusalem have affected the appearance of today's Kidron Valley outside the Golden Gate. On the slopes of the valley are Jewish, Christian and Moslem cemeteries. The ancient Jewish cemetery, the oldest in continuous use anywhere in the world, blankets the western slope of the Mount of Olives. The Christian cemetery lies deep within a wall at the bottom of the valley. The Moslem cemetery covers the hillside below and adjacent to the Golden Gate, along the eastern wall of the Old City. For centuries, the faithful of these religions have wanted to be buried as close as possible to the Golden Gate and the Mount of Olives. The thousands of graves paving the Valley of Judgment bear witness to the faith of the dead, their remains silently waiting in the dry earth like Rose of Jericho seeds waiting for the rain of the resurrection and the last judgment.[1]

"Golden Gate" is actually the Christian name for the eastern gate of Jerusalem. This name was probably derived from New Testament references to a gate known as the Beautiful Gate (Acts 3:2, 10). How did "Beautiful" become "Golden"? In the earliest Greek New Testament, the word for "beautiful" is *oraia*. When Jerome translated the New Testament into Latin in the fourth century, he changed the Greek *oraia* to the similar-sounding Latin *aurea*, rather than to the Latin word for "beautiful." So the Latin Vulgate text read "Golden Gate" instead of "Beautiful Gate."[2]

"Beautiful or Golden," I thought to myself as I proceeded on my walk that spring morning. "It doesn't matter. It's both!" When I knelt down in front of the Golden Gate to take a picture, I was filled with these pleasant thoughts. I was unaware

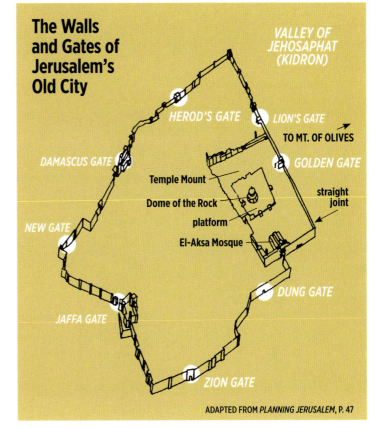

The Walls and Gates of Jerusalem's Old City

VALLEY OF JEHOSAPHAT (KIDRON)

HEROD'S GATE

LION'S GATE

TO MT. OF OLIVES

DAMASCUS GATE

GOLDEN GATE

Temple Mount

straight joint

Dome of the Rock

platform

El-Aksa Mosque

NEW GATE

DUNG GATE

JAFFA GATE

ZION GATE

ADAPTED FROM *PLANNING JERUSALEM*, P. 47

that my feet were gradually sinking into the muddy earth of the Moslem cemetery. The heavy night rain had not yet evaporated, but I was concentrating on the view in my camera, not my sinking feet. Suddenly the earth gave way beneath me. I felt as though I was part of a rock slide. Down I went into a hole eight feet deep.

I was disoriented but uninjured. I picked myself up and tried to focus my eyes in the dim light that came through the hole above my head. I suddenly realized that I was standing amidst the bones of 30 to 40 human skeletons apparently thrown together in a mass burial. Some of the bones were still connected by cartilage, which indicated interment within the last hundred years or so—relatively recently in Middle Eastern chronology. I wondered if the burial of such a large number of people in an unmarked grave meant that these people had died suddenly as a result of some disaster—battle, famine, or plague?

Once I realized that enough stones had fallen into the tomb with me to construct a platform from which I could chin myself and thereby get out, I was able to concentrate more closely on my surroundings. I was amazed to see an ancient wall below the Golden Gate exposed in front of me. The Gate itself is built into a turret that protrudes about six feet from the wall. The underground stones of the wall

How to Understand the Golden Gate

The Golden Gate is located in a turret protruding from the eastern wall of the Old City of Jerusalem. The two arched portals of the Golden Gate are now mortared closed, but if you could walk through them, you would find yourself on the Temple Mount, which is located in the southeastern corner of the Old City. In short, the southern part of the eastern wall of the Old City is also the eastern wall of the Temple Mount, and if it were open, the Golden Gate would lead into the Old City directly onto the Temple Mount.

On the interior (western side) of the Gate is an elaborate structure (see p. 499) that includes domed chambers that may be entered from steps leading down from the Temple Mount.

Outside the Golden Gate is a Moslem cemetery. It covers the slope down to the Kidron Valley (also called the Valley of Jehosaphat).

In the drawing opposite, we see, above ground, the Golden Gate and the eastern wall. We also see several structures below ground—in particular, the sealed Lower Gate below the Golden Gate, an underground eastern wall, and a massive curving wall in front (east) of the Lower Gate.

The author of this article stumbled into the large tomb in front of the left portal of the Golden Gate. At the bottom of the tomb, on the face of the wall, he observed wedge-shaped stones, indicating the top of an arch. In the drawing above, the stones that he actually saw are drawn in solid lines inside the tomb. If the partial arch he saw is, in fact, complete, it forms an arched gateway exactly under the left portal of the Golden Gate. Presumably, a similar arched portal is under the right portal of the Golden Gate, thus forming a double-portaled Lower Gate. Except for the stones in the left arch of the Lower Gate that were actually observed, the Lower Gate is drawn with dotted lines to show that it is a reconstruction.

The Lower Gate was built on a stone foundation and was set into an earlier city wall. The present 16th-century A.D. wall was built on top of this earlier wall. Two to three courses of this earlier wall may still be seen above ground level and are shown in the drawing as rectangular stones with rough, projecting faces and 3- to 6-inch margins around their edges. These stones are much larger than and different from the masonry in the wall built on top of them.

To see the earlier, largely underground wall from another viewpoint, look at the cross-section drawing (below). This drawing shows a vertical slice through the present eastern wall of the Old City at the point where the Golden Gate leads into it. In this cross-section drawing, the courses of the earlier wall are numbered. Courses numbered 1 and 2 are seen above ground on the right and left (outside and inside) of the Golden Gate. They can indeed be seen even today (see p. 498). Courses numbered 3 and 4 are underground, but are above the arched entrances of the Lower Gate. Courses numbered 5 through 10 form the rest of this lower wall into which the Lower Gate was built. The floor of the Lower Gate is at the bottom of course number 10. Courses 11 through 17 form the foundation wall, which was underground even when the Lower Gate was above ground. Course number 17 sits on bedrock. A less massive wall built by Suleiman the Magnificent (1537–1541) sits on course number 1 of the earlier wall.

Return now to the first drawing. Forty-one feet *below* ground level and 46 feet in front

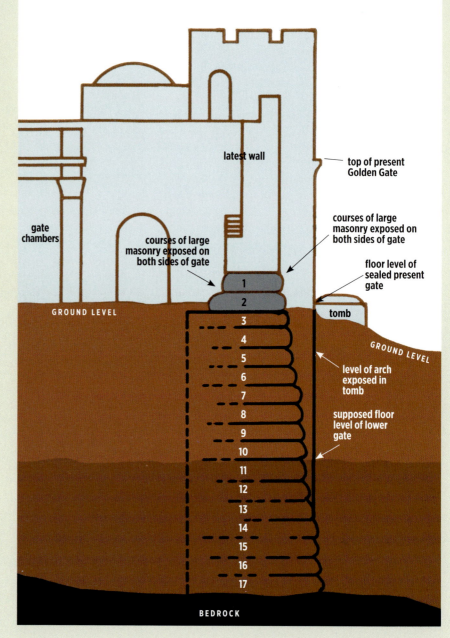

- latest wall
- top of present Golden Gate
- gate chambers
- courses of large masonry exposed on both sides of gate
- courses of large masonry exposed on both sides of gate
- floor level of sealed present gate
- tomb
- GROUND LEVEL
- GROUND LEVEL
- level of arch exposed in tomb
- supposed floor level of lower gate
- BEDROCK

of the eastern wall of the Old City is a wall discovered in 1867 by Captain Charles Warren. Warren encountered the wall after he sank a shaft 143 feet east of the Golden Gate and then burrowed westward underground along bedrock toward the Temple Mount. This underground wall obstructed his progress, so he tried to chisel through it in order to reach the Old City wall. After penetrating 5.5 feet into the underground wall and failing to come out on the other side,

he decided to tunnel south to try to get around the wall. After tunneling 14 feet south without coming to the end, Warren turned around and dug north for 55 feet until an earthfall in the tunnel stopped him. Shortly before he was forced to stop tunneling, Warren observed that this underground wall obstructing his progress had started to curve west toward the Golden Gate and the Old City wall.

Warren further observed that the masonry

in this curving underground wall resembles the masonry of the earlier Old City wall exposed above ground in courses numbered 1 and 2 on either side of the Golden Gate. It also resembles the masonry in the seven lower courses immediately north of the Straight Joint (see p. 500).

The author uses these comparisons of masonry to try to date the earlier wall and the Lower Gate that was built into it.

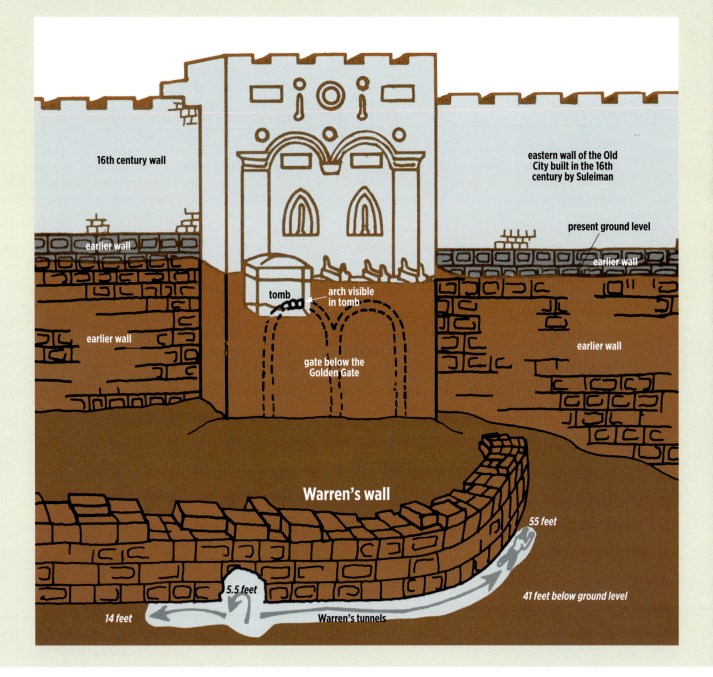

16th century wall

eastern wall of the Old City built in the 16th century by Suleiman

present ground level

earlier wall

earlier wall

earlier wall

tomb

arch visible in tomb

gate below the Golden Gate

earlier wall

Warren's wall

55 feet

41 feet below ground level

5.5 feet

14 feet

Warren's tunnels

south of the turret were large and imposing. Then I noticed with astonishment that on the eastern face of the turret wall, directly beneath the Golden Gate itself, were five wedge-shaped stones neatly set in a massive arch spanning the turret wall. Here were the remains of an earlier gate to Jerusalem, below the Golden Gate, one that apparently had never been fully documented.[3]

I attempted a few pictures, though I had to use time exposures because I had no flash equipment. Then I scurried out of the hole and returned to school.

The next day I again went to the Golden Gate, but this time with flash equipment. Unfortunately, the caretakers of the cemetery had acted with efficiency quite uncharacteristic of the Middle East. The tomb into which I had fallen had already been repaired!

In 1972, while showing the tomb to my brother, I noticed a new hole in the tomb. I had previously told Dr. George Giacumakis, now president of the Institute of Holy Land Studies in Jerusalem and a member of BAR's Editorial Advisory Board, of my experience at the tomb. Happy for the opportunity to photograph the tomb and arch under better conditions, I returned with Dr. Giacumakis, Professor Roy Hayden of Oral Roberts University, and Ginger Barth, a member of the Institute staff. We lowered ourselves into the tomb and re-photographed the wall and the stones of the arch. Shortly thereafter, the tomb was cemented over permanently. That tomb and others directly in front of the Golden Gate were then enclosed by a protective iron fence in 1978. It is unlikely that anyone will have an opportunity in the foreseeable future to examine the remains of this ancient gate to Jerusalem. That being the case, it is especially important to give a detailed description of both the visible upper gate and the lower gate beneath it.

How old is the gate below the Golden Gate? Could it have been the gate through which Jesus entered the Holy City? Unfortunately, it is difficult to date this underground gate precisely. All that can be said with confidence is that the Lower Gate—as I shall identify the gate below the Golden Gate—is older than the Golden Gate itself.

Without the possibility of an archaeological excavation there are only two clues to estimating the age of the Lower Gate: First, the relationship of the arch of the Lower Gate to the gate above it; second, the relationship of the Lower Gate to the lower courses of masonry just above ground along the eastern wall of the Old City.

The Golden Gate is the oldest of all the present gates of the Old City. Six of the other seven present gates* were built by Suleiman the Magnificent from 1539 to 1542, when he rebuilt the walls of Jerusalem. Jaffa Gate, Damascus Gate, Zion Gate, Lion's (Saint Stephen's) Gate, Dung Gate, and Herod's Gate all were built by Suleiman. The New Gate was added in modern times. The Golden Gate was the only ancient gate preserved when Suleiman reconstructed the walls of Jerusalem.

Most scholars believe that the Golden Gate with its beautiful double arches was built in the Byzantine Period.[4] In a soon-to-be-published paper on the gates to the Temple Mount, Meir Ben-Dov will argue, however, that the Golden Gate was built in the Early Arab Period, not long after the Arabs captured Jerusalem in 638 A.D. Ben-Dov calls attention to the similarities between the Golden Gate and the other entrances to the Temple Mount (or *Haram esh-Sharif* as it is called in Arabic) built during the Early Arab Period. Ben-Dov also notes the absence of crosses in the ornate arches, an indication, he says, that the Golden Gate was constructed after the Byzantine period.

The arch of the Lower Gate is under the southern arch of the present Golden Gate. Both arches seem to be on precisely the same line. Moreover, both gates are on the same vertical plane—built into a turret that extends 6 feet outward from the wall line.

Some scholars have suggested that the Lower Gate dates to the period just preceding the Byzantine—the Late Roman Period. Beginning in 130 A.D., Hadrian rebuilt Jerusalem as a Roman colony named Aelia Capitolina. Could this Lower Gate have led to Hadrian's Temple of Jupiter built over the destroyed Jewish Temple? Two arches most scholars date to Aelia Capitolina are visible in the Old City today. One is the gate beneath the Damascus Gate. The other is the arch that passes through the convent of the Sisters of Zion, the Ecce Homo arch, so-called because when it was discovered, it was attributed to the time of Jesus and identified as the place where Pilate said "Behold, the man" ("Ecce homo"). These two Aelia Capitolina arches are composed of stylized concentric arcs that recede slightly from the top of the arch as their radii become smaller. The arch beneath the Golden Gate, on the other hand, is constructed of smooth, wedge-shaped stones. This difference in masonry makes it difficult to argue that the arch of the Lower Gate dates to the Late Roman period. The masonry of the Lower Gate is certainly very different from the two known arches

---

*I do not count the sealed gates, such as the Hulda Gates (Double and Triple) or the Single Gate on the southern side of the Temple Mount, the Postern and "Unnamed Gate" on the east, the Tanner's Gate on the south, the Late Roman entryway on the west, or the Roman gate under the Damascus Gate.

that are commonly dated to this period.

The gate below the Golden Gate could conceivably be Herodian (37 B.C. to 70 A.D.) but this too is unlikely. Josephus, the first-century historian, clearly states that the eastern Temple enclosure wall was the only one that Herod did not rebuild. (*The Jewish War* V, 184–189 [v. 1]).

A comparison of the Lower Gate with the wall into which it is built might help date the gate. Unfortunately, most, but not all, of this wall is underground.

In the 16th century, when Suleiman began to build the wall on either side of the Golden Gate, he found that both sides of the gate were leaning outward and needed strengthening. To buttress the gate, he built perpendicular arches on the interior, and on the exterior he replaced some older stones with wider ones in the corners.

North and south of the Golden Gate, Suleiman built a new wall on the line of an earlier wall. This earlier wall, built of large handsome ashlars 2.5 feet high and 4 to 5 feet long, can still be seen for two or three courses above ground (below the line of Suleiman's masonry). Each ashlar has a recessed margin three to six inches wide. Inside the marginal draft, the face of the stones projects about 6 inches (see p. 498).

The ashlars in this earlier wall do not join tightly together; they are separated by uneven spaces. This odd construction suggests that the stones were restacked after an earlier collapse. The arch I found is about four courses below this early wall adjacent to the Golden Gate. The floor of the underground gate is probably about eight courses below the arch that surmounts the gate. Thus, the arch of the Lower Gate probably belongs to the gateway constructed into this massive lower wall.

This ancient wall may have been a double wall. A wall discovered in 1867 by Captain Charles Warren may have been part of the outer wall of this double wall. The story of Warren's exploration of this outer wall is full of 19th-century romance and excitement. Warren was commissioned by the London-based Palestine Exploration Fund to explore the entire Temple Mount area.[5] But when Warren arrived in Jerusalem, the local governor denied him permission to conduct large-scale digging; the governor feared that excavations might dangerously weaken the Haram esh-Sharif enclosure wall.

Warren determined to be as inconspicuous as possible—he went underground. First he sank deep shafts in several places adjacent to the Temple Mount enclosure walls. In this way Warren explored the walls of the Temple Mount below ground. On the east side, however, the Moslem cemetery just

ZEV RADOVAN

ROMAN GATE BENEATH THE DAMASCUS GATE. Recently cleared, this gate led into second century A.D. Roman Jerusalem, named Aelia Capitolina. The arch, formed by receding concentric rings, closely resembles the Ecce Homo arch, but differs distinctly from the arch of wedge-shaped stones beneath the Golden Gate. From these stylistic comparisons scholars conclude that the buried gateway beneath today's Golden Gate was built at a different time than these other arches and does not date to Roman Jerusalem.

outside the wall prevented his sinking a shaft adjacent to the wall. To avoid the cemetery, he had to sink a shaft some distance further to the east and then drive an underground tunnel back to the wall.

Warren sank his shaft in the lower Kidron Valley, 143 feet east of the Golden Gate. When he reached bedrock, he began tunneling westward along the bedrock up the slope. However, he was forced to come to an abrupt halt 46 feet east of the present wall when he encountered another, massive wall parallel to the present east wall. Warren tried to tunnel over the wall, but it proved too high and he feared that some of the tombs in the cemetery overhead might cave in on him if he continued. He

GARO NALBANDIAN

A 19TH CENTURY LITHOGRAPH of the "Ecce Homo" arches (left). Once attributed to the time of Jesus and identified as the place where Pilate said "Behold, the man" (*Ecce Homo*) (John 19:5), this three-part gateway is now dated to Aelia Capitolina, the second century A.D. Roman Jerusalem rebuilt by Hadrian on the ruins of the city destroyed in 70 A.D. Here we see the large central archway and one of its two smaller flanking arches. Since the last century, when this lithograph was made, the Sisters of Zion convent was built, incorporating the small arch and a portion of the larger central one into its chapel. The remainder of the central arch spans the street known as the Via Dolorosa, outside the convent.

ANCIENT ARCHWAY FORMING APSE of Sisters of Zion chapel (right). This massive arch and the niche to its right appear in the lithograph (opposite) to the left of the large central arch. Here, in the upper right of the picture we see one edge of the large central span of this second century Roman triumphal arch in Jerusalem. The distinct difference in style between these Ecce Homo arches and the arch in the gateway below the Golden Gate suggests that the Lower Gate was built at a different, probably earlier, time.

GARO NALBANDIAN

tried to chisel through the wall, but abandoned this time-consuming effort when, having chiseled 5.5 feet into it, he found yet another course of masonry blocking his way.

Then Warren tried to tunnel around this obstructing wall in his effort to reach the eastern wall of the Temple Mount. First he tunneled south along the obstructing wall for 14 feet and then decided it might be shorter if he dug north. At last, when the tunnel had reached a length of 55 feet, the wall began turning west. Warren's expectation of reaching the eastern temple enclosure soared! But a sudden underground landslide made further progress too dangerous, and Warren was forced to abandon the effort. There seemed to be no way to tunnel around this massive obstructing wall.

Although Warren was unable to reach the eastern Temple Mount enclosure wall, he did make his usual careful observations. The most important of these, for our purposes, is that the massive underground wall 46 feet in front of the Golden Gate resembled the two or three lower courses of masonry exposed above ground on either side of the Golden Gate. Warren described the masonry of the underground wall as follows: "...large quarry-dressed blocks...so far similar to the lower course seen in the sanctuary wall near the Golden Gate, that the roughly dressed faces of the stones project about six inches beyond the marginal drafts, which are very rough."

Warren measured the ashlars in the underground wall and found that they were similar in size to the ashlars in the two or three courses exposed above ground in the eastern wall on either side of the Golden Gate. Warren did note one difference, however. Instead of lying side by side, the

stones in the underground wall were as much as a foot apart with the space between them filled with smaller rocks and plaster. Warren had examined the part of the wall that rested on bedrock; at that level, a rough foundation wall was apparently all that was required.

From the similarity in the ashlars, as well as the fact that Warren's underground wall takes a 90 degree turn west directly toward the Golden Gate, we can assume that the wall Warren found is associated with the lower two or three courses of masonry exposed above ground on either side of the Golden Gate.

Warren also compared the masonry in the lower two or three courses of the eastern wall adjacent to the Golden Gate with the masonry in the eastern wall to the right (north) of the famous "straight joint." The "straight joint" is a vertical seam in the masonry of the eastern wall of the Old City, 105 feet north of the southeastern corner of the Temple Mount. The straight joint or straight seam was obviously created by an addition to the eastern wall on its southern end. The addition, most are agreed, was built by Herod the Great, to extend the

TWO COURSES OF LARGE ROUGH ASHLARS. These stones are visible just above ground level north (above) and south (below) of the Golden Gate. The ashlars, each about 2.5 feet high and 4 to 5 feet long, are unevenly spaced, an indication that the wall had collapsed and was then restacked. These courses resemble the masonry north of the so-called straight joint (see photo on p. 500) and the masonry in the underground wall east of the Golden Gate discovered more than a century ago by Captain Charles Warren.

southern end of the Temple Mount.

But who built the wall north of the straight joint? The question has significance here because the masonry appears to be the same as that in the lowest two or three courses visible above ground on either side of the Golden Gate, as well as that of the large ashlars with marginal drafts Warren found below ground in the wall that curved toward the Golden Gate.

The masonry north of the straight joint appears to have two building phases, though the stones in both phases have the same appearance. The lowest seven courses are arranged in alternating rows of headers (short facings) and stretchers (long facings); the stones themselves are tightly joined. Above these seven courses, however, the pattern of alternating rows of headers and stretchers is abandoned, and the stones are not snugly fitted together—as if the upper courses had once collapsed and were then restacked, like the two or three exposed courses of masonry adjacent to the Golden Gate.

Scholars disagree as to who built the wall north of the straight joint. Some, like Professor Michael Avi-Yonah, who died in 1973, attribute the masonry to Herod the Great. The Herodians, Avi-Yonah said, used more than one kind of masonry. Herod, the king, built the wall to the right of the straight joint. To its left, one of Herod's descendants, in the so-called Herodian period, later added the "Royal Portico" to the southern end of the Temple Mount, using a different kind of masonry. (In support of Avi-Yonah's theory is the observation by Josephus that an earlier portico built by Herod the Great burned and was rebuilt later.)

ZEV RADOVAN

There are several difficulties with Avi-Yonah's dating. There is no suggestion in the literary sources that either Herod or his successors ever did any building (such as the underground wall Warren found) along the eastern side of the Temple platform. Josephus records that Herod Agrippa II (53–66 A.D.) considered raising the height of the east wall in order to employ 18,000 men left without work after completion of the construction of the Temple. The people "urged the king to raise the height of the east portico. This portico was part of the outer temple, and was situated in a deep ravine [The Kidron]. It had walls four hundred cubits long and was constructed of square stones, completely white, each stone being twenty cubits long and six high. This was the work of King Solomon, who was the first to build the whole temple. The king [Agrippa] reasoned that it is always easy to demolish a structure but hard to erect one, and still more so in the case of this portico, for the work would take time and a great deal of money. He therefore refused this request of theirs; but he did not veto the paving of the city with white stone." (*Jewish Antiquities* XX, 219–223, [7]).

If, as Avi-Yonah says, the eastern temple enclosure

THE ELABORATE WESTERN SIDE of the Golden Gate, viewed from the Temple Mount. On the horizon to the east is the Mount of Olives. As part of his massive rebuilding of the walls of Jerusalem around 1540, Suleiman the Magnificent built arches to buttress the leaning walls of the Golden Gate.

wall was constructed by Herod, how could it have been in need of renovation in 64 A.D. and how could it have appeared so ancient that it was believed by the people to be 1,000 years old, from King Solomon's time? This account in Josephus forces us to conclude that until the eve of the destruction of the Temple, the eastern walls and porticoes remained old, and were, therefore, called "Solomon's Porticoes." (See also Acts 5:12.)

Basing their conclusions on archaeological evidence, many scholars date the masonry north of the straight joint to a period earlier than the Herodian. However, they disagree as to just how much earlier.

For example, Dr. Yoram Tsafrir[6] suggests that the masonry to the right of the straight joint dates from the Hellenistic Period and is possibly the work of Alexander Yannai (103–76 B.C.). There are

THE STRAIGHT JOINT. A vertical seam interrupts the lower courses of masonry in the eastern wall of the Old City, 105 feet north of the southern end of the wall. The straight joint marks the transition between an older section of wall on the right (north) and later construction on the left (south). This later addition was probably built by Herod the Great in the first century B.C., to enlarge the earlier and smaller Temple Mount. However it is less certain when the older, northern wall was constructed.

The rough-faced stones to the north of the straight joint resemble those in the two or three lowest courses of the eastern wall on either side of the Golden Gate (see p. 498), as well as those in the curved wall discovered underground by Captain Charles Warren east of the Golden Gate. If we could date the masonry north of the straight joint it would help us to date these other walls as well as the gate beneath the Golden Gate, which is related to them. Scholars' conclusions about when and by whom the wall north of the straight joint was built differ, however, by as much as 1,000 years—from the time of Herod to the time of Solomon.

similarities between this wall and the Alexandrium and Machaerus fortresses also believed to have been constructed by Yannai. And Tsafrir suggests another possible builder from the Hellenistic Period—Simon the Just, High Priest from 219–196 B.C., might have built this eastern wall. Warren's underground second wall of similar masonry parallel to this eastern wall presents an intriguing correlation to Simon's building projects mentioned in Ben Sira 50:1–2: "Simon the high priest, son of Onias, in his life repaired the house [of God], and in his time fortified the temple. He laid the foundations for the *high double walls*, the high retaining walls for the temple enclosure." Though the meaning of "double walls" is obscure, the reference here may be to Warren's wall along the eastern temple enclosure.

Other scholars, such as Dame Kathleen Kenyon[7] and Maurice Dunand, whom Kenyon calls "the doyen of archaeology of the Phoenician coast,"[8] have opted for an even earlier date—in the Persian period (the end of the sixth century B.C.)—for the masonry to the right of the straight joint. They base this dating on similarities with Persian period walls found in Sidon and Byblos. A few years before her death in 1978, Kenyon wrote that the wall dated to the period of the return to Zion from Babylonian captivity, when the Jews reconstructed Jerusalem (2 Chronicles 36:23, Ezra 1:2–3, 6:5–8). For example, in *Digging Up Jerusalem*, Kenyon stated that the wall was a result of several reconstructions occurring within the Persian period. Originally, she suggested, the wall may have been built by Zerubabel on the earlier site of Solomon's southeast Temple podium of the Temple Mount.

However, if Zerubabel, on his return from exile, had difficulty building even a modest Temple (as the Biblical documents indicate), he could scarcely have completed a wall as impressive as this early eastern wall. At least one scholar, Dr. Ernest Marie Laperrousaz[9], has suggested dating the lower courses right of the straight joint to the time of King Solomon. Laperrousaz relies on the similarity between this masonry and that of the Phoenicians. (The Bible tells us that Solomon employed Phoenician masons to construct the Temple.) If Laperrousaz is right, then the Lower Gate may be Solomonic!

In any event, the dating of the masonry right (north) of the straight joint is probably the best clue we have to dating the two or three lowest courses of the wall adjacent to the Golden Gate. And the date of these lowest courses would be the best indication of the date of the gate below the Golden Gate, for the Lower Gate appears to have been built into the courses of this earlier wall.

Perhaps the most important implication of the presence of the Lower Gate below the threshold of the Golden Gate is that this area has long been identified as a location for the eastern entrance into the Temple Mount. Many Jerusalem maps show a Temple gate due east of the Dome of the Rock in the Haram esh-Sharif. The Golden Gate, however, is located about 350 feet north of this point. We now know that the location of the present Golden Gate was determined by an earlier gate.

The precise dating of the Lower Gate must, for the present, remain problematic. Only excavation could determine the exact relationship of the Lower Gate to the lower courses exposed in the eastern wall. The very existence of the arch implies that a gateway at this elevation would have cut through at least eight to ten courses of this ancient masonry.

The best archaeological evidence for dating the Lower Gate seems to be the masonry to the right of the straight joint. Most scholars date this masonry on archaeological and historical grounds to sometime

before the Herodian period. The Lower Gate would, therefore, also date to a period earlier than the Herodian. How much earlier, we cannot be sure. But a date as early as the reign of King Solomon is not impossible. It is even possible that such a gate, revered through the ages, continued to be used for a thousand years or more and was thus the gate through which Jesus entered the Holy City. ◪

[1] See "The Rose of Jericho," BAR, September/October 1980.

[2] For a thorough discussion of whether the "Beautiful Gate" of Acts 3:2, 3:10 is the eastern city gate or an interior Temple gate leading from the Court of the Gentiles on the east to the Court of Israel, see Jack Finegan, *The Archaeology of the New Testament* (Princeton University Press, 1969), pp. 129–130.

[3] A report that the tomb in front of the Golden Gate was partially destroyed by a bomb in the June 1967 Israeli-Arab war can be found in a pamphlet by Eli Schiller called *The Golden Gate* (Ariel Publishing House, 1975 [Hebrew]), pp. 6–7.

[4] See K. Creswell, "Early Muslim Architecture," and Spencer Corbett, "Some Observations on the Gateways to the Herodian Temple in Jerusalem," *Palestine Exploration Quarterly* (January–April 1952).

[5] For an account of another phase of Warren's explorations, see "Jerusalem's Water Supply During Siege—The Rediscovery of Warren's Shaft," BAR, July/August 1981.

[6] See Yoram Tsafrir, "The Location of the Seleucid Akra in Jerusalem," *Revue Biblique*, Vol. 82, p. 177.

[7] See M. Dunand, "Byblos, Sidon, Jerusalem," *Vetus Testamentum*, XVII, 1968; and Kathleen Kenyon's works *Digging Up Jerusalem* (1974) and *Royal Cities of the Old Testament* (1971).

[8] Kathleen M. Kenyon, *Digging Up Jerusalem*, (New York: Praeger Publishers, 1974), p. 112.

[9] See "*A-t-on Dégagé l'angle sud-est du Temple de Solomon?*" in *Syria*, L. (1973).

See the Queries and Comments section of the May/June 1983 issue for corrections and a number of letters we received in response to this article.

Related Reading

Meir Ben-Dov, "Herod's Mighty Temple Mount," BAR, November/December 1986.

Kathleen Ritmeyer and Leen Ritmeyer, "Reconstructing Herod's Temple Mount in Jerusalem," BAR, November/December 1989.

Dan Bahat, "Jerusalem Down Under: Tunneling Along Herod's Temple Mount Wall," BAR, November/December 1995.

David Jacobsen, "Sacred Geometry: Unlocking the Secrets of the Temple Mount, Part 1," BAR, July/August 1999; David Jacobsen, "Sacred Geometry: Unlocking the Secrets of the Temple Mount, Part 2," BAR, September/October 1999; Asher S. Kaufman, "Kaufman Responds to Jacobsen," BAR, March/April 2000; Leen Ritmeyer, "Ritmeyer Responds to Jacobsen," BAR, March/April 2000.

Strata: "Exclusive New Photos of Ancient Jerusalem's Eastern Gate," BAR, March/April 2008.

FEW PLACES BETTER ILLUSTRATE the layered history that archaeology uncovers than the little ridge known as the City of David, the oldest inhabited part of Jerusalem. For example, to tell the story of the Pool of Siloam, where Jesus cured the blind man, we must go back 700 years before that—to the time of the Assyrian monarch Sennacherib and his siege of Jerusalem.

Hezekiah, the Judahite king at that time, could see the Assyrian siege coming. Protective steps were clearly called for, especially to protect Jerusalem's water supply. The only source of fresh water at this time was the Gihon Spring, near the floor of the adjacent Kidron Valley. So Hezekiah decided on a major engineering project—he would construct a tunnel under the ridge on which the City of David lay to bring the water of the spring to the other, less vulnerable, side of Jerusalem. It was dug by two teams of tunnelers working from opposite ends, meeting in the middle—it's still a mystery how they managed to meet, but they did. A memorial plaque was carved in the tunnel wall to commemorate the feat—the famous Siloam Inscription, now in the Istanbul Museum (it was discovered in Ottoman times). Water flowed through the tunnel from the spring to the Pool of Siloam at the other end. It is still known as Hezekiah's Tunnel, and it is still a thrill for tourists to walk through its 1750-foot length.

Where Jesus Cured the Blind Man

HERSHEL SHANKS

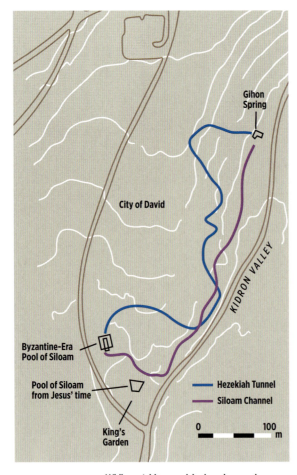

Gihon
Spring

City of David

KIDRON VALLEY

Byzantine-Era
Pool of Siloam

Pool of Siloam
from Jesus' time

King's
Garden

— Hezekiah Tunnel
— Siloam Channel

0   100
         m

PRECEDING PAGES: While watching municipal workers replace a sewer pipe in the City of David, south of Jerusalem's Temple Mount, archaeologist Eli Shukron noticed that the construction equipment had revealed two ancient steps. Shukron quickly notified his colleague Ronny Reich, who identified the steps as part of the Pool of Siloam from the late Second Temple Period (first century B.C.-first century A.D.), as further excavations soon confirmed. It was at the Pool of Siloam, according to the Gospel of John, that Jesus cured the blind man (John 9:1-11). The newly discovered pool is adjacent to an area referred to as the King's Garden and is just southeast of what had long been called the Pool of Siloam (see plan above). The other pool, however, does not date to Jesus' time but to the fourth century (a photo of this later Pool of Siloam appears on p. 508).

The waters of Siloam are mentioned by the prophet Isaiah, a contemporary of Hezekiah's, who refers to "the gently flowing waters of Siloam" (Shiloah in Hebrew) (Isaiah 8:6). When the exiles returned from Babylon and rebuilt the walls of Jerusalem, Nehemiah tells us that a certain Shallun rebuilt "the wall of the Pool of Shiloah by the King's Garden" (Nehemiah 3:15).

In Jesus' time the Pool of Siloam figures in the cure of a man who had been blind from birth. Jesus spits on the ground and mixes his saliva with the mud, which he smears on the blind man's eyes. He then tells the man "to wash in the Pool of Siloam." When

the blind man does so, he is able to see (John 9:1-7).

We still haven't found the Pool of Siloam from Isaiah's and Hezekiah's time. We're not even sure where it was. The same is true regarding the pool in Nehemiah's time. In the Byzantine period the empress Eudocia (c. 400-460) built a church and a pool where the water debouches from Hezekiah's Tunnel to commemorate the miracle of the blind man. Early in the last century archaeologists found the remains of that church, over which today sits a mosque. The church and the pool are mentioned in several Byzantine pilgrim itineraries. Until last year, it was this pool that people meant when they talked of the Pool of Siloam.

Now we have found an earlier pool, the pool as it existed in Jesus' time—and it is a much grander affair.

As with so much in archaeology, it was stumbled on, not part of a planned excavation. In June 2004 archaeologists Ronny Reich and Eli Shukron were digging in the area of the Gihon Spring where Hezekiah's Tunnel begins. Far to the south, between the end of the rock ridge that forms the City of David and a lush green orchard that is often identified as the Biblical King's Garden, is a narrow alley through which a sewer pipe runs carrying waste from the valley west of the City of David into the Kidron Valley east of the City of David. The city authorities needed to repair or replace this sewer and sent workers with heavy equipment to do some excavating. Eli was watching the operation, when suddenly he saw two steps appear. He immediately halted the work and called Ronny, who came rushing down. As soon as Ronny saw the steps, he exclaimed, "These must be steps going down to the Pool of Siloam during the Second Temple Period." He took a few pictures and wrote a report to Jon Seligman, the district archaeologist for Jerusalem. A quick response was called for because the winter rains were fast approaching and the sewer pipe had to be repaired or replaced. Ronny and Eli were quickly authorized to excavate the area on behalf of the Israeli Antiquities Authority. The more they excavated, the more steps they found, and the wider the steps became.

They have now excavated the entire length of the steps on the side adjacent to the rock ridge of the City of David. There are in fact three short segments of descending stairways of five steps each. The first leads down to a narrow landing. The second leads to another landing and the third leads down to the final level (so far). The size of the pool itself would vary, depending on the level of the water. When it was full, it probably covered all of the steps. The landings served as a kind of esplanade for people to stand on when the steps were submerged in water.

HERSHEL SHANKS

THREE SETS OF STAIRS (above), each with five steps, have been uncovered at the New Testament-era Pool of Siloam. The excavators have exposed an area 225 feet long on one side of the pool and have reached both corners of that side (one corner is shown at right). The corners are somewhat greater than 90 degrees, indicating that the pool was not a square but a trapezoid.

The archaeologists also uncovered the two stepped corners at either end of these steps. So we know how wide the pool was at this point: more than 225 feet. We also know that the steps existed on at least three sides of the pool.

The corners are not exactly at right angles, however; they are a little more than 90 degrees. The pool appears to have been a trapezoid, widening apron-like as it descends into the valley. How far into the valley the pool extended, the archaeologists are not sure. Ronny's best guess is that it is about the same as the width of the pool on the side they have uncovered.

Many times archaeologists are unsure of the date of what they find. But in this case, there is no question. Ideally, archaeologists want two dates: the date of construction and the date when the

HERSHEL SHANKS

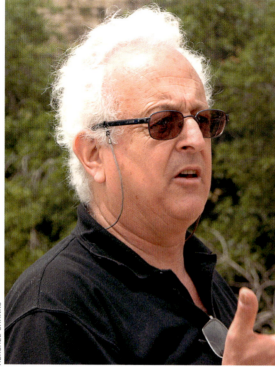

HERSHEL SHANKS

RONNY REICH was the first to identify the steps as part of the Pool of Siloam from the time of Jesus. Now the leading archaeologist specializing in Jerusalem, Reich worked with the late Nahman Avigad in the Old City's Jewish Quarter and has also dug at the western wall of the Temple Mount. His excavations at the Gihon Spring have revolutionized our understanding of the city's ancient water supply system.

facility went out of use. Here the archaeologists are fortunate to have both.

The pool had two phases. The stone steps are part of the second phase. Under the stone steps and in places where the stones are missing, the excavators were able see that in the first phase the steps were plastered. Only in the second phase were the steps faced with stones. The excavators went over the early steps with a metal detector, and in four places it beeped, revealing four coins *in the plaster*. These coins would date the first phase of the pool.

They were all coins of Alexander Jannaeus (103-76 B.C.), one of the later Hasmonean (Jewish) kings who were succeeded in 37 B.C. by Herod the Great. The excavators cannot be sure precisely how long these coins were in circulation before being embedded in the plaster of the first phase of the Pool of Siloam. But they can say with some assurance that the pool was constructed in the late Hasmonean period or early Herodian period. They may know more precisely if they dig under the steps and find a coin from Herod's time. Then the pool would be Herodian.

We also know from coins how long the pool was in use. Near one corner of the pool they excavated part of a plaza or terrace and found nothing but late Second Temple pottery (which ended with the Roman destruction of Jerusalem in 70 A.D.). Most significantly, they found a dozen coins from the

ARALDO DE LUCA/CORBIS

Jesus cures the blind man (John 9:1-11)

As he walked along, he saw a man blind from birth. [2]His disciples asked him, "Rabbi, who sinned, this man or his parents, that he was born blind?" [3]Jesus answered, "Neither this man nor his parents sinned, he was born blind so that God's works might be revealed in him. [4]We must work the works of him who sent me while it is day; night is coming when no one can work. [5]As long as I am in the world, I am the light of the world." [6]When he had said this, he spat on the ground and made mud with the saliva, and spread the mud on the man's eyes, [7]saying to him, "Go, wash in the pool of Siloam" (which means Sent). Then he went and washed and came back able to see. [8]The neighbors and those who had seen him before as a beggar began to ask, "Is this not the man who used to sit and beg?" [9]Some were saying "It is he." Others were saying, "No, but it is someone like him." He kept saying, "I am the man." [10]But they kept asking him, "Then how were your eyes opened?" [11]He answered, "The man called Jesus made mud, spread it on my eyes, and said to me, 'Go to Siloam and wash.' Then I went and washed and received my sight."

JASON CLARK

period of the First Jewish Revolt against Rome. The
revolt lasted from 66 to 70 A.D. The excavated coins
date from years 2, 3 and 4 of the revolt. The pool was
therefore used until the end of the revolt, after which
it was abandoned.

period of the First Jewish Revolt against Rome. The
revolt lasted from 66 to 70 A.D. The excavated coins
date from years 2, 3 and 4 of the revolt. The pool was
therefore used until the end of the revolt, after which
it was abandoned.

This area, the lowest spot in all Jerusalem, was
not inhabited again until the Byzantine period.
Every year the winter rains flowing down the valley
deposited another layer of mud in the pool. And
after the Roman destruction of the city, the pool
was no longer cleaned. Over the centuries a thick
layer of mud accumulated and the pool gradually disappeared. The archaeologists found it under nearly
10 feet of mud in places.

When Byzantine Christians returned to the area
in the fourth century, they assumed the Pool of
Siloam referred to in the New Testament was at
the end of Hezekiah's Tunnel, so they built their
pool and a commemorative church where the
tunnel comes out of the rock. This pool figures in
numerous 19th-century engravings. As late as the
1970s, Arab women still washed clothes in this pool.
It is well worth a visit.

THE SILOAM POOL as it might have looked during the New
Testament era is shown here in an artist's rendition. Bathers would
have enjoyed a view of the Kidron Valley, just east of the City of
David. In the Gospel of John, when Jesus cures the blind man, he
tells him, "Go to Siloam and wash" (John 9:11). The pool probably
served as a *miqveh*, a Jewish ritual bath.

What function the Pool of Siloam served in Jesus'
time is not entirely clear. Undoubtedly, thousands
of pilgrims would come to Jerusalem on the three
Biblically ordained pilgrim festivals—Passover, Weeks
(Pentecost, or Shavuoth) and Tabernacles (Succoth).
They may well have camped in the adjacent Kidron
Valley and been supplied with drinking and cooking
water from the pool. The water in the pool would
also qualify as a *miqveh*, for ritual bathing, points out
Reich, who is a leading expert on *miqvaot*. Indeed its
naturally flowing spring water was of the highest level
of sanctity. The water in a *miqveh* is usually standing
water, even though it is required to flow into the
pool naturally. But here the spring flowed continuously, refreshing the water. However, ritual bathing in
a *miqveh* must be in the nude. Perhaps there was some

HERSHEL SHANKS

means of providing privacy.

Whether the Pool of Siloam in Hezekiah and Isaiah's time was located in the same place as in Jesus' time remains a question. Even if it was in the same spot, it may have been a different size. Ronny and Eli would like to make a cut under the steps, which would give some indication of an earlier pool. If they find Iron Age pottery (tenth–sixth century B.C.), they can conclude that the Pool of Siloam from Hezekiah's and Isaiah's time was in this same location. However, Ronny and Eli do not want to dig into the verdant orchard that now fills the unexcavated portion of the New Testament-era Pool of Siloam. Besides, it belongs to the Greek Orthodox Church, which, like Ronny

A WOMAN KNEELS to do her laundry (photo at left) in what had long been known as the Pool of Siloam. Byzantine-era Christians assumed this pool was the Biblical Siloam and built a church here; this pool was a popular destination for pilgrims and was the subject of a 19th-century illustration by W.H. Bartlett (below). Thanks to the recent discovery, we now know that the Biblical Pool of Siloam was just southeast of this site.

How Historical Is the Gospel of John?

The Gospels, the first four books of the New Testament, tell the story of the life of Jesus. Yet only one—the Gospel of John—claims to be an eyewitness account, the testimony of the unnamed "disciple whom Jesus loved." ("This is the disciple who is testifying to these things and wrote these things, and we know that his testimony is true" [John 21:24]). Matthew, Mark and Luke are so alike in their telling that they are called the Synoptic Gospels, meaning, "seen together"—the parallels are clear when they are looked at side by side. Matthew and Luke follow the version of events in Mark, which is thought by scholars to be the earliest and most historically accurate Gospel. John, however, does not include the same incidents or chronology found in the other three Gospels, and the fact that it is so different has spurred a debate over whether John's Gospel is historical or not.

Several hypotheses have attempted to explain why so much of Jesus' life not portrayed in the Synoptics is present in John and vice versa. One hypothesis claims that John recorded many of the events that occurred before the arrest of John the Baptist, while the Synoptics all have Jesus' ministry beginning only after the arrest. Another holds that John was written last, by someone who knew about the other three Gospels but who wished to write a spiritual gospel instead of an historical one. There is also the possibility that the author of John did not know of Mark and hence did not have the same information.

One of the facts in dispute among the four Gospels is the length of Jesus' ministry. According to the Synoptics, it lasted only about a year, while John has Jesus ministering between two and three years. The Jesus of John's telling also knew Jerusalem well and had traveled there three or four times. The Synoptics, however, have Jesus visit Jerusalem only once. In John, Jesus had friends near Jerusalem, including Mary, Martha and Lazarus of the town of Bethany, which is just outside of the city on the east slope of the Mount of Olives.

The author of John also knew Jerusalem well, as is evident from the geographic and place name information throughout the book. He mentions, among others, the Sheep Gate Pool (Bethesda), the Siloam Pool and Jacob's Well. The geographic specificity lends credence to John's account.

Another aspect of John that may be more historically accurate than the Synoptics is the account of the crucifixion and the events that led up to it. The Synoptics say that Jesus' Last Supper was the Passover meal—held that year on a Thursday evening (Jewish holidays begin at sunset)—and they would have us believe that the Sanhedrin, the high court, gathered at the beginning of a major holiday to interrogate Jesus and hand him over to the Romans. John, in contrast, has Jesus handed over for crucifixion on "the day of Preparation of Passover week, about the sixth hour." According to John, the Last Supper is not a Passover meal (because the holiday that year did not start until Friday evening), and Jesus is crucified and buried before Passover begins. In John's account Jesus becomes the Passover sacrificial lamb, which was offered the afternoon before the Passover holiday. Some scholars suggest that John may be more historical regarding the crucifixion than the other three Gospels.

Given John's familiarity with Jerusalem and its environs, it is very possible that he had visited the Pool of Siloam, which he mentions in connection with the story of the curing of the blind man (a story that appears only in John's Gospel). It is that pool that has only recently been uncovered, as described in the accompanying article.

For more on the question of John's historical reliability, see D. Moody Smith, "John: Historian or Theologian?" Bible Review, October 2004.

FOUR COINS, INCLUDING the one shown here, embedded in the plaster of the newly discovered Siloam Pool, show that the pool was in existence at the time of Jesus. All four date to the rule of Alexander Jannaeus, one of the later Hasmonean kings, who ruled from 103 to 76 B.C.

and Eli, would not want the orchard destroyed. But they would like to make a very small cut through the trees to see how deep the pool is and to learn whether there are Iron Age remains beneath. Perhaps the church, appreciating the significance of this place, will permit this. The church's orchard suddenly has great significance for the history of its faith. ◧

For reader letters and corrections in response to this article, see Queries and Comments in the January/February 2006 issue of BAR. In addition, the Pool of Siloam is presumed to be trapezoidal in shape, based on the edges that were revealed in excavation, not a rectangle as depicted in our reconstruction drawing on p. 507.

Related Reading

Strata: "Ritual Bath or Swimming Pool?" BAR, May/June 2008; Queries and Comments: "Nude in the *Mikveh*?" BAR, September/October 2008.

Urban C. von Wahlde, "The Puzzling Pool of Bethesda," BAR, September/October 2011.

11

Understanding the Deaths of John and Jesus

From the site of the Baptist's gruesome beheading to the only known archaeological remains of a victim of Roman crucifixion, these articles offered stunning details about the Gospels' most famous deaths.

John the Baptist and Jesus were both executed at the hands of the ruling authorities—the former by beheading and the latter by crucifixion. What can archaeology tell us about the setting and circumstances of these grisly executions?

SEPTEMBER/OCTOBER 2012
Machaerus—Where Salome Danced and John the Baptist Was Beheaded

Machaerus is one of a string of desert palace-fortresses mounted by Herod the Great on the eastern border of his empire. Machaerus is the only one, however, east of the Jordan River. Visually the site and its remains are eye-popping, but they are also special historically: Here is where Salome danced and John the Baptist was beheaded.

The story is told in Matthew 14:1–12 and supplemented by Josephus. Although the sources speak of Herod, it is actually Herod the Great's son Herod Antipas who is the major actor in the story. It all began when John the Baptist denounced the marriage of Herod Antipas and Herodias (she was divorced from Herod Antipas's brother). The Baptist condemned the marriage as unlawful. When Hedodias's daughter Salome danced for Herod Antipas at Machaerus, he was so entranced that he promised to give her anything she might ask for. At her mother's instigation, Salome asked for the Baptist's head on a platter. And so it was: John the Baptist was brought to Machaerus in chains and beheaded.

The site was later besieged by the Romans during the First Jewish Revolt of 66–70 C.E., but, unlike Masada, a negotiated settlement saved the mountain-top site from destruction. But the residents were required to leave.

Machaerus was excavated beginning in the late 1970s by the Franciscan archaeologists Virgilio Corbo and Michele Piccirillo, but both died before completing a final report. The excavation was then continued in 2009 by the Hungarian archaeologist who continues to work at the site and wrote this report, Gyozo Vőrős. He embraces the latest archaeological techniques, including ground penetrating radar and eddy current detectors with variable antennas that can reveal underground structures 12 feet below the surface.

JANUARY/FEBRUARY 1985
Crucifixion—The Archaeological Evidence

The only identifiable victim of crucifixion whose remains have been excavated was recovered in Jerusalem by Israeli archaeologist Vassilios Tzaferis of the Israel Department of Antiquities and Museums, now the Israel Antiquities Authority.

The large iron nail is still embedded in the victim's overlapping heels, together with bits of the olive wood cross on which he was nailed. What can this tell us about the position of the victim on the cross and crucifixion in general? Tzaferis reports in this chapter's second article.

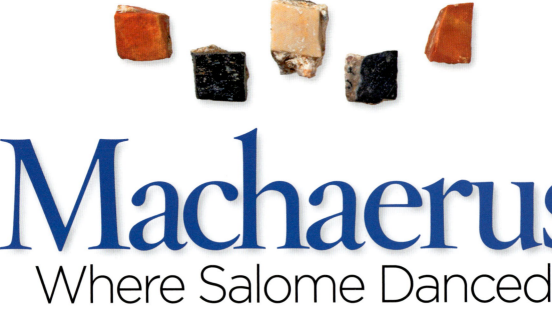

Machaerus

Where Salome Danced and John the Baptist Was Beheaded

GYŐZŐ VÖRÖS

SALOME DANCED AT MACHAERUS. And John the Baptist was beheaded there. The gospel story is supplemented by the Jewish historian Josephus: It all began when Herod Antipas (King Herod the Great's son who ruled Galilee and Perea between 4 B.C. and 39 A.D.; see article in September/October 2012 issue) lusted after his brother's wife Herodias. Herod Antipas persuaded Herodias to divorce her husband and marry him. This union was denounced as unlawful by John the Baptist,[1] which naturally made Herodias furious with him. During her first marriage, Herodias had borne a daughter named Salome, who danced for her new step-father, Herod Antipas, at his famous birthday party at Machaerus. Herod Antipas was so pleased with her dance that he "promised an oath to grant her whatever she might ask" (Matthew 14:7; see also Mark 6:23). "Prompted by her mother," Salome asked for the head of John the Baptist on a platter. "Out of regard for his oaths and for the guests, he commanded it to be given; he sent and had John beheaded in the prison" (Matthew 14:8–10; see also Mark 6:24–28). According to Josephus, the Baptist was brought to

Machaerus in chains and put to death.[2]

I think we can identify the very location of the party where Salome danced. But that is getting ahead of the story.

Machaerus is one of the fortified royal palaces most often associated with Herod the Great, although they are actually of Hasmonean origin (except for Herodium, which was built and named by Herod). There were at least seven of these fortresses, from Alexandrium (also known as Alexandreion or Sartaba) in the north to Masada in the south. In between, from north to south, were Doq, Cypros, Hyrcania, Herodium (Herodion) and Machaerus. Excluding Machaerus, which sits on

CARE TO DANCE? While Machaerus is best known from Josephus as the setting of Salome's dance and John the Baptist's subsequent execution (a story also told in the Gospels), archaeology at the palatial fortress tells a longer tale. The site was occupied in three primary phases under Hasmonean, Herodian and Zealot leadership. Comparative studies of other contemporaneous Judean fortresses west of the Dead Sea and Jordan River often reveal striking parallels to the history, artifacts and architecture of Machaerus.

the eastern edge of the Dead Sea, all of these sites are located west of the Jordan River and the Dead Sea. Those west of the Jordan form a kind of wall protecting Jerusalem. All, including Jerusalem, are visible from Machaerus's high perch over the Dead

MASADA

MACHAERUS

HERODIUM

Sea (see photo below). Machaerus was thus the first to face an enemy from the east and could warn the others of the danger. According to Pliny the Elder, Machaerus was the strongest citadel in Judea after Jerusalem.[3]

Herod the Great was a notoriously unpopular ruler, and some think that these palace/fortresses were built to provide Herod with a safe haven in case of rebellion. To assure that he would be mourned, he ordered that "all the principal men of the entire Jewish nation, wheresoever they lived," should be killed on Herod's death.[4] But there was another, outside danger: The Jewish area of Perea, ruled by Herod Antipas after his father's death, lay east of the Jordan at the border of Nabatea, a potential foe. Were the Nabateans to attack, Machaerus would be the first to face the enemy.

If, however, an attack from the north or the south reached Alexandrium or Masada first, Machaerus would receive a signal by smoke during the day or fire by night. The eastern fortress would then send out flares of its own, visible to all of the other western citadels. Even Jerusalem was visible from Machaerus. The smoke of the sacrificial offerings could be seen rising from the altars of the Jerusalem Temple.[5]

The fortress of Machaerus was thus critical to the defense of Judea.

Although Josephus described Machaerus in some detail, its location was forgotten even in ancient times. There is no record of pilgrims going

Matthew 14:1–12

At that time Herod the ruler heard reports about Jesus; and he said to his servants, "This is John the Baptist; he has been raised from the dead, and for this reason these powers are at work in him." For Herod had arrested John, bound him, and put him in prison on account of Herodias, his brother Philip's wife, because John had been telling him, "It is not lawful for you to have

Salome Receives the Head of John the Baptist by Michelangelo Merisi da Caravaggio (c. 1610).

her." Though Herod wanted to put him to death, he feared the crowd, because they regarded him as a prophet. But when Herod's birthday came, the daughter of Herodias danced before the company, and she pleased Herod so much that he promised on oath to grant her whatever she might ask. Prompted by her mother, she said, "Give me the head of John the Baptist here on a platter." The king was grieved, yet out of regard for his oaths and for the guests, he commanded it to be given; he sent and had John beheaded in the prison. The head was brought on a platter and given to the girl, who brought it to her mother. His disciples came and took the body and buried it; then they went and told Jesus.

A VIEW TO LIVE BY. The main defensive advantage of placing a fortified citadel at Machaerus stems from the visibility of its mountainous perch above the Dead Sea. Signals sent from the site could be seen at other defensive fortresses on the other side of the Dead Sea as far as Alexandrium to the north, Masada to the south and Jerusalem to the far west (see map at right and photo below). Machaerus not only warned Judea of attacks from the east, but also stood as an anchor point for relaying warnings from one fortress to the rest. Looking out from Machaerus, one would have been able to see the smoke of sacrificial offerings rising from the Jerusalem Temple.

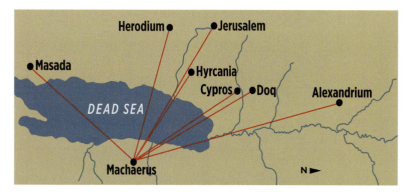

GYŐZŐ VÖRÖS

A LONG WAY UP. The photo above pictures Machaerus from the east in Jordan, and the photo opposite is a view from Israel across the Dead Sea. Josephus describes Machaerus as "a very rocky hill elevated to a very great height, which circumstance alone made it very hard to be subdued."

A LONG WAY DOWN. Author Győző Vörös is shown (at right) excavating ancient debris at the bottom of the 50-foot-deep Hasmonean cistern. In an area with minute rainfall, ancient fortresses needed enormous water reserves in case of a siege.

GYŐZŐ VÖRÖS

to the site when Constantine made Christianity a licit religion in the fourth century. German explorer Ulrich Seetzen rediscovered the citadel at Machaerus only in 1807, and its lower city was first identified by the French Dominican Father Felix-Marie Abel of the École Biblique in 1909.

In 1968 an exploratory trial excavation was conducted by Jerry Vardaman, who later founded the Cobb Institute of Archaeology at Mississippi State University. It lasted for less than a month. The Jordanian authorities canceled the excavation permit, probably because Vardaman's report, written just a year after the Six-Day War in June 1967, described Machaerus as an important site in Judea in Hasmonean (c. 140–37 B.C.) and Herodian times (37 B.C.–44 A.D.).

The most important excavations at Machaerus in the 20th century were conducted by two well-known scholars from the Studium Biblicum Franciscanum in Jerusalem, Virgilio Corbo and Michele Piccirillo, in 1978–1981 and by Piccirillo again in 1992–1993. Although they published several excellent preliminary articles, both scholars passed away before a final report was ever written. Piccirillo did publish the numismatic finds, and Corbo's colleague Stanislao Loffreda published the ceramic finds. Father Corbo concentrated primarily on the architecture of the citadel—his sketched layout was the first publication of the ground plan of the interior of the fortified palace.

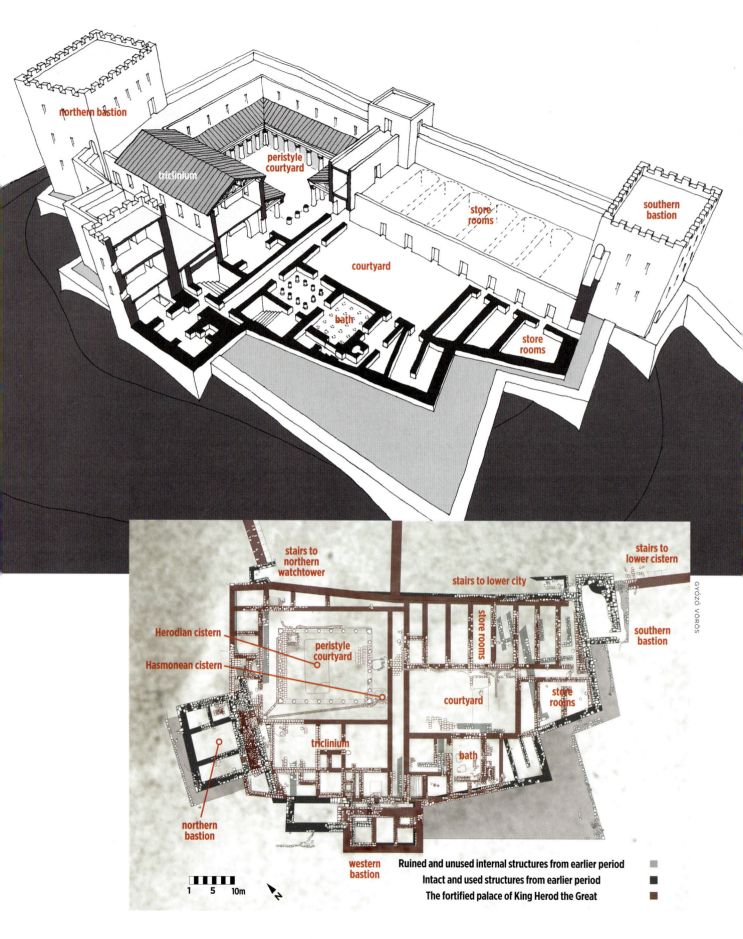

northern bastion

triclinium

peristyle courtyard

store rooms

courtyard

bath

store rooms

southern bastion

stairs to northern watchtower

stairs to lower city

stairs to lower cistern

Herodian cistern

Hasmonean cistern

peristyle courtyard

store rooms

southern bastion

courtyard

triclinium

store rooms

bath

northern bastion

western bastion

GYÓZÓ VÖRÖS

1 5 10m

N

Ruined and unused internal structures from earlier period

Intact and used structures from earlier period

The fortified palace of King Herod the Great

THE EASTERN BASTION OF JUDEA. Both the original construction at Machaerus by Alexander Jannaeus and the later renovated structure of Herod the Great were protected by bastions on three sides. The northern side did not require a bastion as it faced out toward the lower city. Excavations at the western bastion revealed remarkable preservation: Before excavation, the archaeologists expected to find 5 feet of bastion walls; the western bastion, pictured left, has 30-foot-high intact walls.

PLASTER CHIP OFF THE OLD BLOCK. The Herodian-era fortress, like its corollaries to the west, echoes Roman architectural style. Unlike the marble used at Rome or the limestone at Herodium, plaster decorates the Herodian palace at Machaerus. Despite the different materials, the Herodian palace/fortresses are much the same; the citadels of Machaerus and Masada share many characteristics from mosaic decoration and style to storeroom architecture. Only small chips of plaster, such as the one shown at the center of the photo below, survive on the walls at Machaerus.

In 2009, following the untimely death of Father Piccirillo, our team from the Hungarian Academy of Arts, in collaboration with the Jordanian Department of Antiquities, resumed excavations exactly where the Studium Biblicum Franciscanum had left off. A significant result of our excavations was the discovery of the extraordinary depths of the citadel. For example, the interior of the western bastion, previously believed to have walls less than 5 feet tall, included intact walls that were 30 feet high. In another case, we discovered and fully excavated

A HERODIAN PLEASURE PALACE. The size and grandeur of the Herodian palace are apparent in this theoretical cutaway view of the fortress (above opposite, from the south) and in its floorplan (opposite). Alexander Jannaeus's original Hasmonean-period structure mostly consisted of defensive walls with little regard for interior luxury. The major renovations under Herod the Great included a courtyard with a royal garden, a Roman-style bath, a triclinium for fancy dining and formal peristyle courtyard lined with porticoes. The newly redesigned fortress shares architectural similarities with Masada and other fortresses west of the Jordan River and the Dead Sea.

the 50-foot-deep Hasmonean cistern of the citadel (pictured on p. 519), which continued to be used in the Herodian period.

In addition, we used state-of-the-art instruments that included ground-penetrating radar and eddy current detectors with variable antennas. Among the antennas used in the radar surveys, the 400 Mhz GPR antenna (launching 60 electromagnetic pulses per second) can reveal structures more than 12 feet below the surface under dry soil conditions, and the 40 Mhz GPR antenna reveals soil and rock structures up to a depth of 130 feet. The antennas of the eddy current detector operate using different signal strengths and are primarily used for the upper strata of the archaeological layers, down to a depth of 3 feet.

Among our most pleasant tasks were several archaeological and architectural surveys of comparative Hasmonean and Herodian palace/fortresses in Israel. Much of our understanding of Machaerus is based on comparanda from these sites. Not surprisingly, much of the Herodian-period decoration

---

HERSHEL SHANKS

KING OF THE DANCE FLOOR. A semicircular apse (right) marks the spot for the throne of King Herod and his successor Herod Antipas. Located at the axial center of the peristyle courtyard (above), Herod Antipas would have sat in this spot while watching the deadly dance of his step-daughter, Salome. This center of power of the Herodian palace is currently decorated with Ionic columns reconstructed by the Franciscan excavators at Machaerus. Large Doric column prints line the porticoes at the side of the courtyard, however, and the current excavators at Machaerus plan to correct the reconstruction.

HERSHEL SHANKS

at Machaerus is similar to what we had seen at these other sites, which in turn echo contemporaneous Roman style. The architectural decoration of the buildings in Rome were made of marble; in Herodium it was carved limestone; in Machaerus it was plaster. But the style is the same. Often only small chips survived at Machaerus. Like the architecture, the mosaics at Machaerus are reminiscent of the other fortresses. The floor mosaics in the Western Palace of Masada and in the Machaerus apoditerium (the entrance area to the bath) feature matching designs that were plainly made at the same workshop. There are numerous examples of architectural and construction parallels among all the palace/fortresses.

Based on the extensive data from our surveys, instrumental examinations, comparisons with sites west of the Jordan, and excavations (both previous

and our own), we can confidently report that Machaerus was inhabited in three periods: (1) during the time of Alexander Jannaeus (in the Hasmonean period c. 90 B.C.), (2) after being remodeled by Herod the Great (c. 20 B.C.), and (3) by Jewish rebels known as Zealots during the First Jewish Revolt against Rome (66–72 A.D.).

In both the original construction by Alexander Jannaeus and after Herod the Great's renovations, bastions with towers protected the citadel on three sides. The lower city provided the needed protection for the north side of the citadel.

Herod's palace also included a courtyard with a small royal garden, a Roman-style bath, a triclinium for fancy dining and a formal peristyle courtyard enclosed by porticoes on four sides. This final area was the most imposing area of the palace, and it was there that Salome must have danced for Herod Antipas. We even know where the king sat: A semi-circular apse marks the space for King Herod's (and later his son Tetrarch Herod Antipas's) throne in the axial center of the peristyle courtyard.

Part of a stairway (nine steps) confirmed the existence of a second floor above the triclinium. Ten pillar bases in the triclinium supported columns, which in turn supported five arches that served as the underlying backbone of the roof. The palace also included some storerooms similar to those found at

KEEP ON CLIMBING. As if the citadel wasn't already high enough, this extant staircase reveals the existence of a second floor above the triclinium. Ten pillar bases visible in the triclinium supported arches that held up the ceiling and the floor of the upper story.

Masada—a site comparison to be returned to later in this article.

Some of the columns of Herod's peristyle courtyard have been re-erected (the technical architectural term for this is anastilosis). Unfortunately, the columns were mistakenly reconstructed as Ionic columns because the Franciscan excavators found an Ionic capital elsewhere at the site. But examination of the peristyle courtyard revealed Doric columns and several column-prints (Doric columns have no base) on the stylobate of the porticoes. In fact, the columns of the peristyle courtyard were confirmed as Doric by the many column drums: The circumference of the largest Ionic column drum is still smaller than the smallest drum of a Doric column. In the next few years, we hope to reconstruct the peristyle courtyard's columns correctly.

Machaerus's lower city sits on the northeastern slope of the mountain where thousands of people lived, according to Josephus.[6] John the Baptist would have been imprisoned in this lower city before he was beheaded. The Franciscan Fathers excavated

COMPLETING THE PICTURE. A three-dimensional computer model superimposed on an aerial photograph shows the Herodian citadel together with the lower city and aqueduct. While excavation work has focused on the citadel, the lower city is the setting of the most sordid stories from Machaerus. John the Baptist was imprisoned there before he was beheaded, and during the Zealot occupation, the lower city met with a bloody end. A more extensive excavation of the area might well reveal more about the tragic history of Machaerus.

The palatial fortress at Machaerus had a stunning perch above the Dead Sea, leaving an unobstructed, and quite beautiful, view of the fortresses to the west. In these computer-designed architectural reconstructions placed onto the physical landscape, the commanding majesty of the Herodian fortress comes to life again.

only the two side walls of the lower city and the adjacent area. The lower city of Machaerus deserves more extensive archaeological excavation.

This brings us to the third period of occupation at Machaerus—that of the Zealots, the same group of Jewish rebels who occupied Masada during the First Jewish Revolt against Rome. Indeed, in many respects Machaerus is Masada's parallel on the other side of the Dead Sea—in its occupation by the rebels, in the circumvallation siege wall that the Romans built to starve out the rebels and prevent their escape, and even in the beginning of a Roman siege ramp built to reach the fortified site. But there is a little twist at the end.

Josephus describes Machaerus as "a very rocky hill, elevated to a very great height, which circumstance alone made it very hard to be subdued. It was also contrived by nature, that it could not be easily ascended; for it is, as it were, ditched about with such valleys on all sides, and to such a depth, that the eye cannot reach their bottoms."[7]

Josephus's description of the rebels' occupation of Machaerus[8] is confirmed by archaeological evidence. The rebels reinforced the exterior wall of the fortress, which would have been largely destroyed by that time.

The rebels also stocked the site "with an abundance of weapons and engines and studied to make every preparation to enable its inmates to defy the longest siege."[9] As at Masada, the Romans

THE FEARSOME TENTH ROMAN LEGION that attacked Masada also laid siege to Machaerus. The Roman camp pictured above was the base of operations for the siege, which included the beginning of the construction of a massive ramp to reach the summit of the site. While this strategy worked for the Tenth Legion at Masada, the ramp was never completed at Machaerus.

responded with a circumvallation siege wall.

The similarities continue with the still-visible outline of the Roman camps behind the siege wall. The famous *Legio X Fretensis*, the same Tenth Roman Legion that subdued Masada, had attacked Machaerus shortly before. The Tenth Legion used the same techniques at both sites.

At Masada, the Romans erected a massive ramp to gain access to the summit of the site, from which they attacked and easily defeated the rebels.* Faced with the prospect of murder or slavery at the hands of the Romans, the rebels took the lives of their families and then committed suicide, according to Josephus.

The Romans began to build a massive ramp at Machaerus, too, that can still be seen. It was partially built of natural local stones without mortar, but it was never completed. According to Josephus, the Romans captured Eleazar, a young rebel from a large and distinguished family, who had recklessly wandered outside the gate. The Roman general Lucilius Bassus "ordered Eleazar to be stripped and carried to the spot most exposed to the view of the onlookers in the city and there severely scourged him." Josephus tells us that the Machaerus rebels were "profoundly affected by the lad's fate," and "the whole town burst into such wailing and lamentation as the misfortune of a mere individual seemed hardly to justify."

Noting this, Bassus erected a wooden cross as if to prepare for Eleazar's crucifixion. As Bassus had intended, this led to the negotiations that saved Eleazar's life and gave the residents of Machaerus permission "to depart in safety." In these circumstances, the ramp that the Romans were building was never completed and the still-existing uncompleted ramp testifies to the essential veracity of Josephus's account. Unlike the rebels at Masada, the rebels at the Machaerus citadel survived.

Apparently this compact did not apply to the Jews in the lower city of Machaerus. Some Jews tried to escape the Roman siege at night but were caught in their effort to break through the Roman ranks. The Romans proceeded to slay the 1,700 men living there and enslave the women and children.[10] Thus ended the settlement of Machaerus. ▣

* See Dan Gill, "It's a Natural: Masada Ramp Was Not a Roman Engineering Miracle," BAR, September/October 2001.

[1] Under Jewish levirate law, a brother is required to marry his brother's widow, but is forbidden to marry his brother's divorced wife. See Leviticus 18:16; 20:21.

[2] Josephus, *Antiquities* XVIII.119. Josephus's account is reinforced by later Christian authorities. Origen, writing c. 250 states: "For Josephus in the eighteenth book of the *Jewish Antiquities* bears witness to John as the one who was 'the Baptist' and who promised purification for those who were baptized" (*Contra Celsum* 1, 47).

In c. 324 Eusebius likewise confirms the validity of Josephus when he cites the relevant text: "John called the Baptist [...] For Herod slew him [...] On account of Herod's suspicion John was sent in bonds to the above-mentioned citadel of Machaerus, and there slain" (*Ecclesiastical History* 1.11.4–6).

Eusebius was the first who clearly states that the description of Josephus does not contradict the Gospels, but rather is a confirmation of and "testimony" to them. His observation includes the following: "John the Baptist was beheaded by the younger Herod, as is stated in the Gospels. Josephus also records the same fact, making mention of Herodias by name, and stating that, although she was the wife of his brother, Herod made her his own wife after divorcing his former lawful wife [...] The same Josephus confesses in this account that John the Baptist was an exceedingly righteous man, and thus agrees with the things written of him in the Gospels" (*Ecclesiastical History* 1.11.1 and 3).

[3] Pliny, *Natural History*, 5.15, 16.

[4] Josephus, *Antiquities* 17.6, 5 (Loeb ed.).

[5] Cf. Mishnah, *Tamid* 3.8.

[6] Josephus, *Jewish War* 7.208 (Loeb ed.).

[7] Josephus, *Jewish War* 7.6.1 (p. 758, Whiston ed.).

[8] Josephus, *Jewish War* 7.6 (Loeb ed.).

[9] Josephus, *Jewish War* 7.177 (Loeb ed.).

[10] This entire account is based on *Jewish War* 7.190–209 (Loeb ed.).

Related Reading

Morten Hørning Jensen, "Antipas—The Herod Jesus Knew," BAR, September/October 2012.

Crucifixion
The Archaeological Evidence

VASSILIOS TZAFERIS

FROM ANCIENT LITERARY SOURCES WE know that tens of thousands of people were crucified in the Roman Empire. In Palestine alone, the figure ran into the thousands. Yet until 1968 not a single victim of this horrifying method of execution had been uncovered archaeologically.

In that year I excavated the only victim of crucifixion ever discovered. He was a Jew, of a good family, who may have been convicted of a political crime. He lived in Jerusalem shortly after the turn of the era and sometime before the Roman destruction of Jerusalem in 70 A.D.

In the period following the Six Day War—when the Old City and East Jerusalem were newly under Israeli jurisdiction—a great deal of construction was undertaken. Accidental archaeological discoveries by construction crews were frequent. When that occurred, either my colleagues at the Israel Department of Antiquities and Museums or I would be called in; part of our job was to investigate these chance discoveries.

In late 1968 the then Director of the Department, Dr. Avraham Biran, asked me to check some tombs that had been found northeast of Jerusalem in an area called Giv'at ha-Mivtar. A crew from the Ministry of Housing had accidentally broken into some burial chambers and discovered the tombs. After we looked at the tombs, it was decided that I would excavate four of them.

The tombs were part of a huge Jewish cemetery of the Second Temple period (second century B.C. to 70 A.D.), extending from Mt. Scopus in the east

to the Sanhedriya tombs in the northwest. Like most of the tombs of this period, the particular tomb I will focus on here was cut, cave-like, into the soft limestone that abounds in Jerusalem. The tomb consisted of two rooms or chambers, each with burial niches.

This particular tomb (which we call Tomb No. 1) was a typical Jewish tomb, just like many others found in Jerusalem. On the outside, in front of the entrance to the tomb, was a forecourt (which, unfortunately, had been badly damaged). The entrance itself was blocked by a stone slab and led to a large, carved-out cave chamber, nearly 10 feet square (Chamber A on the plan). On three sides of the chamber were stone benches, intentionally left by the carver of the chamber. The fourth wall contained two openings leading down to another, lower chamber (Chamber B on the plan) that was similar in design to the first but had no benches. When we found Chamber B, its entrance was still blocked with a large stone slab.

Each of the two chambers contained burial niches that scholars call *loculi* (singular: *loculus*), about five to six feet long and a foot to a foot and a half wide. In Chamber A, there were four loculi and in Chamber B, eight—two on each side. In Chamber B the two loculi carved into the wall adjacent to Chamber A were cut under the floor of Chamber A.

Some of the loculi were sealed by stone slabs; others were blocked by small undressed stones that had been covered with plaster. In Chamber B, in the floor by the entrance to Chamber A, a child's

Remains of a Jewish Victim of Crucifixion Found in Jerusalem

PINNED TOGETHER by a large iron nail, the heel bones of a young man, 24–28 years old, discovered in a tomb near Jerusalem, present dramatic and heart-rending evidence of crucifixion. The nail was hammered first into the right foot and then the left; the configuration of the bones indicates the contorted posture the victim had been forced into on the cross (see drawing, p. 534).

After piercing both feet, the 7½-inch-long nail penetrated a wood plaque and then the cross; here the nail hit a knot. As it was pounded against the knot, the nail tip curled, securing it so firmly in the cross that it could not be pulled out after the man had died. In order for the entire body to be removed from the cross, the feet had to be amputated, and thus the heel bones, nail, and fragments of the plaque and cross were buried together.

bones had been buried in a small pit. The pit was covered by a flat stone slab, similar to the ossuary lids I shall describe later.

Nine of the 12 loculi in the two tomb chambers contained skeletons, usually only one skeleton to a loculus. However, three of the loculi (Loculi 5, 7 and 9) contained ossuaries. Ossuaries are small boxes (about 16 to 28 inches long, 12 to 20 inches wide and 10 to 16 inches high) for the secondary burial of bones. During this period, it was customary to collect the bones of the deceased after the body had been buried for almost a year and the flesh had decomposed. The bones were then reinterred in an ossuary. The practice of collecting bones in ossuaries had a religious significance that was probably connected with a belief in the resurrection of the dead. But this custom was also a practical measure; it allowed a tomb to be used for a prolonged period. As new burials became necessary, the bones of earlier burials were removed and placed in an ossuary. Reburial in an ossuary was, however, a privilege for the few; not every Jewish family could afford them. Most families reburied

the bones of their dead in pits. The use of stone ossuaries probably began during the Herodian dynasty (which began in 37 B.C.) and ended in the second half of the second century A.D.

Thousands of ossuaries have been found in cemeteries around Jerusalem. Most, like the ones we found, are carved from soft local limestone. The workmanship varies. Some that we found in the tomb have a smooth finish over all their surfaces, including the lids. Others, especially the larger ossuaries, are cruder; the surfaces were left unsmoothed and the marks of the cutting tools are clearly visible.

The ossuaries are variously decorated with incised lines, rosettes and sometimes inscriptions. Ossuary lids are of three types: gabled, flat and convex. We found all three types in our tomb. Often, ossuaries bear scratched marks at one end, extending onto the edge of the lid. These marks served to show how the lid was to be fitted onto the ossuary.

Of the eight ossuaries we found in this tomb, three were *in situ* in loculi in Chamber B; the other five were discovered in Chamber B in the middle of the floor.

We also found a considerable quantity of pottery in the tomb. Because all the pottery was easily identifiable, we were able to date the tomb quite accurately. The entire assemblage can be dated with certainty between the late Hellenistic period (end of the second century B.C., about 180 B.C.) to the Roman destruction of the Second Temple (70 A.D.). However, the bulk of the pottery dates to the period following the rise of the Herodian dynasty in 37 B.C. The assemblage included so-called spindle bottles* (probably used for aromatic balsam), globular juglets (for oil), oil lamps and even some cooking pots.

The skeletal finds indicate that two generations were buried in this tomb. No doubt this was the tomb of a family of some wealth and perhaps even prominence. The eight ossuaries contained the

*A spindle bottle resembles a cylinder that bulges at its midsection.

OSSUARIES DISCOVERED in the Giv'at ha-Mivtar tombs. Made of local limestone, these ossuaries display various incised decorations.

(Top) Concentric circles within a grid of squares may have symbolic meaning, or they may be merely ornamental. This ossuary contained the bones of a woman named Martha, whose name was inscribed on the opposite side.

(Center) A man, a woman, and a child were buried in this ossuary decorated with two six-petaled rosettes within circles. Between the two rosettes an Aramaic inscription reads: *Yhwntn qdrh*, "Jehonathan the potter."

(Bottom) Six-petaled rosettes and concentric circles decorate a small ossuary that contained the bones of two children.

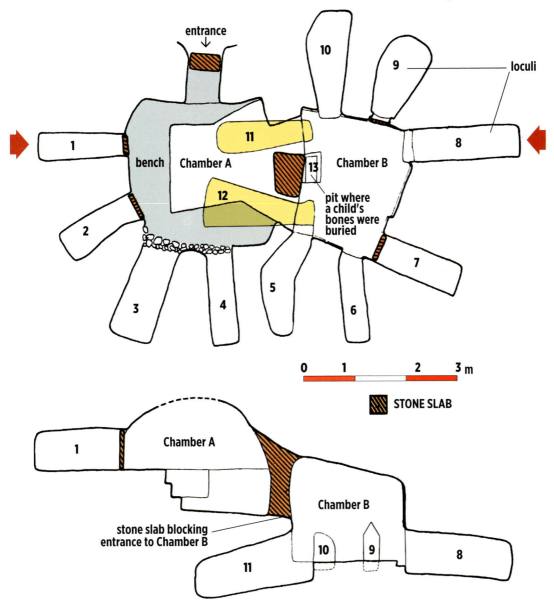

ADAPTED FROM *ISRAEL EXPLORATION JOURNAL* VOL. 20, NUMBERS 1–2, (1970)

entrance

loculi

bench   Chamber A   Chamber B

pit where a child's bones were buried

STONE SLAB

Chamber A

Chamber B

stone slab blocking entrance to Chamber B

TOMB 1 at Giv'at ha Mivtar had two chambers, A and B, that contained a total of 12 loculi, or burial niches. In one wall of chamber A was a large stone slab that blocked the entrance to the lower chamber B. Chamber B was at a sufficiently lower level so that loculi 11 and 12 could be carved under the floor of chamber A.

A cross section view of the tomb (bottom) shows how it would look if an imaginary vertical slice were cut through it between the points marked on the plan with arrows at loculi 1 and 8.

bones of 17 different people. Each ossuary contained the bones of from one to five people. The ossuaries were usually filled to the brim with bones, male and female, adult and child, interred together. One ossuary also held a bouquet of withered flowers.

As we shall see from the inscriptions, at least one

member of this family participated in the building of Herod's temple. But despite the wealth and achievement of its members, this family was probably not a happy one. An osteological examination showed that five of the 17 people whose bones were collected in the ossuaries died before reaching the age of seven. By age 37, 75 percent had died. Only two of the 17 lived to be more than 50. One child died of starvation, and one woman was killed when struck on the head by a mace.

And one man in this family had been crucified. He was between 24 and 28 years old, according to our osteologists.

Strange though it may seem, when I excavated the bones of this crucified man, I did not know how he had died. Only when the contents of Ossuary

SCRATCHED ON AN OSSUARY found in Tomb 1 at Giv'at ha-Mivtar is a symbol that resembles an asterisk. The identical symbol on the lid shows the user how to align the lid when closing the ossuary.

No. 4 from Chamber B of Tomb No. 1 were sent for osteological analysis was it discovered that it contained one three- or four-year-old child and a crucified man—a nail held his heel bones together. The nail was about 7 inches (17–18 cm) long.

Before examining the osteological evidence, I should say a little about crucifixion. Many people erroneously assume that crucifixion was a Roman invention. In fact, Assyrians, Phoenicians and Persians all practiced crucifixion during the first millennium B.C. Crucifixion was introduced in the west from these eastern cultures; it was used only rarely on the Greek mainland, but Greeks in Sicily and southern Italy used it more frequently, probably as a result of their closer contact with Phoenicians and Carthaginians.[1]

During the Hellenistic period, crucifixion became more popular among the Hellenized population of the east. After Alexander died in 323 B.C., crucifixion was frequently employed both by the Seleucids (the rulers of the Syrian half of Alexander's kingdom) and by the Ptolemies (the rulers of the Egyptian half).

Among the Jews crucifixion was an anathema. (See Deuteronomy 21:22–23: "If a man is guilty of a capital offense and is put to death, and you impale him on a stake, you must not let his corpse remain on the stake overnight, but must bury him the same day. For an impaled body is an affront to God: you shall not defile the land that the Lord your God is giving you to possess.")

The traditional method of execution among Jews was stoning. Nevertheless, crucifixion was occasionally employed by Jewish tyrants during the Hasmonean period. According to Josephus,[2] Alexander Jannaeus crucified 800 Jews on a single day during the revolt against the census of 7 A.D.

At the end of the first century B.C., the Romans adopted crucifixion as an official punishment for non-Romans for certain legally limited transgressions. Initially, it was employed not as a method of execution, but only as a punishment. Moreover, only slaves convicted of certain crimes were punished by crucifixion. During this early period, a wooden beam, known as a *furca* or *patibulum* was placed on the slave's neck and bound to his arms. The slave was then required to march through the neighborhood proclaiming his offense. This march was intended as an expiation and humiliation. Later, the slave was also stripped and scourged, increasing both the punishment and the humiliation. Still later, instead of walking with his arms tied to the wooden beam, the slave was tied to a vertical stake.

Because the main purpose of this practice was to punish, humiliate and frighten disobedient slaves, the practice did not necessarily result in death. Only in later times, probably in the first century B.C., did crucifixion evolve into a method of execution for conviction of certain crimes.

Initially, crucifixion was known as the punishment of the slaves. Later, it was used to punish foreign captives, rebels and fugitives, especially during times of war and rebellion. Captured enemies and rebels were crucified in masses. Accounts of the suppression of the revolt of Spartacus in 71 B.C. tell how the Roman army lined the road from Capua to Rome with 6,000 crucified rebels on 6,000 crosses. After the Romans quelled the relatively minor rebellion in Judea in 7 A.D. triggered by the death of King Herod, Quintilius Varus, the Roman Legate of Syria, crucified 2,000 Jews in Jerusalem. During Titus's siege of Jerusalem in 70 A.D., Roman troops crucified as many as 500 Jews a day for several months.

In times of war and rebellion when hundreds and even thousands of people were crucified within a short period, little if any attention was paid to the way the crucifixion was carried out. Crosses were haphazardly constructed, and executioners were impressed from the ranks of Roman legionaries.

In peacetime, crucifixions were carried out according to certain rules, by special persons authorized by the Roman courts. Crucifixions took place at specific locations, for example, in particular fields in Rome and on the Golgotha in Jerusalem. Outside of Italy, the Roman procurators alone possessed authority to impose the death penalty. Thus, when a local provincial court prescribed the death penalty, the consent of the Roman procurator had to be obtained in order to carry out the sentence.

Once a defendant was found guilty and was condemned to be crucified, the execution was supervised by an official known as the *Carnifix Serarum.* From the tribunal hall, the victim was taken outside, stripped, bound to a column and scourged. The scourging was done with either a stick or a *flagellum,* a Roman instrument with a short handle to which several long, thick thongs had been attached. On the ends of the leather thongs were lead or bone tips. Although the number of strokes imposed was not fixed, care was taken not to kill the victim. Following the beating, the horizontal beam was placed upon the condemned man's shoulders, and he began the long, grueling march to the execution site, usually outside the city walls. A soldier at the head of the procession carried the *titulus,* an inscription written on wood, which stated the defendant's name and the crime for which he had been condemned. Later, this *titulus* was fastened to the victim's cross. When the procession arrived at the execution site, a vertical stake was fixed into the ground. Sometimes the victim was attached to the cross only with ropes. In such a case, the *patibulum* or crossbeam, to which the victim's arms were already bound, was simply affixed to the vertical beam; the victim's feet were then bound to the stake with a few turns of the rope.

If the victim was attached by nails, he was laid on the ground, with his shoulders on the crossbeam. His arms were held out and nailed to the two ends of the crossbeam, which was then raised and fixed on top of the vertical beam. The victim's feet were then nailed down against this vertical stake.

Without any supplementary body support, the victim would die from muscular spasms and asphyxia in a very short time, certainly within two or three hours. Shortly after being raised on the cross, breathing would become difficult; to get his breath, the victim would attempt to draw himself up on his arms. Initially he would be able to hold himself up for 30 to 60 seconds, but this movement would quickly become increasingly difficult. As he became weaker, the victim would be unable to pull himself up and death would ensue within a few hours.

In order to prolong the agony, Roman executioners devised two instruments that would keep the victim alive on the cross for extended periods of time. One, known as a *sedile,* was a small seat attached to the front of the cross, about halfway down. This device provided some support for the victim's body and may explain the phrase used by the Romans, "to sit on the cross." Both Erenaeus

COURTESY *ISRAEL EXPLORATION JOURNAL* VOL. 20, NUMBERS 1–2, (1970)

OSSUARY OF YEHOHANAN. About a year after Yehohanan had been crucified, his family reburied his bones in this stone box and scratched his name not once, but several times, into the stone. One of the two inscriptions on this long side of the ossuary reads *Yhwhnn bn hgqwl,* "Yehohanan, son of HGQWL." A clear translation of Yehohanan's father's name is not possible, but it may be a corruption of the name Ezekiel.

and Justin Martyr describe the cross of Jesus as having five extremities rather than four; the fifth was probably the *sedile.* To increase the victim's suffering, the *sedile* was pointed, thus inflicting horrible pain. The second device added to the cross was the *suppedaneum,* or foot support. It was less painful than the *sedile,* but it also prolonged the victim's agony. Ancient historians record many cases in which the victim stayed alive on the cross for two or three or more days with the use of a *suppedaneum.* The church father Origen writes of having seen a crucified man who survived the whole night and the following day. Josephus refers to a case in which three crucified Jews survived on the cross for three days. During the mass crucifixions following the repression of the revolt of Spartacus in Rome, some of the crucified rebels talked to the soldiers for three days.[3]

Using this historical background and the archaeological evidence, it is possible to reconstruct the crucifixion of the man whose bones I excavated at Giv'at ha-Mivtar.

The most dramatic evidence that this young man was crucified was the nail which penetrated his heel bones. But for this nail, we might never have discovered that the young man had died in this way. The nail was preserved only because it hit a hard knot when it was pounded into the olive wood upright of the cross. The olive wood knot was so hard that, as the blows on the nail became heavier, the end of the nail bent and curled. We found a bit of the olive wood (between 1 and 2 cm) on the tip of the nail. This wood had probably been forced out of the knot where the curled nail hooked into it.

When it came time for the dead victim to be

"SIMON, BUILDER OF THE TEMPLE." The inscription on this ossuary found in the same Jewish tomb with the ossuary of Yehohanan tells posterity the part Simon played in history. Eight ossuaries containing the bones of 17 members of Simon and Yehohanan's family were found in this tomb. Since not all families could afford limestone ossuaries for secondary burials, we know that this was a family of some wealth.

victim's position on the cross. Further investigation disclosed, however, that the nail had penetrated both heel bones. The left ankle bone (*sustentaculum tali*) was found still attached to the bone mass adjacent to the right ankle bone, which was itself attached to the right heel bone. When first discovered, the two heel bones appeared to be two formless, unequal bony bulges surrounding an iron nail, coated by a thick calcareous crust. But painstaking investigation gradually disclosed the makeup of the bony mass.*

A word about the conditions under which the bones in the ossuaries were studied might be appropriate here. The medical team that studied the bones was given only four weeks to conduct their examination before the bones were reburied in a modern ceremony. Certain long-term preservation procedures were therefore impossible, and this precluded certain kinds of measurements and comparative studies. In the case of the crucified man, however, the investigators were given an additional period of time to study the materials, and it was during this period that the detailed conditions described here were discovered.

When removed from the tomb chamber, each of the eight ossuaries was one-third filled with a syrupy fluid. Strangely enough, the considerable moisture in the ossuaries resulted in a peculiar kind of preservation of the packed bones. The bones immersed in the fluid at the bottom of the ossuaries were coated with a limy sediment. As a result, the nailed heel bones were preserved in relatively good condition. Nevertheless, the overall condition of the bones must be described as fragile.

Before they were studied, the bones were first dehydrated and then impregnated with a preservative. Only then could they be measured and photographed.

Despite these limiting conditions, a detailed and very human picture of the crucified man gradually emerged. At 5 feet 6 inches (167 cm) tall, this young man in his mid- to late-twenties stood at about the mean height for Mediterranean people of the time. His limb bones were fine, slender, graceful and harmonious. The muscles that had been attached to his limb bones were lean, pointing to moderate muscular activity, both in childhood and after maturity. Apparently he never engaged in heavy physical labor. We can tell that he had never been seriously injured before his crucifixion, because investigators found no pathological deformations or any traumatic bony lesions. His bones indicated no marks of any disease or nutritional deficiency.

The young man's face, however, was unusual. He

removed from the cross, the executioners could not pull out this nail, bent as it was within the cross. The only way to remove the body was to take an ax or hatchet and amputate the feet. Thereafter, the feet, the nail and a plaque of wood that had been fastened between the head of the nail and the feet remained attached to one another as we found them in Ossuary No. 4. Under the head of the nail, the osteological investigators found the remains of this wooden plaque, made of either acacia or pistacia wood. The wood attached to the curled end of the nail that had penetrated the upright of the cross was, by contrast, olive wood.

At first the investigators thought that the bony material penetrated by the nail was only the right heel bone (*calcaneum*). This assumption initially led them to a mistaken conclusion regarding the

*A medical team from the Department of Anatomy at the Hebrew University Hadassah Medical School, headed by Dr. Nico Haas, made an intensive, if brief, study of the bones.

had a cleft right palate—a congenital anomaly which was also associated with the congenital absence of the right upper canine tooth and the deformed position of several other teeth. In addition, his facial skeleton was asymmetric, slanting slightly from one side to the other (plagiocephaly). The eye sockets were at slightly different heights, as were the nasal apertures. There were differences between the left and right branches of the lower jaw bone, and the forehead was more flattened on the right side than on the left. Some of these asymmetries have a direct association with the cleft palate.

The majority of modern medical scholars ascribe a cleft palate (and some associated asymmetries of the face) not to a genetic factor but to a critical change in the manner of life of the pregnant woman in the first two or three weeks of pregnancy. This critical change has frequently been identified as an unexpected deterioration in the woman's diet, in association with psychical stress. Statistically, this malformation occurs more frequently in chronically undernourished and underprivileged families than in the well-situated. But some catastrophe could cause sudden stress in the life of a well-to-do woman as well.

Other asymmetries of the facial skeleton may be attributable to disturbances in the final period of pregnancy or difficulties in delivery. Thus, our medical experts conjectured two prenatal crises in the life of this crucified man: one in the first few weeks of his mother's pregnancy and the other, a most difficult birth.

To help determine the appearance of the face, the team of anatomical experts took 38 anthropological measurements, 28 other measurements, and determined four cranial indices. The general shape of the facial skeleton, including the forehead, was five-sided. Excluding the forehead, the face was triangular, tapering below eye level. The nasal bones were large, curved, tight in the upper region and coarse in the lower part. The man's nose was curved and his chin robust, altogether a mild-featured facial skeleton.

Despite the prenatal anomalies, the man's face must have been quite pleasant, although some might say that it must have been a bit wild. His defects were doubtless almost imperceptible, hidden by his hair, beard and moustache. His body was proportionate, agreeable and graceful, particularly in motion.

What his life was like, we cannot know. But he seems to have come from a comfortable, if not well-to-do family. One of the ossuaries (not the one containing the crucified man) was inscribed in Aramaic on the side: "Simon, builder of the Temple." Apparently at least one member of the family participated in Herod's lavish rebuilding of the Temple on Jerusalem's Temple Mount. Simon may well

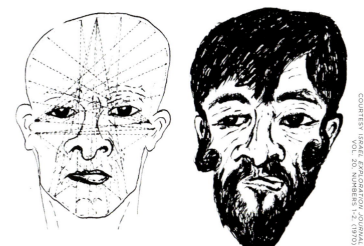

COURTESY ISRAEL EXPLORATION JOURNAL VOL. 20, NUMBERS 1–2, (1970)

FROM DRAWINGS of Yehohanan's skull, an artist has sketched a portrait of the young man who was crucified in the early first century A.D. Yehohanan's face was slightly asymmetrical. This deformity was probably the result of two factors: Yehohanan's mother may have been deprived of food or suffered some severe stress during the first weeks of her pregnancy, and the birth may have been a difficult one.

Yehohanan had a cleft palate, his eyes, nostrils and jaws were at slightly different heights, and his forehead was flatter on the right side than on the left. But hair, beard and moustache probably disguised these irregularities. In fact, Yehohanan was a pleasant looking man whose graceful, muscular and perfectly proportioned body must have compensated for a less-than-perfect face.

have been a master mason or an engineer. Another ossuary was inscribed "Yehonathan the potter."

We may conjecture that during this turbulent period of history, our crucified man was sentenced to die by crucifixion for some political crime. His remains reveal the horrible manner of his dying.

From the way in which the bones were attached, we can infer the man's position on the cross. The two heel bones were attached on their adjacent inside (medial) surfaces. The nail went through the right heel bone and then the left. Since the same nail went through both heels, the legs were together, not apart, on the cross.

A study of the two heel bones and the nail that penetrated them at an oblique angle pointing downward and sideways indicates that the feet of the victim were not fastened tightly to the cross. A small seat, or *sedile* must have been fastened to the upright of the cross. The evidence as to the position of the body on the cross convinced the investigators that the *sedile* supported only the man's left buttock. This seat both prevented the collapse of the body and prolonged the agony.

Given this position on the cross and given the way in which the heel bones were attached to the cross, it seems likely that the knees were bent,

CRUCIFIXION OF YEHOHANAN. Study of the wounds on Yehohanan's skeleton enabled osteologists to reconstruct his position on the cross. His arms were nailed above the wrists to the crossbeam. His legs were bent and twisted to one side, and a small *sedile*, or seat, supported only his left buttock.

COURTESY *ISRAEL EXPLORATION JOURNAL* VOL. 20, NUMBERS 1-2, (1970)

or semi-flexed, as in the drawing (page 534). This position of the legs was dramatically confirmed by a study of the long bones below the knees, the tibia or shinbone and the fibula behind it.

Only the tibia of the crucified man's right leg was available for study. The bone had been brutally fractured into large, sharp slivers. This fracture was clearly produced by a single, strong blow. The left calf bones were lying across the sharp edge of the wooden cross, and the percussion from the blow on the right calf bones passed into the left calf bones, producing a harsh and severing blow to them as well. The left calf bones broke in a straight, sharp-toothed line on the edge of the cross, a line characteristic of a fresh bone fracture. This fracture resulted from the pressure on both sides of the bone—on one side from the direct blow on the right leg and on the other from the resistance of the edge of the cross.

The angle of the line of fracture on these left calf bones provides proof that the victim's legs were in a semi-flexed position on the cross. The angle

of the fracture indicates that the bones formed an angle of 60° to 65° as they crossed the upright of the cross. This compels the interpretation that the legs were semi-flexed.

When we add this evidence to that of the nail and the way in which the heel bones were attached to the cross, we must conclude that this position into which the victim's body was forced was both difficult and unnatural.

The arm bones of the victim revealed the manner in which they were attached to the horizontal bar of the cross. A small scratch was observed on one bone (the *radius*) of the right forearm, just above the wrist. The scratch was produced by the compression, friction and gliding of an object on the fresh bone. This scratch is the osteological evidence of the penetration of the nail between the two bones of the forearm, the *radius* and the *ulna*.

Christian iconography usually shows the nails piercing the palms of Jesus' hands. Nailing the palms of the hands is impossible, because the weight of the slumping body would have torn the palms in a very short time. The victim would have fallen from the cross while still alive. As the evid ence from our crucified man demonstrates, the nails were driven into the victim's *arms*, just above the wrists, because this part of the arm is sufficiently strong to hold the weight of a slack body.*

The position of the crucified body may then be described as follows: The feet were joined almost parallel, both transfixed by the same nail at the heels, with the legs adjacent; the knees were doubled, the right one overlapping the left; the trunk was contorted and seated on a *sedile*; the upper limbs were stretched out, each stabbed by a nail in the forearm.

The victim's broken legs not only provided crucial evidence for the position on the cross, but they also provide evidence for a Palestinian variation of Roman crucifixion—at least as applied to Jews. Normally, the Romans left the crucified person undisturbed to die slowly of sheer physical exhaustion leading to asphyxia. However, Jewish tradition required burial on the day of execution. Therefore, in Palestine the executioner would break the legs of the crucified person in order to hasten his death and thus permit burial before nightfall. This practice, described in the Gospels in reference to the two thieves who were crucified with Jesus (John 19:18), has now been archaeologically confirmed.** Since the victim we excavated was a Jew, we may conclude that the executioners broke his legs on purpose in order to accelerate his death and allow his family to bury him before nightfall in accordance with Jewish custom.

We cannot know the crime of which our victim was accused. Given the prominence and wealth of the family, it is unlikely that he was a common thief.

---

* Early Christian artists, although frequently representing events from the life of Jesus, refrained from drawing scenes of the crucifixion during the first 500 years of Christian history. The earliest Christian representation of the crucifixion dates to the late fifth or early sixth centuries A.D., i.e., about 200 years after crucifixion was legally abolished by the emperor Constantine the Great.

** In John 19:34, a lance is plunged into Jesus' heart. This was not intended as the death blow but as a post mortem blow inflicted in order to testify to the victim's death. Only after this testimonial was obtained was the body removed from the cross and handed over to the victim's relatives for burial. The blow to the heart proved beyond doubt that the victim was indeed dead.

More likely, he was crucified for political crimes or seditious activities directed against the Roman authorities. Apparently, this Jewish family had two or three sons active in the political, religious and social life of Jerusalem at the end of the Second Temple period. One (Simon) was active in the reconstruction of the Temple. Another (Yehonathan) was a potter. The third son may have been active in anti-Roman political activities, for which he was crucified.

There's something else we know about this victim. We know his name. Scratched on the side of the ossuary containing his bones were the words "Yehohanan, the son of Hagakol." 🟊

For further details, see Vassilios Tzaferis, "Jewish Tombs at and near Giv'at ha-Mivtar, Jerusalem," Israel Explor ation Journal 20/1, 2 (1970), pp. 18–32; Nico Haas, "Anthropological Observations on the Skeletal Remains from Giv'at ha-Mivtar," Israel Exploration Journal 20/1, 2 (1970), pp. 38–59; and Joseph Naveh, "The Ossuary Inscriptions from Giv'at ha-Mivtar," Israel Exploration Journal 20/1, 2 (1970), pp. 33–37. See also, for a different hypothesis as to the position of Yehohanan on the cross, Yigael Yadin, "Epigraphy and Crucifixion," Israel Exploration Journal 23 (1973), pp. 18–22. On the history of crucifixion, see Pierre Barbet, A Doctor at Calvary (Image Books, 1963).

[1] Diodorus Siculus XIV:53.

[2] Josephus, *Antiquities* XIV:380–381.

[3] Appian, B. *Civ*. I, 120.

We received a number of interesting letters in response to this article, which can be read in Queries and Comments, BAR, May/June 1985.

Following the publication of the article, a scholarly dispute arose as to the position of the crucified man on the cross. Read about it in Hershel Shanks, Scholars' Corner: "New Analysis of the Crucified Man," BAR, November/December 1985, and in Queries and Comments, BAR, July/August 1986.

Related Reading

Ben Witherington, III, Biblical Views: "Images of Crucifixion: Fresh Evidence," BAR, March/April 2013.

Larry Hurtado, "The Staurogram," BAR, March/April 2013.

Christians and Jews Abroad

The Jewish diaspora and Christian evangelization spread these Biblical faiths far afield from their roots in Israel. These articles explored what happened when these groups came in contact with the rest of the world—and with each other.

Jews and Christians spread far and wide beyond the Holy Land in the early centuries of the Common Era. As they settled throughout the vast Roman Empire, they confronted life in close quarters with pagans—and each other.

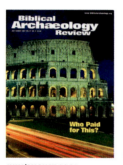

JULY/AUGUST 2001
Financing the Colosseum

More than any other ancient building, the Colosseum represents the grandeur of Rome. But where did the Romans get the money and manpower to build this magnificent amphitheater?

An otherwise-unattested tradition suggests that Jewish prisoners from the failed Jewish Revolt (66–70 C.E.) actually built the Colosseum, apparently based on Josephus's report that the Romans captured nearly a hundred thousand prisoners in their suppression of the revolt.

That the looted Temple treasure provided the enormous sums needed to construct the Colosseum is supported by more extensive evidence, most recently by an inscription in the Colosseum itself. But it is a ghost inscription, a phantom inscription. It is the inscription that isn't there. It was deciphered by Professor Geza Alfoldy of the University of Heidelberg. Although his reconstruction is admittedly conjectural, it has been endorsed by two of the most outstanding scholars of Roman history, Professor Fergus Millar of Oxford and Werner Eck of the University of Cologne.

The inscription was recovered on the basis of holes in a stone to which the inscribed stone was originally attached. This history and an analysis of these nail holes is reported in our article by Professor Louis H. Feldman of Yeshiva University.

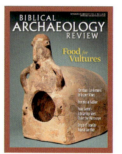

NOVEMBER/DECEMBER 2011
Condemned to the Mines—Copper Production and Christian Persecution

The next article in this chapter begins 200,000 years ago and goes through the time of the Roman persecution of Christians and then the Christian persecution of other Christians regarded as heretics. *Damnatio ad metalla*—condemned to the mines—amounted to a death sentence. For the past 20 years, our authors, American archaeologist Thomas E. Levy and Jordanian archaeologist Mohammad Najjar have been literally mining the desert of Jordan to understand its abundant copper resources. Much of the copper ultimately found its way to Israel during the Biblical periods. By the time the Christians were condemned to these mines, the most easily minable copper had been exhausted and only the less-reachable veins remained. Here early Christians, many of them church dignitaries, were sent to work and die. In these shaft-and-gallery mining operations, a miner might not see daylight for months—if ever.

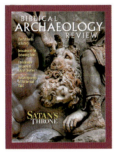

MAY/JUNE 2006
The Spade Hits Sussita

The next article in this chapter actually began 15 years before it was published. In 1990 we published an article entitled "Sussita Awaits the Spade" by Israeli archaeologist Vassilios Tzaferis that described this site high up on a promontory overlooking the Sea of Galilee. Also known as Hippos, Sussita was an important city in the Roman/Byzantine period; it had even been one of the ten cities of the Decapolis. And it had never been extensively excavated.

Fifteen years after the publication of this article, Haifa University Professor Arthur Segal read it and looked at the dramatic photographs of the surface remains. In 749 C.E. Sussita had been destroyed by an earthquake and had never been settled again. By the time of its destruction, it was a Christian city graced with at least five churches. The columns from the most magnificent, probably the cathedral, lay like matchsticks, felled by the earthquake. Then and there Segal decided to attempt to mount an archaeological expedition. Segal, together with his Haifa University codirector Michael Eisenberg, reported to BAR readers after six seasons, reprinted here. The excavation continues to this day. Professor Segal has retired and Eisenberg now leads the excavation team. Subsequent BAR reports have followed on this initial account, but none is quite as exciting as this one.

MAY/JUNE 2010
Godfearers in the City of Love

In its own peculiar way, the last article in this chapter—and this collection—brings Judaism and Christianity together, as well as some gorgeous pagan remains. When the City of Love (Aphrodisias) became known as the City of the Cross (Stavropolis), located in modern Turkey, Christians, Jews and pagans all made their marks on the city's buildings and walls.

A unique 9-foot-high marble pillar from a synagogue in the city is engraved with some 120 names of donors to the synagogue. Most of the names on the inscription are identified as Jews (including proselytes to Judaism) but also people identified as *theosebeis*, so-called Godfearers or sympathizers with Judaism, people who attended the synagogue without formally converting and, in this case, made a contribution in support of the synagogue.

Early Christian fathers sometimes warned their flock not to attend synagogue, in effect testifying to the widespread presence of *theosebeis*. As the names of the *theosebeis* at Aphrodisias attest, these warnings were apparently both necessary and ineffective. Moreover, Christian and Jewish graffiti often appear side by side at Aphrodisias, all as described for BAR by Angelos Chaniotis of the Institute for Advanced Study in Princeton, New Jersey.

Fin

ancing the Colosseum

Where did the money come from to build this magnificent Roman structure? An extremely unusual inscription – one without any extant letters–points to the spoils from the Jerusalem Temple.

LOUIS H. FELDMAN

"SO LONG AS THE COLOSSEUM stands, Rome also stands; when the Colosseum will fall, Rome also will fall; when Rome will fall, the world also will fall" (The Venerable Bede).[1]

The Colosseum is the most striking evidence of the grandeur of ancient Rome—its most massive, impressive and awe-inspiring feat of engineering. Originally known as the Amphitheatrum Flavium, it was the first major all-stone amphitheater in Rome.[2] Since the eighth century, it has been known simply as the Colosseum, apparently because of the colossal statue of the hated Emperor Nero (ruled 54 to 68 C.E.) that had once stood nearby.[3] The statue was placed there by the Emperor Hadrian (ruled 117 to 138), who had removed it from the court of Nero's Golden House.

Nero's connection with the Colosseum, however, is mostly negative. It was erected on a site where the despised emperor had built a lake that was drained after his death.[4] But the clay bottom was hardly fit for a foundation of a structure like the Colosseum, so a concrete ring was sunk into the former lake bottom for support.[5]

The building was constructed during the reigns of three Flavian emperors: The first three tiers of seats were built under Vespasian (ruled 69 to 79). Titus (ruled 79 to 81) added two more tiers. The work was completed under Titus's brother Domitian (ruled 81 to 96).[6] Emperors Nerva (ruled 96 to 98) and Trajan (ruled 98 to 117) made further changes and additions,[7] and the building was restored by the Emperor Antoninus Pius in the middle of the second century.[8]

When completed the Colosseum was 165 feet high, a third of a mile around and had some 80 entrances. According to the Calendar of 354, it had a seating capacity of 87,000 though modern scholars generally regard this figure as exaggerated and reduce it to about 50,000.[9] Spectators could find their seats without difficulty and all of them had a clear view. A canopy protected them from sun and rain. No wonder that the architects of the Harvard Stadium based their design on the Colosseum.

The amphitheater was severely damaged by a fire caused by lightning in 217.[10] It was damaged by another fire, also caused by lightning, in the middle of the third century[11] and by earthquakes in the fifth century.[12] Thereafter it was subject to plunder until the 18th century. Indeed, whole palaces, such as the Cancelleria (the papal chancellery, an enclave in Vatican City completed in the 16th century) and the Palazzo Farnese (a magnificent palace in Rome completed in the 16th century by Cardinal Alessandro Farnese), as well as much of St. Peter's Cathedral in Vatican City, were built from its spoils.

As late as the year 407, when Rome had been ruled by Christian emperors for almost a century, gladiatorial fights were still being staged there, and as late as 523 wild animals were being slaughtered in the arena.

Now the Colosseum is used as an outdoor theater, where as recently as July 20, 2000, the National Theater of Greece put on a new production of Sophocles's tragedy, *Oedipus Rex*.

When Vespasian became emperor in 69 C.E., the empire was in deplorable financial condition because of Nero's extravagance and the fire that devastated Rome in 64. The civil war that had raged during the year preceding Vespasian's accession only added to the economic problems. Unlike Nero, Vespasian was frugal to a fault. Moreover, in contrast to his

THE MAJESTIC COLOSSEUM has stood for nearly 2,000 years as one of Rome's most recognizable—and most visited—landmarks (see photo on previous pages). This ancient amphitheater still draws crowds, but few of them notice the block of stone (right) sitting in one of the theater's entryways as they pass by it on their way inside (above, right). Visible today is a Latin inscription mentioning that the structure was refurbished by one Lampadius, who funded reconstruction efforts in the fifth century C.E. A closer look at the original portions of the stone (center and far left) reveals a series of holes along three pairs of parallel lines, which once held pegs on which were fastened the metal letters of earlier inscriptions. Author Louis Feldman describes how a renowned scholar of "ghost" inscriptions deciphered the original dedicatory inscription made by the emperors Titus and Vespasian when the Colosseum was first built. These reconstructed inscriptions, Feldman goes on to explain, suggest how the Colosseum's massive construction effort was financed.

predecessors, Vespasian did not try to conceal his relatively undistinguished origin. To insure his own popularity (as well as that of his sons, who he was determined should succeed him), Vespasian undertook restorations and repairs that were sorely needed all over Rome. He endowed schools and established a regular annual salary of a hundred thousand sesterces for Latin and Greek teachers of rhetoric, paid for from the public treasury.[13]

According to the second-century writer Suetonius, Vespasian had learned that the emperor Augustus (ruled 27 B.C.E. to 14 C.E.) had cherished a plan for constructing an amphitheater in the heart of Rome.[14] Presumably there Augustus would be able to present on a grand scale the gladiatorial shows that he took particular pride in offering to the Roman people.

The arena with its three tiers was apparently used in Vespasian's reign. A more formal dedication occurred in the year 80. This inauguration lasted 100 days,[15] during which 9,000 animals were killed, 5,000 of them on a single day.[16] The exterior is depicted on several coins of Titus's reign.[17] Spectacles in the Colosseum included gladiatorial bouts, animal hunts, mock sea-battles, re-creations of myths (as in that of Pasiphae, where, according to Martial,[18] a bull actually mounted a woman), and even exhibitions of artificial forests.

The dedication of the Colosseum in 80 doubtless raised the morale of the populace after the volcanic eruption of Vesuvius, the famine and epidemic that followed and the great fire in Rome in 79

and 80. And what a nice touch to build it on the very ground where the despised Nero had enjoyed himself on his lake.

But where did Vespasian and Titus get the money to erect the structure?

The answer might be found in an inscription

that was described for the first time in 1813 by one Carlo Fea.[19] Visitors to the Colosseum, entering by the present main entrance on the west, can still see a large marble block inscribed with four lines of Latin lying on the ground on the right-hand side of the passageway. It has been considerably restored, but two easily identified pieces of it are ancient. In its present position, on the ground, we cannot see the underside of the stone, but it contains a festoon of leaves and animals decorated in a grandiose fashion. The stone must have originally served as an architrave that covered a passageway.[20] The inscription could be seen as one approached and the decoration could be seen as one passed underneath.

The inscription was restored between 1814 and 1822 and again, more accurately, in 1986.[21] It refers to the repair of the building during the reigns of Theodosius II and Valentinian III in 443 or 444.[22]

Salv[is dd.]nn. (= dominis nostris duobus) Theodosio et Placido V[alentiniano Augg.(= Augustis duobus)] / Rufi[us] Caecina Felix Lampadius v(ir) c(larissimus) [et inl(ustris) praef(ectus) urbi] / har̲[e] nam amphiteatri a novo una cum po[dio et pulpito (?) et portis] / p[ost]icis sed et reparatis spectaculi gradibus [ex sumptu suo restituit(?)]. *

"With our two lords, Theodosius and Placidus Valentianus Augusti, being well, Rufius Caecina Felix Lampadius, a most distinguished and illustrious prefect of the city, restored anew at his own expense the arena of the amphitheater together with the podium [the wall around the arena] and platform and rear doors, but also the tiers [of seats] repaired for viewing."

However, scholars, starting with Fea, noticed that between the letters of this inscription there are a number of little holes, at most one centimeter deep and often only a few millimeters deep. There must once have been a previous inscription of metal letters that had been fastened to the marble by pegs, they concluded.

*Square brackets refer to reconstructed and/or assumed text. Parentheses indicate the complete form of abbreviated words.

In 1986, two scholars published a diagram showing the distribution of the holes.[23] The holes form three sets of parallel lines, not all equally long—27 holes in the first line, 22 in the second line, and 18 in the third, for a total of 67. Though visible, they are, for the most part, not well preserved, because the surface of both original fragments was apparently smoothed and deepened at the time the later inscription was engraved, perhaps to make the holes less obvious.

In 1995, Professor Géza Alföldy of the University of Heidelberg published a decipherment of the earlier inscription based on these holes.[24] This is not the first time that original inscriptions have been detected beneath existing inscriptions and reconstructed on the basis of small holes that once attached the letters. Professor Alföldy himself has restored some of these phantom inscriptions, including an inscription on the aqueduct of Segovia in Spain. He has also confirmed an earlier reconstruction of the Vatican Obelisk inscription in St. Peter's Square in Rome, where, as here, the original inscription (of 30 B.C.E.) consisted of metal letters (probably gilded bronze) that were replaced in 14 C.E. by an inscription that was chiselled into the stone.[25] He is thus an expert in so-called "ghost epigraphy."[26]

To this observer, the result of Professor Alföldy's reconstruction is insightful, albeit conjectural. As he himself recognizes, only about half of the holes have survived and a single hole or two could hold a variety of letters.

If all this makes it very difficult, another factor makes it much easier. Roman building inscriptions are extremely formulaic. Were it not for this fact, the task of re-creating this inscription would probably be impossible. Roman building inscriptions generally begin with the name of the ruler who constructed the building, followed by the name of the kind of building and the source of financing, to which various other details may be added.

From the drawing of the holes (see following pages) it is easy to see that there were originally three lines of text and that the inscription must have been quite short—approximately 50 to 70 letters.

Another thing that helps a little is that the later inscription securely establishes the relationship

SEF/ART RESOURCE, NY

between the two fragments with holes, one very small fragment and the other much larger. In other words, the reconstruction of this later inscription, which is comparatively easy, tells us how much space there was between the two original marble fragments.

The two holes in the smaller fragment, one above the other, belong to the beginning of the first line. Their arrangement suggests an *I*, the beginning of the word *Imperator*—just what we would expect in a short building dedication. That exhausts the letters from the small fragment. Then there is a space between the fragments. The space has room for just the two letters MP, which complete the customary abbreviation for *Imperator*, emperor.

On the large fragment, Alföldy has restored a T on the basis of a hole near the bottom of the stem and another at the right hand of the crossbar. The hole for the left end of the crossbar of the T has not survived; it presumably appeared on the missing part of the stone between the two fragments. The T could be the abbreviation for Titus, under whom the building was dedicated in 80. It was customary for the emperor to take the name of his predecessor, in this case Vespasian, as part of his name. On the basis of succeeding holes, Alföldy restores the remainder of this line as CAES (the abbreviation for Caesar) and VESPASI. The last four letters of Vespasianus, the Latin for Vespasian, were on the part of the stone to the right, which has not survived. Similarly, Alföldy adds to this line the abbreviation for the remainder of Vespasian's titulary: AVG, for Augustus.

LIKE FATHER, LIKE SON. The Roman emperors Vespasian (ruled 69 to 79) and his son and successor Titus (ruled 79 to 81) shared at least one common goal: to build a grand amphitheater in Rome. Vespasian (at left) completed the first three tiers of the building and Titus added two more. According to author Feldman, it was Vespasian who ordered a dedication to be fixed above an entranceway, telling all who came that he had built the amphitheater. When Titus augmented the building, he added a T, an abbreviation of his name, to his father's inscription. The new Colosseum inscription was nearly identical to other inscriptions of Titus, such as the coin above that reads, IMP TITUS CAES VESPASIAN AVG PM, "Emperor Titus Vespasian Caesar Augustus Pontifex Maximus" (chief priest, an office each emperor held by default).

The second line apparently contained a long word because there appears to be no word divider in the line. Dedicatory inscriptions often contain little triangles that serve as word dividers. Based on his study of the holes, Alföldy sees no hole for the peg of a word divider. (Note the word divider in the first line between "CAES" and "VESPASI.") Thus, the 18 holes of the second line must belong to the letters of a single word. Here Alföldy has reconstructed AMPHITHEATRV[M]; only the M is missing. Alföldy suggests that on the right was probably the word NOVUM, thus designating the building: "New Amphitheater."

In the third and final line, one would expect a closing formula—a reference to parts of the building, to the recipients of the building (i.e., the Roman people) or to the cost or the source of the financing for the building.

The small fragment tells us where each line of the inscription began, but we don't have that part of the small fragment where the third line begins. We do, however, know how far to the left of the larger fragment the third line began, based on the small fragment. Alföldy concludes that only a couple of letters are missing from the beginning of the third line. If Professor Alföldy is right in conjecturing that this line contained information as to the source of the funding for the building, a word such as *de* or *ex* might well have been the preposition leading to the source of the funding. Alföldy suggests "EX," "from."

The next word is the key to the meaning of the inscription. Alföldy reconstructs MANVBI(I)S— booty! The hole for the base of the left stem of the M is missing—it must have been off the edge of the left side of the large fragment—but the holes for the other four points of the M are there. Then come three holes for the A. Then another three holes, two for the top and bottom of the left stem of the N and one for the point at the right bottom of this letter. This is followed by three holes for the V. Only one hole has survived for the B. Then there are two holes for the I. Two holes, one above the other, held pegs for the last letter of the word, S; one hole was for the upper curve and one for the lower curve of the letter.

Connecting the Dots: Deciphering the Colosseum Inscription

The drawings on these pages explain how scholar Geza Alföldy, a specialist in reconstructing "ghost" inscriptions, was able to deduce the wording on the Colosseum's original dedication. Today, the stone slab bears a fifth-century C.E. inscription carved into the rock that describes a series of repairs to the structure (drawing A; the darker tint indicates the surviving portion of the inscription). But Alföldy and others had noted the presence of holes in the stone along three pairs of parallel lines (drawing B). The holes once held pegs onto which metal letters were fastened. Through meticulous work Alföldy arrived at the phrases that had once adorned

the rock; these are shown superimposed on the inscription visible today (drawing C). Not only did Alföldy determine the original inscription, but he deduced that two emperors, Vespasian (ruled 69 to 79 C.E.) and his son Titus (ruled 79 to 81 C.E.), had a hand in its wording: The first line of Vespasian's dedication read "IMP CAES VESPASIANUS AVG" (Emperor Caesar Vespasian Augustus) (drawing D); Titus, who added two levels to the Colosseum, only needed to add a "T." (for Titus) to make the phrase his own. Titus had the C and the A from "CAES" moved to the right just enough to squeeze in the T and a small triangle that

functioned as a modern period—making it serve as his initial (drawing E; the holes marked in green were added to make the "T." fit; the holes marked in red were the original holes in "CAES"). The result—a "new" dedication attributing the construction of the Colosseum to Titus but still explaining that it was done *ex manubiis*, with the proceeds from the spoils of war. In the accompanying article, author Louis Feldman suggests that the war from which those spoils came was the Great Jewish Revolt against Rome in 66-70 C.E., when Titus destroyed the Jerusalem Temple.

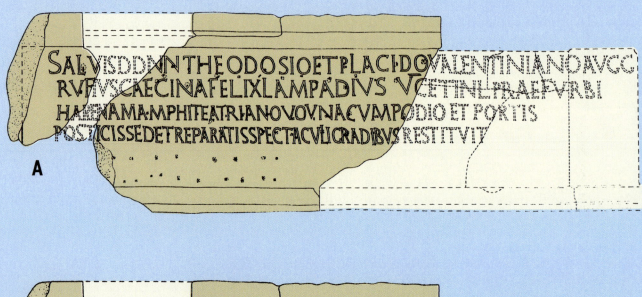

A

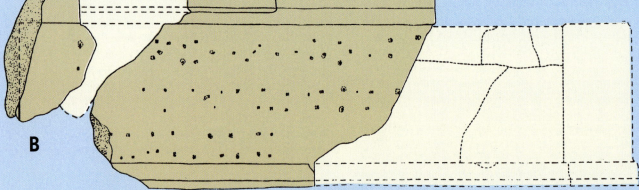

B

C

IMP·T·CAES·VESPASIANVS·AVG
AMPHITHEATRVM·NOVVM
EX·MAN VBIS
FIERI·IVSSIT

D

IMP·CAES·VESPAS IANVS·AVG
AMPHITHEATRVM·NOVVM
EX·MAN VBIS
FIERI·IVSSIT

E

IMP·CAES·VESPAS IANVS·AVG
AMPHITHEATRVM·NOVVM
EX·MAN VBIS
FIERI·IVSSIT

This spells MANVBIS, but the proper spelling is "manubiis"; Alföldy suggests that the I would have extended higher than the other letters, to signify, as is common in Latin inscriptions, a double I. Thus the word properly spelled: MANVBIIS. Apparently, the phrase *ex manubiis* was standard in dedications of monuments, if we may judge from the second-century antiquarian, Aulus Gellius (15.25.1), who remarks that "all along the roof of the colonnades of Trajan's forum there are placed gilded statues of horses and representations of military standards, and underneath is written *Ex manubiis*."

Manubiis means booty. The phrase EX MANVBIIS would indicate the source of the funding for the structure.

This would probably be followed by the well-known formula *fieri iussit*, "[he] ordered to be made."

As reconstructed by Professor Alföldy, the inscription reads:

I[MP(ERATOR)]   T(ITVS)   CAES(AR) VESPASI[ANVS   AVG(VSTVS)]   / AMPHITHEATRV[M NOVVM?] / [EX] MANVBI(I)S (vacat) [FIERI IVSSIT (?)]*

"The Emperor Titus Caesar Vespasian Augustus ordered the new amphitheater to be made from the (proceeds from the sale of the) booty."

Each letter of the inscription would have been created separately. Sometimes they were formed from a mold that included the peg, but at other times they were sawed from a bronze plate; the pegs were later wrought and attached. Letters produced in this way were by no means identical. Often the letters were created by several different craftsmen, introducing additional variations.

One other peculiarity: Note that the T and the C at the beginning of the first line appear crowded together. Alföldy suggests that this was because the T was not there originally. The inscription, except for the T, was placed there by Vespasian before the more formal dedication of the building in 80 C.E. Even during Vespasian's reign games were held there, although the structure was not quite finished. A chronicler writing in the fourth century states that the building was actually dedicated by Vespasian, although it was supplemented by Titus.[27] When Titus succeeded Vespasian in 79 C.E . and added the two top tiers that essentially completed the building, he naturally wanted to include his own name in the dedicatory inscription, which he did by squeezing in the T for Titus.

According to Alföldy, when Titus arranged to have the letter T inserted, the C, the A and the E

*Parentheses indicate the complete form of words that have been abbreviated; brackets indicate words or letters that are omitted but which are suggested by Professor Alföldy.

MANUBIAL TEMPLES. THE Colosseum was not the only grand structure in Rome to be funded from the spoils of victory. It was commonplace for emperors in many periods to use their battle-gained riches to build new temples. Both the Imperial Forum, which encompassed the forums of the emperors (including Augustus's Forum, which held his Temple to Mars Ultor), and the Roman Forum (right), which included the Temple of Concord and the Temple of Castor and Pollux (the three columns visible left of center) were partially funded *ex manubiis*, "from the spoils" of war. (The Colosseum and the Arch of Titus can be seen at far left, in the background of the photograph; see the plan below right for the relationship of the buildings to each other.)

(of CAES) were moved and fastened in the following fashion: The peg that in the first version had held the C was in the second version employed for the T. Above and to the right a new peg was inserted in order to hold the T better. To strengthen the additional punctuation mark (a period), a new peg was inserted after the T. As for the letters CAE, the original A was held by three pegs. In the second version the two left pegs were used for the C. The third peg served to fasten the A. In the upper curve of the C and in the point of the A, a new peg was inserted to hold these letters better. The E in both versions was fastened with one and the same peg. Thus a change was made only in the position of the letters, which in the second version must have been moved somewhat further to the right.

It may at first seem surprising that such a short inscription served as the dedication for such a magnificent building. Alföldy suggests that there was no more room on the architrave above the particular entrance or gateway where this inscription was placed. This suggestion is supported by the fact that the inscription was found at one of the side gates of the Colosseum in the interior of the building. This inscription was probably a very much abbreviated version of a larger inscription on the podium that contained the full nomenclature of the ruler, Imp(erator) Titus Caesar Divi Vespasiani f(ilius) Vespasianus Augustus; it would also have included his full titles of office with the number of times he held that office, as well as the most important individual parts of the building, such as the arena, the podium, the levels and the gates; finally it would have stated that the building was begun by Vespasian and was financed from the *manubiae* (the nominative; *manubiis*, as in *ex manubiis*, is ablative). It would presumably close with a mention of the grandiose spectacles with which the building was dedicated and which are mentioned by later writers.

While Professor Alföldy's reconstruction is admittedly conjectural, it has been endorsed by two of the most outstanding scholars in the field of Roman history and epigraphy, Fergus Millar of Oxford

The Roman Forum

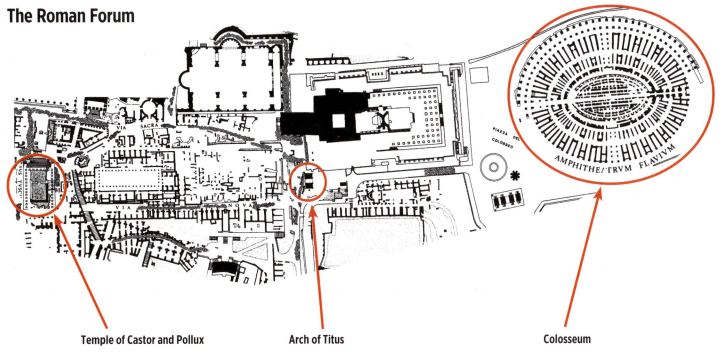

Temple of Castor and Pollux　　　　**Arch of Titus**　　　　**Colosseum**

money that he received from the sale of his spoils (*de manubiis*) to restore the Temple of Concord and of Castor and Pollux.*[34]

Closer to our case, in 63 B.C.E. the Roman general Pompey intervened in a civil war in Judea in which he besieged and finally captured the Jerusalem Temple. Although he did not take any of the Temple treasure, he presented his companions in arms with what Josephus calls "splendid rewards."[35]

The custom seems to have continued during the reigns of the Flavian emperors with whom we are concerned here, as evidenced by the extensive discussion Aulus Gellius devotes to the meaning of the word *manubiae*.

The financial pressure on Vespasian must have been tremendous, if we may trust the testimony of Suetonius,[36] who states that Vespasian found the treasury and the privy purse in such a desperate state that he declared at the beginning of his reign that forty billion sesterces[37] (certainly billions of dollars in modern purchasing power) were needed to set the state upright financially. This enormous deficit is the largest sum of money ever mentioned in antiquity.[38] He was consequently driven by necessity to raise money from military spoils (*manubiae*, precisely the word used in the Colosseum inscription, as reconstructed by Professor Alföldy) and other plunder (*rapinae*).

The next question is from what war Vespasian and Titus would have obtained their *manubiae*. They were of course successive generals of the Roman forces sent to Palestine to suppress the Great Jewish Revolt (66-70 C.E.), which effectively ended with the burning of Jerusalem and the destruction of the Jewish Temple.

Prior to being named general in Judea, however, Vespasian had commanded a legion in Germany and had fought some 30 battles in Britain.[39] But there is no indication that there was much valuable booty to be acquired in either of these places. After leaving the command in Judea to Titus, Vespasian as emperor

University and Werner Eck of the University of Cologne. Eck, whose expertise is precisely in the field of reconstructing inscriptions such as ours that have been removed in order to be replaced by others, writes that Alföldy's reconstruction is truly convincing,[28] and Millar speaks of it as "spectacular" and asserts that no hesitation need be felt over it.[29]

Moreover, Alföldy's reconstruction is also consistent with what we might expect, considering the history and the customs of the time. We focus on what is clearly the most significant word in the restored inscription, *manubiis*, which indicates that the work was paid for from the *manubiae*, that is the sale of booty.[30] Successful Roman generals of the late Republican era, including Marius, Lucullus, Pompey and Julius Caesar, often legally acquired enormous fortunes from the booty they took in their military campaigns.[31] In a document listing his achievements, Augustus states that in his fifth consulship (29 B.C.E.), he gave out of his spoils of war a thousand sesterces to each soldier settled in colonies and that on his own private land he built a temple to Mars and the Augustan Forum;[32] in the temples in the Capitol, he consecrated gifts from the spoils of war that cost him about 100 million sesterces.[33] Augustus's successor Tiberius used the

*According to the *Oxford Classical Dictionary*, "manubiae" refers to funds "raised by an official sale of war booty"; *manubiae* could be used to pay troops, put on games or build public buildings such as temples.

dispatched Petillius Cerealis to put down a revolt in Germany. Vespasian also sent his younger son Domitian to squelch a revolt in Gaul; and he sent Rubrius Gallus to punish the Sarmatians, who had invaded Moesia (modern Serbia and Bulgaria). But these were not achievements of Vespasian himself, and in any case there is no indication that there was in any of these countries much booty to be taken. As for Titus, there is no indication that he had served as a general prior to his service in Judea.[40]

By contrast, we know that the Romans acquired tremendous treasures in their conquest of Judea, especially in Jerusalem, and above all from the Temple, which Herod had renovated at extraordinary expense and which was still being reconstructed almost on the very eve of its destruction in 70 C.E.[41] The *Letter of Aristeas* states that the Temple "was built with a lavishness and sumptuousness beyond all precedent. From the construction of the doorway and its fastenings to the door-posts and the solid nature of the lintel, it was obvious that no expense had been spared."[42]

The Talmud states that "he who has not seen the Temple of Herod has never in his life seen a beautiful building."[43] In his description of the exterior of the Temple, the first-century Jewish historian Josephus

remarks that it lacked nothing that could astound either one's soul or one's eyes.[44] "Being covered on all sides with massive plates of gold," he adds, "the sun was no sooner up than it radiated so fiery a flash that persons straining to look at it were compelled to avert their eyes, as from solar rays."

Moreover, the Temple had been the recipient of countless gifts. Thus, we are told that King Monobazus of Adiabene in northern Mesopotamia had handles made of gold for all the vessels used on the Day of Atonement[45] and that his mother, Helena, set a golden candlestick over the door of the sanctuary.[46] Among Roman leaders who gave valuable gifts to the Temple were Sosius,[47] Marcus Agrippa[48] and Augustus.[49]

We hear specifically of treasures that were delivered over to the victorious Romans by priests, including 1ampstands, tables, bowls and platters, all of solid gold and very massive, as well as many other treasures and sacred ornaments.[50] In particular, Josephus asserts that the altar and lampstand, both made of gold, weighed no less than two talents (approximately 66 pounds).[51] When the Temple was razed the Romans burnt the treasury chambers, "in which lay infinite [*apeiron*, 'boundless'] sums of money, infinite [again the word used is *apeiroi*] piles of raiment, and other valuables; for this, in short, was the general repository of Jewish wealth, to which the rich had consigned the contents of their dismantled houses."[52] The Romans presumably saved for themselves at least some of these valuables.

Many people donated houses and fields to the Temple, which were then sold and the proceeds deposited in the Temple treasury.[53] Moreover, the Temple served as a bank for widows and orphans, who entrusted their deposits to it.[54]

According to Exodus 30:11-16, every male Jew over the age of 20 had to contribute a half shekel to the Temple each year.[55] If, as there is good reason to believe, the number of Jews was somewhere between four and eight million, and if, as apparently was the case, the great majority of Jews faithfully contributed this amount, the total collected must have been enormous.[56] Cicero mentions that in four cities of Asia Minor (a province that was admittedly wealthy but probably not the wealthiest) 220 pounds of gold intended for the Temple were seized by the Roman governor Flaccus in 59 B.C.E.[57]

According to Josephus, in the year 54 B.C.E., Crassus carried off the 2,000 talents that Pompey had left untouched in Jerusalem and was prepared to strip the sanctuary of all its gold, which totaled 8,000 talents.[58] This would have been the equivalent today of perhaps tens of millions of dollars.

During the siege of Jerusalem by the Romans, Josephus relates, gold was so abundant in the city that one could purchase for 12 Attic drachmas what had previously cost 25.[59] Some Jews actually swallowed gold coins to prevent their discovery by the Jewish revolutionaries and then, escaping to the Romans, discharged their bowels.[60] When a rumor ran through the Roman camp that the deserters had come full of gold, an Arab and Syrian rabble cut open no fewer than 2,000 deserters in one night to search their intestines.[61]

When the Romans entered the Temple court, "so glutted with plunder were the troops, one and all, that throughout Syria the standard of gold was depreciated to half its former value."[62]

Moreover, according to Josephus, 97,000 Jews were taken prisoner during the war with the Romans (this may be the source of the tradition, otherwise unattested, that Jews actually built the Colosseum);[63] of those over 17 years of age many were sent to work in Egypt, while those under 17 were sold.[64] The amount thus raised must have been considerable, especially since we may assume that Jews paid large sums of money to ransom their fellow Jews, inasmuch as ransoming of captives is regarded by the rabbis of the Talmud as of paramount importance, so that even money that has been set aside for charitable purposes or for building a synagogue may be used to ransom captives.[65]

A Dead Sea Scroll discovered in 1952 in Qumran Cave 3, engraved on two copper sheets (the so-called Copper Scroll), lists treasures of many tons of silver and gold, as well as other valuables, amounting to approximately 4,500 talents (possibly as much as 100,000 kilograms) or perhaps the equivalent of tens of millions of dollars.[66] Is this imaginary, or is there some basis to this account? John Allegro and, most recently, Al Wolters have argued that a fictional account would not have been laboriously inscribed on such an expensive material nor composed in such a dry bookkeeping style.[67] Wolters, together with the majority of recent scholars, concludes that the treasure is authentic, dates from before 68 C.E., and belonged to either the Qumran community or the Jerusalem Temple.[68] He thinks that the latter is more likely, since the enormous size of the treasure could have come only from the vast wealth of the Temple. Of course, there is no guarantee that even if such a treasure existed it was found by the Romans and transported to Rome.

After Jerusalem was finally conquered, Titus gave orders to his officers to read out the names of all those who had performed any brilliant feat during the war.[69] When their names were called, Titus "placed crowns of gold upon their heads, presented them with golden neck-chains, little golden spears and standards made of silver ... He further assigned to them out of the spoils [laphura, the technical term for spoils taken in war] silver and gold and raiments and other plunder in abundance."

We read, furthermore, that he then descended with his army to the seaport of Caesarea, where he deposited the bulk of his spoils, presumably for transport to Italy.[70] Moreover, upon returning from a visit to Antioch after the capture of Jerusalem, Josephus writes: "Of the vast wealth of the city no small portion was still being discovered among the ruins. Much of this the Romans dug up, but the greater part they became possessed of through the information of the prisoners, gold and silver and other most precious articles, which the owners in view of the uncertain fortunes of war had stored underground."[71]

Josephus says that it is impossible to describe the diversity of riches that were displayed in the triumphal procession in Rome after Jerusalem was destroyed—silver and gold in masses flowing like a river.[72] "The spoils in general," he says, "were borne in promiscuous heaps; but conspicuous above all stood out those captured in the temple at Jerusalem."[73] The reliefs on the Arch of Titus apparently depict only a small portion of the spoil taken by the Romans. According to Josephus, Vespasian deposited the vessels of gold from the Temple in the Temple of Peace that he established in the Roman Forum, but almost nothing has remained of this building.[74] Josephus adds that Vespasian deposited the Law (*nomos*), presumably a Torah scroll, of the Jews and the purple hangings of the sanctuary of the Temple in his palace.

None of our sources, unfortunately, mention the source of the financing for the Colosseum. In Josephus's case, that may have been because of his eagerness to present Titus as generous and mild toward the Jews. Remember that Josephus was a Palestinian Jew living in Rome under the patronage of the emperor when he wrote his history of the Jewish War.

To be sure, Hegesippus, the fourth-century author of a free paraphrase of, significantly, Josephus's *Jewish War*, refers to "the distinguished Josephus, who with his historian's stylus, narrated events up to the burning of the Temple and the *manubiae* of Titus Caesar."[75] He uses the phrase *manubias Titi Caesaris*, "the booty of Titus Caesar," as if it were a household expression.

Moreover, the Colosseum was not the only structure built from the money of the spoils. According to a sixth-century Christian historian, John Malalas, out of the spoils from Judea Vespasian built in Antioch, outside the city gate, what are known as the Cherubim, so called because he placed there the cherubim that Titus had taken from the Temple in Jerusalem.[76] He also built in Antioch the theater of Daphne, inscribing on it "Ex praeda Iudaea," that is, "from the Judean booty,"[77] having destroyed a synagogue that was located at the site, in order to insult the Jews.[78] Malalas also notes that Vespasian built in Caesarea, likewise from the spoils from Judea, a very large odeum, or concert hall, the size of a large theater on a site of what had formerly been a synagogue.[79]

It is true that the various holes in the "ghost inscription" could represent many possible letters and that the reconstruction is therefore conjectural. But the restoration does fit with the formulaic expressions usual in this kind of inscription, and it does fit with the huge amount of booty taken by Titus in the Jewish War. Moreover, for Vespasian and Titus to use their *manubiae* to build the Colosseum was not only the best means to finance this enormous project but also a way to advertise their military achievements.

The philosopher Seneca is quoted by Augustine, alluding to the spread of Judaism in the ancient world, as saying, "*Victi victoribus leges dederunt*," "The conquered have given laws to the victors."[80] If Professor Alföldy's reconstruction of this inscription is valid, the Jews, although conquered, also were the source of the money with which the most magnificent building constructed by the Roman Empire, the Colosseum, was financed.[81]

[1] *Bedae Opera Omnia*, Jacques-Paul Migne, *Patrologia Latina* 94, p. 543; *Bedae Opera* (Cologne, 1612), p. 482.

[2] It is referred to as Amphitheatrum in an inscription of the Arval Brethren from the year 80 (*Corpus Inscriptionum Latinarum* 6.2059=32063=*Inscriptiones Latinae Selectae* 5049) and in the earliest Latin authors who mention the building (Martial, *De Spectaculis* 1.7 and 2.5; Suetonius, *Vespasian* 9.1, *Titus* 7.3, *Domitian* 4.1).

[3] The first appearance of this name is in the *Liber Pontificalis*, the life of Stephen III (Pope 768-772), 1.472. On the debate as to whether the word *Colisaeus* as used by Bede refers to the huge bronze statue (Colossus) of Nero or whether it refers to the Flavian Amphitheater (Colosseum), see Howard V. Canter, "The Venerable Bede and the Colosseum," *Transactions of the American Philological Association* 61 (1930), pp. 150-164, who argues convincingly for the latter view.

[4] Martial, *De Spectaculis* 2.5.

[5] See Robin Haydon Darwall-Smith, *Emperors and Architecture: A Study of Flavian Rome* (Bruxelles: Latomus: Revue d'Études Latines, 1996), p. 78.

[6] So the Chronographer of the year 354, in Theodor Mommsen, ed., *Chronica Minora*, vol. 1, p. 146.

[7] *Corpus Inscriptionum Latinarum* 6.32254-55.

[8] *Scriptores Historiae Augustae*, *Antoninus Pius* 8.2.

[9] Mommsen, *Chronica Minora*.

[10] Dio Cassius 79.25.2-3.

[11] Jerome, *Anno Abrahami* 2268.

[12] Paul the Deacon, *History of Rome* 13.16; *Corpus Inscriptionum Latinarum* 6.32086-89,91-92,94. See Lynne C. Lancaster, "Reconstructing the Restorations of the Colosseum after the Fire of 217," *Journal of Roman Archaeology* 11 (1998), pp. 146-174.

[13] At the time of Caesar (about 50 B.C.E.) an ordinary laborer earned about a thousand sesterces a year. See Jo-Ann Shelton, *As the Romans Did: A Sourcebook in Roman Social History*, 2nd ed. (New York: Oxford Univ. Press, 1998) p. 452.

[14] Suetonius, *Vespasian* 9.1.

[15] Suetonius, *Titus* 7.3; Dio Cassius 66.25; Eutropius 7.21.

[16] Suetonius, *Titus* 7.3; Eusebius [Jerome] *Chronica* (ed. Alfred Schoene, *Eusebi Chronicorum Canonum*, vol. 2 [Berlin: Weidmann, 1876], p. 159); Eutropius 7.21.

[17] See Harold Mattingly, *Coins of the Roman Empire in the British Museum*, vol 2: *Vespasian to Domitian* (London: British Museum, 1930), p. lxxvi, nos. 190-191.

[18] Martial, *Liber Spectaculorum* 5.

[19] Carlo Fea, *Notizie degli scavi nell' Anfiteatro Flavio e nel Foro Traiano* (Rome: Nella stamperia di Lino Contedini, 1813), pp. 3-9.

[20] Géza Alföldy, "Eine Bauinschrift aus dem Colosseum," *Zeitschrift für Papyrologie und Epigraphik* 109 (1995), pp. 195-226.

[21] See Rosella Rea, Tudor Dinca, Alessandra Morelli and Stefano Priuli, *Bulletino della Commissione archeologica communale di Roma* (*BCAR*) 91 (1986), pp. 318ff.

[22] Alföldy, "Eine Bauinschrift," p. 201. He has suggested several corrections, which we have adopted.

[23] Dinca and Morelli, *BCAR* 91 (1986), p. 323.

[24] Alföldy, "Eine Bauinschrift," pp. 195-226.

[25] The original inscription was reconstructed by Filippo Magi, "Le iscrizioni recentemente scoperte sull'obelisco vaticano," *Studi Romani* 11 (1963) pp. 50-56; see also Alföldy, *Der Obelisk aus dem Petersplatz in Rom: ein historisches Monument der Antike* (Heidelberg: Carl Winter Universitätsverlag, 1990; and Alföldy, *Die Bauinschriften des Aquäduktes von Segovia und des Amphitheaters von Tarraco* (Berlin: de Gruyter, 1997).

[26] Another famous example of a phantom inscription is in the Maison Carrée in Nîmes in southern France. For the history of the reconstruction of the original inscription see Jean C. Balty,

Études sur la Maison Carrée de Nîmes (Bruxelles: Latomus: Revue d'Études latines, 1960) pp. 150-177.

[27] Mommsen, *Chronica Minora* 1.146.

[28] Werner Eck, letter 13 October 2000.

[29] Fergus Millar, "The Inscriptions of Rome: Recovery, Recording, and Interpretation," *Journal of Roman Archaeology* 11 (1998), p. 434.

[30] The etymology of this word is disputed. The most likely etymology is that it is derived from *manus* (hand) and *habere* (to have). See Peter G.W. Glare, *Oxford Latin Dictionary* (Oxford: Clarendon Press, 1982), p. 1075, s.v. *manubiae*.

[31] See Israel Shatzman, "The Roman General's Authority over Booty," *Historia* 21 (1972) pp. 177-205. See now Michel Aberson, *Temples votifs et butin de guerre dans la Rome républicaine* (Rome: Institut Suisse de Rome, 1994).

[32] Augustus, *Res Gestae Divi Augusti* 15.3, 21.1.

[33] Augustus, *Res Gestae Divi Augusti* 21.2.

[34] Suetonius, *Tiberius* 20.

[35] Josephus, *Jewish War* 1.154.

[36] Suetonius, *Vespasian* 16.3.

[37] Carol H. V. Sutherland ("The State of the Imperial Treasury at the Death of Domitian," *Journal of Roman Studies* 25 [1935] p. 158 n. 62), states that an emendation by Guillaume Budé to *quadragies*, i.e. four thousand million, has been noted by Maximilian Ihm in his *editio minor* of Suetonius, *Vespasian* 16.3 (Leipzig: Teubner, 1933) 305; but the unanimous reading of the manuscripts is *quadringenties*.

[38] So Tenney Frank, *An Economic Survey of Ancient Rome* vol. 5: *Rome and Italy of the Empire* (Baltimore: Johns Hopkins University Press, 1940), p. 45.

[39] Suetonius, *Vespasian* 4.

[40] Suetonius, *Titus* 4.

[41] Josephus, *Antiquities* 20.219.

[42] *Letter of Aristeas* 84-85.

[43] *Baba Batra* 4a.

[44] Josephus, *Jewish War* 5.222.

[45] Mishnah, *Yoma* 3:10.

[46] On the extraordinary use of gold in the Temple, see Joachim Jeremias, *Jerusalem in the Time of Jesus* (London: SCM Press, 1969), pp. 24-25.

[47] Josephus, *Antiquities* 14.488.

[48] Philo, *Legatio ad Gaium* 37.

[49] Josephus, *Jewish War* 5.562.

[50] Josephus, *Jewish War* 6.387-91.

[51] Josephus, *Against Apion* 1.198.

[52] Josephus, *Jewish War* 6.282.

[53] Tosefta, *Sheqalim* 2:15.

[54] 2 Maccabees 3:10.

[55] Tosefta, *Sheqalim* 1:5

[56] See Salo W. Baron, *A Social and Religious History of the Jews*, 2nd ed., vol. 1 (Philadelphia: Jewish Publication Society, 1952), pp. 370-372, n. 7; and my *Jew and Gentile in the Ancient World* (Princeton: Princeton Univ. Press, 1993), p. 293.

[57] Cicero, *Pro Flacco* 28.68.

[58] Josephus, *Jewish Antiquities* 14.105

[59] Josephus, *Jewish War* 5.550.

[60] Josephus, *Jewish War* 5.420-21.

[61] Josephus, *Jewish War* 5.551-52.

[62] Josephus, *Jewish War* 6.317.

[63] Josephus, *Jewish War* 6.420.

[64] Josephus, *Jewish War* 6.418.

[65] *Baba Batra* 8a-b, *Hullin* 7a.

[66] See Bargil (Virgil) Pixner, "Copper Scroll (3Q15)," *Anchor Bible Dictionary*, ed. David N. Freedman, vol. 1 (New York: Doubleday, 1992), p. 1133. By way of comparison, Appian (*Bella Civilia* 2.101,421) reports that 60,500 talents of silver (approximately 5500 talents of gold) and over 20,400 pounds of gold (approximately 260 talents) were carried in Caesar's triumphal procession and then distributed. Pompey (Appian, *Mithridates* 116, 565), who was by far the richest man in Rome in his day, managed 16,000 talents of silver (approximately 1,455 talents of gold). But this does not take into account the apparently sizable inflation that took place between the time of Caesar and that of the Flavians.

[67] John M. Allegro, *The Treasure of the Copper Scroll* (Garden City: Doubleday, 1960); Al Wolters, "History and the Copper Scroll," in Michael O. Wise et al., eds., *Methods of Investigation of the Dead Sea Scrolls and the Khirbet Qumran Site: Present Realities and Future Prospects* (*Annals of the New York Academy of Sciences* 722 [1994]), pp. 285-298; Wolters, "Copper Scroll," in Lawrence H. Schiffman and James C. VanderKam, eds., *Encyclopedia of the Dead Sea Scrolls*, vol. 1 (New York: Oxford Univ. Press, 2000), pp. 144-148.

[68] See Wolters, "History," pp. 285-92.

[69] Josephus, *Jewish War* 7.13-14.

[70] Josephus, *Jewish War* 7.20

[71] Josephus, *Jewish War* 7.114-15.

[72] Josephus, *Jewish War* 7.132-34.

[73] Josephus, *Jewish War* 7.148

[74] Josephus, *Jewish War* 7.161-162

[75] Hegesippus, *History*, Prologue 1, line 6, in Vincentius Ussani, ed., *Hegesippi Qui Dicitur Historiae Libri V*, vol. 1 (Wien: Hoelder-Pichler-Tempsky, 1932).

[76] Malalas, *Chronographia* 10.45.

[77] Robert E. Glanville Downey ("References to Inscriptions in the Chronicle of Malalas," *Transactions of the American Philological Association* 66 [1935], pp. 55-72) demonstrates, however, that all of Malalas's references to inscriptions may be derived from literary sources rather than from personal observation.

[78] Remains of a theater built near the end of the first century and presumably to be identified with the one mentioned by Malalas were excavated in 1934-1935. See Donald N. Wilber ("The Theatre at Daphne: Daphne-Harbie 20-N," in Richard Stillwell, ed., *Antioch-on-the Orontes*, vol. 2 [Princeton: Princeton Univ. Press, 1938], pp. 57-94), who concludes that Vespasian did, indeed, build a theater at Daphne.

[79] Malalas, 10.46.

[80] *City of God* 6.11.

[81] I want to express my sincere gratitude to Géza Alföldy for inspiring this study and for his great assistance. I also thank E. Badian of Harvard University, Boruch K. Helman of Brookline, Mass., Asher S. Kaufman and Israel Shatzman of Hebrew University and Hershel Shanks, BAR editor, for many helpful suggestions.

We received a number of substantive letters in response to this article. Read them and Louis Feldman's responses in Queries and Comments, BAR, November/December 2001.

Related Reading

Hershel Shanks, *The Copper Scroll and the Search for the Temple Treasure* (Washington, DC: Biblical Archaeology Society, 2007).

Strata: "Jewish Captives in the Imperial City," BAR, January/February 2013.

CONDEMNED
COPPER PRODUCTION

MOHAMMAD NAJJAR AND **THOMAS E. LEVY**

DAMNATIO AD METALLA—condemned to the mines! Tantamount to a death sentence.

For the past 20 years, we have been exploring these mines about 30 miles southeast of the Dead Sea in the Faynan district of Jordan.* In ancient times, these copper mines represented hell on earth to those condemned to work here. Today, the area's

*See Thomas E. Levy and Mohammad Najjar, "Edom & Copper: The Emergence of Ancient Israel's Rival," BAR, July/August 2006.

stark natural beauty and unusual history, both metallurgical and social, draw researchers and eco-tourists from around the world.

The Faynan mines are some of the world's best-preserved ancient mining and metallurgy landscapes. In recognition of this and as part of the Dana Nature Reserve, the area has been declared part of a UNESCO Biosphere.

Faynan is located between the high Jordanian

TO THE MINES
& CHRISTIAN PERSECUTION

plateau, about 5,400 feet above sea level, and the Wadi Arabah, part of the Dead Sea Rift Valley, some 260 feet below sea level, and near the lowest spot on earth. In this middle position, the wadis in the Faynan area have been a major route for human and animal migration since the Paleolithic period more than 200,000 years ago. By the Pre-Pottery Neolithic period (12,000 years ago), people were attracted to the area by another factor—beautiful blue-green veins of copper ore.

The earliest Biblical mention of the site is in Genesis 36:41, where it is spelled Pinon (F and P are the same letter in most Semitic languages) and sited accurately geographically, as located in Edom. (The same reference is found in 1 Chronicles 1:52.)

On the ancient Israelites' trek from Egypt to the Holy Land, they camped here, according to the Bible, although this time it is spelled Punon

PREVIOUS PAGES: HELL ON EARTH. *Damnatio ad metalla* ("condemned to the mines") was the sentence handed down to countless convicted criminals in the Roman Empire, especially Christians in the third–fifth centuries. They were often sent to the copper mines of the Faynan district now in Jordan, south of the Dead Sea between the Jordan plateau and the lowlands of the Arabah Valley (see map and enhanced satellite image below). Laboring in the dark, cramped, poorly ventilated conditions of mines like this room-and-pillar example, the work was tantamount to a death sentence for many persecuted Christians.

(Numbers 33:42).*

In earlier times, the most beautiful rocks were simply collected and the mineral pigments extracted to make jewelry, mostly beads.

In the Old World, the first attempt by people to work copper metal took place by the end of Neolithic period (7500–5700 B.C.E.) when a few copper tools were produced using native copper (probably meteoritic copper). This occurred in the "Eurasian metallogenic belt"—the region that spans the Alps to the Himalayas, before it drops down to the Indian Ocean.[1] Native copper could be collected

* In the annotated index to the authoritative English translation of Eusebius's *Onomasticon*, the site is spelled Phainon, but the entry notes that the site is also known as Phin, Phinon, Fenum, Fin, Fenon, Pinon, Punon, Phaisnon and Feinan. Today, following modern Arabic, it is also spelled Faynan.

from the surface because of its shiny quality, and was perhaps then heated in a fire and hammered (while hot) into a desirable shape.

The first smelting of copper—where heat is used to extract metal from ore—occurred in the Chalcolithic (Copper–Stone) Age, around 4500–3800 B.C.E. This was a major advance in pyrotechnology, involving the intentional use and control of fire and marking the beginning of the copper revolution in the ancient Near East.[2] Israel and Jordan are home to some of the earliest copper smelting sites in the world.

Knowledge of smelting seems to have evolved locally in the southern Levant after several thousands of years of experimentation with pyrotechnology in the Pre-Pottery Neolithic to create lime from crushed limestone, essentially by burning it. At this time, the lime produced was used to coat stone building surfaces as well as skulls of the deceased before they were buried beneath the floor of houses.

By smelting ores, the Chalcolithic craft workers produced a variety of metals from gold to copper. The copper they produced was both pure copper and copper alloy. The alloys consisted of 90 percent copper with 10 percent of other metals such as arsenic, lead and tin. Researchers still don't know where the non-copper alloys were obtained in this early period. These added metals altered the physical properties of the copper; through these additives, the hardness as well as the color of the tools was controlled.

MEDITERRANEAN SEA

Amman

Jerusalem

Gaza

JUDEA

Jordan R.

Umm al-Amad

DEAD SEA

Nessana
Shivta
Avdat

Wadi Arabah

FAYNAN DISTRICT

Khirbat en-Nahas

Petra

N

0   20 mi

Busayra

Khirbat en-Nahas Copper Production Site

THOMAS E. LEVY, UCSD LEVANTINE ARCHAEOLOGY LAB

In the Faynan district where we've been working, two geological strata (or units) of copper-ore deposits have been identified: the Massive Brown Sandstone (MBS) stratum and the Dolomite Limestone Shale (DLS) stratum, referred to locally as the Burj Dolomite-Shale formation. The MBS stratum includes copper ores such as malachite (a green ore especially prized for ornamental items) and cuprite (a copper ore variously colored from red to brown to black). The second common stratum, the Burj formation, contains primarily copper silicates and malachite. Based on analyses of copper objects from the Chalcolithic period, it seems that the MBS stratum was the first to be exploited for smelting purposes and later reopened extensively in the Roman period. However, the Burj ores were the more important source during most periods because Burj ore was not only more abundant but this ore tends to smelt quickly and form slag more readily. And, the copper ore from this stratum naturally contains manganese ores that provide a fluxing agent that lowers the temperature necessary for the reduction of the ores into metallic copper.

Andreas Hauptmann, who has coordinated excavations of ancient mines in the Faynan (as codirector with Gert Weisgerber of an expedition sponsored by the Deutches Bergbau Museum), suggests that by the third millennium B.C.E., a change in the flow patterns of the wadis in the Faynan district created by stronger seasonal floods probably exposed copper ores in the Burj stratum and that this contributed to the intensification of mining activities in the Early Bronze Age.[3] This, in turn, laid the groundwork for industrial mining and metallurgy in the Iron Age (the Biblical period) and Nabatean/Roman period.

The varying intensity of metallurgical activity in different time periods also reflects different forms of social organization. The native copper (ready for use) was available in a very restricted geographic zone; it had little or no impact outside of this limited area. Only in the Chalcolithic period does copper start to become a metal commodity of interregional trade. The smelting seems to have been controlled, however, by elite chiefs living in regions far from Faynan, such as the Beersheva Valley in the northern Negev desert.[4] In this formative period, the copper objects were mostly prestige items such as crowns, scepters and mace heads.

In the Early Bronze I period (c. 3600–3300 B.C.E.) copper was smelted locally in Faynan for the first time. Brick-shaped crucibles for containing the copper have been discovered in Faynan houses in sufficient numbers to cover both domestic and export needs.

Although the beginning of the Early Bronze Age

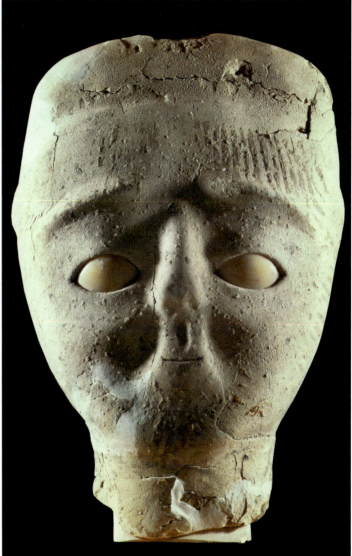

©ERICH LESSING

EARLY PYROTECHNOLOGY. The process of smelting copper seems to have evolved after thousands of years of experimentation with fire. During the Pre-Pottery Neolithic period (8300–5500 B.C.E.), people began to create lime by burning crushed limestone. The lime was then used to produce plaster, with which they coated building surfaces and the skulls of the deceased that were then buried under the floors of their homes. British archaeologist John Garstang discovered this 8,000-year-old plastered skull with painted features and inlaid shells for eyes at Jericho in the 1930s. It may have been used in ancestor worship or to ward off evil.

saw a decline in social complexity, by the Early Bronze Age II–III (c. 3000–2200 B.C.E.), the first "urban revolution" had occurred in the southern Levant, and Faynan metallurgy took on an almost mass-production quality. The Middle East's largest Bronze Age metal manufactory has recently been excavated on a large scale in Faynan at Khirbat Hamra Ifdan.[5]

THOMAS E. LEVY, UCSD LEVANTINE ARCHAEOLOGY LAB

THOMAS E. LEVY, UCSD LEVANTINE ARCHAEOLOGY LAB

EITHER ORE. Experts have identified two geological strata of copper ore deposits in the Faynan district: the Massive Brown Sandstone (MBS) stratum and the Dolomite Limestone Shale (DLS) stratum, or Burj formation. The photo at left shows copper ore nodules from the MBS stratum, which contains the highly prized green malachite as well as reddish-brown cuprite. The photo at lower left shows an ore fragment imbedded in dolomite from the Burj formation. Although the MBS ores appear to have been exploited for smelting earlier in history, the Burj ores became popular because they were more abundant and smelted more quickly.

Only in the Iron Age (c. 1200–900 B.C.E.), however, does copper production peak with the first industrial revolution. At this time the Faynan district became the hub of an ancient metallurgical production landscape. Networks of mines fed copper ore to production centers in Faynan such as Khirbat en-Nahas (Arabic for "Ruins of Copper") where the ore was smelted into ingots. These ingots were objects of trade westward to the Mediterranean coast and southward to the Gulf of Aqaba/Eilat. At Khirbat en-Nahas an Iron Age fortress and more than a hundred buildings were devoted to different aspects of the copper-production industry.

Scholars still do not understand why metal production ceased in Faynan at the end of the ninth century, but it did. It did not re-emerge until Hellenistic-Roman times (c. fourth–first centuries B.C.E.). Coins from this period have been found in the Faynan district in general and at Khirbat Faynan and other copper-bearing sites such as the Wadi Abu Khusheibah and Wadi Abu Qurdiyah.[6]

But in the Nabatean/Roman period (c. first century B.C.E.–fourth century C.E.) and the Byzantine period (c. 324–638 C.E.) copper production resumes at an industrial scale. According to Professor David Mattingly of Leicester University and Dr. Nana Friedman of the Oxford Roman Economy Project, who have studied Faynan administration during the Roman and Byzantine periods, areas rich in copper ore were imperially owned. Both the mining and metallurgy industries were an imperial monopoly.[7] British researchers have surveyed the Roman and Byzantine landscape of the central Faynan valley in great detail and show how it was a landscape organized to produce food and copper under imperial rule.[8]

By the first century C.E., Semites (probably Arab) from the southern Levant and northwest Arabia had evolved into the Nabateans whose socio-economic capital emerged in the hidden desert valleys of Petra, about 25 miles southeast of Faynan. The Nabatean kingdom extended westward into the Negev desert of Israel at impressive sites such as Shivta, Avdat and Nessana, and southward into the Hijaz desert in Saudi Arabia at the magnificent site of Mada'in Salih.[9] Like others before them, the Nabateans produced metallic copper from copper ores in nearby Faynan. Most of the mines in Umm al-Amad high above the Wadi Faynan and in the Wadi Abu Khusheibah are yet to be excavated, but judging from the abundance of Nabatean pottery sherds, these mines were probably operative during the Nabatean period. As it was in the earlier Iron Age, in the Roman period all the mines in Faynan were owned by the state. Ancient historical sources can tell us a lot about how the mines were operated. The copper was mined and smelted by slaves and war captives. They were supervised either by soldiers or by contractors to whom the slaves were leased. To prevent flight and even conversation between the supervising guards and the miners, garrisons of foreign soldiers with no knowledge of local languages were entrusted to guard the mines.[10]

In addition to slaves and war captives, at one point criminals were added to the work force.

By this time, the best veins of copper had been exhausted. Equally important, by the third and fourth centuries C.E., the superior ores of Spain were exhausted. Naturally the demand for Faynan copper increased. Previously neglected poor ores from the MBS stratum in the Faynan area suddenly became more valuable. Earlier mines from the Chalcolithic through the Iron Age were reopened, enlarged and reworked. Even earlier slag was recycled to "squeeze" every drop of copper from it. To make the poor copper deposits of Faynan economically profitable, the condemned miners were simply pushed to the limit of human endurance—and beyond.

Greek and Roman philosophers considered mining "a violation of the earth," and a search for wealth in the "home of the dead." They believed that mining "sometimes [caused the earth] to split open or to shake."[11] Mining on the Italian peninsula was prohibited.[12]

Simultaneous with these developments in the third, fourth and even fifth centuries, Christians were often gruesomely persecuted, first by pagan Roman emperors and then by Christian emperors who regarded other Christian sects as heretics. *Damnatio ad metalla*—condemnation to the mines— became a widely imposed punishment. Being condemned to the mines was apparently worse than scourging and carding, as the case of Silvanus, bishop of Gaza, illustrates. He was, according to Eusebius (c. 263–339 C.E.), a multiple offender. The first time his punishment was scourging. By the second time, he was an old man, and his punishment was "[carding] combs on his sides." The third time he was sent to the copper mines.[13] In another account, Eusebius identifies the copper mines where Bishop Silvanus was sent: "the copper mines in Phaeno."[14]

On one occasion, a mandate was issued, according to Eusebius, that "all those in the mines who had become enfeebled through old age or sickness, and those who were not able to work, should be put to death by the sword; and God's martyrs, being all together forty in number, were beheaded all in one day."[15] Their leader was Silvanus, "a man truly blessed and beloved of God."

SMELTING FOR STATUS. Copper smelting, the process of heating ore to extract metal, first occurred in the Chalcolithic period (c. 4500–3800 B.C.E.) and marked the start of the copper revolution. Israel and Jordan are home to some of the earliest copper-smelting sites in the world. Copper became an important trade commodity and was used in the Chalcolithic period mostly for "prestige items" such as crowns, scepters and maces. This copper scepter with ibex heads is part of the famous Nahal Mishmar hoard, a collection of largely copper artifacts from the Chalcolithic period that were discovered in a cave west of the Dead Sea.

Of all the copper mines, Faynan was especially feared, the worst in the whole Roman Empire. The reasons were many. First was the nature of the Faynan geology. The fragmentation of the ore deposits required oversized mine galleries; despite all efforts, the ceilings were unstable and miners were often crushed at work. Second, the inhuman treatment of the miners in Faynan contributed to its terrible reputation.

The Christian historian Theodoret, in the later fourth century, reports that 19 monks were whipped and tortured and then "sent to the *metalla* of Phenneusus [Faynan] and Proconesus."[16] Shortly thereafter, Theodoret reports that a deacon was similarly "sent to the mines at Phenneusus, which are copper mines."[17]

Essentially three methods of mining the copper were used at Faynan during the Iron Age and Roman period. The most common was the shaft-and-gallery technique. The miners would first dig

a vertical shaft, the Romans often near an existing double-shaft Iron Age mine. The new shaft would go somewhat deeper than the copper vein. Galleries (tunnels) would then branch off the shaft in different directions. Once the copper-ore deposit at this level was exhausted, the shaft was deepened and new galleries at deeper levels were excavated. At Wadi Al-Abyad Andreas Hauptmann's team found ten mines with four levels of galleries.[18]

In 1989 the German expedition led by Gert Weisgerber and Andreas Hauptmann excavated a "triple-shaft" mine with two Iron Age shafts, a reopening of the mine in the Roman period, and a third shaft from the Roman period. Pottery and coins allowed the modern excavators confidently to date each of the shafts.

The second type of mining operation is known as a room-and-pillar gallery mine. This type of operation begins with a cave in the hillside that has a broad but shallow entrance area. The miners would then cut narrow galleries in different directions, following the veins of ore. As they expanded the cave, the miners would leave sturdy pillars to support the roof of the cave; hence the term "room-and-pillar."

This type of mine was known to ancient writers as mining with "arched supports." Pliny describes mines with "arched supports" at frequent intervals that could bear "the weight of the mountain above."[19]

BIG BUSINESS. In the early Iron Age (1200–900 B.C.E.), copper production reached its peak and became heavily industrialized. The ore was brought from the mines to copper-production centers such as Khirbat en-Nahas ("Ruins of Copper"), where it would be smelted and then traded abroad in ingots. Over a hundred buildings at Khirbat en-Nahas were used for copper production. In this four-room workhouse, excavators found more than 350 grinding and pounding tools used to extract ore from the bedrock.

THOMAS E. LEVY, UCSD LEVANTINE ARCHAEOLOGY LAB

INTO DARKNESS. The most common method of copper mining in the Iron Age and Roman period was the shaft-and-gallery technique, in which a shaft was dug down and then tunnels, or galleries, branched out from these for mining the ore. Two of the shafts in this "triple-shaft" mine date to the Iron Age, but they were reopened and a third shaft dug during the Roman period.

Another type of mine was called the room-and-pillar gallery mine (also pictured on pp. 556–557). Here the mine began with a low, broad cave entrance in a hillside (right). The miners then enlarged the cave, following the ore deposits, until the mine resembled a large hall. They left pillars of uncut stone to support the roof and prevent collapse while they mined.

These caves look like halls filled with pillars. The Bedouin refer to one Roman room-and-pillar gallery mine in the rugged terrain above Faynan as Umm al-Amad, "Mother of the Pillars."

Umm al-Amad was the first mine of this type to be documented—by the famous American explorer, surveyor and archaeologist (and also a rabbi), Nelson Glueck, in the 1930s.[20] The German geologist Hans Kind discovered another set of these mines in the Wadi Abu Khusheibah in the 1960s.[21] We visited these mines recently with University of California, San Diego, graduate student Erez Ben-Yosef, who is researching archaeometallurgy in Faynan.[22]

We have recently identified a third type of mine, which we call a copper-pit mine field. In our survey of the area, we found hundreds of plate-like depressions about 23 feet in diameter that we believe date to the early Iron Age (c. 1200–900 B.C.E.). These plate-like depressions are very similar to what Israeli archaeologist Beno Rothenberg found in the Timna copper mines in southern Israel just north of Eilat. They were excavated into the relatively loose earth at the base of slopes. The excavated earth included copper nodules from prehistoric times that eroded

THOMAS E. LEVY, UCSD LEVANTINE ARCHAEOLOGY LAB

THOMAS E. LEVY, UCSD LEVANTINE ARCHAEOLOGY LAB

A DIFFERENT KIND OF MINE FIELD. Najjar and Levy have recently identified a third type of mining, called a copper-pit mine field. In a survey of the Faynan area (aided by satellite photos), they discovered hundreds of shallow round depressions measuring about 23 feet in diameter (see above and left). These pit mines, similar to the copper mines at Timna in Israel, were dug into relatively loose earth to provide easy access to naturally broken-up copper ore. These mines date to the early Iron Age and were much easier to work in than the shaft-and-gallery or room-and-pillar types where convicted Christians labored under the Roman and early Byzantine rulers. After the pit mines were abandoned, they were gradually filled with wind-blown sediment much lighter in color than the surrounding black rock, making them easy to identify.

from copper ores formed in earlier eras. These pits were thus an easily accessible source of naturally broken copper ore.[23]

Once the miners of these depressions were finished with their work and left, the plate-like depressions gradually filled up with wind-blown loess sediment. This sediment now enables us to identify these pits rather easily because the color of the sediment markedly differs from the black dolomite rocks surrounding them. The pits also naturally collect surface runoff water during the rare winter rains, making the plate-like scars of the ancient mines suitable for small-scale gardening by semi-nomadic Bedouin, even in this extremely arid zone.[24] These mines are similar to primitive pit mines used to extract gold

and other minerals in the Congo today.

Mining in these pits during the Iron Age was far less difficult and far less hazardous than the shaft-and-gallery and room-and-pillar gallery mines of the Roman period—when Christians were condemned to the mines.

The tool kits of the condemned Christians included hammers, chisels and wedges to loosen the host rock surrounding the copper ore. Ropes for climbing and baskets for the ore were also provided. The miners worked with the aid of light from oil lamps and may not have seen daylight for months. The Greek historian Diodorus (first century B.C.E.) tells us that the condemned miners in Egypt were "fettered with chains and kept busy at their work without ceasing, both by day and night."[25]

Ventilation in the underground facilities at Faynan was a serious problem. Because the shafts and galleries were narrow and the copper-ore dust was poisonous, most of the miners would either die naturally or be crushed when cracks, running in every direction, suddenly gave way. Ancient pollution studies of Nabatean, Roman and Byzantine copper mining and smelting activities show that in antiquity both producers and consumers (plants and animals) would have been subjected to potentially toxic heavy metals in Faynan.[26] The tunnels were cut through the rock not in straight lines, but wherever a vein of ore led. Because of the twists and turns, it was especially dark inside. First-century Roman historian Strabo reports, "In addition to the anguish of the work, they say that the air in the mines is both deadly and hard to bear. Workers are continually consumed by sickness and death."[27]

Damnatio ad metalla was a common sentence (especially during the Great Persecution of Christians in 303–311 C.E.). Shortly after his victory at the Milvian Bridge in 312 C.E. under what he said was the sign of the cross, the Roman emperor Constantine made Christianity a licit religion (although he himself was not baptized until his death bed). But this did not bring an end to Christian persecution. As one scholar has written, "A variety of sources indicates that condemnation to mines and quarries for religious offense persisted at least through the fourth and fifth centuries."[28] Constantine soon ruled that those Christians he considered heretics were not "true" Christians. *Damnatio ad metalla* continued to be a punishment for being the wrong kind of Christian—especially on the wrong side of the Arian controversy regarding the true nature of Christ.

In the heat of summer, these thoughts are often on our minds as we explore the Wadi Faynan and its famous—or infamous—copper mines. It is ironic that today we researchers and our students love working in the Faynan mining district. We can't wait to get back into the field next year. ⌷

[1] For a "global snapshot" of the beginning of Old World metallurgy, see D. Wengrow, *What Makes Civilization? The Ancient Near East and the Future of the West* (Oxford: Oxford University Press, 2010).

[2] T.E. Levy, *Journey to the Copper Age—Archaeology in the Holy Land* (San Diego: San Diego Museum of Man, 2007).

[3] A. Hauptmann, *The Archaeo-metallurgy of Copper—Evidence from Faynan, Jordan* (New York: Springer, 2007), p. 43.

[4] T.E. Levy, and S. Shalev, "Prehistoric Metalworking in the Southern Levant: Archaeometallurgy and Social Perspectives," *World Archaeology* 20 (1989), pp. 353–372.

[5] T.E. Levy, R. B. Adams, A. Hauptmann, M. Prange, S. Schmitt-Strecker and M. Najjar, "Early Bronze Age Metallurgy: A Newly Discovered Copper Manufactory in Southern Jordan," *Antiquity*

[6] H. Kind, D.K.K.J. Gilies, A. Hauptmann and G. Weisgerber, "Coins from Faynan, Jordan," *Levant* 37 (2005), pp. 169–195.

[7] See D.J. Mattingly, *Imperialism, Power, and Identity: Experiencing the Roman Empire* (Princeton, NJ: Princeton Univ. Press, 2011) and H.A. Friedman, "Industry and Empire: Administration of the Roman and Byzantine Faynan" (University of Leicester: unpublished PhD, 2008).

[8] D. Mattingly, P. Newson, O. Creighton, R. Tomber, J. Grattan, C. Hunt, D. Gilbertson, H. el-Rishi and B. Pyatt, "A Landscape of Imperial Power: Roman and Byzantine Phaino," in G. Barker, D. Gilbertson and D. Mattingly, eds., *Archaeology and Desertification—The Wadi Faynan Landscape Survey, Southern Jordan*, vol. 6 (Oxford: Oxbow Books, 2007), pp. 305–348.

[9] For overviews of the Nabatean kingdom in the Negev and Hijaz, see M. Babelli, *Mada'in Saleh* (Riyadh: M. Babelli, 2007) and M. Evenari, L. Shanan and N. Tadmor, *The Negev—The Challenge of a Desert*, 2nd ed. (Cambridge: Harvard Univ. Press, 1982).

[10] Diodorus of Sicily, *History* 3.12–13.

[11] Pliny, *Natural History* 33.1–3.

[12] Id. at 3.138.

[13] Eusebius, *Martyrs in Palestine*.

[14] Eusebius, *Ecclesiastical History*, 8.13.

[15] Eusebius, *Martyrs in Palestine*; the account in *Ecclesiastical History* also recites that Sylvanus was beheaded at Phaeno.

[16] Theodoret, *Hist. Eccl.* 4.22.26.

[17] Theodoret, *Hist. Eccl.* 4.22.28.

[18] G. Weisgerber and A. Hauptmann, "Early Copper Mining and Smelting in Palestine," in R. Maddin, ed., *The Beginning of the Use of Metals and Alloys* (Cambridge, MA: MIT Press, 1988), pp. 52–62, and A. Hauptmann, *The Archaeometallurgy of Copper: Evidence from Faynan, Jordan*, p. 146.

[19] Pliny, *Natural History* 21.70

[20] Nelson Glueck, *The Other Side of the Jordan* (New Haven: American Schools of Oriental Research, 1940).

[21] H.D. Kind, "Antike Kupfergewinnung zwischen Rotem und Totem Meer," *Zeitschrift des Deutschen Palästina-Vereins* 81 (1966), pp. 56–73.

[22] We thank Erez Ben-Yosef for organizing our short survey of the mines in Wadi Abu Khusheibah.

[23] B. Rothenburg, "Explorations and Investigations in the Mines of the Timna Valley (Israel): Paleomorphology as Key to Major Problems in Mining Research," *Glasnik Srpskog arheološkog društva* 22 (2005), pp. 133–148.

[24] See Erez Ben-Yosef, Thomas E. Levy and Mohammad Najjar, "New Iron Age Copper-Mine Fields Discovered in Southern Jordan," *Near Eastern Archaeology* 72, no. 2 (2009), p. 8.

[25] Diodorus of Sicily, *History* 3.12–13.

[26] F.B. Pyatt, G. Gilmore, J.P. Grattan, C.O. Hunt and S. McLaren, "An Imperial Legacy? An Exploration of the Environmental Impact of Ancient Metal Mining and Smelting in Southern Jordan," *Journal of Archaeological Science* 27 (2000), pp. 771–778.

[27] Strabo, *Geography* 12.3.40.

[28] Mark Gustafson, "Condemnation to the Mines in the Later Roman Empire," *Harvard Theological Review* 87, no. 4 (1994), p. 422.

One of our readers pointed out an omission, about Pesach Bar-Adon, the excavator of the Chalcolithic hoard pictured in this article. Read her note in Queries and Comments, BAR, March/April 2012.

Related Reading

Thomas E. Levy and Mohammad Najjar, "Edom and Copper," BAR, July/August 2006.

THE SPADE HITS SUSSITA

BAR Article–"Sussita Awaits the Spade"–Leads to Excavation

ARTHUR SEGAL
AND
MICHAEL EISENBERG

FIFTEEN YEARS AGO, I (Arthur Segal) sat in my study reading an article in BAR by Vassilios Tzaferis about Sussita, a dramatic site overlooking the Sea of Galilee that had been destroyed in a violent earthquake in 749 C.E. and had never been resettled. The columns of a church at the center of the site were still lying on the ground like toothpicks, just where they had fallen 1,250 years ago.

The site had been surveyed at the end of the 19th century by the German engineer and excavator Gottlieb Schumacher, who located the main street, a city gate, the remains of walls and towers, as well as a monumental Roman structure. In 1937 members of Kibbutz Ein Gev, led by the redoubtable Mendel Nun, an expert on the entire region surrounding the Sea of Galilee and now in his ninth decade, identified the two anchorages of the city. After Israeli independence in 1948, the Israel Defense Forces (IDF) built a frontier outpost here facing the Syrian border, unfortunately causing considerable damage to the site. In the 1950s a rescue excavation of areas exposed by the IDF uncovered a church, baptistery and what was probably a monastery.[1] In the 1990s an Israeli-German expedition conducted a number of surveys and trial excavations over the traces

PRECEDING PAGES: COMMANDING a dramatic view of the Galilee, Sussita sits atop a thousand-foot-high hill. A zigzag road leads to the site from the west. The oblong-shaped site is 2,000 feet long and 700 feet wide. During the New Testament era, Sussita was a member of the *Decapolis*, a group of ten cities governed according to the principles of a Greek city-state (polis). A stunning cross (inset) is preserved on the chancel screen marking an area at the end of the southern aisle of the Northwest Church, where rites for saints were held (see p. 576).

LIKE FALLEN MATCHSTICKS, the columns of an ancient church lie on the ground on the ridge of Sussita, about a mile east of the Sea of Galilee. The columns had been toppled by an earthquake in 749 C.E. This photo served as an illustration in a 1990 BAR article entitled "Sussita Awaits the Spade," which noted that although the site had been surveyed in the past it had never undergone a major excavation. That article spurred Arthur Segal to propose to his colleagues that they lead a dig at the site. After six seasons of excavation, he and his co-author report on their discoveries in the accompanying article.

of the aqueduct leading to Sussita and its internal water system.[2] But that was it. No major excavation of the site. The BAR article was tantalizingly entitled "Sussita Awaits the Spade."*

As I finished reading the article, I asked myself how it could be possible that no one was interested in excavating one of the best-preserved and most beautiful classical sites in the country. A few days later, I proposed to my colleagues at the University of Haifa that we adopt Sussita as a project of our Department of Archaeology. We have now finished our sixth season of excavation, and it is time to report to BAR readers.[3]

Sussita is located on the eastern side of the Sea of Galilee (Kinneret in Hebrew), a little over a mile from the shore. The site itself is flat with an oblong shape about 2,000 feet long and 700 feet wide. A saddle on the east links it to the Golan Heights. The site has many advantages. It is close to the lake, but rises a thousand feet above it. It is near the road that circles the eastern shore of the Sea of Galilee and at the same time dominates it, so the inhabitants of Sussita could view and exert control over the entire area that spreads to the east and southeast of the lake. At the base of the steep northern and southern slopes run the Ein Gev stream and the Sussita stream.

The crest of the mountain contains a little over 20 acres and is surrounded by a strong wall that follows the line of the cliffs. In some places the wall passes over the edge of the abyss and actually appears to be part of the cliffs. The city had two gates, one at the eastern end and another at the western end. Within, a network of streets intersects at right angles

*BAR, September/October 1990.

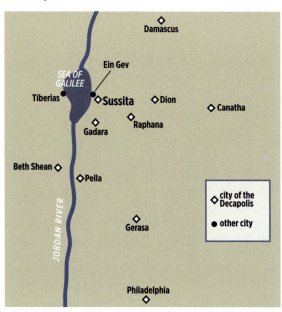

THE HEART OF SUSSITA appears in this aerial view taken from the north; in the foreground is a church that the excavators call the Northwest Church [7] (see photo, p. 575); beyond it, in the center of the photo, is the temenos of the city's main sanctuary during the Hellenistic period [6] (late second century B.C.E.) (see photo, p. 573); and at top is the *decumanus* [9] and the forum [4] (see photos, pp. 570–571).

The plan at right shows Sussita's major features: the *decumanus*, or the major east-west road [9]; the east gate [1]; the Cathedral [2]; the Northeast Church [3] (see photo, p. 574); the forum [4]; the *kalybe* [5], an open-air temple that featured a statue of the emperor; the Hellenistic compound [6] (see photo, p. 573); the Northwest Church [7]; and the west gate [8].

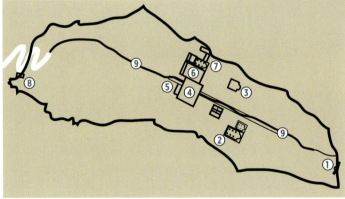

creating *insulae* in which public buildings and residential quarters were constructed. Even today, a visitor can clearly see the main thoroughfare of the city that traverses its entire length from east to west. This street, the *decumanus maximus*, was lined with impressive columns, some of which are still at the site.

Sussita traces its origins to the period after the death of Alexander the Great in 323 B.C.E., when his empire was divided among the Ptolemies in Egypt and the Seleucids in Syria, leaving them to fight over the hinterland between. Palestine changed

hands several times. Pottery from our excavations found beneath a Hellenistic compound indicates that the site was first inhabited by the Ptolemies in the third century B.C.E. Whether it was a semi-urban settlement or simply an outpost fortress is still uncertain, although the latter seems more likely. When it was captured by the Seleucids (we also found pottery from this level), it was given the name Hippos. The full Greek name was Antiochia Hippos. This suggests that a semi-urban settlement was established only in the Seleucid period, most

likely by Antiochus III or Antiochus IV.

In the last half of the second century B.C.E., the successful Jewish revolt against the Seleucid ruler Antiochus IV Epiphanes (a victory still celebrated in the Jewish festival of Hanukkah) led to the creation of the first independent Jewish state since the Babylonians destroyed Jerusalem in 586 B.C.E. A series of Hellenistic Jewish kings known as the Hasmonean dynasty then ruled the country. One of the last Hasmonean rulers, Alexander Jannaeus, conquered the area of Hippos between 83 and 80 B.C.E., according to the ancient historian Josephus,[4] and the city became known as Sussita, which means "Horse" in Aramaic (just as the earlier name, Hippos, means "horse" in Greek). We really can't account for this name.

The short-lived independent Jewish kingdom was brought under Roman rule by Pompey in 63 B.C.E. Pompey renewed the settlement of Hellenistic cities like Sussita east of the Sea of Galilee and included them in *Provincia Syria*, which he founded.

Sussita was subsequently included in the group of ten cities known as the *Decapolis*, literally "ten cities." These cities formed a broad settlement bloc stretching from Philadelphia (today Amman) in the south to Damascus in the north, and from Beth-Shean in the west to Canatha (today Kanawat, in Syria) in the east. Beth-Shean, incidentally, is the only city of the *Decapolis* west of the Sea of Galilee. The cities of the

THE FORUM IS shown in a general view in the photo (above), while the photo at upper right shows the remains of several columns and a cracked column base; at lower right is a semi-circular base for a statue or a memorial plaque.

The forum was a grand public space; it was paved with basalt flagstones and was lined on at least two sides with colonnades. The columns were made of gray granite and supported a roof, thus providing a shaded walkway along the edges of the forum. The bases that supported the columns were round and made of white marble; they sat on square pedestals made of local limestone. The semi-circular statue base, which measures 6 feet in diameter, was also made of limestone. Such semi-circular bases are common in Greece and Asia Minor but have never before been found in ancient Israel. The decision to erect a statue or plaque in Sussita's forum could only have been made by the city's council and indicates a high level of local governance.

Decapolis, contrary to widespread view, never created a city league based on the model of the Delian League formed by Athens against the Persians in the fifth century B.C.E. The *Decapolis* was instead merely a group of cities that, besides their shared location within a certain geographical area, conducted their lives according to the principles of a *polis** and

---

*A polis (city state in Greek) was an independent entity in which every citizen, i.e., an adult male being a member of an "ecclesia" (general assembly), could elect or be elected to any of the city's governing bodies, but mainly to the *boule*, the city council, whose members (200–700, on average, according to the size of the population), elected the officials, especially the *strategoi*, who ran the city's affairs.

HERSHEL SHANKS

HERSHEL SHANKS

of trade and competition. The term used for Sussita in a Jewish source as the "bane of Tiberias"[9] must have originated from the competition between the two cities.[10]

Although the references are scant, it is safe to assume that Sussita, like the other cities of the Decapolis, flourished and thrived during the second and third centuries C.E. as the *Pax Romana* brought quiet, open borders and wide-ranging commercial links. The main public buildings, the ruins of which are much in evidence in the urban landscape of Sussita, were most probably erected during this time, expressing the city's pride as well as loyalty to the Roman Empire.

In the Byzantine period (beginning in the fourth century C.E.), ancient Palestine was divided into three districts. Sussita was one of the cities of *Palaestina Secunda*, which included the Galilee, and most of the population was Christian. From the writings of the church fathers, we learn that, in this period, the city was the seat of an *Episcopus* (bishop). The five churches located so far in Sussita confirm the range and depth of Christianization that the city underwent.

Archaeological evidence shows that the transition from the Byzantine to the early Arab period (the Umayyad Caliphate) in the seventh century C.E. was not accompanied by a destruction. The churches continued to exist and flourish even during the seventh and early-eighth centuries. The wealth of Umayyad pottery and coins found in the area of the Northwest Church confirms the continued existence of this church until the mid-eighth century C.E.

Sussita came to an end in a catastrophic earthquake in 749 C.E. The destructive force of this earthquake is evident in the fallen columns, crushed walls and the small finds scattered over the area, all testifying to the fact that the shock was sudden and devastating. The city was abandoned and has never been inhabited since.

Now let's take an archaeological tour of the city. We enter by the eastern gate—over the saddle from the Golan Heights. (The route to the western gate that faces the Galilee follows a zigzag, snake-like route to overcome a thousand-foot difference in height over a steep and rocky slope in less than one mile; it is not in use today because it is so steep and dangerous.) The road over the saddle is carved into soft limestone and on both sides are clearly visible remains of mausoleums, or, to use the Greek or Latin plural, *mausolea*. Building stones from these structures (mostly limestone, some basalt) are scattered about, surveyed but unexcavated; sections of architraves, engaged half-columns, capitals and bases, all fashioned with great care, testify to the

constituted an outstanding Greek cultural entity in an area that was mainly Semitic.

Herod the Great ruled Judea as a Roman vassal monarch (he was confirmed by the Roman Senate) beginning in 37 B.C.E. Shortly thereafter, Augustus, the Roman emperor, extended the borders of the Herodian kingdom, transferring Sussita, among other areas, to Herod's rule. The citizens of Sussita were bitterly vexed at this decision; they wished to remain part of *Provincia Syria*.[5] After Herod's death in 4 B.C.E., Sussita reverted to the Province of Syria.[6]

But the city continued to be home to a Jewish minority,[7] and a number of Jewish villages existed around Sussita as the hub.[8]

Relations between Jewish Tiberias on the southwestern shore of the lake and Hellenistic Sussita were

"GOOD LUCK AELIUS CALPURNIANUS" begins a 13-line inscription in Greek that covers one side of a white marble column found in Sussita's forum plaza. The man was a high official in the Roman provincial administration; the inscription also mentions his wife, Domitia Ulpia, and bears a date of the Pompeian era that corresponds to 238/239 C.E. The inscription refers to Domitia as "Matrona Stolata," a title that suggests that she was granted the right to conduct her financial and legal affairs independently of her husband. The inscription indicates that the provincial administrative system of the Roman Empire had successfully spread Greek Hellenistic culture to Sussita, just as it had spread it in scores of cities throughout its domain.

magnificence of the original structures. Pieces of sarcophagi are also strewn about. This was no doubt the burial place of the city's elite.

A second cemetery on a slope south of the city served the rest of the inhabitants. They used a totally different system of burial. Here, the graves form a system of rock-carved tombs. Unlike the *mausolea*, however, each tomb has a central burial chamber in which three of the walls (all but the entrance wall) have burial niches (*loculi*) carved into them. The number of niches in each burial chamber varies from three to eleven. The burial chambers were usually sealed by doors made of dressed and ornamented stone, the broken pieces of which still lie around.

The existence of two cemeteries, one for the wealthy people of Sussita and one for the rest of the residents, reflects in a clear, spatial way the social relationships of the *polis*. We hope one day to excavate both of these cemeteries.

The East Gate has a single passageway, about 10 feet wide with towers on either side, one round and one square. The round tower was incorporated into the city wall, creating a killing field in front of the passageway. We have also exposed a section of the city wall into which the round tower was integrated.

Two Prominent Citizens

εὐτυχῶς·
Αἰλίος Καλπουρ-
νιανὸς ἀπὸ
κορνουκ(λαρίων) τοῦ κα-
θολικοῦ δ( ) καὶ
Δομέτια Οὐλ-
πία ματρ(ῶνα) στολ(ᾶτα)
σύνβιος αὐ[τοῦ]
τὸν πρεσβέᾳ
τῇ κυρίᾳ πα-
τρίδι· ἔτι
βτ
Δεῖος η̄ .

"Good Luck Aelius Calpurnianus, the former cornicularius (in the office) of the procurator summanum nationum, and Domitia Ulpia, matrona stolata, his wife (erected the statue of) the ambassador, to the native city. In the year 302 (in the month of) Dios (day) 8."

The wall is built of carefully dressed ashlars with delicate margins and smooth, slightly raised bosses that are typical of the first century C.E. and have been discovered in *Provincia Arabia*, Syria and the northern part of Israel. Hence, we feel comfortable dating the gate to the first century C.E. The towers probably rose to a height of three stories, with the upper one serving as a station for catapults.*

This round tower—including the method of construction, the way the layers were placed and the type of stone dressing—closely resembles the round towers at Tiberias and Gadara (on the Sea of Galilee), which are better preserved and therefore easier to visualize.

Inside the gate a few flagstones hint at a plaza that led to the eastern end of the *decumanus maximus*. We intend to excavate this area in the near future.

The *decumanus maximus*, the main street of the city, traversed the full length of the city. On either side the street was lined with a colonnade of gray granite columns imported from Aswan in Egypt. Each column weighs nearly five tons and is about 15 feet high.

The importation of hundreds of columns and

SACRED SPACE. This area, across the *decumanus* from the forum, was home to several of Sussita's religious structures over many centuries. Shown here is the area from the Hellenistic period (late second century B.C.E.), when it served as a *temenos*, or religious compound. The surviving column bases, column drums and elegantly carved Corinthian capitals (believed to be the earliest ever found in Israel) testify to the area's past grandeur. The Hellenistic temple here was made of limestone and was likely destroyed in 83 B.C.E., when the Hasmonean ruler Alexander Jannaeus conquered the city. A smaller temple, made of basalt, was erected on the site during the Roman period, probably at the end of the first century B.C.E. or early C.E. Atop the ruins of that temple, in the late-fifth or early-sixth century C.E., rose a Byzantine-era church (see photos on p. 574) that used many of the building stones of its predecessors.

their installation along the colonnaded street (as well as in the forum; see below) must have been extremely expensive, not to mention the logistic and engineering skills required for their transfer up to the site and subsequent erection. The ability of a medium-sized city like Sussita to plan, finance and carry out such a project surely arouses admiration. It was probably undertaken sometime in the second century C.E.

Near the midpoint of the *decumanus maximus* was the urban center of Sussita. Adjoining the *decumanus maximus* on the south lay the forum; on the northern side was the main sanctuary (*temenos*) of Sussita. This compound continued to function in its original capacity from the Hellenistic down to the Byzantine period, when a church—what we call the Northwest Church—was built upon the remains of pagan temples.

---

*The Roman Army used several types of siege weapons for discharging missiles. The largest was the *onager*, also called a *scorpio*. This siege machine could hurl massive stones. The Jewish historian Josephus states that at the siege of Jerusalem the machines of Legio X Fretensis hurled stones that weighted a talent (more than 50 pounds) a distance of two furlongs (about 1,400 feet [*The Jewish War* V, 6,3]). The smaller machines, to which the Roman architect Vitruvius gives the general term of catapult (*catapulta*) were of various sizes. The smaller ones were called *scorpiones* and the larger, *ballistae*. (See G. Webster, *The Roman Imperial Army* [London: Rowman and Littlefield Publishers, Inc., 1985, 3rd ed.], pp. 243–244.)

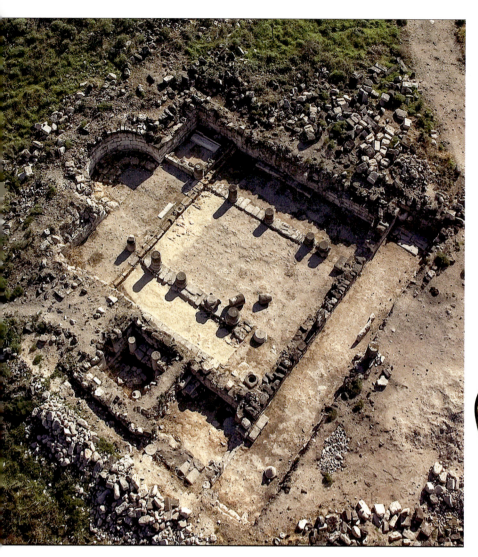

BEARING CONSULAR ROBES and a crown, a figure decorates a coin minted in about 601 C.E. (below). Coins are crucial for dating the Northwest Church; this one belongs to the Byzantine era, but most of the recovered coins date to the Umayyad, or early Arab, period (630–750 C.E.). From the numismatic evidence, the excavators determined that the Northwest Church continued to function even after the Muslim conquest of the Holy Land and was not destroyed until the earthquake of 749 C.E.

Found just last summer, the elegant Byzantine-era structure at left is called by the excavators the Northeast Church and lies just 150 feet from the Northwest Church (see plan, p. 569). Though smaller than its counterpart, the Northeast Church also is divided into thirds by columns and features a semi-circular apse at the end of the central nave.

In the summer of 2005, we excavated the junction between the forum and the *decumanus maximus*. There we uncovered a pair of piers, facing each other and meticulously executed in basalt stone. They apparently belonged to a decorative gate that must have stood here proclaiming to passersby that they were about to enter the forum.

The forum is paved with basalt flagstones. Colonnades lined two sides of the forum (north and east; the southern side remains unexcavated). The columns supported entablatures, above which were roofs, creating shady roofed promenades along the northern and eastern sides of the forum. The columns were made of the same gray granite as the columns lining the *decumanus maximus* and were crowned with Corinthian capitals of white marble. The columns were placed on Attic bases made of white marble, which in turn were set on square pedestals made of local limestone. The use of three types of stone so different from each other

was hardly fortuitous. The architects clearly showed great sensitivity for the aesthetic aspects of the forum layout.

On the southern part of the forum, a well-preserved stairway leads to an underground water reservoir with impressive barrel-vault roofing. The bottom part is carved into the rock surface, the upper part is built of limestone. It is one of the largest and best-preserved reservoirs in the area. Water was brought into the underground reservoir from an aqueduct more than 15 miles long. Some of the stone piping is still visible, especially near an eastern gate of the city, as are fragments of a built channel that passes under the *decumanus maximus* on its way to the reservoir under the forum plaza.

In the northern part of the forum plaza between the fallen columns lying on the pavement, we discovered a D-shaped (semicircular) podium of limestone about 6 feet in diameter. Podiums (*podia*) like this are widespread in Greece and Asia Minor, but were

A COLORFUL MOSAIC decorates the Northwest Church. Its floor contains simple floral and geometric patterns, and the walls, columns and even the capitals were colored. Painted plaster covered the walls, and some even bore murals depicting flowers, fruits and leaves.

never before found in Israel. They served mostly for statues or memorial tablets to commemorate the exploits of one of the citizens or of some high-ranking visitor. Such a monument in the central city plaza could not be the act of an individual. The decision to place this kind of monument in a public area could only have been made by the city council, the *boule* of Hippos-Sussita. The Sussita podium is clear testimony to the organization of its urban government and cultural character.

Fronting on the plaza on the west side were two monumental structures. One appears to have been a decorative gate. All that remains of it are the foundations, and its exact design is unknown.

The other structure, however, is a monumental building built of basalt ashlars of superior quality. Even before excavation it stood to a height of more than 10 feet and was the best-preserved structure on the site. What purpose it served has been a puzzle. Gottlieb Schumacher, who surveyed the building in 1885, thought it was a synagogue. More-recent scholars speculated that it might be a *nymphaeum*—a large, decorative, architecturally intricate fountain—like the *nymphaea* that graced so many Roman cities (for example, Beth-Shean). This suggestion was based on the decorative eastern façade of the building, in the center of which is a semicircular niche nearly 20 feet wide. The lower part of the niche is stepped; the upper part, which did not survive, was a half-dome, with some of its stones lying scattered at the foot of the building.

At first we, too, thought it was a *nymphaeum*, but we soon found that neither there nor in its immediate vicinity was there any kind of water installation, pipes or channels that would indicate its function as a *nymphaeum*. In addition, the building did not have a decorative water pool typical of all *nymphaea*.

We finally decided that the structure was a *kalybe*, an open-air temple, in which a statue of the emperor stood in the niche. Buildings of this kind have been discovered in many cities throughout the region, invariably erected at sites in city centers and facing public streets or the main colonnaded thoroughfare.

What is uniquely common to *kalybe* structures, wherever they might be, is that they are open buildings with a broad façade and a central niche for the emperor's statue. In contrast to temples dedicated to the gods, the *kalybe* temples were not set up in sacred compounds separate from the rest of the city area, but were erected with an explicit link to the forum or to the colonnaded street. The emperor's statue was in full view for all to see. This type of temple was an innovation in the urban panorama in the eastern provinces of the Roman empire. The salient presence of these *kalybe* temples in the very heart of the city and their accessibility and relationship to daily city life are all blunt and powerful expressions of the presence of imperial rule represented by the image of the emperor.

Just how closely Sussita was integrated with Rome is demonstrated in an unusual inscription discovered in the forum plaza. It was found on a white marble column a few yards from the semicircular podium. We have finally deciphered it; the text is printed in the box on page 572. The 13-line Greek inscription mentions a high-ranking official in the financial administration of the province, most probably *Provincia Syria-Palaestina*, named Aelius Calpurnianus and his wife Domitia Ulpia. It is dated according to the Pompeian era, the equivalent of 238/239 C.E. These two Sussita citizens with Roman names and belonging to the city nobility commemorated themselves in Greek. Aelius Calpurnianus's family

apparently received Roman citizenship during the reign of the emperor Hadrian (whose family name was Aelius), while his wife, Domitia Ulpia, was granted Roman citizenship during the reign of Trajan, whose full name was Marcus Ulpius Traianus (hence the name Ulpia). Domitia also bore the Latin title "Matrona Stolata." The precise meaning of this title is still unclear; it seems to record her special status as an independent woman who is permitted to conduct legal and financial affairs in her own name, without her husband's authorization.

In any event, this inscription clearly indicates that some Sussita citizens had attained the highest ranks in Roman provincial administration. It also reflects the degree to which Sussita had absorbed Greek Hellenistic culture within the system of Roman provincial administration. This phenomenon is not unique to Sussita alone, but appears in other cities of the Decapolis, as well as in other parts of the Roman Empire. Indeed, not long

ago a Latin inscription was found at Caesarea that mentions a certain Valerius Calpurnianus, perhaps a relative of our Aelius Calpurnianus. It is difficult not to speculate on the enormous success of the Roman Empire in creating around the Mediterranean basin a unified and standard system of administration that was one of the central components of its cultural uniformity during the second and third centuries C.E. Roman administration in the eastern provinces of the empire rested upon urban nobility in hundreds of *poleis* that fostered Greek cultural identity but that also saw themselves as an inseparable part of the Roman Empire.

On the other side of the *decumanus maximus*, opposite the forum, was an extensive religious compound or *temenos*. We have excavated only a small part of this area, but enough to reveal that, during the Hellenistic period (late second century B.C.E.), there was already a temple there. The column bases, column drums and Corinthian

CARVED WITH CROSSES, a chancel screen (photo at left) demarcates an area at the end of the southern aisle of the Northwest Church as a *martyrion*, where rites for saints were held. The photo at right shows a track on which a chancel stood. Beyond the chancel screen, four small columns (below) frame a red limestone *reliquarium*, which held the bones of a saint.

Church) consists of a prayer hall and a courtyard atrium in front that is paved with basalt flagstones. Parallel with its four walls were four porticoes of columns that created a central courtyard and four shaded corridors. The column drums are fixed upon Attic bases crowned with pseudo-Ionic capitals. The architecture of the prayer hall and atrium resembles that of many contemporaneous churches and synagogues in the Galilee, Golan and Hauran regions. But we were astonished to find, near the southernmost of the three doorways leading into the prayer hall, a theater seat made of basalt. What is a theater seat doing in a Byzantine church? It probably came from Sussita's theater, which has not yet been located. We have an idea where it is, and we intend to excavate there to test the theory.

The central entrance to the church leads into the nave, the two secondary entrances lead into the aisles, separated from the nave by rows of columns. At the end of the nave is a semi-circular apse.

Unexpectedly, the two aisles are not the same. At the end of the northern aisle is a small apse, while the end of southern aisle is rectangular. This lack of symmetry in the internal arrangement of the prayer hall is very rare in churches of this region. In its earliest phase, the church was monoapsidal. On the north and south side of the central apse there were two rectangular shaped chambers. At a later stage a small apse was added to the northern aisle, while the shape of the south chamber remained unchanged.

In the central apse was a podium (the *bema*) that was separated from the rest of the prayer hall by a chancel screen placed between chancel posts. The church furniture—of white marble—is mostly well

capitals are mute testimony to what once stood here. To the best of our knowledge, these Corinthian capitals are the earliest ever found in Israel. The Hellenistic temple was probably destroyed when Alexander Jannaeus, the Hasmonean ruler of Judea, conquered the city around 83 B.C.E. Later, as early as the first century C.E., a smaller temple was built here of basalt stone, instead of the limestone of the earlier temple. Over the ruins of the Roman temple, a Byzantine church was erected at the end of the fifth or the beginning of the sixth century. It made extensive use of the building stones from both the Hellenistic temple and the Roman one.

The Byzantine church over the ruins of the ancient temples symbolized the victory of Christianity over paganism. A substantial part of the church walls were built of large limestone blocks from the Hellenistic temple; the columns of the church were set on marble bases that had once belonged to the Roman temple.

This church (we refer to it as the Northwest

preserved and has been reconstructed and placed in its original positions.

The floor of the prayer hall is paved with a colorful mosaic of simplified floral and geometrical patterns. The remains of the plaster on the walls, columns and even the capitals reveal that they were colored, giving the interior of the church a bright, attractive look. Some of the walls were covered not only with layers of ordinary painted plaster but also with simple murals, such as leaves, fruits and flowers. The dominant colors were red, blue, green and yellow.

A chamber south of the central apse served as the *martyrion*, where rites for saints were held. Entry into this chamber is through a doorway between two chancel screens and tall posts that created a kind of gate. On one of the two tall posts, three silver crosses remained undamaged and in their original locations *in situ*. Other finds in the *martyrion* included a bronze oil lamp in the shape of a dove which hung on a chain and two round bronze candelabra (in Greek, *polykandela*).

Near the eastern wall of the *martyrion* was a red limestone *reliquarium*, a receptacle for preserving the bones of a saint. On top of it was another smaller *reliquarium* with a gabled lid made of marble. In the center of the lid was a hole in which we found a bronze stick used for anointing ceremonies.

An annex to the church functioned as a *diakonikon* for storing food and tools. Among the metal findings here were sickles, scissors, an almost perfectly preserved Umayyad bronze decanter, scores of oil lamps and coins. A few of the coins were from the Byzantine period but most were from the Umayyad period. These coins are extremely important for dating the church. The church apparently continued to function throughout the Umayyad (Arab) period, only to be destroyed in the earthquake of 749 C.E. The collapse of the arches that supported the roof of the *diakonikon* and the way in which the amphorae and jars were scattered when they fell from wooden shelves evidence a life that ended abruptly.

To conclude on a somewhat mundane note, in our 2005 season we discovered in what we call the Northeast Church[11] (about 150 feet from the Northwest Church) an amulet assuring its wearer that he or she will have healthy digestion and no stomach problems. It consists of a medallion made of hematite and set in a beautifully executed gold frame with one Greek work engraved in the center—"Digest" (*Pepte*).

The excavation of Sussita is still in its initial stages. The first six seasons have unearthed only a small bit of what is hidden at the site. You are invited to come and uncover it with us. 🔲

Uncredited photos courtesy of Hippos-Sussita Excavations.

[1] These excavations were conducted by Claire Epstein, Emmanuel Anati, Michael Avi-Yonah and Aaron Shulman.

[2] Participating in this project were Ze'ev Meshel, Tsvika Tsuk, Z. Felbush and Y. Peleg.

[3] The excavations were conducted by the Zinman Institute of Archaeology at the University of Haifa in cooperation with the Research Center for Mediterranean Archaeology of the Polish Academy of Sciences, the National Museum in Warsaw, and the Concordia University in St. Paul, Minnesota. The project is headed by Prof. Arthur Segal and the co-directors of the Sussita expedition are Prof. Jolanta Mlynarczyk, Dr. Mariusz Burdajewicz and Prof. Mark Schuler.

[4] *Antiquities* 13:394–397.

[5] *Antiquities* 17:217; *War* 1:396.

[6] *Antiquities* 17:320; *War* 2:97.

[7] Jerusalem Talmud, *Ketubot* 12:4; Babylonian Talmud, *Rosh Hashana* 2:1.

[8] Tosefta, *Shevi'it* 4:10; Tosefta, *Ohalot* 18:4.

[9] *Lamentations Rabba*, Buber edition, 46a.

[10] Jerusalem Talmud, *Shevi'it* 8:3.

[11] The Northeast Church was excavated by a team from Concordia University, St. Paul, Minnesota, headed by Prof. Mark Schuler.

The 15th season of ongoing excavations at Hippos/Sussita concluded in 2014. The project was directed by Arthur Segal and codirected by Michael Eisenberg, both of the University of Haifa's Zinman Institute of Archaeology, until 2012, at which time Eisenberg took over as sole director.

Since publication of the BAR article, the excavations have revealed the city's main forum, an odeion (a small, theater-like structure) and the remains of a high-quality mausoleum in the necropolis that dates to the second century C.E. According to Eisenberg, dozens of such mausoleums were built on both sides of the saddle ridge for the city's wealthy inhabitants.

The first volume of the excavation report is now available: Arthur Segal, Michael Eisenberg, Jolanta Mlynarczyk, Mariusz Burdajewicz and Mark Schuler, *Hippos (Sussita) of the Decapolis: The First Twelve Seasons of Excavations (2001-2011), Volume I* (Haifa: The Zinman Institute of Archaeology, 2013). The second volume is due to be published in 2015.

Related Reading

Vassilios Tzaferis, "Sussita Awaits the Spade," BAR, September/October 1990.

Mendel Nun, "Ports of Galilee," BAR, July/August 1999 (see p. 458 of this book for another article by Nun).

Michael Eisenberg, Archaeological Views: "What's Luck Got to Do with It?" BAR, November/December 2010.

Michael Eisenberg and Arthur Segal, "Hercules in Galilee," BAR, November/December 2011.

Godfearers
in the
City of Love

ANGELOS CHANIOTIS

In Roman times, Aphrodisias in the southwest of Asia Minor (modern Turkey) was the city of Aphrodite, goddess of love. It was also a city of marble, abundantly available in excellent quality from nearby quarries. The monumental marble gate of the sanctuary of Aphrodite (the tetrapylon) has now been magnificently restored. Beyond are the meager remains of the goddess's temple.

Sometime after the city became largely Christian in the late fifth century C.E., the temple of Aphrodite was transformed into a Christian basilica. By the seventh century, the name of the city had become an embarrassment and it was changed to Stavropolis ("City of the Cross"). In the Byzantine period, Stavropolis was the seat of the bishop of Caria.

In addition to the ruins of the temple of Aphrodite, the city boasts one of

PREVIOUS PAGES: CITY OF LOVE. Set on a lush plateau amid the picturesque mountains of southwestern Turkey, the ancient city of Aphrodisias is renowned for its impressive marble monuments, including this towering and recently restored tetrapylon gate that gave access to the city's main sanctuary to Aphrodite, the goddess of love. (The more meager remains of the goddess's temple, later turned into a church, can be seen in the distance at left.) By the fourth and fifth centuries C.E., Aphrodisias had become a cosmopolitan city inhabited by not only adherents to the city's traditional Hellenic pagan faiths, but also various Christian sects and a vibrant Jewish community. As our author explains, a new study of an old inscription sheds fresh light on the incredible and often complex interchange of faiths, ideas and communities during late antiquity.

the best-preserved stadiums in antiquity, an impressive theater and a building complex dedicated to the worship of the Roman emperors (the *Sebasteion*).

The modern visitor to Aphrodisias (it is once again called by its Roman name) admires the buildings, their splendid decoration and the many free-standing sculptures that once adorned the city's public spaces. Thanks to its high-quality marble quarries, Aphrodisias was one of the most important centers of sculpture in the Roman East. A large part of the population was connected with this trade, and many worked as quarrymen, masons and sculptors. They used the implements of their work not only to make the statues and reliefs for which Aphrodisias is famous, but also to engrave texts and images on the walls and columns of public buildings. Perhaps that explains why so many graffiti (informal inscriptions or drawings carved on public walls and monuments) survive at Aphrodisias—indeed, more graffiti are found here than at almost any other contemporaneous site.

In the fluting of one of the less-impressive columns of the *Sebasteion*, for example, you will see the partly erased drawing of a seven-branched candelabra (menorah) flanked by a palm branch (*lulav*) and ram's horns (*shofar*), a common trio of Jewish

iconography. On another column of the *Sebasteion* is a Hanukkah menorah with nine candles instead of seven.*

Graffiti are notoriously difficult to date, but it is reasonable to assume that these drawings were made sometime in late antiquity (mid-fourth–sixth centuries C.E.), when the *Sebasteion* was no longer used for the cult of the emperor. At that time, the rooms (*tabernae*) in the *Sebasteion*'s two porticoes were transformed into shops for tradesmen. The Jewish symbols must have marked shops belonging to Jews. At the entrance to another one of these shops is a reused marble plaque with the faint remains of two *menorot*, one flanked by what appear to be a *lulav* (palm branch) and *etrog* (a lemon-like fruit), both of which are used on the Jewish festival of Sukkot.

Two *menorot* have also been preserved on columns of the west portico of the South Market, which was restored in the late fifth century C.E., and a drawing of *menorot* accompanied by a short prayer was found among the ruins of the city's theater. A piece of a broken clay oil lamp found in the North Market preserves a part of a menorah that once decorated the lamp. Another menorah was engraved on the shoulder of a jar that was probably used in a Jewish home to store agricultural products.

Another unusual bit of evidence of the presence of a Jewish community in Aphrodisias comes from the theater-like room in the Roman town hall (*bouleuterion*) that was used for entertainment in late antiquity. From inscriptions found in the theater, we know that one section of seats was reserved for the *Hebraioi* and their elders (*palaioi*).

Like the Jews, the city's Christians were also carving graffiti on the walls of public buildings—but crosses instead of *menorot*.

We must add to this mixture the persistence of ancient pagan religion and its more recent adaptations by philosophers such as Asklepiodotos of Alexandria who promoted an intellectual version of polytheistic Hellenic religion. In an honorary epigram for Pytheas, a prominent political figure, its author provocatively reminds his fellow citizens that his fatherland was still the city of Aphrodite.

Most of the scholarly discussion of religious conditions in Aphrodisias has focused on the conflict between Christians and pagans, or among different Christian groups that tried to impose their orthodoxy with political support from Constantinople. In fact,

*The menorah in the Jerusalem Temple had seven branches. Eight of the branches of the Hanukkah menorah commemorate the eight days of the festival, which in turn commemorate the miracle by which the oil that was enough only for one day lasted for eight days in 164 B.C.E. after the Temple was cleansed of the desecration of Antiochus IV. The light in the ninth branch is used to light the other eight.

MARVELOUS MARBLES. Located only a few miles from some of the richest marble quarries in the ancient world, Aphrodisias was famous not only for its gleaming monuments, but also for the beauty and craftsmanship of its many marble sculptures. The marble relief panel above, which once decorated the halls of the city's *Sebasteion*, shows a battle-clad Aeneas, the legendary Trojan hero and ancestor of Rome's founders, fleeing the sack of Troy with his elderly father Anchises perched on his shoulder and his young son Iulus (also called Ascanius) in tow. (The story of Aeneas's flight from Troy and subsequent voyage to Italy is famously told in Virgil's epic *The Aeneid*.) The trio's escape is watched over by Aeneas's divine mother, Aphrodite (also pictured at right), the goddess of love who was worshiped in the temple of Aphrodisias and whose beauty was often inspiration for the city's sculptors.

ANGELOS CHANIOTIS

ANGELOS CHANIOTIS

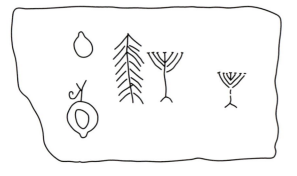

SIGNS OF THE TRIBE. A close look at the numerous graffiti carved into the walls and columns of ancient Aphrodisias reveals just how prevalent Jews and Jewish traditions were among the city's population. Jewish tradesmen and merchants of the fourth to sixth centuries, for example, set up shop in the abandoned rooms and colonnaded halls of the city's ancient *Sebasteion* (opposite, above), originally built as a monument to the cult of the emperor. Among the graffiti-carved marble ruins of their stalls, one can spot the distinctive symbols of Jewish art and iconography, including one column inscribed with a seven-branched candelabra (menorah) that has been partially erased (above left). On another column is a typical nine-branched Hanukkah menorah (above); and on a marble plaque located at the front of another shop are carved the faint images of two *menorot,* a palm branch (*lulav*) and the *etrog* fruit—clear signs that the store was owned by a Jew (center left; see drawing at left). Jewish graffiti are even found on items of everyday household use, like a large round storage jar decorated with a picture of a menorah (opposite, below).

the situation was far more complex and cannot be fully understood without taking into consideration the Jewish communities.

I believe the Jews of Aphrodisias have hardly played any part in discussions of the city's religious conflicts and ambiguities in late antiquity because the most important piece of evidence regarding the Jewish community has been erroneously dated by most scholars to a much earlier period.

I speak of a remarkable artifact—a tall, nearly rectangular marble block now kept in the garden of the

Aphrodisias excavation house. It is more than 9 feet high and measures 1.5 feet on each side (see photo on p. 587). It is engraved on two adjacent sides with a quite extraordinary inscription—a list of at least 120 donors, apparently to the city's synagogue. The donor list includes the names of both born Jews and recent converts to Judaism (proselytes), as well as unconverted members of the synagogue community (*theosebeis,* or "Godfearers").

The marble block was excavated in 1976 during construction work for the Aphrodisias museum. The

text of the inscription was published in 1987 with an excellent commentary by Joyce Reynolds and Robert Tannenbaum.[1] After discussing the various options, Reynolds and Tannenbaum opted for a date around 200 C.E. (in the Severan period), but without excluding other possibilities (fourth or fifth century). They recognized the position they favored "is not, unfortunately, susceptible of proof. It may be wrong; but it seems to us likely." This quite explicit caveat has been overlooked by most scholars who have discussed the text in connection with the history of Judaism. Until recently, with few exceptions,[2] the attribution of the text to the early third century has become canonical, excluding this very important document from discussions of the Jewish population of late antiquity.

The question of chronology has important historical implications. If it dates to about 200, to the period of the Severan emperors, then it must be understood in the context of that time, the time when the first great treatise on Jewish law, the Mishnah, was created, and when Aphrodisias was a typical Hellenistic city of the Roman East. If it dates to late antiquity (mid-fourth–sixth centuries C.E.), it must be understood in an entirely different context. Then the context is the religious interaction among Christians, Hellenists and Jews after the establishment of imperial Christianity. Unfortunately, this has hardly been addressed in discussions of the inscription.

I believe the arguments for a later date are compelling. The evidence is sometimes technical, however, so I have relegated the details to an endnote.[3] Many of the names in the inscription, for example, were common only in late antiquity.

This inscription is the longest Jewish inscription written in the Greek language ever found in the Jewish diaspora. In the initial publication, the text was assumed to be one inscription, but, as we shall see, it is really two inscriptions. Both texts, however, record the names, as previously noted, not only of Jews (including proselytes), but also of *theosebeis*, so-called Godfearers, or sympathizers to

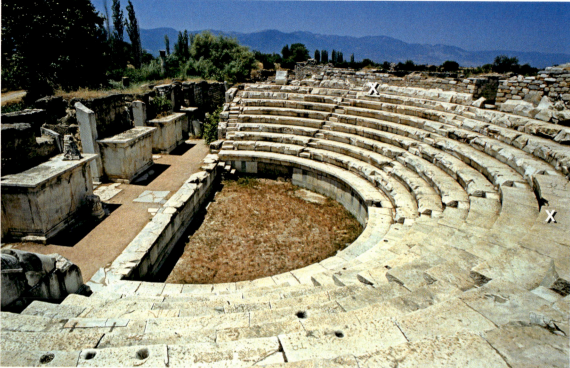

RESERVED SEATING. APHRODISIAS'S theater-like *bouleuterion* (above), which functioned as the city's town hall during Roman times, had by the fifth century become a venue for various public events, including lectures and musical and theatrical performances. Jews, like some of the factional and religious communities living at Aphrodisias, had seating areas reserved for them. Poorly preserved Greek inscriptions such as the one at left, carved into the seats marked in the photograph above, indicate areas specifically reserved for the Hebrews (*Hebraioi*) and their elders (*palaioi*).

Judaism. This indicates that a very significant part of the population regularly attended the synagogue and practiced Jewish rituals.

The rectangular marble block is inscribed on two adjacent faces. The two faces are slightly different in size, however; one is about half an inch wider than the other. We will call the wider one Face I and the narrower one Face II. Of the other two faces, one is carefully smoothed (like Face I and Face II), but the other is not. The rough, uninscribed side was apparently the back of the stone, originally intended to remain unseen, probably placed against a wall. The size and shape of the block strongly suggests its original function as a doorjamb. Perhaps it stood at the entrance to the city's synagogue.

The text on Face II bears a heading, but there is no trace of a heading on Face I. This might suggest a single text beginning on Face II and proceeding to Face I. But, indeed, that is not the case. Since the top of the block has been broken off, it is possible

that a separate heading could have been written on the lost part of Face I (possibly on a molding).

A clear difference in the writing distinguishes the inscription of Face I from Face II. The writing on Face I has a clean and neat appearance, as one expects for the front of a monument. The engraver started writing at the very top of the block, carefully engraving letters with standard, uniform letter heights within set guidelines. This face also has a drafted margin down both sides (see photos on pp. 588–589).

There are no such guidelines for the engraver on Face II. The letter heights vary. In a few cases the text goes beyond the right-hand margin. The first line, certainly written together with the rest of the text, is carved along a slightly oblique orientation. Another difference: The inscription on Face II starts about 5 inches from the top.

The clear difference between the two faces is very easy to explain: Face I was written first, while the stone was still lying on the ground. This made it easy for the engraver to draw the guidelines and to start inscribing the text at the very top of the block, as he could bend over the stone and did not have to climb a ladder to reach the top. Sometime later, after the block had been set up, another engraver inscribed the second text on Face II. His work was impeded by the height of the block and by the fact that it was standing. This explains why he had to start his inscription at a lower level, why his lines are not horizontal and why the script gives the impression that less care was given to the carving. The engraver of Face II was not less experienced, paid worse or simply idle; he was working under unfavorable conditions.

Although the second inscription is later, it is impossible to say how much later. Both date within late antiquity (c. 350–500 C.E.), and we can definitely rule out a date around 200 C.E.[4]

Let us now turn to the inscription itself. Face II begins with an invocation:

> May God help the *patelládes* (or the *patellâs*, or the *pátella*).

Unfortunately the last part of the last word is not preserved. *Pátella* usually means a dish or a plate and *patellâs* designates the profession of the "fast food sellers." These general meanings can be reconciled with different explanations—perhaps the term refers to a professional association of cooks, cook-shop customers or a soup kitchen for the poor. It may also have a funerary character or refer to a synagogue banquet hall initiated by a burial society. The huge block was found within the city wall, between the *Sebasteion* and one of the gates that lead outside of the city to the cemeteries. The text clearly has a funerary context (see below). The most plausible suggestion is that we are dealing with a burial society associated with the synagogue.

The text continues:

> Below are listed the members of the association (*dekania*) of those who are "fond of learning" (*philomatheis*), also known as those who continually praise God [or, who continually invoke

SUPPORTING THE SYNAGOGUE. Standing more than 9 feet high, this massive marble pillar may have originally functioned as a doorjamb at the main entrance of the Jewish synagogue of Aphrodisias. Two of its faces are inscribed in Greek with the names of at least 120 donors who commissioned the memorial, making it one of the longest Jewish inscriptions written in Greek that has ever been found. But while many Jewish names appear on the stone, a surprising number of donors to the synagogue identified themselves as recent converts to Judaism (proselytes) or as *theosebeis*, "Godfearers," a little-known group of gentiles and even Christians who were sympathetic to Judaism and participated in synagogue life.

God's blessing] (*paneulog[ountes]*), who erected this memorial, at their personal expense, for the liberation of the people (*plethos*) from grief.

The association (*dekania*), whose members initiated the donation, was certainly Jewish. The *philomatheis* ("fond of learning") were students of the Torah.

The text also identifies the specific titles of various officials in the Jewish community: *prostates*, the president of the community; *archon*, a member of the board; *archidekanos*, president of an association; and *psalmologos*, a psalm singer.

Face I lists more than 55 Jews and 52 Godfearers. Face II lists 14 men with predominantly Hebrew names (including three proselytes) and two Godfearers.

Many of the donors on Face I are also identified by their professions. Occupations mentioned in the text include greengrocer, fuller, bronzesmith, goldsmith and carpenter.

It is clear that people of very diverse social strata, from humble workers to members of the council, were attracted to Judaism.

Most of the donors on both faces have Biblical names—Jacob, Joseph, Joshua, Judah, Samuel—clearly indicating their Jewish identity. Other names are Greek translations of Hebrew names: Heortasios corresponds to Haggai, Theodotos to Jonathan and Nathaniel, Theophilos to Eldad. Still others had rare names related to religious or moral values, such as love of God, good behavior and willingness to offer consolation. More than half of the Jews had adopted names with a religious message. They used their names as a means of identity and separation (see box on p. 592).

What does this inscription tell us about the Jewish community of Aphrodisias in late antiquity? Jews were apparently prominent citizens as well as craftsmen. They used Biblical names. Proselytes were proud of their Judaism and made contributions to the synagogue, thus proving that despite the measures of the imperial administration, proselytism continued into the fourth and early fifth centuries. Jews who converted were not fearful of identifying themselves as proselytes. This was also true of the *theosebeis*, Godfearers.

The term *theosebeis* is found as early as the Septuagint translation of the Psalms (115:11,13, 118:2–4, 135:20). Similar terms, "those who fear God" and "those who venerate God," are found in the New Testament (Luke 7:1–10; Acts 10:22,28, 13:16,26), referring to gentiles who were attracted to Judaism. The Godfearers in the Aphrodisias inscription reflect the continuation of religious

TOP OF FACE I

TOP OF FACE II

UNEARTHED IN 1976, the inscribed pillar (above and opposite) was originally dated to the early third century C.E., but closer inspection of the inscription reveals that it was first carved and erected several hundred years later, probably in the mid-to-late fourth century. The pillar includes not one inscription, but two. The stone's slightly wider, front face (Face I) is engraved with a clean, neat inscription that follows horizontal guidelines and is written within drafted vertical margins (top). The inscription on the adjacent face (Face II) is far less precise, with varying letter heights, words that extend into the margins and an initial line awkwardly carved at a different angle from the rest of the text (above). These two distinct carving styles suggest that the inscription on Face I was carved first, when the stone was still lying flat on the ground and fully accessible to the engraver, while the text of Face II was carved at a later date, once the pillar had already been installed in the synagogue and the engraving had to be completed from atop a ladder.

ANGELOS CHANIOTIS

STILL KICKING. Well into late antiquity, the traditional Hellenic cults continued to thrive in Aphrodisias, even though many pagan rituals had ostensibly been banned by the Christian emperors of Byzantium. In the mid-fifth century C.E., the pagan philosopher Asklepiodotos of Alexandria (likely depicted in the portrait shown opposite) moved to Aphrodisias to establish a school of classical learning and philosophy, where he is said to have performed miracles regularly and composed hymns in honor of the city's pagan gods. Even some members of the city's ruling elite, including local governors, are known to have taken part in sacrifices and rituals aimed at restoring the pagan cults of old.

competition and exchange into late antiquity. The *theosebeis* are usually identified as a group of sympathizers of Judaism, who attended the synagogue without being fully converted. It has been suggested that they were worshipers of *Theos Hypsistos* ("the Highest God") and should be associated with a group that the literary sources call "those who venerate the God" (*sebomenoi ton theon*).[5] Whether all references to *theosebeis* in the literary sources and inscriptions denote a single group is arguable. But the references do evidence an extremely important religious phenomenon in late antiquity: the crossing of religious boundaries. Individuals were interested in the religious beliefs and rituals of others; they debated the faith of others; and sometimes they converted to the religion of others, as the proselytes' names show.

It was a time of great religious diversity. From 311 C.E., Christianity was "tolerated" in the Roman Empire. Within a few years it became the religion of the emperors and received their support, although Christians were divided by dogmatic conflicts. Like the Jew s, Christians also expressed their religious devotion in their names. Indeed, the majority of the names of Christians in Aphrodisias in this period reveal their religious identity. They adopted names of apostles, evangelists and angels, for example, Ioannes, Loukas, Michael, Petros, Stephanos, as well as names related to the Lord (Kyriakos). Some of their names reference Christian religious values or cultic peculiarities, such as Iordanes (an allusion to

RIGHT: PART OF THE MIX. By the late fifth century C.E., Christians, supported by Byzantine emperors, dominated Aphrodisias and had even rebuilt the ancient temple of Aphrodite as a Christian basilica. Within a hundred years, the city, no longer comfortable with its close association with the pagan goddess of love, was renamed Stavropolis, the City of the Cross. Until that time, Christians, though segmented by their own dogmatic quarrels, were simply part of the everyday make-up of this cosmopolitan city of Asia Minor. And like the Jews and Hellenists living around them, Christians carved their own graffiti into Aphrodisias's marble monuments, including these simple drawings of Byzantine crosses found near the gate of one of the city's markets (right) and in the converted temple of Aphrodite (above).

baptism), Athanasios (a reference to the immortality of the soul), Anastasios (an expression of the hope of resurrection) and Eustathios and Eudoxia, references to the firm and correct faith.

Among early Christians we also find representatives of all social strata. The Christianization of the "city of Aphrodite," however, was a slow process. The resistance of the last polytheists remained strong until the early sixth century. The pagan philosopher Asklepiodotos of Alexandria came to Aphrodisias around 450 C.E. and found a flourishing group of polytheists.[6] A large house near the city's *Sebasteion* is decorated with images of the intellectuals of classical antiquity and their disciples; among them are the

ANGELOS CHANIOTIS

ANGELOS CHANIOTIS

More than Just Names

The myriad Jewish, Christian and pagan names carved into the marble ruins of ancient Aphrodisias, especially the "donors' inscription," tell us a lot about society in late antiquity in this part of the world.

First, the names tell us that religion was a central issue in the public and social life of the Aphrodisians. Jews tended to be named either after major prophets or figures from the Hebrew Bible, or in association with specific moral values connected with their religion. Similarly, Christians named their children after various apostles and angels from the New Testament, or as a reflection of a principal belief of their faith. Parents who worshiped in the Hellenic pagan sanctuaries of Aphrodisias continued the traditional name-giving practices, which reflected, among other things, civic values and the worship of Greek gods.

Second, the names, read in context, reflect the competition among religions at this time. As the religious nature of some of the names indicates, each religion was fostering homogeneity and solidarity in its ranks.

Finally, the names in the "donors' inscription" tell us not only about the complexity of religious identity at this time, but of the competition among religions for adherents.

Listed below are some of the more common names used by members of the various religious communities at Aphrodisias.

JEWISH	CHRISTIAN	PAGAN
IAKOB (JACOB)	PETROS (PETER)	APELLAS (MAN OF THE ASSEMBLY)
ROUBEN (REUBEN)	LOUKAS (LUKE)	ASKLEPIODOTOS (GIFT OF ASKLEPIOS)
HEORTASIOS (HAGGAI; RELATED TO THE FEAST)	ANASTASIOS (RESURRECTION)	HERMIAS (UNDER THE PATRONAGE OF HERMES)
THEODOTOS (JONATHAN/ NATHANIEL; GOD-GIVEN)	IORDANES (BAPTISM)	PHILIPPOS (FOND OF HORSES)
CHARINOS (HANAN; GRACE)	ATHANASIOS (THE IMMORTAL SOUL)	PYTHEAS (RELATED TO PYTHIOS [APOLLO])
	EUDOXIOS (FIRM AND CORRECT FAITH)	ZENON (UNDER THE PATRONAGE OF ZEUS)

images of the pagan "holy men" Pythagoras and Apollonios of Tyana. Asklepiodotos is said to have composed hymns and to have performed miracles—all this in a period in which pagan rituals were punishable by death.

As late as 482 C.E., pagans were performing sacrifices and expecting the restoration of the old cults.[7] It seems that several members of the elites, including local governors, were still devoted to the old religion.

The Jews did not live in isolation in Aphrodisias. Their religious symbols were engraved in the most prominent places. Their representatives had reserved seats in the town hall. Several members of the council identified themselves as "Godfearers" and joined the Jews in the donation that is recorded in the earlier face of the impressive donors' inscription. And some gentiles became proselytes.

If the early Christian fathers, like John Chrysostom and Ephraim the Syrian, never tired of warning their Christian flock not to attend the synagogue, it is because many Christians did. Some of the men listed in the donors' inscription at Aphrodisias may in fact be members of Christian families. A *theosebes* on Face I has the characteristic Christian name Gregorios, which alludes to the duty of the Christian to be alert and watchful (*gregorein*) with regard to sins. The father of a proselyte on Face II bears the name Eusebios, more often used by Christians than any other group.

Perhaps the most valuable aspect of the Aphrodisias donors' inscription is its evidence of the religious ambiguities of late antiquity.

[1] Joyce Reynolds and Robert Tannenbaum, *Jews and Godfearers at Aphrodisias* (Cambridge: Cambridge Philological Society, 1987).

[2] Helga Botermann, "Griechisch-jüdische Epigraphik: Zur Datierung der Aphrodisias-Inschriften," *Zeitschrift für Papyrologie und Epigraphik* 98 (1993), pp. 187–192; Marianne Palmer Bonz, "The Jewish Donor Inscriptions from Aphrodisias: Are They Both Third-Century, and Who Are the Theosebeis?" *Harvard Studies in Classical Philology* 76 (1994), pp. 281–299; Stephen Mitchell, "The Cult of Theos Hypsistos Between Pagans, Jews, and Christians," in Polymnia Athanassiadi and Michael Frede, eds., *Pagan Monotheism in Late Antiquity* (Oxford: Oxford Univ. Press, 1999), p. 117, note 108; Glen W. Bowersock and Louis H. Feldman, *Jew and Gentile in the Ancient World. Attitudes and Interactions from Alexander to Justinian* (Princeton: Princeton Univ. Press, 1993), p. 577, note 138; Angelos Chaniotis, "The Jews of Aphrodisias: New Evidence and Old Problems," *Scripta Classica Israelica* 21 (2002), pp. 209–242; Walter Ameling, *Inscriptiones Judaicae Orientis II* (Tübingen: Mohr Siebeck, 2004), pp. 69–123; Margaret H. Williams, "Semitic Name-use in Roman Asia Minor and the Dating of the Aphrodisias Stele Inscriptions," in Elaine Matthews, ed., *Old and New Worlds in Greek Onomastics* (Oxford: Oxford Univ. Press, 2007), p. 191.

[3] For instance, six names (Acholios, Adolios, Anikios, Heortasios, Oxycholios and Patrikios) appear in the record at least one generation after the Constitutio Antoniniana of 212 C.E. Another four names (Amantios, Anysios, Eupeithios and Manikios) are not attested until at least one century after the early date. A few other cases should suffice. In the case of Eusebios, 90 percent of the attestations of this name in inscriptions and papyri are after c. 200. In the case of Eutropios, it is 95 percent. In the case of Gregorios, 97 percent.

The inscription on Face I cannot have been inscribed earlier than the fourth century; such a date can best be reconciled with the letterforms and the mention of councilors (*bouleutai*) among the "Godfearers." The inscription on Face II is certainly later than Face I.

The sign *s*, used to abbreviate words or names, is attested in this function in inscriptions only from the fourth century onwards. The formulaic expression *theos boethos* is not attested earlier than the fourth century and became common only after c. 350. The word *palatinos*, probably a designation of status, makes most sense in the context of late antiquity. The presence of three proselytes would be surprising only a few years after the reinforcement of the early-third-century anti-conversion laws under Septimius Severus.

Conversely, what we would expect if the inscription dated to the mid-third century is not there. After the award of Roman citizenship to all free inhabitants of the empire (with the Constitutio Antoniniana of 212 C.E.), the recipients of citizenship added to their name the Latin names Marcus Aurelius. None of the some 123 persons listed in the two texts has this name. Consequently, the texts were written either before 212 C.E. or long after that date, when Roman citizen nomenclature had been abandoned for a single-name system (fourth or fifth century).

Joyce Reynolds herself observed that the letterforms in the inscription can be reconciled with a date any time between c. 200 and c. 450 C.E. Although she preferred the earlier date, she never concealed the fact that the arguments for an early date are not conclusive.

[4] Perhaps we can narrow the dates even further. The donation of the 55 Jews and 52 *theosebeis* on Face I probably belongs to the short period of religious tolerance between Galerius's tolerance decree (311 C.E.) and the more aggressive measures for the establishment of Christianity under Theodosius I (380 C.E.). The more advanced letterforms and the larger number of Biblical names on Face II support the assumption that the second text was inscribed later, probably sometime in the early fifth century. In 418 C.E. imperial legislation banished Jews from imperial administration and prosecuted conversion to Judaism (see Gary Gilbert, "Jews in Imperial Administration and Its Significance for Dating the Jewish Donor Inscription from Aphrodisias," *Journal for the Study of Judaism* 35, no. 2 (2004), pp. 169–184). Although the three proselytes probably converted to Judaism earlier than this date, they could have made their donation later.

[5] Mitchell, "The Cult of Theos Hypsistos Between Pagans, Jews, and Christians"; Dietric Alex-Koch, "The God-fearers Between

Facts and Fiction: Two Theosebeis-Inscriptions from Aphrodisias and Their Bearing for the New Testament," *Studia Theologica* 60 (2006), pp. 62–90.

[6] Charlotte Roueché, *Aphrodisias in Late Antiquity* (London: Society for the Promotion of Roman Studies, 1989), pp. 85–93; Polymnia Athanassiadi, *Damascius, the Philosophical History. Text with Translation and Notes* (Athens: Apamea, 1999), pp. 202–233, 248–249, 284–285, 348–349.

[7] Glen Bowersock, *Hellenism in Late Antiquity* (Cambridge: Cambridge Univ. Press, 1990), p. 3.

Related Reading

Mark R. Fairchild, "Turkey's Unexcavated Synagogues," BAR, July/August 2012.

John Byron, Archaeological Views: "A Tale of Two Slaves," BAR, July/August 2013.

Mark R. Fairchild, "Why Perga?" BAR, November/December 2013.